MICAH

THE OLD TESTAMENT LIBRARY

Editorial Advisory Board

WILLIAM P. BROWN
CAROL A. NEWSOM
BRENT A. STRAWN

Daniel L. Smith-Christopher

Micah

A Commentary

WESTMINSTER
JOHN KNOX PRESS
LOUISVILLE · KENTUCKY

© 2015 Daniel L. Smith-Christopher

First edition
Published by Westminster John Knox Press
Louisville, Kentucky

15 16 17 18 19 20 21 22 23 24—10 9 8 7 6 5 4 3 2 1

All rights reserved. No part of this book may be reproduced or transmitted in any form or by any means, electronic or mechanical, including photocopying, recording, or by any information storage or retrieval system, without permission in writing from the publisher. For information, address Westminster John Knox Press, 100 Witherspoon Street, Louisville, Kentucky 40202-1396. Or contact us online at www.wjkbooks.com.

Unless otherwise specified, quotations of Micah are the author's translation. Other Scripture quotations not identified are from the New Revised Standard Version of the Bible, copyright © 1989 by the Division of Christian Education of the National Council of the Churches of Christ in the U.S.A., and used by permission, yet "YHWH" may replace "the LORD." Those marked NJPS are from *The TANAKH: The New JPS Translation according to the Traditional Hebrew Text*, copyright 1985 by the Jewish Publication Society, and used by permission. The list of abbreviations identifies other versions briefly cited. After NRSV verse numbers, differing MT or LXX versification may appear in brackets or parentheses.

Book design by Jennifer K. Cox

Library of Congress Cataloging-in-Publication Data

Smith-Christopher, Daniel L.
   Micah : a commentary / Daniel L. Smith-Christopher.—First edition.
      pages cm.—(The Old Testament library)
   Includes bibliographical references and index.
   ISBN 978-0-664-22904-7 (hardback)
   1. Bible. Micah—Commentaries.   I. Title.
   BS1615.53.S65 2015
   224'.9307—dc23
                                                                    2015012974

∞ The paper used in this publication meets the minimum requirements of the American National Standard for Information Sciences—Permanence of Paper for Printed Library Materials, ANSI Z39.48-1992.

Most Westminster John Knox Press books are available at special quantity discounts when purchased in bulk by corporations, organizations, and special-interest groups. For more information, please e-mail SpecialSales@wjkbooks.com.

For
Zsa Zsa, always,

and for
Jordan and Sydney:

. . . be like Micah.

CONTENTS

Acknowledgments xi

Abbreviations xiii

Bibliography xvii

Introduction 1

  Contexts for Micah and for *Reading* Micah 2

    International Context: Policies of Neo-Assyrian Mesopotamia 3

    Mesopotamian Empires and Their Western Interests 5

    Eighth-Century Regional Contexts: Biblical History from the Lowlands 8

    Hezekiah's Revolt against Assyria: God's Protection, or Trapped "like a Bird in a Cage"? 12

    Excursus 1: LMLK Jar Stamps, Pillar Figurines, and Military Preparations in the Shephelah 14

    Moresheth as Frontier Town: Local Issues and Economy 15

    Plows and Swords: An Economics of Eighth-Century Rural Palestine 18

    Antimilitary Populism as the Ideological Context for Reading Micah 20

    Micah's Revolt and the Politics of Jeremiah 26

    Micah versus Isaiah? 28

    Is the Book of Micah a Revolutionary Text? 30

  Literary Observations on the Book of Micah 31

    Versions of the Text 31

    Organization of the Book: The Coherence of Micah 32

    Judgment and Hope/Salvation as Guiding Principles in Reading Micah? 34

	Micah as Drama?	37
	Jan Wagenaar's Analysis	37
	The Coherence of Micah: Summary and Observations	38
	Micah among the Twelve	40
	Reading the Whole Book of Micah as Coherent	43
	Trauma and the Redaction of Micah	44

COMMENTARY

Micah 1:1	Superscription	45
	Excursus 2: Micaiah ben Imlah	46
Micah 1:2–7	Call to Court: Accusations against the Capital Cities	48
	Excursus 3: Feminist Analysis of Micah 1:6 and Beyond	57
Micah 1:8–9	The Initial Lament with Warning	61
Micah 1:10–16	The Impact of the Policies of Destruction	67
Micah 2:1–5	The Oppression of the Ruling Elite	79
Micah 2:6–7	Micah Anticipates His Opponents' Objections	90
Micah 2:8–13	Micah Condemns the Judean Military Elite and Denounces Their Prophetic Supporters in Judah	94
Micah 3:1–4	Micah Accuses the Political and Military Leadership of Economic Cannibalism	107
Micah 3:5–8	Against the Corrupt Prophetic Advisers	113
Micah 3:9–12	Micah Warns the Central Leadership of Coming Judgment	121
	Excursus 4: The Judgments against Samaria and Jerusalem	125
Micah 4:1–5	Micah's Vision of the Economy of Peace	128
	Excursus 5: The Peace Passage: Reading Micah 4:1–5 in "Contexts"	139
Micah 4:6–10	Building a New Society out of Crisis	145
	Excursus 6: The "Lame" in the Greek Version	147
Micah 4:11–5:1	An Exilic-Era Insertion on Future Restoration (4:11–14 MT)	155

	Excursus 7: "Being Watched" in Micah and Biblical Literature	157
Micah 5:2–5a	The Ideal King (5:1–4a MT)	165
Micah 5:5–6	A Curse and Warning against Assyria (5:4–5 MT)	171
Micah 5:7–15	Judah over (or among?) the Nations (5:6–14 MT)	176
	Excursus 8: A Lion among the Beasts	179
Micah 6:1–5	God Reconvenes the Trial	188
Micah 6:6–8	The Prophet Advises the Accused	192
Micah 6:9–16	God's Accusations of Injustice and Sentence	198
Micah 7:1	The Farmer-Prophet's Anguish	206
Micah 7:2–6	The Prophet Describes an Unjust and Disintegrating Society	208
Micah 7:7–13	The Vindication to Come	214
Micah 7:14–20	A Final Prayer for Deliverance	219
Index of Scripture and Other Ancient Sources		**229**
Index of Subjects and Authors		**253**

ACKNOWLEDGMENTS

Few books of the Bible can match Micah for generating so many questions from such a small amount of text. Consisting of a mere seven chapters, Micah has inspired a strikingly large amount of commentary and analysis from an equally impressive variety of perspectives. In preparing the work that follows, many of these studies were read with appreciation. This particular commentary is part of a series that, unlike some commentaries, does not feature detailed interaction with all scholarly work. The economy of references in this work, therefore, is not a fair indication of my indebtedness to previous scholarship on Micah. I recognize my indebtedness to all the works that I have read with great appreciation, beginning with James Luther Mays's previous OTL volume on Micah, which is, I hope, supplemented, yet certainly not replaced, by my offering here. I have tried to provide an extensive bibliography by way of acknowledgment of the large number of scholars whose work I have found always interesting and often challenging. I am particularly indebted to my OTL editor William P. Brown and also to the editorial staff at WJK—Dan Braden, S. David Garber, Bridgett Green, Gary Lee, Tina Noll, and Kellyann Falkenberg Wolfe—whose work was meticulous and always helpful.

It is a wonderful honor to contribute to the Old Testament Library, and because of that, I would like to take this rare opportunity to express some important notes of thanks. I owe a great debt of gratitude to my Mennonite teachers at AMBS in Elkhart for creating such an intellectually rich atmosphere of learning there and warmly welcoming an exiled Quaker, most especially to Millard Lind and Jacob Enz (of blessed memory) who, with Arthur O. Robert's help, first sparked my love for Old Testament. I wish to also thank John Barton, who guided me with a steady and supportive hand through my DPhil work at Oxford. I appreciate the continued advice from friends and colleagues, whose work I continue to find inspiring, especially Stephen Breck Reid, Andrew Mein, Aliou Niang, Sue Gardiner, R. S. Sugirtharajah, and Gregory Cuellar. Thanks to Neil and Ruth Snarr for treasured friendship and to Rev. Alistair Macrae for a wonderful Australian journey of learning.

I want to also express my gratitude to Jon Berquist for his original invitation to write this commentary. To my colleagues and friends at Loyola Marymount

University who have provided me a warm and welcoming academic home these last twenty-seven years, I cannot thank you enough.

I hope that some of the words of this commentary are useful to your work, Rev. Donald Tamihere, which I also offer to you in gratitude for what I have learned from you and the rest of my extended Maori family: *Nga mihi mutunga kore ki a koe e toku hoa aroha.*

Finally, of course, a note of thanks to my always supportive family—my late father, R. Dean; my mother, Virginia, who first told me to read the Bible; and my brother, David, and Susanne for always being encouraging.

Although I owe a great deal to these and many others who have supported and contributed to my work, all remaining mistakes or misjudgments remain entirely my own.

ABBREVIATIONS

AB	Anchor Bible
ABD	*Anchor Bible Dictionary.* Edited by D. N. Freedman. 6 vols. New York, 1992.
ACCS	Ancient Christian Commentary on Scripture
ANE	ancient Near East(ern)
ANEP	*The Ancient Near East in Pictures Relating to the Old Testament.* Edited by J. B. Pritchard. Princeton: Princeton University Press, 1954.
ANET	*Ancient Near Eastern Texts Relating to the Old Testament.* Edited by James B. Pritchard. 3d ed. Princeton: Princeton University Press, 1969.
AOTC	Abingdon Old Testament Theological Commentary
BAR	*Biblical Archaeological Review*
BASOR	*Bulletin of the American Schools of Oriental Research*
BBB	Bonner biblische Beiträge
Bib	*Biblica*
BibInt	*Biblical Interpretation*
BHS	*Biblia Hebraica Stuttgartensia.* Edited by K. Elliger and W. Rudolph. Stuttgart, 1983.
BN	Biblische Notizen
BZAW	Beihefte zur Zeitschrift für die alttestamentliche Wissenschaft
CBQ	*Catholic Biblical Quarterly*
CBQMS	Catholic Biblical Quarterly Monograph Series
CBR	*Currents in Biblical Research*
CC	Continental Commentaries
CEB	Common English Bible
CHANE	Culture and History of the Ancient Near East
CTU	*The Cuneiform Alphabetic Texts from Ugarit, Ras ibn Hani, and Other Places.* Edited by M. Dietrich, O. Loretz, and J. Sanmartín. ALASP 8. Münster: Ugarit-Verlag, 1995. 2d, enlarged ed. of *KTU: Die keilalphabetischen Texte aus Ugarit.*

	Edited by M. Dietrich, O. Loretz, and J. Sanmartín. AOAT 24/1. Neukirchen-Vluyn, 1976.
DH	Deuteronomistic History
ESV	English Standard Version
FO	*Folia orientalia*
FOTL	Forms of Old Testament Literature
FS	Festschrift
GKC	*Gesenius' Hebrew Grammar.* Edited by E. Kautzsch. Translated by A. E. Cowley. 2d ed. Oxford, 1910.
HAT	Handbuch zum Alten Testament
HBS	Herders Biblische Studien
HSM	Harvard Semitic Monographs
HTR	*Harvard Theological Review*
Int	*Interpretation*
JBL	*Journal of Biblical Literature*
JBQ	*Jewish Bible Quarterly*
JHS	*Journal of Hellenic Studies*
JQR	*Jewish Quarterly Review*
JSOT	*Journal for the Study of the Old Testament*
JSOTSup	Journal for the Study of the Old Testament: Supplement Series
JSS	*Journal of Semitic Studies*
KAT	Kommentar zum Alten Testament
KJV	King James Version
KTU	*See CTU*
LHB/OTS	Library of Hebrew Bible/Old Testament Studies
LXX	Septuagint
MT	Masoretic Text and its versification
Mur.	Murabbaʿat
NETS	*A New English Translation of the Septuagint.* Edited by A. Pietersma and B. G. Wright. Oxford University Press, 2007.
NIBCOT	New International Biblical Commentary on the Old Testament
NICOT	New International Commentary on the Old Testament
NIV	New International Version
NJB	New Jerusalem Bible
NJPS	*Tanakh: The Holy Scriptures: The New JPS Translation according to the Traditional Hebrew Text*
NRSV	New Revised Standard Version
NYT	*New York Times*
OBO	Orbis biblicus et orientalis
OTE	*Old Testament Essays*
OTG	Old Testament Guides
OTL	Old Testament Library

PEQ	*Palestine Exploration Quarterly*
PN	personal name
REB	Revised English Bible
ResQ	*Restoration Quarterly*
RSV	Revised Standard Version
SBL	Society of Biblical Literature
SBLDS	Society of Biblical Literature Dissertation Series
SBLMS	Society of Biblical Literature Monograph Series
SBLSymS	SBL Symposium Series
SBS	Stuttgarter Bibelstudien
SBT	Studies in Biblical Theology
S-C	translation by the author, Smith-Christopher
sg.	singular
TBT	*The Bible Today*
TTZ	*Trierer theologische Zeitschrift*
VT	*Vetus Testamentum*
VTSup	Supplements to Vetus Testamentum
WBC	Word Biblical Commentary
ZAW	*Zeitschrift für die alttestamentliche Wissenschaft*

BIBLIOGRAPHY

Commentaries in Series

Achtemeier, E. 1996. *Minor Prophets I.* NIBCOT 17. Peabody, MA: Hendrickson.
Alfaro, J. 1989. *Justice and Loyalty: A Commentary on the Book of Micah.* International Theological Commentary. Grand Rapids: Eerdmans.
Allen, L. C. 1976. *The Books of Joel, Obadiah, Jonah, and Micah.* NICOT. Grand Rapids: Eerdmans.
———. 2008. *Jeremiah: A Commentary.* OTL. Louisville: Westminster John Knox.
Andersen, F., and D. Freedman. 2000. *Micah.* AB 24E. New York: Doubleday, 2000.
Baltzer, K. 2001. *Deutero-Isaiah.* Hermeneia. Minneapolis: Fortress.
Bartelt, A. 1996. *The Book around Immanuel: Style and Structure in Isaiah 2–12.* Biblical and Judaic Studies from the University of California, San Diego 4; Biblical and Judaic Studies 4. Winona Lake, IN: Eisenbrauns.
Ben Zvi, E. 2000. *Micah.* FOTL 21B. Grand Rapids: Eerdmans.
Berges, U. 1998. *Das Buch Jesaja: Komposition und Endgestalt.* HBS 16. Freiburg: Herder.
Carroll, R. P. 1986. *Jeremiah: A Commentary.* OTL. Louisville: Westminster John Knox.
Cha, J. 1996. *Micha und Jeremia.* BBB 107. Weinheim: Beltz Athenaum.
Dietrich, W. 2001. "1 and 2 Kings." Pages 232–66 in *The Oxford Bible Commentary.* Edited by J. Barton and J. Muddiman. Oxford: Oxford University Press.
Ferreiro, A., ed. 2003. *The Twelve Prophets.* ACCS 14. Downers Grove, IL: InterVarsity.
Gray, J. 1970. *1 and 2 Kings.* OTL. Philadelphia: Westminster.
Hillers, D. 1984. *A Commentary on the Book of the Prophet Micah.* Hermeneia. Minneapolis: Fortress.
Hobbs, T. R. 1989. *A Time for War: A Study of Warfare in the Old Testament.* Old Testament Studies 3. Wilmington, DE: Glazier.

Holladay, W. 1989. *Jeremiah*. Hermeneia. Minneapolis: Fortress.
Kang, S. M. 1989. *Divine War in the Old Testament and in the Ancient Near East*. BZAW 177. Berlin: de Gruyter.
King, P. 1988. *Amos, Hosea, Micah: An Archaeological Commentary*. Philadelphia: Westminster.
Limburg, J. 1988. *Hosea–Micah*. Interpretation. Atlanta: John Knox Press.
March, W. 2000. "Micah." Pages 660–64 in *HarperCollins Bible Commentary*. San Francisco: HarperCollins.
Mason, R. 1991. *Micah, Nahum, Obadiah*. OTG. Sheffield: Sheffield Academic Press.
Mays, J. 1976. *Micah: A Commentary*. OTL. Philadelphia: Westminster.
McComiskey, T. 2009. "Micah." Pages 395–445 in vol. 7 of *The Expositor's Bible Commentary*. Edited by T. Longman III and D. E. Garland. Rev. ed. Grand Rapids: Eerdmans.
McKane, W. 1998. *The Book of Micah: Introduction and Commentary*. Edinburgh: T&T Clark.
Miscall, P. 1993. *Isaiah*. Sheffield: JSOT Press.
Oberforcher, R. 1995. *Das Buch Micha*. Neuer Stuttgarter Kommentar 24/2. Stuttgart: Verlag Katholisches Bibelwerk.
Paul, Shalom M. 1991. *Amos*. Hermeneia. Minneapolis: Fortress.
Robinson, T. H. 1954. "Micha." Pages 127–52 in *Die zwölf kleinen Propheten: Hosea bis Micha*. Edited by T. H. Robinson and F. Horst. HAT 14. Tübingen: Mohr Siebeck.
Rogerson, J. W. 2003. "Micah." Pages 703–7 in *Eerdmans Commentary on the Bible*. Edited by J. D. G. Dunn and J. W. Rogerson. Grand Rapids: Eerdmans.
Rudolph, W. 1975. *Micha-Nahum-Habakuk-Zephanja*. KAT 13/3. Gütersloh: Gerd Mohn.
Simundson, D. 1996. "Micah." Pages 530–89 in vol. 7 of *The New Interpreter's Bible*. Nashville: Abingdon.
———. 2005. "Micah." Pages 297–347 in *Hosea, Joel, Amos, Obadiah, Jonah, Micah*. AOTC. Nashville: Abingdon.
Smith, R. 1984. *Micah–Malachi*. WBC. Waco: Word.
Smith-Christopher, D. 2002b. "Daniel and Additions to Daniel." Pages 17–194 in vol. 7 of *The New Interpreter's Bible*. Nashville: Abingdon.
Sweeney, M. 2000–2001a. *The Twelve Prophets*. Vols. 1–2. Berit Olam. Collegeville, MN: Liturgical Press.
Utzschneider, H. 2005. *Micha*. Zürcher Bibelkommentare. Zurich: Theologischer Verlag.
Waltke, B. 2007. *A Commentary on Micah*. Grand Rapids: Eerdmans.
Wildberger, H. 1991. *Isaiah 1–12*. Translated by Thomas Trapp. CC. Minneapolis: Fortress.

Williamson, H. 2001. "Micah." Pages 595–99 in *The Oxford Bible Commentary*. Edited by J. Barton and J. Muddiman. Oxford: Oxford University Press.
Wolff, H. 1990. *Micah: A Commentary*. CC. Minneapolis: Augsburg.

Monographs and Collected Volumes

Abrams, R.H. 1969. *Preachers Present Arms*. Newton: Herald Press.
Allen, B. 1996. *Rape Warfare: The Hidden Genocide in Bosnia-Herzegovina and Croatia*. Minneapolis and London: University of Minnesota Press.
Avalos, H., S. Melcher, and J. Schipper, eds. 2007. *This Abled Body: Rethinking Disabilities in Biblical Studies*. Leiden: E. J. Brill.
Ayoub, Mahmoud. 1978. *Redemptive Suffering in Islam*. Berlin: de Gruyter.
Bach, A. 1997. *Women, Seduction, and Betrayal in Biblical Narrative*. Cambridge: Cambridge University Press.
Barstow, A. L., ed. 2000. *War's Dirty Secret: Rape, Prostitution, and Other Crimes against Women*. Cleveland: Pilgrim Press.
Barton, J. 1986. *Oracles of God: Perceptions of Ancient Prophecy in Israel after the Exile*. London: Darton, Longman, & Todd.
Bissett, J. 1999. *Agrarian Socialism in America: Marx, Jefferson, and Jesus in the Oklahoma Countryside, 1904–1920*. Norman: University of Oklahoma Press.
Blenkinsopp, J. 1988. *Ezra and Nehemiah*. OTL. Philadelphia: Westminster.
Bohak, G. 2008. *Ancient Jewish Magic*. Cambridge: Cambridge University Press.
Bosshard-Nepustil, E. 1997. *Rezeptionen von Jesaja 1–39 im Zwölfprophetenbuch: Untersuchungen zur Literarischen Verbindung von Prophetenbüchern in Babylonischer und Persischer Zeit*. OBO 154. Freiburg, CH: Universitätsverlag; Göttingen: Vandenhoeck & Ruprecht.
Briant, P. 2002. *From Cyrus to Alexander: A History of the Persian Empire*. Translated by Peter Daniels. Winona Lake, IN: Eisenbrauns.
Burbank, G. 1976. *When Farmers Voted Red: The Gospel of Socialism in the Oklahoma Countryside, 1910–1924*. Westport, CT: Greenwood.
Callaway, P. R. 2011. *The Dead Sea Scrolls for a New Millennium*. Eugene, OR: Cascade Books.
Campbell, A., and M. O'Brien. 2000. *Unfolding the Deuteronomistic History: Origins, Upgrades, Present Text*. Minneapolis: Fortress.
Carr, D. M. 2014. *Holy Resilience: The Bible's Traumatic Origins*. New Haven: Yale University Press.
Chavalas, M. 2006. *The Ancient Near East: Historical Sources in Translation*. Blackwell Sourcebooks in Ancient History. Malden, MA: Blackwell.
Christensen, D. L. 1975. *Transformations of the War Oracle in Old Testament Prophecy*. Harvard Dissertations in Religion 3. Missoula: Scholars Press.

Clifford, R. 1972. *The Cosmic Mountain in Canaan and the Old Testament.* HSM 4. Cambridge, MA: Harvard University Press.

Cogan, M. 1974. *Imperialism and Religion: Assyria, Judah and Israel in the Eighth and Seventh Centuries B.C.E.* SBLMS 19. Missoula, MT: SBL, Scholars Press.

Cook, J. 1983. *The Persian Empire.* New York: Schocken.

Cuffey, K. 2015. *The Literary Coherence of the Book of Micah: Remnant, Restoration, and Promise.* LHB/OTS 611. London: Bloomsbury/T&T Clark.

Dever, W. 2005. *Did God Have a Wife? Archaeology and Folk Religion in Ancient Israel.* Grand Rapids: Eerdmans.

Dubovský, P. 2006. *Hezekiah and the Assyrian Spies: Reconstruction of the Neo-Assyrian Intelligence Services and Its Significance for 2 Kings 18–19.* Rome: Editrice Pontificio Istituto Biblico.

Eisen, R. 2011. *The Peace and Violence of Judaism: From the Bible to Modern Zionism.* New York: Oxford University Press.

Elsmore, B. 1989. *Mana from Heaven: A Century of Maori Prophets in New Zealand.* Reed: Auckland.

Faris, J. C. 2003. *Navajo and Photography: A Critical History of the Representation of an American People.* Salt Lake City: University of Utah Press.

Foucault, M. 1977. *Discipline and Punish: The Birth of the Prison.* New York: Vintage.

Fretheim, T. 1984. *The Suffering of God.* Fortress: Minneapolis.

Frye, R. 1962. *The Heritage of Persia.* London: Weidenfeld & Nicolson.

Fullerton, W. M. 1914. *Problems of Power.* New York: C. Scribner's Sons.

Gallagher, W. R. 1999. *Sennacherib's Campaign to Judah: New Studies.* Leiden and Boston: E. J. Brill.

Goffman, E. 1961. *Asylums: Essays on the Social Situation of Mental Patients and Other Inmates.* New York: Doubleday.

Grabbe, L. L. 2007. *Ancient Israel: What Do We Know and How Do We Know It?* London: T&T Clark.

Graham-Stewart, M. 2006. *Out of Time: Māori and the Photographer 1860–1940.* Auckland: John Leech Gallery.

Hagstrom, D. 1988. *The Coherence of the Book of Micah: A Literary Analysis.* SBLDS 89. Atlanta: Scholars Press.

Hallo, W. W., and K. L. Younger, eds. 1997. *Canonical Compositions from the Biblical World.* Vol. 1 of *The Context of Scripture.* Leiden: E. J. Brill.

———, eds. 2000. *Monumental Inscriptions from the Biblical World.* Vol. 2 of *The Context of Scripture.* Leiden: E. J. Brill.

———, eds. 2002. *Archival Documents from the Biblical World.* Vol. 3 of *The Context of Scripture.* Leiden: E. J. Brill.

Hasel, G. F. 1974. *The Remnant: The History and Theology of the Remnant Idea from Genesis to Isaiah*. 2d ed. Andrews University Monographs, Studies in Religion 5. Berrien Springs, MI: Andrews University Press.

Haupt, P. 2007. *The Book of Micah*. Analecta Gorgiana 68. Reprint of Chicago: University of Chicago Press, 1910. Piscataway, NJ: Gorgias.

Heschel, A. 2007. *The Prophets*. Peabody, MA: Hendrickson.

Hillers, D. 1964. *Treaty-Curses and the Old Testament Prophets*. Biblica et orientalia 16. Rome: Pontifical Biblical Institute.

Holloway, S. 2002. *Aššur Is King! Aššur Is King! Religion in the Exercise of Power in the Neo-Assyrian Empire*. CHANE 10. Leiden: E. J. Brill.

———. 2006. *Orientalism, Assyriology and the Bible*. Hebrew Bible Monographs 10. Sheffield: Sheffield Phoenix Press.

Horgan, M. 1979. *Pesharim: Qumran Interpretation of Biblical Books*. CBQMS 8. Washington, DC: Catholic Biblical Association of America.

House, P. 1990. *The Unity of the Twelve*. Bible and Literature Series 27. Sheffield: Almond.

Houston, W. 2006. *Contending for Justice: Ideologies and Theologies of Social Justice in the Old Testament*. LHB/OTS 428. London: T&T Clark.

Jacobs, M. 2001. *The Conceptual Coherence of the Book of Micah*. JSOTSup 322. Sheffield: Sheffield Academic Press.

Jenson, P. P. 2008. *Obadiah, Jonah, Micah: A Theological Commentary*. LHB/OTS 496. London: T&T Clark.

Jones, B. 1995. *The Formation of the Book of the Twelve: A Study in Text and Canon*. SBLDS 149. Atlanta: Scholars Press.

Jonker, G. 1995. *The Topography of Remembrance: The Dead, Tradition, and Collective Memory in Mesopotamia*. Leiden and New York: E. J. Brill.

Kalimi, I., and S. Richardson, eds. 2014. *Sennacherib at the Gates of Jerusalem: Story, History and Historiography*. CHANE 71. Leiden and Boston: E. J. Brill.

Keel, O., and C. Uehlinger. 1998. *Gods, Goddesses, and Images of God in Ancient Israel*. Minneapolis: Fortress.

Kern, P. 1999. *Ancient Siege Warfare*. Bloomington: Indiana University Press.

Kitamori, K. 1965. *The Theology of the Pain of God*. Richmond: John Knox, 1965.

Kuhrt, A. 1995. *The Ancient Near East, c. 3,000–330 BC*. 2 vols. London and New York: Routledge.

Laniak, T. 1998. *Shame and Honor in the Book of Esther*. SBLDS 165. Atlanta: Scholars Press.

Leick, G., ed. 2007. *The Babylonian World*. New York: Routledge.

Lipschitz, O. 2005. *The Fall and Rise of Jerusalem*. Winona Lake, IN: Eisenbrauns.

Liverani, M. 2014. *The Ancient Near East: History, Society and Economy*. London and New York: Routledge.

Loretz, O. 1984. *Der Prolog des Jesaja Buches (1,1–2,5): Ugaritologische und kolometrische Studien zum Jesaja-Buch*. Ugaritisch-biblische Literatur 1. Altenberge: Akademische Bibliothek; Soest: Bestellungen an CIS-Verlag.

Lydon, J. 2005. *Eye Contact: Photographing Indigenous Australians*. Durham, NC, and London: Duke University Press.

Martínez, F. G., ed. 1996. *The Dead Sea Scrolls Translated: The Qumran Texts in English*. Translated by W. G. E. Watson. 2d English ed. Grand Rapids: Eerdmans.

Mazar, A. 1990. *Archaeology of the Land of the Bible, 10,000–586 BCE*. New York: Doubleday.

McKay, J. 1973. *Religion in Judah under the Assyrians*. SBT 26. London: SCM.

Metzner, G. 1998. *Kompositionsgeschichte des Michabuches*. Frankfurt: Peter Lang.

Moltmann, J. 1974. *The Crucified God*. Fortress: Minneapolis.

Moss, C. R., and J. Schipper, eds. 2011. *Disability Studies and Biblical Literature*. New York: Palgrave Macmillan.

Neusner, J. 1962. *A Life of Rabban Yohanan Ben Zakkai, ca. 1–80 C.E.* Leiden: E. J. Brill.

Niditch, S. 1993. *War in the Hebrew Bible*. Oxford: Oxford University Press.

Nogalski, J. 1993. *Literary Precursors to the Book of the Twelve*. BZAW 217. Berlin: de Gruyter.

Olyan, S. M. 2008. *Disability in the Hebrew Bible: Interpreting Mental and Physical Differences*. Cambridge and New York: Cambridge University Press.

O'Toole, L., J. R. Schiffman, and M. L. Kiter, eds. 2007. *Gender Violence: Interdisciplinary Perspectives*. New York: New York University Press.

Péristiany, J. G. 1966. *Honour and Shame: The Values of Mediterranean Society*. Chicago: University of Chicago Press.

Petersen, D. 1981. *The Roles of Israel's Prophets*. JSOTSup 17. Sheffield: Sheffield Academic Press.

Petrotta, A. 1991. *Lexis Ludens: Wordplay and the Book of Micah*. Frankfurt: Peter Lang.

Pham, Xuan Huong Thi. 1999. *Mourning in the Ancient Near East and the Hebrew Bible*. JSOTSup 302. Sheffield: Sheffield Academic Press.

Premnath, D. N. 2003. *Eighth Century Prophets: A Social Analysis*. St. Louis: Chalice.

Purver, A. 1764. *A New and Critical Translation of All of the Books of the Old and New Testaments: With Notes Critical and Explanatory*. 2 vols. London: Richardson & Clark.

Rad, G. von. 1991. *Holy War in Ancient Israel*. Translation of the 3d German ed., 1958. Grand Rapids: Eerdmans.

Renaud, B. 1977. *La formation du livre de Michée: Tradition et actualisation*. Études bibliques. Paris: Gabalda.

———. 1987. *Michée, Sophonie, Nahum.* Sources bibliques. Paris: Gabalda.
Rogerson, J. W. 1984. *Old Testament Criticism in the Nineteenth Century: England and Germany.* London, SPCK.
———. 2010. *A Theology of the Old Testament: Cultural Memory, Communication, and Being Human.* Minneapolis: Fortress.
Roux, G. 1964. *Ancient Iraq.* London: Penguin.
Runions, E. 2001. *Changing Subjects: Gender, Nation and Future in Micah.* Playing the Texts 7. Sheffield: Sheffield Academic Press.
Sakenfeld, K. 1978. *The Meaning of Hesed in the Hebrew Bible.* HSM 17. Missoula: Scholars Press.
Schultz, R. L. 1999. *The Search for Quotation: Verbal Parallels in the Prophets.* JSOTSup 180. Sheffield: Sheffield Academic Press.
Schwartz, M. 1976. *Radical Protest and Social Structure: The Southern Farmers' Alliance and Cotton Tenancy, 1880–1890.* Chicago: Chicago University Press.
Sharp, G. 2005. *Waging Nonviolent Struggle: 20th Century Practice and 21st Century Potential.* Boston: Extending Horizons Books.
Shaw, C. 1993. *The Speeches of Micah: A Rhetorical-Historical Analysis.* JSOTSup 145. Sheffield: Sheffield Academic Press.
Smith, M. S. 2002. *The Early History of God: Yahweh and the Other Deities in Ancient Israel.* Biblical Resource Series. Grand Rapids: Eerdmans.
———. 2010. *God in Translation: Deities in Cross-Cultural Discourse in the Biblical World.* Grand Rapids: Eerdmans.
Smith-Christopher, D. 2002a. *A Biblical Theology of Exile.* Minneapolis: Fortress.
Soelle, D. 1983. *The Arms Race Kills Even without War.* Minneapolis: Fortress.
Spieckermann, H. 1982. *Juda unter Assur in der Sargonidenzeit.* Göttingen: Vandenhoeck & Ruprecht.
Stansell, G. 1988. *Micah and Isaiah: A Form and Tradition Historical Comparison.* SBLDS 85. Atlanta: Scholars Press.
Stern, E. 2001. *The Assyrian, Babylonian, and Persian Periods, 732–332 B.C.* Vol. 2 of *Archaeology of the Land of the Bible.* New York: Doubleday.
Stiebert, J. 2002. *The Construction of Shame in the Hebrew Bible: The Prophetic Contribution.* JSOTSup 346. Sheffield: Sheffield Academic Press.
Stock, C. 1996. *Rural Radicals: Righteous Rage in the American Grain.* Ithaca, NY: Cornell University Press.
Stolper, M. 1985. *Entrepreneurs and Empire: The Murašû Archive, the Murašû Firm, and Persian Rule in Babylonia.* Leiden and Istanbul: Nederlands Historisch-Archaeologisch Instituut te Istanbul.
Strawn, B. 2005. *What Is Stronger than a Lion? Leonine Image and Metaphor in the Hebrew Bible and the Ancient Near East.* OBO 212. Göttingen: Vandenhoeck & Ruprecht.

Utzschneider, H. 1999. *Michas Reise in die Zeit: Studien zum Drama als Genre der prophetischen Literature des Alten Testaments*. SBS 180. Stuttgart: Verlag Katholisches Bibelwerk.

Van de Mieroop, M. 2004. *A History of the Ancient Near East, ca. 3000–323 B.C.* Oxford: Blackwell.

Vanderhooft, D. S. 1999. *The Neo-Babylonian Empire and Babylon in the Latter Prophets*. HSM 59. Atlanta: Scholars Press.

Volkan, V. 1997. *Bloodlines*. New York: Farrar, Straus & Giroux.

———. 2002. *The Third Reich in the Unconscious: Transgenerational Transmission and Its Consequences*. New York: Brunner-Routledge.

Wagenaar, J. 2001. *Judgement and Salvation: The Composition and Redaction of Micah 2–5*. VTSup 85. Leiden: E. J. Brill.

Weems, R. 1995. *Battered Love*. Minneapolis: Fortress.

Westermann, C. 1967. *Basic Forms of Prophetic Speech*. Philadelphia: Westminster.

Willi-Plein, I. 1971. *Vorforman der Schriftexegese innerhalb des Alten Testaments*. BZAW 123. Berlin and New York: de Gruyter.

Williamson, H. 1994. *The Book Called Isaiah*. Oxford: Clarendon.

Wolff, H. 1981. *Micah the Prophet*. Translated by Ralph D. Gehrke. Philadelphia: Fortress.

Würthwein, E. 1979. *The Text of the Old Testament: An Introduction to the Biblia Hebraica*. Grand Rapids: Eerdmans.

Yadin, Y. 1963. *The Art of Warfare in Biblical Lands*. New York: McGraw-Hill.

Yoder, J. H. 1994. *The Politics of Jesus*. 2d ed. Grand Rapids: Eerdmans.

Yong, A. 2011. *The Bible, Disability, and the Church*. Grand Rapids: Eerdmans.

York, T., and J. Barringer, eds. 2012. *A Faith Not Worth Fighting For: Addressing Commonly Asked Questions about Christian Nonviolence*. Eugene, OR: Cascade Books.

Younger, K. L., Jr. 1990. *Ancient Conquest Accounts: A Study in Ancient Near Eastern and Biblical History Writing*. JSOTSup 98. Sheffield: JSOT Press.

Ziegler, J., ed. 1984. *Duodecim Prophetae*. Vol. 13 of *Septuaginta: Vetus Testamentum Graecum*. 2d ed. Göttingen: Vandenhoeck & Ruprecht.

Articles or Chapters

Allen, L. C. 1973. "More Cuckoos in the Textual Nest: At 2 Kings XXIII. 5; Jeremiah XVII. 3,4; Micah III. 3; VI. 16 (LXX); 2 Chronicles XX. 25 (LXX)." *Journal of Theological Studies* 24:69–73.

Anderson, B. 1992. "A Worldwide Pilgrimage to Jerusalem." *Bible Review* 8/3:14, 16.

Barker, K. 1998. "A Literary Analysis of the Book of Micah." *Bibliotheca sacra* 155:437–48.

Becking, B. 2002a. "The Exile Does Not Equal the Eschaton: An Interpretation of Micah 4:1–5." Pages 1–7 in *The New Things: Eschatology in Old Testament Prophecy; Festschrift for Henk Leene.* Edited by F. Postma, K. Spronk, and E. Talstra. Maastricht: Uitgeverij Shaker Pub.

———2002b. "Expectations about the End of Time in the Hebrew Bible: Do They Exist?" Pages 44–59 in *Apocalyptic History and Tradition.* Edited by C. Rowland and J. Barton. London and New York: Sheffield Academic Press.

Ben Zvi, E. 1998. "Micah 1:2–16: Observations and Possible Implications." *JSOT* 77:103–20.

———. 1999. "Wrongdoers, Wrongdoing and Righting Wrongs in Micah 2." *BibInt* 7:87–100.

Biddle, M. 2000. "'Israel' and 'Jacob' in the Book of Micah: Micah in the Context of the Twelve." Pages 146–65 in *Reading and Hearing the Book of the Twelve.* Edited by J. D. Nogalski and M. A. Sweeney. SBLSymS 15. Atlanta: Scholars Press.

Bleibtreu, Erika. 1991. "Grisly Assyrian Record of Torture and Death." *BAR* 17:01.

Bohak, G. 2009. "Prolegomena to the Study of the Jewish Magical Tradition." *CBR* 8:107–50.

Borowski, O. 1995. "Hezekiah's Reforms and the Revolt against Assyria." *Biblical Archaeologist* 59:148–55.

Brin, G. 1988. "The Significance of the Form *mah-ṭṭôb* [in Mic 6:8]." *VT* 38:462–65.

———. 1989. "Micah 2, 12–13: A Textual and Ideological Study." *ZAW* 101:118–24.

Broshi, M. 1993. "Judeideh Tell." Pages 837–38 in vol. 3 of *The New Encyclopedia of Archaeological Excavations in the Holy Land.* Edited by E. Stern. New York: Simon & Shuster.

Brown, S. 2003. "Micah 2:1–11." *Int* 57:417–19.

Bryant, D. 1978. "Micah 4:14–5:14: An Exegesis." *ResQ* 21:210–30.

Byrne, R. 2004. "Lie Back and Think of Judah: The Reproductive Politics of Pillar Figurines." *Near Eastern Archaeology* 67/3:137–51.

Campbell, E. 1998. "A Land Divided: Judah and Israel from the Death of Solomon to the Fall of Samaria." Pages 273–319 in *The Oxford History of the Biblical World.* Edited by M. Coogan. Oxford: Oxford University Press.

Carreira, J. 1981. "Micha: Ein Ältester von Moreschet?" *TTZ* 90:19–28.

Carroll, R. P. 1992. "Night without Vision: Micah and the Prophets." Pages 74–84 in *The Scriptures and the Scrolls.* Edited by F. G. Martínez et al. Leiden: Brill.

———. 1996. "Whorusalamin: A Tale of Three Cities as Three Sisters." Pages 67–82 in *On Reading Prophetic Texts: Gender-Specific and Related Studies* in Memory of Fokkelien van Dijk-Hemmes. Edited by B. Becking and M. Dijkstra. Leiden: E. J. Brill.

Cathcart, K. 1968. "Notes on Micah 5:4–5." *Bib* 49:511–14.

———. 1978. "Micah 5:4–5 and Semitic Incantations." *Bib* 59:38–48.

Cathcart, K., and K. Jeppesen. 1988. "Micah 2:4 and Nahum 3:16–17 in the Light of Akkadian." Pages 191–200 in *Fucus: A Semitic/Afrasian Gathering in Remembrance of Albert Ahrman*. Edited by Y. L. Arbeitman. Amsterdam/Philadelphia: John Benjamins Publishing.

Chaney, M. 2006. "Micah—Models Matter: Political Economy and Micah 6:9–15." Pages 145–60 in *Ancient Israel: The Old Testament in Its Social Context*. Edited by P. F. Eisler. Minneapolis: Fortress.

Cogan, M. 1998. "Into Exile: From the Assyrian Conquest of Israel to the Fall of Babylon." Pages 321–65 in *The Oxford History of the Biblical World*. Edited by M. D. Coogan. New York: Oxford University Press.

Cohen, M. 1979. "The Prophets as Revolutionaries." *BAR* 5:12–19.

Cook, S. 1999. "Micah's Deuteronomistic Redaction and the Deuteronomist's Identity." Pages 216–31 in *Those Elusive Deuteronomists*. Edited by L. S. Schearing and S. L. McKenzie. Sheffield: Sheffield Academic Press.

Crocker, P. 1995. "Micah 5:1: What and Where Is the 'City of Troops'?" *Buried History* 31:21–24.

Day, P. L. 2000. "The Bitch Had It Coming to Her: Rhetoric and Interpretation in Ezekiel 16." *BibInt* 8:231–54.

De Moor, J. 2000. "Micah 7:1–13: The Lament of a Disillusioned Prophet." Pages 149–96 in *Delimitation Criticism: A New Tool in Biblical Scholarship*. Edited by M. C. A. Korpel and J. M. Oesch. Assen: Van Gorcum.

Dempsey, C.1994. "Economic Justice in Micah." *TBT* 32:272–76.

———. 1999. "Micah 2–3: Literary Artistry, Ethical Message, and Some Considerations about the Image of Yahweh and Micah." *JSOT* 85:117–28.

———. 2014. "Micah 1:1–16 and 7:1–10: A Poet's Cry of the Heart in the Midst of Tragic Vision." Pages 36–48 in *Why? . . . How Long? Studies on Voice(s) of Lamentation Rooted in Biblical Hebrew Poetry*. Edited by L. S. Flesher et al. London: Bloomsbury.

Denton-Borhaug, K. 2010. "War Culture and Sacrifice." *Feminist Theology* 18:175–91.

Dever, W. 1995. "Social Structure in Palestine in the Iron II Period on the Eve of Destruction." Pages 416–30 in *The Archaeology of the Holy Land*. Edited by T. E. Levy. London: Leicester University Press.

Edelman, D. 2008. "Hezekiah's Alleged Cultic Centralization." *JSOT* 32:395–434.

Fales, F. 2008. "On Pax Assyriaca in the Eighth–Seventh Centuries BCE and Its Implications." Pages 17–36 in *Isaiah's Vision of Peace in Biblical and Modern International Relations: Swords into Plowshares*. Edited by R. Cohen and R. Westbrook. New York: Palgrave MacMillan.

———. 2014. "The Road to Judah: 701 B.C.E. in the Context of Sennacherib's Political-Military Strategy." Pages 223–48 in *Sennacherib at the Gates of Jerusalem: Story, History and Historiography*. Edited by I. Kalimi and S. Richardson. Leiden and Boston: E. J. Brill.

Friedlander, I. 1916. "The Present Position and the Original Form of the Prophecy of Eternal Peace in Isaiah 2:1–5." *JQR* 6:405–13.

Fuerst, W. 1982. "A Study of Prophetic Disagreement." *TBT* 20:20–25.

Fuller, R. 2000. "Minor Prophets." Pages 554–57 in vol. 1 of *The Encyclopedia of the Dead Sea Scrolls*. Edited by L. H. Schiffman and J. C. VanderKam. Oxford: Oxford University Press.

Garfinkel, Y. 1988. "2 Chr 11:5–10 Fortified Cities List and the *lmlk* Stamps: Reply to Nadav Naʾaman." *BASOR* 271:69–73.

Genot-Bismuth, J. 1980. "Pacifisme Pharisien et sublimation de l'idée de guerre aux origines du Rabbinisme." *Revue de theologie et de philosophie* 4:73–89.

Gordon, R. 1978. "Micah VII 19 and Akkadian *kabāsu*." *VT* 28:355.

Grabbe, L. 2003. "Prophetic and Apocalyptic: Time for New Definitions—and New Thinking." Pages 107–33 in *Knowing the End from the Beginning*. Edited by R. Haak and L. Grabbe. London: Continuum.

Grelot, P. 1986. "Michee 7:6 dans les evangiles et dans la literature rabbinique." *Bib* 67:363–77.

Guillaume, P. 2007. "A Reconsideration of Manuscripts Classified as Scrolls of the Twelve Minor Prophets (XII)." *Journal of Hebrew Scriptures* 7:2–12.

Haak, R. D. 1982. "A Study and New Interpretation of *qsr npš*." *JBL* 101:161–67.

Haran, M. 1985. *Temples and Temple-Service in Ancient Israel: An Inquiry into Biblical Cult Phenomena and the Historical Setting of the Priestly School*. Winona Lake, IN: Eisenbrauns.

———. 1988. "Temple and Community in Ancient Israel." Pages 18–25 in *Temple in Society*. Edited by M. V. Fox. Winona Lake, IN: Eisenbrauns.

Hardmeier, C. 1991. "Die Propheten Micha und Jesaja im Spiegel von Jeremia XXVI und 2 Regum XVIII–XX: Zur Prophetie-Rezeption in der nachjoschijanischen Zeit." Pages 172–89 in *Congress Volume: Leuven, 1989*. Edited by J. A. Emerton. VTSup 43. Leiden: E. J. Brill.

Hoffman, Y. 2008. "The Wandering Lament: Micah 1:10–16." Pages 86–98 in *Treasures on Camel's Humps: Historical and Literary Studies from the Ancient Near East Presented to Israel Ephaʿal*. Edited by M. Cogan and D. E. Kahn. Jerusalem: Hebrew University, Magnes Press.

Holladay, J. 1970. "Assyrian Statecraft and the Prophets of Israel." *HTR* 63:29–51.

———. 1998. "The Kingdoms of Israel and Judah: Political and Economic Centralization in the Iron IIA-B (ca. 1000–750 BCE)." Pages 368–98 in *The Archaeology of Society in the Holy Land*. Edited by T. E. Levy. London: Leicester University Press.

Hostetter, E. 1994. "Prophetic Attitudes toward Violence in Ancient Israel." *Criswell Theological Review* 7/2: 83–89.

Hutton, R. 1987. "Eating the Flesh of My People: The Redaction History of Micah 3:1–4." *Proceedings of the Eastern Great Lakes Biblical Society and Midwest Region of the Society of Biblical Literature* 7:131–42.

———. 1999. "What Happened from Shittim to Gilgal? Law and Gospel in Micah 6:5." *Currents in Theology and Mission* 26:94–103.

Jacobs, M. 2006. "Bridging the Times: Trends in Micah Studies since 1985." *CBR* 4:293–329.

Jaruzelska, I. 1994. "People Pronouncing Sentences in Court: Amos 5, 7–12, 16–17: An Attempt at Sociological Identification." *FO* 30:77–94.

Jeppesen, K. 1978. "New Aspects of Micah Research." *JSOT* 8:3–32.

———. 1984a. "Micah V 13 in the Light of a Recent Archaeological Discovery." *VT* 34/4:462–66.

———. 1984b. "The Verb *yāʿad* in Nahum 1:10 and Micah 6:9?" *Bib* 65: 571–74.

———. 1999. "'Because of You!': An Essay about the Centre of the Book of the Twelve." Pages 196–210 in *In Search of True Wisdom: Essays in Old Testament Interpretation in Honour of R. E. Clements*. Edited by E. Ball. JSOTSup 300. Sheffield: Sheffield Academic Press.

Jeremias, J. 2003. "Micha 1: Vom Lokalereignis zur Weltgeschichte." Pages 137–49 in *"Einen Altar von Erde mache mir—": Festschrift für Diethelm Conrad zu seinem 70. Geburtstag*. Edited by J. F. Diehl, R. Heitzenröder, and M. Witte. Waltrop: Hartmut Spenner.

Kalimi, I. 2014. "Sennacherib's Campaign to Judah: The Chronicler's View Compared with His 'Biblical' Sources." Pages 11–50 in *Sennacherib at the Gates of Jerusalem: Story, History and Historiography*. Edited by I. Kalimi and S. Richardson. Leiden and Boston: E. J. Brill.

Kallikuzhuppil, J. 1985. "Liberation in Amos and Micah." *Bible Bhashyam* 11:215–23.

Kapelrud, A. 1968. "The Number Seven in Ugaritic Texts." *VT* 18:494-499.

Kegler, J. 1992. "Prophetic Speech about the Future." Pages 69–109 in *The Meaning of Peace: Biblical Studies*. Edited by P. B. Yoder and W. M. Swartley. Louisville: Westminster/John Knox.

Kletter, R. 1999. "Pots and Politics: Material Remains of Late Iron Age Judah in Relation to Its Political Borders." *BASOR* 314:19–54.

Kloner, A. 1996. "Mareshah." *ABD* 4:523–25.

Kotter, W. R. 1992. "Gilgal." *ABD* 2:1022–24.

Laato, A.1995. "Assyrian Propaganda and the Falsification of History in the Royal Inscriptions of Sennacherib." *VT* 45:198–226.

Larsen, M. 1979. "The Tradition of Empire in Mesopotamia." Pages 75–105 in *Power and Propaganda: A Symposium on Ancient Empires*. Edited by

M. T. Larsen. Mesopotamia: Copenhagen Studies in Assyriology 7. Copenhagen: Akademisk Forlag.

Lescow, T. 1972a. "Redaktionsgeschichtliche Analyse von Micha 1–5." *ZAW* 84:46–85.

———. 1972b. "Redaktionsgeschichtliche Analyse von Micha 6–7." *ZAW* 84:182–212.

Lewis, T. 2008. "'You Have Heard What the Kings of Assyria Have Done': Disarmament Passages vis-à-vis Assyrian Rhetoric of Intimidation." Pages 75–100 in *Isaiah's Vision of Peace in Biblical and Modern International Relations: Swords into Plowshares*. Edited by R. Cohen and R. Westbrook. New York: Palgrave Macmillan.

Limburg, J. 1997. "Swords into Plowshares: Text and Contexts." Pages 279–93 in *Writing and Reading the Scroll of Isaiah: Studies of an Interpretive Tradition*. Edited by C. C. Broyles and C. A. Evans. Leiden: E. J. Brill.

Lipschitz, O. 2012. "Archaeological Facts, Historical Speculations and the Date of the LMLK Storage Jars: A Rejoinder to David Ussishkin." *Journal of Hebrew Scriptures* 12/4. http://www.jhsonline.org/Articles/article_166.pdf.

Luria, B. Z. 1989. "For the Statutes of Omri Are Kept." *JBQ* 2:69–73.

Maclean, J. 2002. "Micah 3:5–12." *Int* 56:413–16.

Marrs, R. R. 1988. "Micah and the Task of Ministry." *ResQ* 30:1–16.

———. 1999. "Micah and a Theological Critique of Worship." Pages 184–203 in *Worship and the Hebrew Bible: Essays in Honour of John T. Willis*. Edited by M. P. Graham, R. R. Marrs, and S. L. McKenzie. JSOTSup 284. Sheffield: Sheffield Academic Press.

McKane, W. 1995. "Micah 1:2–7." *ZAW* 107:420–34.

———. 1997. "Micah 2:1–5: Text and Commentary." *JSS* 42:7–22.

Melcher, S. 2007. "With Whom Do the Disabled Associate? Metaphorical Interplay in the Latter Prophets." Pages 115–29 in *This Abled Body: Rethinking Disabilities in Biblical Studies*. Edited by H. Avalos et al. SBL Semeia Studies 55. Atlanta: SBL.

Miller, C. 1982. "Micah: A Word for Our Time." *TBT* 20:13–17.

Moberly, R. 2003. "Does God Lie to His Prophets? The Story of Micaiah ben Imlah as a Test Case." *HTR* 96:1–23.

Mulvey, L. 1999. "Visual Pleasure and Narrative Cinema." Pages 833–44 in *Film Theory and Criticism: Introductory Readings*. Edited by L. Braudy and M. Cohen. New York: Oxford University Press.

Na'aman, N. 1979. "Sennacherib's Campaign to Judah and the Date of the LMLK Stamps." *VT* 29:61–86.

———. 1986. "Hezekiah's Fortified Cities and the LMLK Stamps." *BASOR* 261:5–21.

———. 1995. "'The House-of-No-Shade Shall Take Away Its Tax from You' (Micah I 11)." *VT* 45:516–27.

———. 2008. "Let Other Kingdoms Struggle with the Great Powers—You, Judah, Pay the Tribute and Hope for the Best: The Foreign Policy of the Kings of Judah in the Ninth–Eighth Centuries BCE." Pages 55–74 in *Isaiah's Vision of Peace in Biblical and Modern International Relations: Swords into Plowshares*. Edited by R. Cohen and R. Westbrook. New York: Palgrave Macmillan.

Neiderhiser, E. 1981. "Micah 2:6–11: Considerations on the Nature of the Discourse." *Biblical Theology Bulletin* 11/4:104–7.

Otto, E. 1992. "Micha/Michabuch." *Theologische Realenzyklopädie* 22:695–704.

Pannell, R. 1988. "The Politics of the Messiah: A New Reading of Micah 4:14–5:5." *Perspectives in Religious Studies* 15:131–43.

Patton, C. L. 2000. "'Should Our Sister Be Treated Like a Whore?': A Response to Feminist Critiques of Ezekiel 23." Pages 221–38 in *The Book of Ezekiel*. Edited by M. Odell and J. Strong. Atlanta: SBL.

Peterson, D. 1998. "The Book of the Twelve." Pages 95–128 in *The Hebrew Bible Today: An Introduction to Critical Issues*. Edited by S. L. McKenzie and M. P. Graham. Louisville: Westminster John Knox.

Piro, J. 2008. "Foucault and the Architecture of Surveillance: Creating Regimes of Power in Schools, Shrines, and Society." *Educational Studies* 44:30–46.

Pixley, G. 1991. "Micah—A Revolutionary." Pages 53–60 in *The Bible and the Politics of Exegesis: Essays in Honor of Norman K. Gottwald on His Sixty-Fifth Birthday*. Edited by D. Jobling, P. L. Day, and G. T. Sheppard. Cleveland: Pilgrim Press.

Pratt, W. C. 1988. "The Farmers Union and the 1948 Henry Wallace Campaign." *Annals of Iowa* 49:349–70.

———. 1996. "The Farmers Union, McCarthyism, and the Demise of the Agrarian Left." *Historian* 58: 329–42

Reicke, B. 1967. "Liturgical Traditions in Mic. 7." *HTR* 60:349–67.

Rudmon, D. 2001. "Zechariah 8:20–22 and Isaiah 2:2–4//Micah 4:2–3: A Study in Intertextuality." *BN* 107–108:50–54.

Savran, G. 2009. "Multivocality in Group Speech in Biblical Narrative." *JHS* 9:25. http://www.jhsonline.org/cocoon/JHS/a127.html.

Schniedewind, W. 1998. "The Geopolitical History of Philistine Gath." *BASOR* 309:69–77.

Schwendemann, W. 1996. "Weisung vom Zion (Mi 4,1–5)." *Bibel und Kirche* 51:163–65.

Sedlmeier, F. 1998. "Die Universalisierung der Heilshoffnung nach Micha 4, 1–5." *TTZ* 107:62–81.

Sinclair, L. A. 1983. "Hebrew Text of the Qumran Micah Pesher and Textual Traditions of the Minor Prophets." *Revue de Qumran* 11:253–63.

Slayton, J. 1992. "Shittim." *ABD* 5:1222.

Smith-Christopher, D. 2002c. "Ezekiel in Abu Ghraib: Rereading Ezekiel 16:37–39 in the Context of Imperial Conquest." Pages 141–58 in *Ezekiel's Hierarchical World: Wrestling with a Tiered Reality*. Edited by S. Cook and C. Patton. SBLSymS 31. Atlanta: SBL.

———. 2009. "Engendered Warfare and the Ammonites in Amos 1:13." Pages 15–40 in *Aspects of Amos: Exegesis and Interpretation*. [FS John Barton.] Edited by A. Mein and A. Hagedorn. LHB/OTS 536. Cambridge: Cambridge University Press.

Stade, B. 1881. "Bemerkungen uber das Buch Micha." *ZAW* 1:161–72.

Stager, L. 1996. "The Fury of Babylon: Ashkelon and the Archaeology of Destruction." *BAR* 22:56–77.

Strydom, J. 1993. "Micah of Samaria: Amos's and Hosea's Forgotten Partner." *OTE* 6:19–32.

Sweeney, M. 2001b. "Micah's Debate with Isaiah." *JSOT* 93:111–24.

———. 2004. "Portrayal of YHWH's Deliverance in Micah 2:12–13 Reconstructed." Pages 315–26 in vol. 2 of *God's Word for Our World: Biblical Studies in Honor of Simon John DeVries*. Edited by J. H. Ellens, D. L. Ellens, I. Kalimi, and R. Knierim. LHB/OTS 389. London: T&T Clark.

Talmon, S. 1971. "Typen der Messiaserwartung um die Zeitwende." Pages 571–88 in *Probleme biblischer Theologie: Gerhard von Rad zum 70. Geburtstag*. Edited by H. W. Wolff. Munich: Kaiser.

Turkowski, L. 1969. "Peasant Agriculture in the Judean Hills." *PEQ* 101:21–33.

Tushingham, A. 1992. "New Evidence Bearing on the Two-Winged LMLK Stamp." *BASOR* 287:61–65.

Uffenheimer, B. 1984. "Ancient Hebrew Prophecy—Political Teaching and Practice." *Immanuel* 18:7–21.

———. 1994. "Isaiah's and Micah's Approaches to Policy and History." Pages 176–88 in *Politics and Theopolitics in the Bible and Postbiblical Literature*. Edited by H. G. Reventlow, Y. Hoffman, and B. Uffenheimer. Sheffield: JSOT Press.

Ussishkin, D. 1976. "Royal Judean Storage Jars and Private Seal Impressions." *BASOR* 223:1–13.

———. 2013. "Lachish." Pages 63–75 in vol. 2 of *The Oxford Encyclopedia of the Bible and Archaeology*. Edited by D. M. Master. Oxford: Oxford University Press.

———. 2014. "Sennacherib's Campaign to Judah: The Archaeological Perspective with an Emphasis on Lachish and Jerusalem." Pages 75–103 in *Sennacherib at the Gates of Jerusalem: Story, History and Historiography*. Edited by I. Kalimi and S. Richardson. Leiden and Boston: E. J. Brill.

Utzschneider, H. 2004. "Micha und die Zeichen der Zeit: Szenen und Zeiten in Mi 4,8–5,3." Pages 265–82 in *Schriftprophetie: Festschrift für Jörg Jere-

mias zum 65. Geburtstag. Edited by F. Hartenstein, J. Krispenz, and Aaron Schart. Neukirchen-Vluyn: Neukirchener Verlag.

Van der Woude, A. S. 1969. "Micah in Dispute with the Pseudo-Prophets." *VT* 19:244–60.

Vargon, S. 1992. "Gedud: A Place-Name in the Shephelah of Judah." *VT* 42:557–64.

Wagenaar, J. 1996. "The Hillside of Samaria: Interpretation and Meaning of Micah 1:6." *BN* 85:26–30.

———. 2000. "'From Edom He Went Up . . .': Some Remarks on the Text and Interpretation of Micah II 12–13." *VT* 50:531–39.

Warren, N. J. 2014. "A Cannibal Feast in Ezekiel." *JSOT* 38:501–12.

Watson, W. 1984. "Allusion, Irony and Wordplay in Micah 1,7." *Bib* 65:103–5.

Weitzman, S. 2002. "The Samson Story as Border Fiction." *BibInt* 10:158–74.

Wessels, W. 1997a. "Wisdom in the Gate: Micah Takes the Rostrum." *OTE* 10: 125–35.

———. 1997b, "Conflicting Powers. Reflections from the Book of Micah." *OTE* 10:528–44.

———. 1998. "Micah 1, an Apt Introduction to Power Talks." *Skrif en kerk* 19:438–48.

———. 1999. "Micah 4 and 5: A Battle of Words and Perceptions." *OTE* 12:623–41.

———. 2000. "Cheating at the Market Place—Impressions from Micah 6:9–16." *Skrif en kerk* 21:406–415.

———. 2003. "Micah 7:8–20: An Apt Conclusion to the Book of Micah." *Verbum et Ecclesia* 24:249–59.

———. 2009. "Empowered by the Spirit of Yahweh: A Study of Micah 3:8." *Journal of Biblical and Pneumatological Research* 1:33–47.

Williamson, H. 1997. "Marginalia in Micah." *VT* 47:360–72.

Willis, J. 1968a. "A Note on *wā'ōmar* in Micah 3:1." *ZAW* 80:50–54.

———. 1968b. "Micah IV 14–V 5—A Unit." *VT* 18:529–47.

———. 1969a. "The Structure of the Book of Micah." *Svensk exegetisk årsbok* 34:5–42.

———. 1969b. "The Structure of Micah 3–5 and the Function of Micah 5:9–14 in the Book." *ZAW* 81:191–214.

———. 1969c. "The Authenticity and Meaning of Micah 5:9–14." *ZAW* 81:353–68.

———. 1997. "Isaiah 2:2–5 and the Psalms of Zion." Pages 295–316 in vol. 1 of *Writing and Reading the Scroll of Isaiah: Studies of an Interpretative Tradition*. Edited by C. C. Broyles and C. A. Evans. VTSup 70/1; Formation and Interpretation of Old Testament Literature 1/1. Leiden: E. J. Brill.

Wilson, I. D. 2012. "Judean Pillar Figures and Ethnic Identity in the Shadow of Assyria." *JSOT* 36:259–78.

Wolff, H. 1986. "Prophets and Institutions in the Old Testament." *Currents in Theology and Mission* 13:5–12.

———. 1992. "Swords into Plowshares: Misuse of a Word of Prophecy?" Pages 110–26 in *The Meaning of Peace: Biblical Studies*. Edited by P. Yoder and W. Swartley. Louisville: Westminster/John Knox.

Wood, J. R. 2000. "Speech and Action in Micah's Prophecy." *CBQ* 62:645–62.

Zajonc, R. 1965. "Social Facilitation." *Science* 149:269–74.

Zapff, B. 2003. "The Perspective on the Nations in the Book of Micah as a 'Systematization' of the Nations' Role in Joel, Jonah, and Nahum? Reflections on a Context-Oriented Exegesis." Pages 292–312 in *Thematic Threads in the Book of the Twelve*. Edited by P. L. Redditt and A. Schart. Berlin and New York: de Gruyter.

INTRODUCTION

Interpretation of texts arises out of a dialogue between past and present. Part of becoming aware of this dialogue involves directly addressing contemporary assumptions and models for reading a text. In his important 1984 commentary on Micah, for example, Delbert Hillers proposes that the book may have arisen out of a "millenarian" movement active in any number of the various historical contexts proposed for all or parts of the book (4–8). On the other hand, Hans W. Wolff (1990) famously proposes that Micah should be read as the work of an "elder" from a small agricultural village, whose words were taken as "prophetic," but whose actual identity may not have been very similar to those ancient figures known as "prophets" in ancient Israelite society. Going even further, Robert Carroll wonders if Micah is to be considered a prophet in any sense and proposes that only later editorial activity "made" his words into those of a prophet as opposed to simply a gifted village speaker, a "poet" (1992). Even though I disagree somewhat with all of these proposed ancient contexts and identities for Micah, the instinct to seek a sociopolitical context for Micah (i.e., the man, the words of the book, and their social contexts) is quite correct, and I will also be forthright about the historical contexts within which I am conducting my analysis of Micah.

I propose reading the book of Micah as an ancient Israelite "critical populist," whose attitudes were fueled partially by his location as a "lowlander," specifically from a village (Moresheth, about 23 miles southwest of Jerusalem) of the Shephelah (the foothills, what I am calling the "lowlands"), and partially by his fiery criticism of the Jerusalem elite. This criticism differentiates Micah from Isaiah, a prophet far closer to Judean political power (cf. Peterson 1998, 113–14). Indeed, central to Micah's critique is his anger at the war policies of the Jerusalem elite surrounding King Hezekiah. These policies were economically disastrous for those whom Micah refers to as "my people," his fellow villagers, who often bore the brunt of military reprisals against the self-serving adventurism of the Jerusalem crown. Part of defending this ancient Hebrew "populist antimilitarism" involves locating the book of Micah in a tradition of prophetic condemnation of war policies before Micah's time as well as after Micah's time. The prime example of this is Jeremiah's similar attitude toward the folly of military resistance to the Neo-Babylonian forces. Further critical views are occasionally reported, as in the late writings of Chronicles, where memories (or revivals?) of such a critique were perhaps safer to make public!

Contexts for Micah and for *Reading* Micah

In any modern analysis of the Bible, all serious scholars today acknowledge the historical context of the biblical texts. In previous decades, however, it was not typical to acknowledge another horizon: the contemporary context of *the scholar's own historically and socially informed reading of* the biblical text. Yet, in looking back, hardly anyone can now deny that there was surely unacknowledged significance to writing about Old Testament theology in Germany in the 1930s and 1940s (Rogerson 2010, 11; cf. idem 1984), or even reading Micah in the turbulent 1970s in Chicago (the context for James Luther Mays's widely appreciated previous volume on Micah in this series [1976]).

Biblical scholarship no longer ignores the social contexts of both readers and texts. It is now routine in biblical studies to provide a self-identification of the commentary or theology writer's possible contexts, such as the acknowledgment by John Rogerson of his own "context" for reading the texts and interpreting them theologically (2010, 10–12). The use of consciously chosen cognitive models and social comparisons drawn from other historical locations can also be illuminating and instructive. This must certainly include candor about the contemporary context of reading, and we are now justifiably suspicious of allegedly "objective" readings of ancient history. In the worst cases such claims reflect the language of hidden agendas, or in the best cases merely betray unacknowledged social assumptions.

I choose to be explicit about my own approach to Micah. As I write this commentary, I am committed to historical-critical biblical scholarship *and* a declared sympathy with movements in the twenty-first century for seeking greater and more equitable distribution of the earth's resources to peoples who have been systematically suppressed, as well as movements that seek to ameliorate those inequitable situations without violence. I aspire to present a commentary that is not only enlightening about the book of Micah and a contribution to the important legacy of the Old Testament Library, but also enlightening and encouraging to Bible readers among peoples African American, Asian American, Native American, Maori, Aboriginal Australian, Ainu Japanese, and others who have known only too well what it means to mourn, to seek justice, or to bitterly condemn those who "plan evil on their beds" (Mic 2:1).

I also write this commentary as a biblical scholar who was born to, and remains by conviction a member of, the Society of Friends (Quakers). However, my work is deeply influenced by the rich biblical scholarly tradition of my friends and teachers, the Mennonites. It is thus no accident that one of the main themes I have sought to explicate in the book of Micah is the ancient impact of militarism in society. Any accusation of "reading into" Micah such themes is a charge by now rather banal. Feminist scholars find issues of concern to women (both ancient and modern) in the Bible not because they "read into" the texts important issues that are not there. Rather, they often find these issues in the text because they alone think to look for them. They are alert to ask new questions of the familiar (and sometimes unfamiliar) texts.

If I am asked whether my commitments as a Christian devoted to nonviolent social change have "influenced" my reading of the book of Micah, I can only reply that I certainly hope so. I will go further. In my own review of the extensive literature on the book of the prophet Micah, it has become patently clear to me that a certain strong bias has already dominated a great deal of Micah studies. According to this socially conservative assumption, Micah as a historical prophet could not possibly have questioned the authority of Jerusalem, nor questioned the king's military and economic policies, nor proposed a radical critique of both king and country on the basis of a radical faith in the God of Israel. I argue precisely for this kind of radical criticism as a key to Micah's thought, or at least to the book we now have that bears his name. Along the way, I happily acknowledge those occasions where other colleagues seem to have suspected something similar in their own reading of Micah.

Along with acknowledging one's own contemporary context, the scholar who reads Micah becomes immersed in *four other contexts*. The socioeconomic contexts of Micah the prophet and Micah the book are centrally important. By this I mean the historical period and place identified in 1:1 of the book as the context of Micah the prophet as well as the continued contexts of the editorial activity that carry Micah's discourse into subsequent periods of Israelite history (e.g., "in Babylon" in 4:10 and possibly a similar chronological reference to "gathering" the "remnant" in 2:12–13). A variety of perspectives are available for examining this complex context for the book of Micah. I have chosen to highlight three historical contexts: *international*, *regional*, and *local*, the latter especially in terms of economic issues. The fourth context is a proposed orientation from which to read Micah: as *rural, antimilitary populism*.

International Context: Policies of Neo-Assyrian Mesopotamia

It is important to survey the larger geopolitical context and the human impact of the massive physical and economic violence of Neo-Assyrian, Neo-Babylonian, and indeed Persian imperial designs. At the outset, careful readers recognize that an earlier tradition of interpreting the Neo-Assyrian Empire was dependent on ancient public propaganda generated by the empire to instill both fear and obedience. The language of this material is decidedly threatening and militaristic, including the iconographic representations of conquest in Neo-Assyrian palatial reliefs (e.g., destruction images depicting Lachish, originally featured in the Assyrian palace of Nineveh). This results in a decidedly dark image of the Neo-Assyrian age. So, for example, Jonker writes that the first millennium was

> terrorized by the Assyrians. Their diplomatic policy of "peace" involved deportation and demolition. . . . Deportations totally disrupted life in the inhabited world in the first millennium. It was not enough for the conquerors to raze every sign of human habitation to the ground, not enough to cut down the trees and burn the crops in what today would be described as a scorched-earth policy; they [also] disinterred the dead and denuded the earth by removing the fertile topsoil. . . . We know of 157 mass deportations undertaken by Assyrian dictators, by means of which they intended to do their utmost to eradicate any traces of the memory of their opponents; they were not content until nothing remained. (1995, 47–48)

Others have stated that the central goal of the Assyrian Empire was "to secure a constant flow of goods from the periphery to the center" (Larsen 1979, 100). Warfare in the Assyrian economy was practiced to ensure sufficient captured manpower and resources to fuel the expanding needs of an ancient empire (Kern 1999, 58). By the seventh century, Assyria was in control of the entire Fertile Crescent, including Egypt (Kuhrt 1995, 473).

It is widely recognized that a major change occurred in the imperial ambitions of the Neo-Assyrian Empire under the reign of Tiglath-Pileser III (745–727 B.C.E.). When historians refer to the "reforms" of Tiglath-Pileser III, there is often discussion of "efficiency" and "control," but for our analysis the importance of these reforms is found in Tiglath-Pileser III having "doubled the size of the army, revamped the provincial administration, and conducted a major campaign of deporting conquered peoples to other regions of the Empire" (Chavalas 2006, 384). Those who resisted were severely punished by torture, rape, beheading, and being flayed, with their corpses left for public display (Van de Mieroop 2004, 218). In considering such grotesque suffering, however, any reading of the prophet Micah asks us to wonder who among the Judeans actually suffered the brunt of such Assyrian punishments. Surely it involved large numbers of the Judean villagers who were pressed into duty, despite their desires for peaceful farming (Mic 2:8–9; 3:1–5; see commentary).

It is, furthermore, necessary to clarify that the Neo-Assyrian Empire did have very real diplomatic concerns. A recent "balancing" of our assessment of Neo-Assyrian imperial policies seeks not to reduce the horrors of Assyrian military practice (although Holloway has raised important questions about contemporary "Orientalist" bias, and anti-Ottoman polemics caught up in 19th–20th-century scholarly descriptions of ancient Mesopotamian empires [2002; 2006, 1–41]), but to emphasize that there were also reasoned policies of international relations sought by the Assyrian royal administration. Liverani points out that Tiglath-Pileser III battled against those whom he believed had betrayed agreements and treaties (2014, 485), and Fales discusses the nature of "Pax Assyriaca" in light of ancient texts other than those designed to intimidate. In these texts, Fales writes, "It may be shown that the recourse to armed conquest and physical coercion was far from indiscriminate, and in fact was considered by the Assyrians themselves as an option to be weighed against other, diplomatic, strategies in order to gain the submission of foreign polities" (2008, 18). Furthermore, Fales notices the Neo-Assyrian use of diplomatic language of "good relations" and "peacemaking" used to describe "the diplomatic dealings of the Assyrian state with a foreign entity, with the relevant verb *salamu,* 'to be in peace'" (18). Finally, the Neo-Assyrian practice of placing local business colonies (yet also armed and provided with policing forces) even had the notable impact of encouraging elements of the local economies, such as Phoenician shipping or the "commercial emporia" of Philistine cities in their trade with Egypt (22). One might also add the apparent economic flourishing of the elite of the Assyrian client states of Israel and Judah in the late ninth and eighth centuries B.C.E., leading up to the turbulent events of growing resistance to the Neo-Assyrian Empire in the last third of the eighth century. In sum, reading ancient empires as people who "cannot be reasoned with," or who "only understand violence," was as dangerous then as it is today. Capacity for violence is not necessarily an incapacity for diplomacy.

The importance of these differing perspectives—threatened violence but also reliable possibilities for stable diplomacy and trade—serves to highlight our reading the Bible with an eye toward alternative and competing ideologies of religiously and politically reasonable foreign policies vis-à-vis the Mesopotamian regimes of the eighth through the fourth centuries B.C.E. Contrary to frequent contemporary (and often politically motivated) claims for suggesting otherwise, open military resistance was not the only recourse for survival in the face of the ancient empires, as even a casual reading of Jeremiah suggests in relation to the later Neo-Babylonian Empire. Reading Micah forces us to ask who actually benefits (or suffers) from centrally determined policies of war, treaty, or resistance, as in Judah at the end of the eighth century B.C.E. As Micah suggests, the national elite rarely suffered the worst of their policies of military bravado.

Mesopotamian Empires and Their Western Interests

Among the changes introduced by Tiglath-Pileser III just before the time of Micah's concern are clear signs of increased central control and a reduced local authority. Many Assyrian districts were made smaller, thus requiring the appointment of more administrators or governors. Outside Assyria, Tiglath-Pileser III turned more territories into provinces, and they too were given new leadership answerable only to the monarch. In addition, there was an increase in communications by means of runners traveling to and from the king. We have documentation of "Orders of the king" sent to local rulers, who were also responsible for raising the annual tribute, maintaining local order, and providing troops. Perhaps most notably, Tiglath-Pileser III also professionalized a standing army, thus maintaining forces that were not based on conscripts supplied by local rulers. Roux has wondered, however, whether the heavy increase of foreign elements in this standing military may not ultimately have weakened the Assyrian forces, since foreign conscripts may not have been as trustworthy as the Assyrian peasants supplied by the wealthy local elite as in previous generations (1964, 284).

Conquest, of course, has violent impacts on people, both physically and economically. The levels of Assyrian control varied from vassal (with local leadership) to province, which involved a much tighter level of control and financial burden of tribute. Damascus became a province in 732 B.C.E.; the lands of Ammon, Moab, and Edom were vassals in 730. Israel (northern territories) became a vassal in 738, and portions were broken off and became provincial areas later—including Gilead and Megiddo in about 732. A reduced area of Israel became a province with the Assyrian conquests of 722. Judah, on the other hand, was also a vassal already by 733. Directly west of Judah, along the coast, the Philistine city-states of Ekron, Ashdod, Ashkelon, and Gaza were vassal entities by 732, and many were reduced to provincial direct rule by 720 or 712 (Van de Mieroop 2004, 234; Liverani 2014, 412). The apparent goals were to carve up the territories into ever smaller units and increase the imperial grip on power with more levels of authority.

Thus it is possible that the rapid succession of usurpations in Israel between 745 and 722 is to be explained by the internal instability within Israel created by conflicting attempts to cope with Assyrian demands (Kuhrt 1995, 466). Liverani suggests that Assyrian policies toward Phoenician port cities was based largely on Assyrian interest in limiting local trade with Philistines and Egyptians in hopes of concentrating "the majority of goods in Assyria" (2014, 432). Thus Assyrian conquest was motivated by massive exploitation and central imperial business interests, which meant that "tributary states constantly revolted despite heavy-handed Assyrian responses" (Van de Mieroop 2004, 251).

Biblical history verifies this economic interest. When Scripture briefly introduces readers to Tiglath-Pileser III, the perfunctory references to economic extraction are clear:

> King Pul of Assyria came against the land; Menahem gave Pul a thousand talents of silver, so that he might help him confirm his hold on the royal power. Menahem exacted the money from Israel, that is, from all the wealthy, fifty shekels of silver from each one, to give to the king of Assyria. So the king of Assyria turned back, and did not stay there in the land. (2 Kgs 15:19–20)

This is followed by the brief account of Ahaz, king of Judah, appealing to Tiglath-Pileser III for assistance against the coalition of Rezin of Aram and Pekah of Israel (2 Kgs 16:7–8): "Ahaz also took the silver and gold found in the house of the LORD and in the treasures of the king's house, and sent a present to the king of Assyria." Again, one is struck by the tribute-extractive interests of the Assyrian monarch. Sargon II (721–705) seems to have seized power in a coup against Shalmaneser V, faced internal problems as a result, and thus carried on the policies of his predecessor, Tiglath-Pileser III (Kuhrt 1995, 597–98). We will focus on the period of Sennacherib in more detail below; in this initial survey suffice it to report the comments of many historians that the end of the Neo-Assyrian Empire came with startling speed. In 640, the Neo-Assyrian regime was at its height under Ashurbanipal, but "thirty years later the Assyrian Empire was finished. What exactly happened is unclear" (Van de Mieroop 2004, 250). Because some texts in Micah are likely from a later period, the historical survey necessarily continues.

In 609 and 605, the last Assyrians fell to the rising Neo-Babylonian forces, and Nebuchadnezzar began to entertain ambitions to control Egypt as well. This required controlling the land bridge between his home territories and Egypt, namely, Palestine! Nebuchadnezzar eventually controlled this territory in 598/7. At that point, young King Jehoiachin of Judah surrendered. According to Nebuchadnezzar's inscriptions, he appointed in Jerusalem "a king of his liking, took heavy booty from it [Judah], and brought it into Babylon" (*ANET* 564). Babylonian control over Palestine lasted from 597 until 539, when the imperial control of Palestine changed from Babylonian to Persian rule.

The Persian conquest and the end of the Neo-Babylonian regime also came with legendary swiftness (Isa 45). Cyrus II, after unifying the Persian tribes and defeating the Medes, conquered the city of Babylon in 539 B.C.E. Biblical sources about the early Persian period indicate that the Persians were initially understood to be generous "liberators" in returning exiles to their homelands, including the Jews. However, recent work on the Persian period reveals that this supposedly "enlightened rule" was greatly exaggerated, and Neh 9:36–37 paints an entirely darker picture of later Persian rule over the Jews in Palestine.

In sum, the nature of imperial economics in the ancient Near East from the Neo-Assyrian Empire to the Persian Empire is reasonably clear. With regard to the Neo-Babylonian policies under Nebuchadnezzar, Vanderhooft describes the "brute facts of subjugation" and surmises that Nebuchadnezzar's western ventures had monetary motivations as well (1999, 61–114). Similar to the massive building projects of the Assyrians, which required so much externally sourced resources, the Neo-Babylonian rulers engaged in large-scale imperial building projects, which required resources. But at what human cost for those who stood in their way? Writing of Babylon's "fury," Stager refers to the empire's "scorched-earth" policy by citing evidence of fiery destruction: Nebuchadnezzar created "a veritable wasteland west of the Jordan River" (1996).

As noted, the claim is often made that the Persians were far more humane. Were the Jewish Diaspora communities better off under the Achaemenid administrations? Stolper's analysis of the Murašu archive, a set of business documents, is suggestive:

> In both . . . tenure and commercial practice, Achaemenid administration put new faces on old patterns. The Murašu texts point to some results of this policy: a tendency toward concentration of wealth, and a tendency toward relative impoverishment at the lowest ranks of the state-controlled agricultural sector, despite indications of overall prosperity in the province. (1985, 154)

The Persian "economy" was essentially designed to hoard precious metals. Alexander, so it appears, was stunned by the amounts of bullion he found stashed at Susa, Ecbatana, and Persepolis, but it can hardly be said that the Persian or the Hellenistic rulers were interested in "encouraging business" or spreading wealth among the populace. Frye, for example, states that taxes were ubiquitous in Persian territories, including tolls and fees of all kinds, as well as forced labor: "Life for the common person must have been at times oppressive. The local public works were probably financed by local taxes, while gold and silver streamed into the king's coffers" (1962, 114–15). Cook comments that labor and production were so widely organized in Persian territories (even sheep raising was tightly controlled) that he wonders how anything like a private enterprise could have ever existed (1983, 89–90).

The point is simply this: irrespective of the very real differences between the political and ideological regimes from the eighth century B.C.E. until and after Alexander's conquests from 333 till his death in 323 B.C.E., we must always attend to the stubborn similarities of ancient imperial designs toward power and control over wealth, territory, and human resources. On these matters, little difference appears in practice and results. Some Hebrews may have prospered, but the biblical literature (e.g., prophetic texts, later apocalyptic texts, Diaspora stories) hardly suggests that this was the common fate of living under Near Eastern empires.

Eighth-Century Regional Contexts: Biblical History from the Lowlands

As we have seen, the eighth century B.C.E. was a period of serious socioeconomic pressure on the rulers of Judah and Israel, and these pressures often led to instability in the central governing powers. Let us begin with an examination of the rulers of the northern and southern kingdoms in reference to Neo-Assyrian rulers, paying particular attention to the changes brought about by the rise of Tiglath-Pileser III in Assyria:

Table 1. Rulers of northern and southern kingdoms alongside Neo-Assyrian rulers

Judah	Israel	Assyria
Azariah/Uzziah 783–742	Jeroboam II 786–746	Adad-Nirari III 810–783
		Shalmaneser IV 783–773
(period of prosperity and success in local wars)		Ashur-dan III 773–755
		Ashur-nirari V 755–745
	(instability in Israel) Zechariah 746? (less than a year)	
	Killed by Shallum (745? less than a year)	Tiglath-Pileser III 745–727 (begins aggressive policies)
Jotham 742–735 (began as coregent)	Menahem (kills Shallum) 745–737	
Ahaz 735–727 (or 715?) (allies with Assyria)	Pekahiah 737–736 Pekah (kills Pekahiah) 736–732	
	Hoshea (kills Pekah) 732–723	Shalmaneser V 727–722
Hezekiah 727 (715?)–687		Sargon II 722–705 Sennacherib 705–681

Clearly, the book of Micah, a text that purports to have its origins from a prophet who lived "in the days of Jotham, Ahaz, and Hezekiah" (beginning ca. 742 B.C.E.), must be read in the contexts of the Assyrian threat to the lands of the Eastern Mediterranean coastline, including Palestine. Notice the particular instabilities in the north (Israel) just before and immediately following the aggressive policies of Tiglath-Pileser III. Biblical historians often suggest that the instability of the northern state "must have arisen over how to participate in the constantly changing power game" (A. Campbell and O'Brien 2000, 313). The supposed periods of "quiet and prosperity" in the first half of the eighth century (typically seen in the reigns of Uzziah and Jeroboam II) are entirely a matter of perspective. So we ask, Prosperous *for whom*?

Just before these allegedly "prosperous years" under Uzziah and Jeroboam II, the kings of Israel (Jehoash, 802–786) and Judah (Amaziah, 800–783) were engaged in serious conflict. No doubt emboldened by his successes against the Edomites (2 Kgs 14:7), the Judean Amaziah challenged Jehoash, who taunted him in reply, calling him a "thornbush" and telling Amaziah to simply be satisfied with his conquests of the Edomites (vv. 9–10). But Amaziah did not listen and challenged Jehoash. The result was a devastating defeat for Amaziah's Judah; Jerusalem was captured and most likely required to pay tribute (cf. 2 Kgs 18:14; 23:35; 25:15—"gold and silver" as typical tribute). Thus what we see is arguably Assyrian-like policies on the smaller scale of Palestine! Even more significant, however, is the fact that Amaziah was then assassinated by unnamed Judeans who "made a conspiracy against him" (2 Kgs 14:19).

At this point Uzziah (= Azariah: the name is spelled either way, giving rise to speculation on which may be a throne name) is enthroned at age 16, and 2 Kings then turns to discuss his counterpart in the north, Jeroboam II. While the text condemns him for the "sins of Jeroboam son of Nebat" (2 Kgs 14:24), it rather grudgingly acknowledges that he was quite successful in restoring territory because God determined to care for the Samarian people (2 Kgs 14:26–27). Similarly, Uzziah's long reign is not commented upon in detail by the Deuteronomistic Historian, but the Chronicler (2 Chr 26) fills in more detail, suggesting a massive military and economic buildup during his reign. Notable in Uzziah's reign, according to 2 Chr 26:6–7, is an indication of battles with the Philistines and descriptions of battle sites near the town of Micah:

> He went out and made war against the Philistines, and broke down the wall of Gath and the wall of Jabneh and the wall of Ashdod; he built cities in the territory of Ashdod and elsewhere among the Philistines. God helped him against the Philistines, against the Arabs who lived in Gur-baal, and against the Meunites.

Gath is only about six miles northwest of Micah's village of Moresheth, with the fortress of Lachish about five miles to the southwest. Conflicts in this area certainly involved local Judean villagers, according to 2 Chr 26:9–16, including conscripts from the Shephelah region.

Uzziah was succeeded by Jotham, of which the Deuteronomistic Historian provides only scant description, but again the Chronicler is more forthcoming (27:3–6). Notable, however, is the final note about Jotham in 2 Chr 27:7, "Now the rest of the acts of Jotham, and all his wars and his ways, are written in the Book of the Kings of Israel and Judah." In the Chronicler, David is not allowed to build the temple because of his "wars" (1 Chr 22:8), and Asa is punished by the curse of "wars" (2 Chr 16:9). Jotham, too, is noted for "his wars." Before continuing, let us turn to the northern kingdom.

As recognized, the instability in the northern kingdom became serious by the mid-eighth century. Shallum assassinated Zechariah, the son of Jeroboam II, after only six months (2 Kgs 15:10 S-C, "in broad daylight!"). Shallum, in turn, is killed by Menahem within one year. Menahem, however, becomes a vassal of Tiglath-Pileser III, which requires massive payments that Menahem, in turn, exacts from the "wealthy" by taxing them (v. 20). With financial and foreign policies such as these, it seems hardly surprising that Menahem's son, Pekahiah, was then killed by a military officer, Pekah, and it seems hard to avoid the impression that these political assassinations are directly related to the Samarian policies to appease Assyria (Kuhrt 1995, 466).

It is the usurper Pekah, after all, who instigates further conflict with Judah in support of a revolt against Assyria. The so-called Syro-Ephraimite War refers to the events described in 2 Kgs 16, when King Ahaz of Judah calls on Assyrian assistance against Pekah and his ally, Rezin of Damascus. The defeat of Rezin is specifically mentioned by Tiglath-Pileser III's own annals: in language similar to Sennacherib's description of Hezekiah of Jerusalem, Tiglath-Pileser boasts that he trapped Rezin in Damascus "like a bird in a cage" (Hallo and Younger 2002, 284–86). These territories north of Samaria are then conquered by Tiglath-Pileser and divided into Assyrian provinces of Megiddo, Dor, and Gilead (2 Kgs 15:29).

Edward Campbell, however, points out the importance of the alternative picture provided by the Chronicler with regard to these events (1998, 315). According to 2 Chr 28, Pekah actually campaigned in Judah in an alliance with Aram; furthermore, this later historical source suggests that Ahaz, king of Judah, was actually killed by Pekah, along with a "great slaughter" (lit., "great strike, blow") that included 120,000 Judeans. When Pekah then tried to take "200,000" (!) captive Judeans and resettle them in Israel, he was confronted by the prophet Oded and a significant insurrection, led by northern tribal leaders who not only opposed Pekah's military actions but also clothed, fed, and "anointed" the captives (medical care, presumably) and returned them to Judea through Jericho. *This insurrection against the military policies of the central leadership gives further indication to readers not to presume that the military and foreign policies of the top leaders always had the approval or support of the rural countryside.* The insurrection was from the people, the very source of the soldiers and commodities expected to support the opportunism of the central powers. This insurrection is even more interesting, assuming any kind of accurate memories provided by the Chronicler, because the Chronicler describes it as part of the historian's apparent defense of Pekah's actions against Judah. Notably for us, Chronicles then describes even more violence that Ahaz faced:

> For the Edomites had again invaded and defeated Judah, and carried away captives. And the Philistines had made raids on the cities in the Shephelah and the

Negeb of Judah, and had taken Beth-shemesh, Aijalon, Gederoth, Soco with its villages, Timnah with its villages, and Gimzo with its villages; and they settled there. (2 Chr 28:17–18)

Hoshea then killed Pekah. Although Hoshea feigned loyalty to Assyria, the Deuteronomistic Historian accuses him of duplicity in plotting with Egypt against Assyria, political moves that Hoshea probably initiated after the death of Tiglath-Pileser III (727 B.C.E.), which likely gave him hope of breaking free from Assyrian constraints (2 Kgs 17:1–5). This revolt, in turn, brought Shalmaneser to Samaria, and the resounding defeat is associated with the fall of the northern kingdom in 722. However, Sargon II (the brother of Shalmaneser) also claimed responsibility for the defeat of Samaria, and it is entirely possible that both brothers were involved in ways that allowed Sargon II to later boast when he was in sole control.[1]

The Deuteronomistic Historian (2 Kgs 17) gives some detail about the movement of peoples into the northern territory by Sargon II (only referred to here as "king of Assyria"); yet for this time, archaeology also indicates a movement of population southward, significantly expanding Jerusalem, and also settlements in nearby territories (cf. Smith 1984).

Hezekiah's Revolt against Assyria: God's Protection, or Trapped "like a Bird in a Cage"?

After an apparent gap in the biblical descriptions, the texts then skip to the events of the Assyrian attacks on Jerusalem in 702/701 B.C.E. The Assyrian king quartered his armies at Lachish after defeating "the fortified cities" of Judah (again, only 5–6 miles from Micah's village); from there he sent his officers to offer terms of surrender to Jerusalem. As the text of 2 Kgs 18–19 now reads, Hezekiah initially provided tribute payments (2 Kgs 18:14–16), but the narrative continues to describe a later confrontation at Jerusalem with the officers sent by the Assyrian king. Many commentators have proposed that the entire account in 2 Kings suggests that Sennacherib was not happy with the tribute payments and demanded more—thus overstepping his authority against God's chosen city and therefore bringing on God's miraculous reprisal against the Assyrian armies. For many scholars, this odd sequence (tribute paid, then further hostile encounter) suggests a combination of sources, and even versions, of what actually occurred. Furthermore, in the famous speech before

---

1. Grabbe discusses the famous disagreement in the Assyrian records with regard to the actual conqueror of Samaria, either Shalmaneser V (see 2 Kgs 17:3–6) or Sargon II (*ANET* 284–85). Grabbe notes that the archaeological evidence suggests not an actual destruction but a massive deportation and that a deportation may be what Sargon was actually referring to in 722, rather than a conquest accomplished perhaps by Shalmaneser (2007, 149).

the walls of Jerusalem, the Assyrian officer (the Rabshakeh) offers terms of surrender that include, notably, the promise that Judean vassals of Assyria will prosper and "eat from your own vine and your own fig tree" (2 Kgs 18:31; cf. Mic 4:4). Moreover, the text emphasizes (2 Kgs 18:26–27) that the Assyrians intentionally used a language understandable to the general population (perhaps conscripting a captured Judean or even a sympathizer? or with knowledge provided from a sophisticated Assyrian intelligence system? see Dubovský 2006). It seems probable that the Assyrians hoped for yet another native insurrection against the central Judean power by appealing to the interests of the populace—even promising agricultural productivity and relative peace. *The book of Micah may well represent precisely the kind of insurrectionist thinking that the Neo-Assyrian armies hoped to instigate.*

There is a growing literature on the relation of the texts of 2 Kings, Isaiah, the Neo-Assyrian accounts, and many later accounts of Sennacherib's famous campaign in Judah (esp. Gallagher 1999; Kalimi and Richardson 2014). For example, recent work tends to divide the material in 2 Kgs 18:13–19:37 into at least two sources: a proposed shorter version of events called A (2 Kgs 18:13–16), which has now been joined to a longer version marked B (2 Kgs 18:17–19:37; see Kalimi 2014, 23–25). Version B appears to be a theological development, intended to present Hezekiah in a more positive light, while version A simply and curtly recounts the negative results of Hezekiah's attempted defiance of Assyria.

The B account is paralleled in Isa 36–39, focusing on Isaiah's promise to Hezekiah that the Assyrians will not be successful. The B account further suggests that God sends an angel to defeat the Assyrian armies (2 Kgs 19:35), while Sennacherib's own inscriptions speak of Hezekiah being trapped "like a bird in a cage" but avoid mentioning the fact that Jerusalem itself did not fall. Did something actually happen? Did Sennacherib fail? Laato summarizes the contrasting descriptions of the event itself and concludes, after establishing the tendencies toward exaggeration in Neo-Assyrian annals as a balance to the usual criticism of the biblical record, that Herodotus's suggestion about a plague breaking out makes the most sense (1995). In short, the Assyrians failed in their goal of actually conquering Jerusalem. On the other hand, Fales suggests that Sennacherib would have considered his Judean campaign "a complete success" given the restoration of Assyrian hegemony over the entire area, forced allegiances, and amounts of tribute and booty (2014, 248). Fales observes that Sennacherib's decision not to physically invade Jerusalem is consistent with other Neo-Assyrian tactics with regard to capital cities. What seems clear in the debate between a proposed A source and B source, however, is the presence of clearly divided opinion about Hezekiah's actions. Source A simply recounts Hezekiah's humiliating apology ("I have done wrong . . ."; 2 Kgs 18:14) and payment of tribute; it seems to represent a negative opinion—and thus a viewpoint that, we will argue, is clearly reflected in Micah's opposition to Hezekiah's actions.

One further aspect of Hezekiah's attempted revolt is tied to the fascinating debates surrounding the significance and meaning of the troves of LMLK ("belonging to the king") jar stamps and now also the so-called pillar figurines, basically fertility dolls (amulets?) of eighth–seventh-century Judah.

Excursus 1: LMLK Jar Stamps, Pillar Figurines, and Military Preparations in the Shephelah

It is widely presumed that the hundreds of jar-handle stamps labeled LMLK (and some labeled with four different settlements) found in eighth-century levels of Judean archaeological sites are from jars that likely stored wine, oil, and possibly grain. Over 300 were found in Jerusalem itself. The significance of these numerous jar-handle stamps continues to be debated.

The jar handles have been found predominantly in the Shephelah region and in the hill country of the north in Judah—in short, precisely along a line of defense that a Judean ruler would anticipate needing to supply in preparing for an Assyrian attack "from the north" and along the coastal plains, where armies could travel to stage an assault up the hills toward Jerusalem itself (and precisely the Assyrian routes of Tiglath-Pileser III, Sargon II, and Sennacherib in 701). Over 350 of the jar stamps were found in Lachish alone (Naʾaman 1986; Lipschitz 2012), and about 40 were found in Tell Judeidah (Broshi 1993; Stern 2001), the proposed site of Micah's town, Moresheth, among other locations where the handle stamps were found. Notably, a small number were even found in the ruins of Gath, supporting arguments that Gath was among the border towns that often changed hands between Philistine and Judean control and were likely in Hezekiah's control for part of his reign.[2] The fertility figurines, also, come from this same general area: "Approximately ninety-six percent of the provenanced pillar figurines (822 of the 854 total specimens, but we now have over 1000 . . .) have surfaced within the geographic parameters traditionally ascribed to Judah during the eighth to seventh centuries BCE" (Byrne 2004, 139).

Were these jars stored by Hezekiah in the late eighth century B.C.E. in anticipation of the many siege battles from Assyrian invasion(s)? Naʾaman, among many others, especially following Ussishkin (1976), is certain that they were. Borowski believes that many other aspects of Hezekiah's "religious reforms" are directly related to his anticipated battles with Assyria (1995). Notably, Naʾaman disputes the argument that the LMLK jars indicate royal storehouse activity, and thus normal "peacetime" economic activity, because "*lmlk* jars were never found in royal stores, as should be the case for the produce of crown lands; rather they were found in private houses" (1986, 14). In any case, the number of the jar handles found at Tell El-Judeideh, Gath, and the very large numbers at Lachish may attest to the strategic significance of these places as outposts

---

2. Schniedewind dates the LMLK stamps at Gath to Sargon's campaign of 713–712 B.C.E. rather than Sennacherib's campaign against Judah in 701/702 (1998, 76).

that were being prepared by Hezekiah in the face of an Assyrian onslaught, which did come in 703–701 B.C.E.[3]

Recently, however, the debates about the jar stamps have been joined to the equally intriguing debates over the so-called pillar figurines in the same areas and in the same time periods. These female images typically feature exaggerated breasts being held by the arms and/or hands of the figure. There is clear evidence for mass production of these figurines (e.g., the use of molds) as well as evidence for simple handmade varieties of the same image. Byrne has recently reiterated the argument that the enlarged breasts are likely to be associated with birth and breast-feeding; thus they are presumed to be fertility symbols, possibly with some kind of magical powers to encourage fertility (2004).[4] Byrne speculates that these figurines, rather than representing a "folk religious" belief in magic contrary to the "official religion" of the Jerusalem royal house, may well represent evidence of further official religious policies of increasing birthrates, either in anticipation of losses to Assyrian invasions, or just as likely to produce soldiers. Byrne provocatively suggests that the number of figurines found in Jerusalem itself (405, or nearly half of the total examples found thus far) indicates official tolerance of the "use" of these figurines at the very least, or perhaps even official encouragement of the reproductive results from distributing such magical artifacts. Such a population policy would have striking resonance with Micah's bitter complaint about the loss of children (2:9). Compare modern moves to make reproduction itself a battlefront for militarized ethnic battles, such as the late twentieth-century conflicts of Bosnia and Serbia (see Smith-Christopher 2009; Barstow 2000; O'Toole, Schiffman, and Kiter 2007; B. Allen 1996).

Moresheth as Frontier Town: Local Issues and Economy

Micah is identified as coming from Moresheth. Despite the fact that Jerusalem has heretofore had the lion's share of attention even in Micah studies—the importance of these events to the Shephelah (lowlands; cf. Jer 17:26) is significant on a number of levels and especially to our reading of Micah, his ideology, and the book's message. The mention of Moresheth, for example, already makes sense in the light of villages and cities named in Mic 1: Gath, Adullam, and Lachish. The location of Moresheth is (almost) unanimously identified by modern archaeologists as the site now called Tell Judeideh, some 23–25 miles southwest of modern Jerusalem.[5] More significant, however, is its proximity to

---

3. Lipschitz (2012), however, has questioned Ussishkin's focus on the period of preparation for 701 B.C.E. and has suggested that most of the LMLK stamps were in use over a much larger period of time, although certain "private stamps" may still show signs of a significant preparation for the onslaught of 701 B.C.E. For a response, see Ussishkin 2014.

4. We are only beginning to seriously study Jewish magic in both ancient and later periods. For a fascinating overview, see Bohak 2008; 2009.

5. The identifications of the site as Moresheth begin already at the end of the third century C.E. with Eusebius (*Onomasticon* 134.10), and there are charming early legends about the location of a Byzantine church built on the "tomb of Micah" after pious Christians "discovered" the body of Micah and respectfully interred him where the church stands at Al-Bassal. This is some distance, however, from Tell Judeideh. There are criticisms of this identification. See Vargon 1992, 557–64.

Lachish, which was the second most important city in Judah after Jerusalem.[6] In fact, Stern points out that Moresheth was built along an "inner line" of defensive towns (he proposes a less densely populated "outer line" further down from the foothills) in the Shephelah (2001, 143).

Although not excavated recently, Tell Judeideh was examined in 1899–1900 as part of a series of excavations in nearby villages. It appears to have signs of settlement beginning in the Bronze Age, was abandoned, and then was rebuilt in the First Temple period (Broshi 1993). Stern cites evidence of continued occupation into the seventh century by identification of a few seals and figurines that are not typical of the earlier periods (2001, 148). Notably, however, small trading weights were also discovered, suggesting the kind of local agricultural business that was of central concern to Micah. The site was finally destroyed in the Neo-Babylonian period, no doubt as part of Nebuchadnezzar's campaigns in 587/586 B.C.E. The location is 398 meters above sea level, and some have pointed to the possibility that the village was often viewed as a "suburb" of the Philistine city Gath, which is a reason occasionally given for why it appears as "Moresheth-gath," as in Mic 1:14. "Gath," however, probably means "winepress," and there are other sites using the term: Gath-hepher (Josh 19:13; 2 Kgs 14:25), Gath-rimmon (Josh 19:45; 21:24–25). It is more important to notice the site as under the control of Lachish.

Lachish, so close to Micah's home village, had not only major military importance in the conflicts with Assyria but also an economic significance. The city was among the district administrative centers that has been described by archaeologists as a site of "special military importance," featuring a palace fortress and "densely built domestic houses" (Ussishkin 2013, 69–71). The economic importance of Lachish, however, is further supported by the fact that it was rebuilt and reoccupied after the destruction by Sennacherib. Mazar notes (somewhat ironically) that the seventh century was a "period of prosperity" for Lachish (1990, 438).

In terms of the violent history of Lachish, our sources include the graphic and grisly depictions of the fall of the city's defenses in horrific battle scenes from Nineveh, showing the invasions of Sennacherib in 701 B.C.E. (*ANEP* 130–31). We have every reason to keep in mind the horrific threats of violence that living along the "defensive line" must have meant to Micah and his people. Even if we take into consideration the tendencies toward exaggeration in ancient Near Eastern battle descriptions and "read" the visualizations of Assyrian conflict as propaganda (Laato 1995; Holloway 2002; Younger 1990), the context of fear is palpable. Na'aman states that it is in Stratum IV, representing the ninth

---

6. Mazar points out that while eighth- to seventh-century Jerusalem occupied some 150 acres, by far the largest settlement in Judah, Lachish was 20 acres (1990, 409–17), yet Ussishkin notably calls Lachish "the largest and most massive edifice known today from ancient Judah" (2014, 77).

and eighth centuries, that "massive fortifications were constructed" (1986, 6). Na'aman reassigns the list in 2 Chr 11:5–10 to the time of Hezekiah, when "Gath," specifically, would have been under Judean control.

In sum, the evidence points to Moresheth as existing in a classic border region, pulled between competing central powers, often changing hands, and reflecting the cultural as well as political influences of rival powers (cf. Weitzman 2002). Furthermore, the proximity of Gath and the Philistine peoples suggests an awareness of the Other that may have been more unusual than in Jerusalem itself, where war policies can be formulated ("on their beds," Mic 2:1), amid blissful ignorance of needing to deal with ongoing consequences for peoples living in the borderlands. Edelman also suggests the possibility of interaction between Judean and Philistine villages under the "watchful eyes" of the Assyrian economic umbrella (2008, 401).

In his significant metastudy, Raz Kletter (1999) tries to bring together the various archaeological reports about the distribution of more than one kind of artifact, including the LMLK stamps, as well as rosette stamps, horse-and-rider figurines, and female figurines (often presumed to be Asherah figurines in a "folk religion" of Judah). Kletter's main task is to suggest the possibilities for these artifact-distribution maps for the ongoing discussions of locating the political and ethnic borders of Judah. However, what seem particularly important for Micah studies are his observations about this borderland, this frontier between coastal Philistia and the Judean Shephelah. Kletter's study reveals a distinct mixing of regional styles in precisely these locations (e.g., Judean weights at Gath, "coastal figurines at Lachish"); he also notices the constant state of debate in the scholarly literature about the status of Philistine cities like Gath in relation to Judean control (1999, 26). The very debate about where the boundaries are to be located indicates the shifting borderland or frontier status of precisely this area. When we add to this Sennacherib's specifics about his campaigns in 701, the picture becomes even more interesting. At Ekron, Sennacherib's battle descriptions speak of capturing those who tried to revolt.[7] He "hung their bodies on watchtowers." Finally, he detached lands from the coastal plains and put territories into the hands of handpicked allies in the areas of Ashdod, Ekron, and Gaza (Hallo and Younger 2002, 302–3; cf. Chavalas 2006, 344–50). Not only do we thus have a written accompaniment to Nineveh's horrific reliefs depicting Lachish's fall; we also have land changing hands precisely along the borderlands of Philistia and the Judean Shephelah— Micah's territories.

Micah therefore comes from a part of Judah that is a frontier of violence between Philistines, Judeans, and invading Mesopotamians and Egyptians,

---

7. Schniedewind notes that the rise of Ekron is to be taken as a measure of the destruction of Gath in Sargon's campaigns of 712 (1998, 73).

even more than secluded Jerusalem, located up in the hills. Hence Sennacherib occupies the Shephelah but sends representatives to negotiate a surrender of Jerusalem, according to 2 Kgs 18, no doubt hoping to avoid the costs of the uphill campaign. Is it any wonder, then, that Micah directs his rage against "the mountains" (i.e., Jerusalem; 1:4; 6:1) from the "badlands" of the Shephelah in the late eighth century?

In short, what is notable about this series of references to biblical historiography is that it does not depend on detailed knowledge of events, which are hard to verify, but on the "impressions" of the time period in which we are interested. Time and again, we read references to violence in the Shephelah, the mustering of troops, and collections of tribute or taxation. Without even trying to be comprehensive, we can paint a striking picture by using textual references to horrific violence or economic pressures (including mustering armies and rations for military actions), especially involving the Shephelah/Lachish area throughout this period. (See table 2.)

When this is read while simultaneously gazing at the reliefs of Lachish battle scenes that adorned Sennacherib's palace at Nineveh, is it any wonder that Micah "mourns," "wails," and rages against the powers he blames for the destruction of his communities, those he calls "my people"? (cf. Dempsey 2014). Micah is, as we shall see, deeply concerned about endless warfare and the human and economic costs of these constant battles and preparations for battle. The problem with Micah studies heretofore has been an understandable but now inexcusable focus on Jerusalem and the "central powers" when our attention should be on the Shephelah, especially Lachish, and the state of the region where Micah's attention would naturally have been focused: Moresheth, Micah's home!

Plows and Swords: An Economics of Eighth-Century Rural Palestine

In modern biblical studies, we have seen a revival of serious interest in trying to be specific about the economic context of prophetic literature—especially with regard to the meaning of "justice," the "poor," loss of "houses" and "fields," and so forth. In his recent study, Houston helpfully outlines many of the competing social and economic models for describing the situation that gave rise to eighth-century prophetic accusations of injustice toward the poor or peasant farmers of Judah and Israel (2006). Was the system a form of sharecropping? Was rising class conflict a response as an elite began to dominate a rural poor by overcoming an older distributive ideal in Mosaic practice? Was the monarchy moving toward letting a centralized elite control ever more expansive amounts of territory? Or was it a patronage system, where unequal power relations, including economic relations, are maintained within a culturally specific mythology of family or kinship ties and obligations, which can include loyalty to agreed

Context for Micah and for Reading Micah

Table 2. Violence in the lowlands
(approximate dates; S = south, Judah; N = north, Israel)

790	Amaziah (S) battles Edom and challenges Israel.
786/5	Jehoash (N) defeats Amaziah (S) at Beth Shemesh (10 miles from Moresheth).
785	Jerusalem is sacked.
785–759	Massive military buildup under Uzziah (S), including state building projects in the Shephelah, state-run farms, and mustering of soldiers.
785–759	Uzziah initiates battles in Philistia and mentions Gath (5 miles from Moresheth).
759–745	Jotham (S) fights Ammon, fortifies towns (in highlands), fights many wars.
735	Pekah (N) does "great slaughter" in Judah; tries to take many Judean hostages.
735	Philistines raid Judean Shephelah and capture many villages near Moresheth.
734	Pekah (N) and Rezin (Aram) lay siege to Ahaz in Jerusalem.
734	Tiglath-Pileser III (Assyria) comes against Philistia.
734–725	Ahaz (S) taxes his people heavily to pay Assyrian tribute payments.
722	Assyrian conquest of Israel (N) sends large numbers of refugees south.
716	Sargon II (Assyria) likely campaigns against Philistia (Younger 1990).
713–712	Sargon II likely campaigns against Philistia; fall of Ashdod (Younger 1990).
705–701	Hezekiah (S) fortifies his line against Assyria, including the Shephelah (probable time of the hundreds of LMLK jars at Lachish and towns).
702–701	Sennacherib conquers Lachish and quarters Assyrian armies in the Shephelah.

relations (covenanted in various forms) and can even be expressed in terms like "love" and "care" issuing from the powerful to the dependent? Houston helpfully analyzes each proposal in detail (cf. also Premnath 2003), but for our purposes we do not need a *precise* socioeconomic system to be defined (e.g., Ben Zvi 1999, 88–89). The main problem with our inability to be precise about these socioeconomic relations of eighth-century Samaria and Judah is that this lack of precision can distract us from what we *can* know about socioeconomic relations in this time period:

1. Clear archaeological evidence shows the growth of powerful secondary sites in addition to Jerusalem in the south and Samaria in the north. We are particularly interested in the importance of Lachish, near Micah's home.
2. Elite wealth is certainly in evidence, such as the famous ivories of Samaria and the ostraca that record taxation of wine and oil (see Dever 2005, 424). It is precisely the ability of the royal Judean family to offer apologies and tribute payments that interest Sennacherib (e.g., "ivory beds," in Hallo and Younger 2002, 302–3; cf. Amos 6:4).
3. The LMLK stamps are clear evidence for royal involvement in distributing resources such as wine and oil, and probably grain, whether for military preparation or not, possibly including the official encouragement of fertility through talisman-like pillar figurines.
4. Biblical texts from the prophets reflect, even if we cannot be precise about the economic relations involved, a clear anger about perceived exploitation by powerful elites, mistreating those defined as weak and vulnerable: the "poor" (*dallîm* or *'ănîyîm*, Isa 3:15; 14:30; *'ebyônîm*, Amos 4:1); "my people," "women," and "children" (Mic 2:8–9); "widow and orphan" (Isa 1:17; Jer 7:6).
5. The biblical texts reveal that these exploitative practices are not the unintended results of otherwise honest economic activity (peripheral damage) but come from policies planned to seek permanent economic advantages without regard to human costs (Mic 2:1; 3:11; Amos 6:1–6; Isa 32:6)
6. Finally, these exploitative actions play havoc with the basics of life: houses and fields (Isa 5; Mic 2:2, 9).

Antimilitary Populism as the Ideological Context for Reading Micah

Finally, we do not fully appreciate the radicalism of this prophet unless we add one critical element to a discussion of his "context," a context that is a key to reading the book of Micah: the exploitation of people and resources and the resulting economic inequalities, which are created precisely by the royal and elite buildup of the military. Previous suggestions point the way. For example, in passing Dever observes that Micah represents a "populist" attitude toward economic relations in Judean and Samarian society (2005, 288). Wolff famously

Context for Micah and for Reading Micah

argues that Micah was actually a village "elder," appealing on behalf of his rural-based kin and their village economies, arguing for a more just distribution of resources and against a growing elite expropriating local power, resources, and economies (1981; 1990). Sweeney suggests that the book "points to a man who knows firsthand the terrors of war and the brutality of life in an ancient city under siege.... His constant criticism of Israel's and Judah's leadership indicates the perspective of a man who lives in an outlying village that suffers as a result of the decisions made in Samaria and especially in Jerusalem" (2000, 340). This commentary builds on all of these proposals, although I argue that what has been missing in the previous analysis of Micah the person *and* Micah the book is a major emphasis on the specifically military expropriations that were part of the context of late eighth-century Shephelah existence. Therefore the most effective way to understand Micah in his historical, geographical, and ideological context is to read his message as a regionally oriented religious and political challenge to the oppressive economic and military interests of the central elite of Jerusalem. Micah's message should be read from the "interested perspective" of Micah's own agriculturally based lowland region. Micah represents an attitude of ancient localism that sees primary loyalties to family, clan, and region, rather than identifying completely with the fate of the "national" elite in a dominant city.

Thus Micah exhibits a certain inherent suspicion of centralized militarism, a suspicion that has often been a characteristic of many examples of "populist" attitudes in history. Such attitudes are not based in any moralistic pacifism (although sometimes such attitudes can accompany these views) but rather represent a political resistance to serving interests far removed from home. In more recent history, this has sometimes been associated with labor's antiwar sentiments, typical of the International Workers of the World (IWW, the so-called Wobblies). Other examples include the little-known Green Corn Rebellion in August 1917. That rebellion united Oklahoma tenant farmers (black and white!) against conscription for the American entry into World War I. They intended to march on Washington, swearing to live on "green corn" along the way, but they were savagely repressed within a week of the uprising (Bissett 1999, 150–53; Burbank 1976, 133–56). Finally, one may cite Fred Stover, the fiery leader of the Iowa Farmers Union who opposed the Cold War, the Korean War, and Vietnam until his death in 1990 (Pratt 1988, 1996). American farming history has no shortage of Micahs.

Like the ancient poetry of the book of Micah, one of the best sources for this kind of populist antimilitary ethos is precisely in folk songs from both American and European history. Examples are not difficult to find, such as the late Hazel Dickens's haunting Appalachian song "Will Jesus Wash the Bloodstains from Your Hands?" and the antiwar sentiments of "Down by the River Side" (a classic Negro spiritual already recorded in 1920 by the Fisk Jubilee Singers), which features lyrics taken directly from Isa 2 // Mic 4:

> Gonna lay down my sword and shield
> Down by the river side . . .
> Ain't gonna study war no more.

Further examples must include Edwin Starr's electrifying 1970 cover of a Temptations anti-Vietnam War tune, "War—What Is It Good For?" One can also cite the far less familiar words of the later verses of "The Internationale," whose lyrics suggest a French "Micah" from the nineteenth century:

> The state oppresses and the law cheats.
> The tax bleeds the miserable. . . .
> The kings make us drunk with their fumes.
> Peace among ourselves, war to the tyrants!
> Let the armies go on strike,
> Stocks in the air, and break ranks.
> If these cannibals insist
> On making heroes of us,
> Soon they will know our bullets
> Are for our own generals!
>   (Fullerton 1914, 227)

A careful reading of the biblical book before us strongly suggests that the prophet from Moresheth would have sung along with the French composition *avec brio* ("with gusto"; cf. Mic 3:1–4)!

In fact, to argue that militarism is a central theme in Micah is too easy. To begin, the sheer number of references to violence, weapons, and warfare (or the contrast of peace and well-being) is striking in the book of Micah, as in this preliminary list:

1:3	"Treading" upon the earth (military metaphor).
1:8	Micah speaks of becoming a prisoner of war ("naked").
1:13	Chariots at the fortress of Lachish.
1:15	A coming conqueror.
1:16	Exile.
2:4	Captors take land.
2:8	People forced to fight; peace taken from people who have "no thought for war" (NRSV).
3:5	Prophets-for-pay encourage war when they are hungry.
3:10	Leaders build cities with bloodshed.
3:11	Well-paid false prophets preach security.
4:3	God's judgments arbitrate between nations.
4:3	Weapons are fashioned into farm tools.
4:3	Nations no longer prepare for war.
4:4	Peoples will sit under their own vines and fig trees.

Context for Micah and for Reading Micah 23

4:8	Jerusalem will be conqueror again (words from false prophets?).
4:10	People exiled to Babylon.
4:11	Nations encircle Judah.
4:13	Jerusalem will conquer other nations (from Micah or prophetic opponents?).
5:1	Zion under siege.
5:4	Promise of true "rest" and "security" under new Ruler.
5:5–6	Threat against Assyrian invasions.
5:8	Jerusalem will conquer foes.
5:10	God will destroy all horses and chariots.
5:15	Judgment will come on nations.
6:4	God brought the people from Egypt.
6:5	God protected the people against Balaam on the route through Moab.
6:14	Resources are handed over to imperial taxation.
7:2	People plan bloodshed.
7:10	Enemies will boast over the defeat of Judah.
7:12	Enemies will gather in Judah/Zion.
7:16–17	Nations will be ashamed of their "power" and repent.

The importance of this becomes clearer when we ask, What did preparations for battle mean for Micah and his fellow lowlanders? A presumption that has gone unexamined far too long about the book of Micah goes something like this: "The prophet Micah was a nationalist urgently advising loyalty to Jerusalem and the plans of its central administration." In our reading of the book of Micah, we will see that there is serious reason to question this presumption of nationalistic loyalty in Micah, a presumption that may have more to do with the values of modern readers than with the text itself.

While it is certainly true that some early prophets encourage wars (Christensen 1975, 21–72), we have already noticed the evidence for internal insurrections *against* some wars planned by the central powers of the northern and southern kingdoms, and we need to recognize the times when prophets or even local elders forbid or oppose violence by the central power:

- In 1 Kgs 12:22–24, Shemaiah forbids war against Jeroboam.
- In 1 Kgs 22:17–18, Micaiah ben Imlah stops a conflict by predicting disaster so that people can "go home in peace."
- In 2 Kgs 6:20–23, Elisha forbids the slaughter of the Arameans.
- Despite one prophet encouraging Jehu's slaughter of the house of Ahab in 2 Kgs 9, Hosea condemns such violence in Hos 1:4.
- In 2 Chr 28:9–15, tribal leaders of the north (and the prophet Oded) "rise up" and forbid slaughter or enslavement of Judeans under Pekah.

In fact, we have reason to suspect that the basis for at least some of the antimilitary ethos evident in some parts of the Deuteronomistic History is not some kind of ancient "pacifism" but rather a "populist" realization of the economic impact of warfare preparation. The key, ironically enough, appears in a close reading of one of the most famous passages in Micah—the Peace Passage at the beginning of chapter 4, but with particular attention to vv. 3–4:

> They will hammer their swords into plows,
>   and their spears into vineyard shears.
> A nation will not lift up a sword against a nation,
>   and they will no longer train for war. (v. 3b)
> A man will dwell under his vine and his fig tree,
>   and will no longer fear. (v. 4a)

Amid the scholarly interest in this powerful imagery, readers have tended to miss the details as we are taken up in prosaic rapture over the (all-too-rare) biblical sentiment for an era of disarmed peace. But on sober reflection, the imagery itself is the key. In short, what if Micah is *not* merely waxing poetic? What if Micah is quite literal? Weapons *should* be refashioned into farming tools! Preparations for war are contrasted with the business of family farms. Micah prefers his own vine and fig tree—precisely what the Rabshakeh promises! Is Micah (who, in contrast to Isaiah, actually uses the "vine and fig tree" image) advocating that the central powers should take the deal offered by Assyria (2 Kgs 18:31//Isa 36:16; cf. Mic 4:4, a sentiment not found in the parallel passage of Isa 2:2–4)? Plausibly Micah has always considered Hezekiah's revolt to be the Jerusalem elite's dangerous folly.

Furthermore, we also cannot fully appreciate the vision of 4:1–5 without taking into consideration the warnings about the future of kingship in the famous "antiroyalist" passage in 1 Sam 8. This text mentions that the "sons" of the people will become commanders, but then elaborates that the "sons" will also be forced to plow and reap the fields of the central power, which is immediately followed by "and to make his implements of war and the equipment of his chariots" (1 Sam 8:12). That is, those who plow and reap will also make implements of war. This is conceptually the obverse of Mic 4:1–5! Indeed, virtually all of vv. 12–17 in 1 Sam 8 refers to the militarization of Hebrew agricultural society! The description of 1 Sam 8 also reminds us of, if anything, the typical lists of tribute from Neo-Assyrian annals—such as the resources that Sennacherib mentions among the "tribute payments" demanded from conquered western Judean and Philistine cities in 701: "ivory beds, . . . bows and arrows, countless trappings and implements of war, daughters, palace women, male and female singers" (Hallo and Younger 2002, 302–3).

In short, what Sennacherib wants is precisely what the monarchs of Israel also want. Thus 1 Sam 8 suggests that the changed conditions amount to tribute payments from the people to the central royal establishment and concludes with a clear reference to the command society of Egypt in v. 18, when the people "cry out" as they did under Egyptian slavery (cf. Exod 2:23). Readers will see that Micah reads very much like this.

If Micah is an elder, then it seems entirely consistent that, as a local leader, he grows weary of the constant military buildup of the royal houses—a militarization that exploits village farmers and extracts not only commodities but also the soldiers themselves, the "sons" and "daughters" (1 Sam 8:11, 13). Furthermore, if this is true, then there is a strong argument to be made against one of the most widely held canons of Micah scholarship: the proposed "contradiction" between the treatment of Jerusalem in 3:12 and the Peace Passage of 4:1–5. If Jerusalem/Zion is to be "plowed as a field" (3:12, echoing that Samaria will be planted with vineyards in 1:6), how is this a *contradiction* to weapons being hammered into farming tools? Jerusalem and Samaria, in short, are no longer the source of constant mustering and extraction of military preparations. Rather, they become fields to be plowed and vineyards to be tended—something actually *useful* in the eyes of Micah the farmer! Micah even envisions the nations coming to work on the newly reclaimed Jerusalem farm!

If there is a *unique* theme running through the book of Micah, it certainly is not the theme of social justice, or criticism of the cult in favor of justice, or criticism of false prophecy or exploitation by a ruling elite: all these themes can be identified in other prophetic texts. Instead, it is precisely Micah's populist-based criticism of the social destructiveness of relentless military buildup, mustering, and extraction. If Micah argues that Jerusalem should be "plowed as a field" and thus become a place for making farming tools from weapons, such imagery is entirely consistent with Micah's love for striking, imaginative, and provocative imagery.

I propose that readers may have missed this precisely because of the debate over the famous Peace Passage in 4:1–5. The lines of the debate have tended to focus on whether the passage is a kind of pacifist/universalist message of love and reconciliation between nations (and thus whether such a sentiment could even be found in this era), or whether the nations come to Zion and are forced to destroy weapons because the Hebrew people are militarily ascendant, and everyone else cowers under a forced, even if miraculously imposed, Pax Israelitica. This specious argument is based only on a carefully selected group of comparatively violent texts and thus is not open to other textually supported comparisons (most notably Zech 8:20–23).

This is also why so much attention has been focused on the meaning of the prologue to the passage: "In the end of days," or "In the latter days" (4:1). The more convincing the argument that this passage represents a stunning vision of world peace and reconciliation, *the more the passage is safely relegated to the distant future and thus dismissed as a mere pipe dream of Micah* (and Isaiah), or the dream of a later editor, or even (with van der Woude 1969) another of the promises of one of Micah's opponents regarding Zion's inviolability! What is rarely proposed, however, is that Micah is dead serious: he proposes a refusal to continue to send their sons and daughters "up the hill" to Jerusalem, a refusal to constantly produce the arrays of weaponry for Jotham, Ahaz, and Hezekiah's (and probably Uzziah's) ever-impressive armories. "In the latter days" does not mean, "I realize this will never happen," as it is usually taken to imply (at least to modern readers), but rather "I propose this as the ideal of God that will come—and I hope sooner than later." *If 3:12 is read with 4:1–5*, Micah invites the nations to reject war and their elite war masters for the peaceful commerce of agriculture and suggests that they all start with his own elite's city: Jerusalem!

In short, the typical choices of either a form of Hebrew pacifism on the one hand, or an example of a Pax Israelitica conquest on the other—these are not the only two options. I propose that Micah is no pacifist, but a close reading of the book suggests that he, and his editors, are enraged and weary with incessant warfare and simply want to get back to the farm and the more equitable distribution of commodities that this would allow! His is a populist critique of militarism, more in line with populist, labor-inspired criticisms of warfare as a form of "capitalist control of the masses." It is a message very close to the motto of the early twenty-first-century movement of antiwar farmers: "Farms, Not Arms!" One of the tasks of this commentary is to defend, in detail, this general reading of the book of Micah in the comments that follow.

Micah's Revolt and the Politics of Jeremiah

One of the most important indications of the historicity of Micah the man, and at least part of the material that now constitutes the book of Micah, is the citation of Micah by the supporters of Jeremiah in the sixth century B.C.E.

> Then the officials and all the people said to the priests and the prophets, "This man does not deserve the sentence of death, for he has spoken to us in the name of the LORD our God." And some of the elders of the land arose and said to all the assembled people, "Micah of Moresheth, who prophesied during the days of King Hezekiah of Judah, said to all the people of Judah: 'Thus says the LORD of hosts,
>
> > Zion shall be plowed as a field;
> > Jerusalem shall become a heap of ruins,
> > and the mountain of the house a wooded height.'
>
> Did King Hezekiah of Judah and all Judah actually put him to death? Did he not fear the LORD and entreat the favor of the LORD, and did not the LORD change his mind about the disaster that he had pronounced against them? But we are about to bring great disaster on ourselves!" (Jer 26:16–19)

This episode is normally a feature of debates about the historical message of Micah and whether he was a messenger of salvation as well as judgment. Furthermore, John Holladay (1970) and Cha (1996) have argued in detail for many influences from Micah evident in the present book of Jeremiah, and Holladay claims that Mic 3:9–11 is "a gold mine for Jeremiah" but tends to argue that the predominant possibilities for influence come from Mic 1–3 (1970, 50–51). The citation of Micah in defense of Jeremiah, however, is also significant because *Micah's political message is similar to Jeremiah's*, not merely in a threat to the Jerusalem elite but also as an aspect of Jeremiah's wider opposition to conflict with Babylon.

Jeremiah is opposed to the revolt against Babylon. This is not motivated by any love for the Chaldean Empire but rather by a theology suggesting that "bearing the yoke" of Babylon is God's will in the short term (Jer 28). In direct contrast to the false prophet Hananiah (a conflict reminiscent of Micah's opposition to prophets advocating God's sure protection of Jerusalem), Jeremiah asserts an independent political and theological line that counsels nonmilitary resistance until God intervenes to change the circumstances of existence. In Naʾaman's words, "Let Other Kingdoms Struggle with the Great Powers—You, Judah, Pay the Tribute and Hope for the Best" (2008, 55).

Jeremiah does counsel a form of social resistance. Citing the famous "exemptions" from military action in Deut 20, Jeremiah counsels precisely these activities to the exiles in his famous letter (Jer 29):

> Thus says the LORD of hosts, the God of Israel, to all the exiles whom I have sent into exile from Jerusalem to Babylon: Build houses and live in them; plant gardens and eat what they produce. Take wives and have sons and daughters; take wives for your sons, and give your daughters in marriage, that they may bear sons and daughters; multiply there, and do not decrease. But seek the welfare of the city where I have sent you into exile, and pray to the LORD on its behalf, for in its welfare you will find your welfare. For thus says the LORD of hosts, the God of Israel: Do not let the prophets and the diviners who are among you deceive you, and do not listen to the dreams that they dream, for it is a lie that they are prophesying to you in my name; I did not send them, says the LORD.
>
> For thus says the LORD: Only when Babylon's seventy years are completed will I visit you, and I will fulfill to you my promise and bring you back to this place. (Jer 29:4–10)

Jeremiah's theology is embodied in a community that formed immediately after the disaster of 587 B.C.E. at Mizpah, under the appointed "Governor," Gedaliah. It is worthwhile to consider the increasing modern scholarly interest in that community at Mizpah surrounding Gedaliah, which Jeremiah eventually joins before Gedaliah's assassination. In his recent survey of the entire period of the Babylonian conquest and exile, Lipschitz has written of Jeremiah advocating "a political orientation opposed to the policies of those who ruled in Jerusalem" (2005, 87–88).

There is often a disagreement, sometimes a bitter disagreement, among small or minority communities facing a stronger opponent (especially when accompanied by vastly superior firepower). Minorities must always struggle with the reality of subordinate status. The admonition to "resist to the last man" may sound stirring in patriotic songs, but *survival* is also a deeply patriotic notion. Typically the choice is not between quislings (collaborators) and violent revolt (to call one's opponents "quislings," or "cowards," is merely to take a side, not to describe social or historical realities). Just as often, a third option is proposed between total subordination and violence: nonviolent resistance. Both violent and nonviolent resistance are motivated by deeply held compassion for the people in question. A perspective rooted in the knowledge of nonviolence theory and history leads to important new views on some of the prophets (Sharp 2005).

Micah versus Isaiah?

The opposing view to Micah's form of social and spiritual resistance was held by the "Prophets of Nationalist Well-Being (Shalom)." We can see an interesting contrast between Micah's (and Jeremiah's) warnings, as well as the view expressed by Micah's contemporary Isaiah, especially when compared with the Deuteronomistic Historian's accounts of Hezekiah's actual policies in confronting the Assyrian threat.

We have noticed that the discussion of the Assyrian siege of Jerusalem around 701 B.C.E. is reported in two largely parallel texts: Isa 36–38 and 2 Kgs 18–19 (in addition to the widely cited Assyrian inscription on the same event). An important part of these biblical texts is the promise from the prophet Isaiah (in source B of 2 Kings and in Isaiah) that Assyria will be unsuccessful and humiliated. The prophet Isaiah's famous promise is as follows, divided between a poetic oracle of warning directed to the Assyrian emperor and then the promise to Hezekiah:

> But I know your rising and your sitting,
>   your going out and coming in,
>   and your raging against me.
> Because you have raged against me
>   and your arrogance has come to my ears,
> I will put my hook in your nose
>   and my bit in your mouth;
> I will turn you back on the way
>   by which you came.
>   (2 Kgs 19:27–28)

Therefore thus says the LORD concerning the king of Assyria: He shall not come into this city, shoot an arrow there, come before it with a shield, or cast up a siege ramp against it. By the way that he came, by the same he shall return; he shall not come into this city, says the LORD. For I will defend this city to save it, for my own sake and for the sake of my servant David. (2 Kgs 19:32–34)

This is immediately followed by verses describing the demise of Sennacherib. There is one particularly interesting difference between the texts in Kings and Isaiah. In 2 Kgs 18, a brief note describes Hezekiah's initial attempt to avoid the immediate threat of Assyrian attack on Jerusalem. In both Isaiah and 2 Kings, the general episode begins with the same verse, which is 2 Kgs 18:13// Isa 36:1, "Sennacherib of Assyria came up against all the fortified cities of Judah and captured them." *But only the narrative in 2 Kings continues with this brief report, part of the proposed source A*:

King Hezekiah of Judah sent to the king of Assyria at Lachish, saying, "I have done wrong; withdraw from me; whatever you impose on me I will bear." The king of Assyria demanded of King Hezekiah of Judah three hundred talents of silver and thirty talents of gold. Hezekiah gave him all the silver that was found in the house of the LORD and in the treasuries of the king's house. At that time Hezekiah stripped the gold from the doors of the temple of the LORD, and from the doorposts that King Hezekiah of Judah had overlaid and gave it to the king of Assyria. (2 Kgs 18:14–16)

The point is this: the source A may reflect Jeremiah's Realpolitik from the Neo-Babylonian era, now edited into the (earlier) eighth-century Assyrian threat. Isaiah's perspective, a nationalist resistance fueled by a confidence in the inviolability of Zion, shows no interest in Hezekiah's negotiations with the Assyrian armies. The difference between the two texts may reveal the ideological differences between Micah and Isaiah, which plays out in radically different notions of political and social strategies in relation to the Assyrian threat.[8] We have pointed to another tradition, however, that opposes many kinds of violent resistance as greedy folly: inviting the poor to die en masse so that the privileges of the elite may survive! The last question to address, therefore, is whether Micah is a revolutionary text.

---

8. This is also Stansell's argument: Isaiah has more in common with Hananiah, Jeremiah's opponent, while Jeremiah sounds more like Micah (1988, 135). Isaiah supports Zion's inviolability, while Micah resists such a view (65–66). I only add the number of times that the book of Isaiah shows concern with the house of David, promising progeny and the continuance of the line, while Mic 5 speaks of going back to Bethlehem. To start over? Uffenheimer strongly contrasts Isaiah's "utopian" neutrality with Micah's more aggressive call for militant engagement in contemporary international affairs (1984; 1994), while Pannell starkly disagrees with Uffenheimer's conclusion, but nonetheless reads Micah as calling for a nonviolent liberation and resistance (1988).

Is the Book of Micah a Revolutionary Text?

Finally, a number of commentators have asked whether Micah can be read as "revolutionary" (so Pixley 1991). This is a question raised in a significant amount of literature related to the study of Micah among the prophets. Pixley's startling argument is that the destruction of, or violence within, villages and cities enumerated in Mic 1 may well have been the prophet's call for the Judean peasants themselves to rise up against Jerusalem. At no time, Pixley points out, does Micah clearly state that such violent events would be *God's* doing. Micah, in short, is no mere reformer but a revolutionary. Further, Pannell also suggests that Micah's conceptual return to Bethlehem in Mic 5 (a pre-Davidic symbol of God's power to choose a leader) suggests that God is returning to the "source" for a *replacement*, a new messianic leader, to be contrasted with the failures of the present Davidic regime (1988). More recently, Juan Alfaro reads Micah from a perspective largely sympathetic to liberation theology (1989). Finally, the South African Old Testament scholar Wilhelm Wessels points to a very provocative reading of Micah's antimilitarist ethos; I have found his essays to be a rich source of suggestive observations (1997a; 1997b; 1998; 1999; 2003). The question of Micah as "revolutionary" is of obvious importance not only for theologians of the developing world but also for anyone interested in the contemporary pastoral and ethical implications of reading Micah.

Micah can be read as a revolutionary in the sense that he appears to call for a new paradigm, a new regime, or perhaps more to the point, a new social formulation of being God's people in relation to the very real international threats of the Mesopotamian and Egyptian regimes of history. Finally, however, the significance of whether Micah is "revolutionary" (i.e., calling for a radical change in social formations or regimes) relates directly to the tendency of the major commentaries to presume Micah's ultimate loyalty to Jerusalem and its temple, as well as seeing the capital as of ultimate and eternal significance on the one hand, and his presumed loyalty to the house of David on the other. How else can we explain the persistence of commentators who seem to always use the terms *judgment* "and *salvation*" as categories to explain Micah's thought, rather than terms such as *judgment* "and *replacement*," or "the end of the old and the beginning of the new"? The use of these latter terms would suggest a much more radical break with the present conditions. "Judgment and salvation" is a preservationist, reformist interpretation of the book of Micah: it suggests that the regime will simply be modified, perhaps deal with its problems, but ultimately continue. It is clear, however, that this is not a necessary or even the only rational or required way to make sense of the rhetoric of Micah. One way of reading Jer 26, of course, is to accept that plenty of Judeans, including Jeremiah, are ready to read Micah as far less is said to show an attempt to bring the LXX into closer conformity with the MT (Waltke 2007, 18; cf. Würthwein 1979, 54). Based on other finds in the cave, it seems certain that the text was placed in the cave during the Bar Kochba rebellion (132–136 C.E.) and, Würthwein notes, "was already well-worn." Würthwein therefore suggests that the text actually came from soon after the Jewish War of 66–70 C.E. (180). Given the amount of controversy surrounding the reproduction of the Hebrew of Micah, especially the opening sections, it is a pity that we have so little Hebrew material to work with. The Greek texts, frankly, are little help. Wagenaar, for example, argues that any attempt to correct the MT by using the LXX is highly suspect (2001, 60). The LXX often seems to be a free rendering rather than a literal translation of a variant from MT (cf. Jones 1995, 88–90). Sinclair finds only one place where Qumran fragments appear to agree with the LXX against MT (1983, 263).

Furthermore, Leslie Allen also does not believe that either 1QpMic or 4QpMic is much help in improving the text; he suggests that the Greek may only need to be resorted to in 2:7–10; 6:9–12; and 7:11–12 (1976, 253). Furthermore, Allen strongly objects to using the Greek to unravel the famous problems of 1:10–15. In short, a consensus suggests that the LXX is to be used with caution in attempting to reconstruct controversial passages of Micah, but we will nonetheless have occasion to cite interesting aspects of the LXX text, even when it does not necessarily assist in reproducing the Hebrew of Micah. The LXX is, after all, interesting not only as a translation but also as one of the earliest interpretations of Micah, and some LXX readings are significant when considered from that perspective.

Organization of the Book: The Coherence of Micah

One of the most controversial topics in Micah studies is the organization of the book as a whole and whether there is "coherence" to the book as we now have it. While the divisions within books of the Bible are always a source of significant discussion, it seems quite clear from Micah studies in the last century that dividing the book into sections, identifying these sections, and then reassembling them into a proposed "plan" is one of the primary debates associated with the study of this book. It is fair to say that this voluminous discussion is at least partly driven by reactions against late nineteenth- and early twentieth-century scholarship that broke Micah into many fragments and argued that the book was edited and continually supplemented into at least the Neo-Babylonian era. Hellenistic-era editing was argued by Paul Haupt in 1910, but it is a view virtually abandoned today. On the other hand, Andersen and Freedman find nothing in the present text that forces a date after the fifth century and thus after the Persian period (2000, 20).

wedded to the idea of mere "reform." A persistent danger in a Micah, then, is to minimize the break with the past that Micah p the present commentary tries to restore.

Literary Observations on the Book of Micah

Versions of the Text

The only available older Hebrew edition of the *entire* book of Mica Masoretic Text (MT), the critical edition of which (*BHS*) is used for thi mentary and is itself based on the Leningrad Codex. The critical edition Septuagint (LXX, Ziegler 1984) has also been consulted.

It is often presumed that the LXX is based on an alternative version o Hebrew text of Micah (Sinclair 1983), but there are no Hebrew witnesse such a proposed alternative version; some scholars believe that the LXX va tions can be explained as simply a loose translation intended to deal with pe ceived difficulties in Micah, as evident in the text already by the second centur B.C.E. Furthermore, Sinclair believes that the Qumran materials do not suffi ciently diverge from MT as to suggest even a third possible Hebrew tradition of Micah (1983, 263). The most significant older witness to the fuller text of the Hebrew from the Wadi Murabbaʿat differs little from the MT (255).

There are few witnesses to any alternative Hebrew readings of Micah. Among the Dead Sea Scrolls are two sets of fragments of the Hebrew texts of Micah, and in addition two *Pesher* (interpretation) texts that repeat parts of the Hebrew of Micah before offering their sectarian expositions (Fuller 2000). The significant texts include the following:

> *Hebrew texts of Micah*
> 4QXII^g, which generally agrees with the MT
> 4QMic, a small fragment (frg. 5)[9]
>
> *Pesher texts for Micah*
> 1QpMic (1Q14; cf. Martínez 1996, 193–94)
> 4QpMic (4Q168; cf. Martínez 1996, 194–95)

Attention is often paid to the Greek version of many of the Twelve Minor Prophets found at the caves of Naḥal Ḥever in 1952 (8ḤevXIIgr),[10] which

---

9. Fragment 5, said to include a few words from Mic 5:1–2, has at times been attributed to 4QXII^f. See Guillaume (2007). However, Callaway (2011) notes that a rather significant alternative to the MT is included in this fragment; see comments on 5:1–2 below.

10. Andersen and Freedman conclude that the Greek versions are more helpful in studying the text's transmission history than in critically reconstructing the Hebrew (2000, 3).

Jeppesen observed the rising consensus among many studies that the only part of Micah where the prophet himself may be "heard" is in the first three chapters. Yet he went on in his article to challenge this consensus by calling for more caution in dividing the book into small fragments assigned to later periods (1978). It is fair to say, however, that Micah scholarship is still largely guided by the original proposal that the "genuine sayings" are found only in Mic 1–3. This is the view proposed by Stade as early as 1881. Now, however, the increasingly emboldened arguments by some claim that more of Micah may bear eighth-century provenance than previously allowed (so L. Allen 1976).

Mignon Jacobs has collated the various proposals on this question and helpfully outlines the variety of ways in which Micah has often been divided into sections (2006, cf. Cuffey 2015). These sections are then used for charting an editorial history of the book. Jacobs (2001, 62–63) explains that some scholars argue for a sixfold division (she provides only one example of this rather rare argument: 1:2–16; 2:1–13; 3:1–4:8; 4:9–5:15 [14 MT]; 6:1–7:7; 7:8–20); a fourfold division (which varies between three different proposals); a threefold division (which differs only on whether Mic 3 is grouped with Mic 1–2 or Mic 4–5, while all agree that Mic 6–7 constitutes a separate section); and two different twofold divisions (Mic 1–5 and 6–7; or 1–3 and 4–7). This kind of structural analysis, however, can lead to some complex conclusions. For example, in his analysis of Mic 7 alone, De Moor (2000) reports finding (to his "astonishment") no less than twenty different structural patterns (for a 20-verse chapter).

In their highly detailed analysis of Micah, Andersen and Freedman (2000) chart an increased interest in dividing the book into sections of ever-diminishing size (often less than a verse or even a phrase) and then consider the book as a whole by identifying larger sections in Micah. In terms of the larger structure, Andersen and Freedman are among those who accept a threefold division and argue for the following sections (7):

1. The Book of Doom (1:2–3:12)
2. The Book of Visions (4:1–5:15 [14 MT])
3. The Book of Contention and Conciliation (6:1–7:20)

The criteria proposed for the various divisions also vary. Some have suggested the importance of identifying key terms. John Willis, for example, places a great deal of importance on three different occasions of the call to "hear" in 1:2; 3:1; and 6:1 as further indicators of separate sections, in addition to noting that each section begins with a judgment declaration and ends with a hope passage: 2:12–13; 4:1–5:15; and 7:7–20 (1968a; 1968b; 1969a; 1969b; 1969c; 1997; Waltke agrees, 2007, 14). Others point to apparent sectional breaks indicated by contrasting themes and subjects, such as the nearly universally proposed difference between the judgment on Jerusalem given in 3:12, and the hope for Zion/Jerusalem conveyed in the famous Peace Passage in 4:1–5. For example, "Sections 3:12 and 4:1ff. are in so clear opposition to one another that it practically takes one's breath away" (Jeppesen 1978, 8; see also Andersen and Freedman 2000, 18). In the minds of many readers, such differences of view indicate a difference in authorship and perhaps a radical difference in time as well.

Finally, some scholars use these various arguments to suggest a chronology for the book. Zapff (2003, 301–3) cleverly combines the views of Willis (based on the importance of three occasions of "hear" that assist in marking sections, as noted above) and Mays (1976, dividing Micah into two parts: 1–5 and 6–7) by suggesting that the final redactor added the elements noted by Mays onto a structure characterized previously by the threefold division identified by Willis. The result suggests that the later editor was more concerned about the punishment of the nations (toward the ends of chs. 5 and 7) rather than the more compassionate view of nations sharing in salvation, as exemplified by the earlier version.

Furthermore, there are many different arguments about similarity of theme based on the use of vocabulary—shepherding in "hope" sections (2:12; 4:8; 5:4 [3]; 7:14; see Waltke 2007, 12) or the use of "remnant." McKane, for example, argues that Mic 1–3 is a liturgical text to be read after the dedication of the rebuilt temple, around 520–515 B.C.E.; yet he is also impressed with arguments that see Mic 1–3 as largely about judgment and 4–5 largely about salvation. Micah 6:1–7:7 is more in the spirit of Mic 1–3, but contrary to Wolff and others, McKane argues that 7:8–20 does not hold together well enough to be itself a liturgical text (1998, 214–19). Leslie Allen, on the other hand, argues that 4:1–4 may even predate Micah, while 4:6–8 and 7:8–20 may postdate the prophet, but much in the remaining sections of the book may well belong to Micah himself, or close to his time (1976, 251). Sweeney more recently argues for an "arc" of the book that proceeds from punishment to exaltation, or from destruction to rebuilding (2004). If a theme has emerged in these various proposed divisions of the book as a whole, it is surely the importance of judgment and salvation as contrasting subjects addressed by the book as we have it.

Judgment and Hope/Salvation as Guiding Principles in Reading Micah?

It is certainly clear that one of the primary arguments with regard to Micah is precisely the perceived radical difference between hope and judgment. In earlier Micah scholarship, it was common to argue that Micah was cited in Jer 26:18 as solely a prophet of judgment, and thus only the judgment oracles in the book have claim to authenticity, and the hope sections were edited in later. However, many scholars have pointed out not only that a single citation in Jeremiah can hardly carry this kind of weighty conclusion, but also that alternations between judgment and hope are not at all impossible for a single prophet—either at different times in the prophet's life or even directed at different parts of the Hebrew populace (e.g., judgment for the "establishment," "hope" for the remnant, or "my people" after punishment). On the other hand, Williamson argues that these differences suggest editing and simply states, "Much of the book of Micah as we now have it comes from periods long after Micah's day. This is . . . based . . . on the style and thematic content of the work which suit later periods best" (2001, 595).

There are also attempts to identify sections by their adherence to certain literary formats or styles. A format might be, for example, a "chiastic structure" (as for Renaud 1977; 1987; L. Allen 1976). Form-critical approaches represent a particular kind of literary approach that tries to identify established or classic literary forms such as "warning prophecy," "lament song" (1:8–16), "funeral lament" (2:1–5), a "prophetic judgment oracle," or a "theophany" or "epiphany" (1:2–7? see Waltke 2007, 13, but most systematically presented in Ben Zvi 2000). The classic work in identifying these "forms" in prophetic literature in general is Claus Westermann's *Basic Forms of Prophetic Speech* (1967). For Micah studies, the most important work taking up this approach is Ehud Ben Zvi's 2000 commentary.

The limitations of the form-critical approach becomes clear as scholars on Micah often confidently identify a passage as "clearly" belonging to a classic literary type and then immediately proceed to describe how the writer of Micah changes, transforms, or otherwise freely adapts the form in question. In other words, the "fit" is rarely clear without these necessary "adaptations" or "artistic reworkings." Andersen and Freedman, for example, speak of the "oral rhetorical style" of Micah as a way of understanding the various stylistic changes and "unexpected" grammatical forms (2000, 24–27). Although it is clear that such adaptations are attempts to give credit to the writer's unique style, the relationship of "unique style" and "classic forms" raises methodological questions. How "unique" does a passage need to be in order to no longer be truly representative of a "classic style"? And if the authors really are "unique" in their use of "classic styles," how informative are these classic styles in the analysis? The danger is that the use of "classic styles" can detract from the unique message at hand and override the possibility that the writer is saying something unique or even new. Perhaps here is where we most need to be reminded of Alice Bach's warning: "The reader interested in challenging established assumptions needs to resist genre stereotyping as it leads to one-note readings, and intellectual inertia" (1997, 77).

Furthermore, ideas about the "message" or "coherence," and even the suggested dates of various portions of the book of Micah, often turn on a point that usually receives only cursory attention: the assumptions with regard to the identity of Micah. If Micah is an elder from the village of Moresheth, disputing with the leadership of Jerusalem, then this assumption certainly does have serious implications for what parts of the book of Micah coherently, or even reasonably, lend themselves to this kind of context. This is why I have given considerable attention to this question here in the introduction.

Finally, in an influential study, the Dutch scholar A. S. van der Woude argues coherently for the presence of a debate in the book of Micah, particularly in chapters 4–5 (1969). Here, he argues, Micah is taking on the nationalist "false" prophets who speak with confidence about Zion's inviolability. In reference to Mic 4, van der Woude asks:

> The question arises whether any prophet or pupil of a prophet, or redactor could have got it into his head to juxtapose words of doom and words of weal in such a clumsy and confusing way. Verse 9 speaks of weal (by implication), vs. 10 of doom, vs. 11–13 of weal, while vs. 14 proclaims doom. . . . In my opinion the passage in question contains neither more nor less than a disputation between the pseudo-prophets and Micah, in which the words of the arguing parties are juxtaposed. (1969, 249)

This proposal has gained many adherents who believe that such a dialogue explains what is otherwise a troubling inconsistency in arguments. To take a good example of later uses of van der Woude's argument, we can cite Wessels, who has continued this argument (as have many others)[11] and proposes a division of the material in Mic 4–5 that shows who is speaking (1999, 623–41):

Adversaries	Micah
	4:1–4
4:5	4:6–7
4:8–9	4:10
4:11–13	5:1 (4:14 MT)
	5:2–5a (1–4a)
5:5b–6 (4b–5)	5:7 (6)
5:8–9 (7–8)	5:10–15 (9–14)

---

11. In support of the idea of dialogue even when it is not clearly demarcated in the text, see, e.g., Savran 2009; Carroll 1992; Neiderhiser 1981.

There is certainly some dialogue in Micah, as is clear from reading 2:6–7 and 3:5. The absence of clear markers for a dialogue, however, has always raised suspicions about van der Woude's otherwise compelling arguments.

Van der Woude's argument is not only based on apparent inconsistency of ideas but can also be extended into identifying the actual kinds of arguments used. Although it is rarely pointed out, I find it quite compelling that a passage often assigned to Micah's opponents, the militaristic bravado of 4:13 ("I will make your horns into iron, and make your hooves into bronze"), strongly echoes the sentiment expressed in 1 Kgs 22:11, which is used by a "false prophet" in his debates with Micah's namesake from a century earlier, Micaiah ben Imlah: "Zedekiah son of Chenaanah made for himself horns of iron, and he said, 'Thus says the LORD: With these you shall gore the Arameans until they are destroyed" (also notice the use of a symbolic object, similar to Jeremiah's use of a yoke in Jer 27–28). While I am hesitant to divide the material as precisely as others have done, I agree that we occasionally have the opponents' words cited or alluded to in Micah, and I will clarify those arguments in the commentary that follows.

Micah as Drama?

Related to this important development of "voices" and "layers" in Micah studies, there has emerged a relatively new view, argued by Helmut Utzschneider (2005) and Joyce Rilett Wood (2000). Both claim that Micah is an intentionally dramatic text, "dramatic" not in the sense of being deeply impressive but in the *technical* sense: Micah is a drama reflecting many of the accepted definitions of ancient dramatic texts. Wood, for example, cites many parallels with dramatic style in Aeschylus, while Utzschneider draws on dramatic theory. In some ways, this approach parallels van der Woude's thesis about dialogue in Micah: a dramatic reading of Micah would necessitate the presence of alternative voices driving the central story forward. Utzschneider divides his "drama" into two "acts": 1:2–5:15 (14 MT), and 6:1–7:20 (2005, 16). One of the helpful insights of these two approaches, certainly, is an emphasis on the drama of rhetoric in the book, which would clearly be evident in any public reading of this material.

Jan Wagenaar's Analysis

Finally, readers need to give serious attention to one of the most detailed and careful analyses of Micah to appear in the last fifteen years, the work of Jan A. Wagenaar (2001). While we can only briefly summarize his extensive and impressive analysis, it is one of the most important attempts not only to establish a coherence, but also to chart a historical sequence of the book's development.

Wagenaar sees at least five "stages" in the development of Micah as a book. The original sequence of traditions, the first stage, may be traceable to an oral memory of the prophet's sayings and comprises 2:1–5, 6–11; 3:1–4, 5–8, 9–12. Thus Micah is remembered as a prophet of severe judgment directed against local leaders, exposing the economic oppression of small farmers. These sayings were recorded in the seventh century by circles associated with the prophet Jeremiah, which explains the extensive similarities between Micah and Jeremiah in terms of vocabulary.

A revision of these older sayings may be detected, suggests Wagenaar, in insertions like 2:3a ("against this generation"). He cites a number of other examples to show that the original sayings of Micah were broadened into an indictment against the leading circles of Judah and Jerusalem.

Wagenaar refers to a second stage as *revisions* to the first stage, which include 4:9–10; 5:1 (4:14 MT); 5:10–14 (9–13 MT); and possibly 1:3–5a, as well as the lament over the fall of Jerusalem in 1:8–16. The third stage, which includes 2:12 and 4:6–7a, results in the arrangement noticed by many others where "oracles of doom alternate with oracles of hope" (322). This stage is attributed to the school of Ezekiel and dates from the late exilic period. The fourth stage includes 4:1–5 and deals with the relationships of Judeans to the rest of the world. But a problem appears here. Wagenaar relates the vision of 4:1–5 with the attack on Jerusalem traditions represented by 5:7–8 (6–7 MT), thus reflecting quite different attitudes toward foreigners—a combined vision (peace and conquest) that he sees anticipated in 1:2 and alluded to in 5:15 (14): "The collection of sayings of Micah of Moresheth is thus transformed into a testimony addressed to the nations" (323). This stage is attributed to the same circles that worked on Second and Third Isaiah. The fifth stage is the combination of Mic 1–5 with 6–7, the words of a northern prophet, included by virtue of the first chapter's allusions to Samaria.

Wagenaar's careful reconstruction of a theorized emergence of Micah is heavily dependent on word use in other (mostly later) portions of the Bible, especially Second and Third Isaiah, Zechariah, Jeremiah, and Ezekiel. Rather than seeing these late seventh–sixth-century prophets as responding to an older collection of Micah sayings, Wagenaar reads the Micah construction as a result of editorial work by the same people responsible for these later prophets. If these word-usage comparisons are convincing, then Wagenaar's direction of influence is at least possible. If, however, we are able to establish a coherence based on historical context and a different attitude of a proposed Micah toward the central authorities of his age, then perhaps these kinds of detailed dissections of Micah are not as necessary as previously thought.

The Coherence of Micah: Summary and Observations

The manner in which the debate about literary coherence takes place, somewhat ironically, often leads away from a focus on trying to discern Micah's actual message and the theological significance of that message for the times in which it was written, much less the potential implications for people of faith reading the book of Micah today. In many cases this is because some modern scholars have despaired of ever really understanding that message, or have flatly declared that such a goal is unattainable. Instead, the discussion proceeds along the lines of analyzing literary forms, catchwords, and grammatical stylistics. In short, many analysts measure the book in quantitative rather than qualitative terms. If we can agree that editing and additions occur in the book of Micah, however, I feel compelled to ask: Did the writers actually fill in sections, phrases, or individual terms because they perceived an "incomplete lament form" or an "improper judgment oracle" form? In other words, were materials added to Micah based on the *way* the book of Micah was earlier written? Consistent with some of Wagenaar's analysis, I presume to suggest that ancient editors added to Micah because of agreements or disagreements with *what was stated*. Part of Wagenaar's goal is to measure how Micah's message was expanded and reapplied. I do not dispute the many insights that can be gathered from structural analysis and careful comparison of literary forms, but I further argue that some studies of Micah have consisted of *only* this kind of analysis, with very little attention to the possibility that Micah's message may be unique rather than merely "typical."

Therefore, despite considerable previous interest in questions of literary "coherence" or structural "forms" in Micah studies, in this commentary I seek (to paraphrase Karl Marx) not to change the book of Micah but to understand it! Although I also divide this translation into discernible "sections," I am less concerned with the identification of units and subunits, or the identification of chiastic structures. I am more concerned with the ideology and sentiment contained in the work itself. In that sense, this is predominantly a theological commentary, driven mostly by historical-critical methodologies that are supplemented and also guided by social and ideological questions. Hence identifying literary forms such as "standard theophany," "judgment oracle," or "salvation oracle" is not considered an end in itself in this commentary but will be noted only as it contributes to a proposed and plausible appreciation for what the book is saying. To identify a statement as "typical" of a particular "literary judgment form" and then refrain from seriously discussing *what is being judged* is not a position of academic "neutrality." It avoids discussing a moral issue addressed by an eighth- (or seventh- or sixth-)century writer, whose ideas may well have relevance for modern readers seeking to understand not only ancient Hebrew thought in its great variety but also modern Jewish and/or Christian values and ideas as well. Along these lines, there is one further tendency in recent readings of Micah that does, on the whole, exhibit an interest in Micah's "message": the relation of the book to other shorter prophetic works in the canon.

Micah among the Twelve

Recent work on the Minor Prophets has emphasized the need to read all of these books as part of a gathered collection that was known, already by the time of Sirach (ca. 180 B.C.E.), as "The Twelve" (Peterson 1998; Nogalski 1993; Jones 1995; House 1990; Sweeney 2001a). Note the "folk-blessing" in Sir 49:10:

> May the bones of the Twelve Prophets
>   send forth new life from where they lie,
> for they comforted the people of Jacob
>   and delivered them with confident hope.

Along these lines, one thus wonders whether there is anything significant about the fact that Micah is preceded in this collection by the strikingly universalist message of Jonah, which holds out a hope of transformation for even an enemy city like Nineveh. That book's final sentence has God asking,

> Should I not be concerned about Nineveh, that great city, in which there are more than a hundred and twenty thousand persons who do not know their right hand from their left, and also many animals? (4:11)

Yet this sentiment about Nineveh, one of the primary cities of the Neo-Assyrian Empire, is certainly not shared by the book that *follows* Micah in the canon, which is largely a bitter denunciation of precisely the same city. Indeed, this denunciation occupies all three chapters of the work known to us as Nahum. Compare the final statement of Jonah (above) to the concluding statement of the book of Nahum; after a long series of condemnations of Nineveh and Assyria, the prophet seems to relish the final taunt:

> Your shepherds are asleep, O king of Assyria; your nobles slumber.
> Your people are scattered on the mountains with no one to gather them.
> There is no assuaging your hurt, your wound is mortal.
> All who hear the news about you clap their hands over you.
> For who has ever escaped your endless cruelty?
>
> (3:18–19)

This radical difference between Jonah and Nahum has been recognized throughout the history of rabbinic and Christian interpretation, with some historians wondering if Jonah's "optimism" reflects an earlier period, while Nahum's "pessimism" comes from a later period. In short, the book of the Twelve speaks to different times rather than different attitudes. As Zapff clarifies, this kind of interpretation goes back at least to Pirke Rabbi Eliezer (ninth century C.E.), a work arguing that the repentance of Assyria in Jonah was

Literary Observations on the Book of Micah 41

short-lived, necessitating the eventual destruction of Assyria as announced in Nahum (Zapff 2003, 292–312). I am concerned, once again, that the drive for a coherent message for all the books together succeeds only in silencing the unusual, especially the radicalism of Micah, when compared to other prophetic voices in the Twelve, and even in the Hebrew Bible as a whole.

There is also debate about the arrangement of the Twelve, and whether any interpretation of the Twelve as a whole depends on a particular sequence. For example, 4QXII^g famously features Jonah at the very end, rather than immediately preceding Micah. Although Jones argues for this as representing an original sequence of the Twelve, he also claims that there was an original group of three, Hosea-Amos-Micah, and that the Twelve was "built" around this original core to produce the final product we know today (Jones 1995). Others argue that the DSS sequence in 4QXII^g represents an exception and that the MT sequence must be preserved (Zapff 2003, 294–95). Certainly ending the series with a hopeful note such as Jonah would have interesting implications for the "message" of the whole, if there is one, but it is difficult to disagree with many scholars that placement of Jonah remains a kind of wild card in this argument, so unusual are its arguments and satirical message. Jones may well be correct, however, that the witness of 4QXII^g suggests that Jonah was the last addition (1995, 221–42; but answered by Zapff 2003). Was adding Jonah a hope expressed by a late editor who rounded off the entire series on the note of radical compassion? There is even the possibility that some books (again Jonah is most often suggested) were written precisely to place them in the collection (Zapff 2003, 310–12).

Zapff is particularly intrigued with the possibility that Jonah is in dialogue with the violent nationalism of Joel and Nahum (noting, for example, similar catchphrases like Jonah 3:9 and Joel 2:14). This raises interesting questions, then, about the role of Micah "between" the two debating perspectives. Zapff argues that Micah mediates between the two positions, or at least places them in a sequence. In his view, Micah as a whole is to be read as follows:

- The judgment of Israel leads to a judgment of the nations.
- The judgment of nations leads them to return the people to Zion.
- Many of the nations also come.
- But the nations that stubbornly refuse to come will be punished.

This outline cleverly integrates the messages of Jonah (forgiveness to nations who repent) and Nahum (punishment for those who do not), yet with a remaining problem that the "message" of either salvation or destruction still involves the same people: Assyria, and is strikingly similar to Isa 60–62. Surely the message would have been clearer, however, if two *different* peoples/nations were in view, one who repented and another who did not. However, Zapff's intriguing thesis does show how it may be possible to "read" elements of the books in the Twelve with an eye to a metamessage that comes from the combination of the books, whereby the whole is greater than the sum of the parts.

Consequently, the nature of the relationship may indicate as much a dialogue as a unity. Paul House points to thematic connections between Micah and the six books preceding it, even though he argues that the direct connections with the immediately previous work, Jonah, are "not significant" (1990, 85). Micah, he argues, alludes to Hosea's use of prostitution as a slur against the leadership of the people and also agrees with Joel regarding the threat of a conqueror. Ethical transgressions are reminiscent of Amos, and Micah's warning against the gloating of enemies is reminiscent of Obadiah's accusations against Edom. Finally, Jonah may be alluded to in Mic 4:1–5 (House 1990, 85). Ultimately, House argues, Micah is part of a U-shaped trajectory of the messages of the Twelve prophets. The message descends into bitter denunciation (where Micah is among the strongest, at the bottom of the U) but then rises to hope for the future in Haggai through Malachi.

I certainly agree that the present sequence of Jonah-Micah-Nahum, irrespective of wider-ranging connections with other books, is significant. But it is difficult to come to firm conclusions. If Micah is largely read as a prophet who bitterly condemns the abuses of the Jerusalem elite and even advocates a nonmilitary response to Assyrian overtures, then the message of Jonah seems entirely appropriate in partnership with Micah. If, on the other hand, Micah's revolutionary perspective was considered so distasteful that it had to be "balanced," then Nahum was perhaps attached for this reason. Finally, however, it is hard to avoid the possibility that we, the readers, are invited to an ongoing dialogue, if not debate, in the juxtaposition of Jonah-Micah against Nahum. One might therefore suggest that Nahum can be read as yet another example of the ultranationalist prophets who were precisely Micah's opponents!

Even though I acknowledge that reading Micah in the wider contexts of the book of the Twelve is an important consideration, I can only conclude that a clarification of Micah's message remains a necessary prelude before taking up the question of Micah's relation to the Twelve in earnest. Most studies that address the relationship among the Twelve prophetic books and the possible metamessages of the collection *as a whole* are entirely dependent on conclusions about the more specific messages of the constituent books. In short, it is a different project to go from an analysis of Micah itself, to then see it in a relationship with the books surrounding it. The latter question belongs more to the earliest stages of history of interpretation—a fascinating topic, of course, but beyond this commentary.

Literary Observations on the Book of Micah 43

Reading the Whole Book of Micah as Coherent

In this commentary I will have occasion to raise questions about the assumptions typically proposed for dividing Micah into sections and assigning those sections to different time periods, thus allowing for the possibility that these sections are motivated by different ideas and ideologies. I believe, however, that the contemporary interpreter's own assumptions about ideological coherence can be challenged along the way. Yair Hoffman, for example, argues that since we are

> aware of the likelihood that the prophetic books are the final product of long and complicated redactional activity, it would be methodologically wrong to presuppose such authenticity in prophecies dealing with more than one specific topic. In such prophecies, an opposite methodological point of departure should be preferred, namely: the variety of topics may testify to redactional activity that created the alleged coherence. (2008, 87)

It is a reasonable suggestion—but it depends on identifying the topics and whether specific passages are part of a similar theme/topic or whether they introduce radically different ideas. The obvious issue, however, is that changing the alleged "theme" or "topic" can dramatically challenge ideas about whether texts actually fit together or not. For example, taking up one of the central arguments of this commentary, I challenge the widely held view that Mic 3:12, with its judgment against Jerusalem (a judgment that echoes 1:6 against Samaria), is *radically incompatible* with "streaming to Zion" and beating swords into plowshares in 4:1–5. On the contrary, from a proposed critical, antimilitarist, and thus anti-Jerusalem perspective—the very perspective I believe Micah takes— the two sentiments concur rather dramatically! Jerusalem will be plowed—and we want to pound our swords into the very plowshares that will help do the job! Perhaps then the nations can meet to unlearn war when Hezekiah's militarist Jerusalem is removed! *Suggesting that these ideas are radically incompatible avoids the otherwise startling possibility of Micah's radically critical ideology.* In the commentary I raise the possibility of hearing a stridently surprising voice of Micah by expressing some skepticism toward the previous consensus on divisions of texts and themes within the book of Micah. I argue that many (certainly not all) of the arguments about the "incoherence" of the message of Micah may reflect a discomfort with (or incredulity toward) the revolutionary implications of a Micah whose words *can* be put together under a proposed general coherence suggested by the central texts of 1:6; 2:8; 3:12; and 4:1–5. Indeed, some of the proposed later additions to Micah are clearly intended to support and maintain the radical witness of the older Micah so that its message is not forgotten.

Trauma and the Redaction of Micah

There is one final warning. In biblical studies today, more than ever before, we are aware of the impact of traumatic events on individuals and groups (Carr 2014). Trauma studies is an important part of historical-critical analysis, especially when massive military events are the subject of analysis. What does this mean for reading Micah? We will see that it matters a great deal. But before leaving the issue of "coherence" and editing in Micah, it is valuable to seriously consider recent work on transgenerational trauma. The Turkish-American psychologist and theorist Vamik Volkan suggests the mechanics of how traumas can be passed on for generations:

> The memory of the past trauma remains dormant for several generations, kept within the psychological DNA of the members of the group and silently acknowledged within the culture—in literature and art, for example—but it reemerges powerfully only under certain conditions. For instance, a political leader may reignite a dormant group memory that affects collective thinking, perceptions, and actions. (1997, 46)

Furthermore, these events then become part of social identity—and obviously also religious tradition itself:

> Because the traumatized self-images passed down by members of the group all refer to the same calamity, they become part of the group identity, an ethnic marker on the canvas of the ethnic tent. (Volkan 1997, 45)

Transgenerational trauma serves to caution us against the typically unexamined presumption by many biblical scholars that different time periods must result in presuming radically different attitudes, perspectives, or viewpoints in the proposed additions to a book. Not necessarily. Later additions to a book—especially if they were added by persons who were part of a community deeply influenced by the earlier writings of the book—may well continue to share quite similar ideas. Transgenerational trauma studies, therefore, suggest that even where we may have a strong basis for considering a passage to be a later addition to a biblical book, *this is not necessarily a strong argument for a radically different perspective in that later material.* Later material may simply reapply the older ideas in new situations. The success of these arguments, of course, rests on the historical-critical arguments I present in the commentary.

COMMENTARY

Micah 1:1 The Superscription

1 The word of YHWH, which came to[a] Micah the Moresheti,[b] against[c] Samaria and Jerusalem, which he saw[d] in the days of Jotham,[e] Ahaz, and Hezekiah,[f] kings of Judah.

a. The Hebrew suggests that YHWH's word "happened" to Micah, using the common verb "to be" (*hyh*). The Greek translation uses the *aorist* (past) form of the basic term "to occur" as well (*ginomai*).

b. Most English translations prefer "from Moresheth," but the translation above preserves more of the Hebrew idiom and is a familiar form in American English (e.g., "the New Yorker," "the Bostonian"). Whether this identification of a place (as opposed to a father or ancestor) means that Micah is particularly identified as a "rural" person is an intriguing conjecture. Does Moresheth mean "possession" from *yrš*?

c. The prefix can mean "concerning" or "about," but it can also take the meaning "against," which certainly anticipates the mood of the book (cf. Andersen and Freedman 2000, 125, noting that the same form is rendered with *kata* = "against" in Isa 1:1 LXX; cf. *GKC* 383).

d. "Which he saw" (*'ăšer-ḥāzâ*; cf. Isa 2:1). Isaiah also begins with a reference to a "vision" (*ḥăzôn*, 1:1; cf. Hab 1:1). It is certainly not the case that "visions" were more characteristic of "false prophets" (cf. Ezek 13:6 in reference to *ḥāzû šāwĕ'*, lying or false visions), and it should not be removed from Micah as a later addition. How a "word" can be "seen" is a question better dealt with in discussions of poetic style.

e. Surprisingly, Uzziah is not listed but rather his son and coregent for over 25 years (759–733), Jotham, relatively unknown in the biblical historical narrative.

f. Wolff argues that this form of the name is late, perhaps 4th century (1 Chr 4:41; 2 Chr 28:27), as opposed to the form noted in 2 Kgs 16:20; 18:1–21 (1990, 34).

[1] Micah's name means "Who is like Yah[weh]?" The name is derived from a question seeking to raise the God of Israel above all else. Waltke notes forms of such comparative "phrase names" in pagan literature, such as "Who is like [the god] Sin?" in Akkadian literature (2007, 38). A similar question occurs toward the end of the book (7:18, *mî-'ēl kāmôkā*, "Who is a god like you?"),

which may be a late addition when the book was made a part of the collection of shorter prophetic writings later known in the (pre-Christian) Hebrew traditions as "the Twelve." However, it also forms a "bookend" that matches the opening of the book. Another form of the same name "Micah" appears to be connected to another prophet, known as Micaiah ben Imlah (*mîkāyĕhû ben-yimlâ*), whose story appears in 1 Kgs 22. Wolff believes that the names of the kings are an example of "advanced theological reflection" indicative of Deuteronomistic editing (1990, 34).

Excursus 2: Micaiah ben Imlah

There is more in common between Micah the Moresheti and Micaiah ben Imlah than the name. The unique phrase in Mic 1:2a ("Listen, all of the peoples") appears also in 1 Kgs 22:28b, certainly establishing some connection (Wolff 1990, 35). The story of Micaiah ben Imlah, notably, deals with the question of true and false prophecy, which the book of Micah also takes up. Furthermore, Micaiah ben Imlah clearly had strong conflicts with the ruling powers of Israel over a military issue, in this instance because Micaiah ben Imlah's attitude toward conflict was at variance with the "four hundred prophets" assembled by Ahab to justify his military expeditions against Aram. Finally the false prophet Zedekiah is said to have made "horns of iron" to represent the power of the united Israelite and Judean forces, and then Zedekiah used this image to symbolize their predicted victory (1 Kgs 22:11). It seems important, then, that Mic 4:13 (using the same term for "horns") is often taken to be the words of a false prophet, or a later addition to the book, speaking of "iron horns" used against the enemies of the Hebrew people as well. There may be some influences on the book of Micah from the story of Micaiah precisely because of the similarity of names (see Jer 26:18, where both forms of the name are attested in some texts).

What we are particularly interested in, however, is the prophetic legacy of standing against the central powers on behalf of those who suffer from the leaders' hegemonic policies of taxation and militarism (see introduction above). Stansell also observes that comparing the two prophetic stories/texts raises further common themes: Who is the true prophet? Which prophet really has the spirit of God? In both cases "shalom" is used by the false prophets (Mic 3:5, and implied of false prophets in 1 Kings 22:28). Stansell concludes that Micah is thus opposed to the Davidic tradition associated with this notion of Zion's inviolability, a view suggesting that Jerusalem will always have "shalom" because of God's protection (1988, 68, 78). Finally, Moberly (2003) argues that the Micaiah ben Imlah story may well have been artificially set in the time of Ahab; perhaps it comes from a later period and thus is originally associated with one of Ahab's descendants. This would place the association between the two figures even closer.

We have already noticed the significance of Micah's village, Moresheth. The geography makes sense in the light of settlements named in Mic 1: Gath, Adullam, and Lachish. The site is usually identified as Tell Judeideh, some 23–25 miles SW of modern Jerusalem (see introduction).

Micah 1:1 The Superscription

As explained in the introduction, recent emphases on reading the Minor Prophets in the context of a collection known already by around 180 B.C.E. as "the Twelve" raises questions about the opening identifications provided in all of these writings. For example, one would expect all the opening lines of the Twelve to have been brought into more strict conformity if these books were the result of extensive editing into a "set" of short books to be read together. Such a clear harmonization of opening lines is not obvious, however. Andersen and Freedman speak of "enough resemblance" to suggest a "template" (2000, 103), but there are some interesting differences. Although Micah's opening is virtually the same as that found in Hosea, Joel, and Zephaniah (Jonah's opening is *nearly* the same), others of the Twelve have significantly different opening sentences and forms. Obadiah, notably, begins with a reference to a "vision";[1] and Nahum begins as a *maśśā'* ("oracle") concerning Nineveh (cf. Mal 1:1; Isa 13:1). Somewhat surprisingly, Amos begins with an indication that these are "the words of Amos," perhaps to be contrasted with the emphasis in Micah on the word of God (Renaud 1977, 19). In Zechariah, the same formula for "the word of YHWH" eventually appears, but not in the very beginning, as in Micah, Hosea, Joel, and Zephaniah.

The introduction clearly suggests that this word "came to" Micah or "occurred" to him, but then states that he "saw" the "word," which may suggest that Micah had visions. This is yet another point of some discussion in the critical literature, particularly from scholars who wish to differentiate Israelite prophets from "visionaries." Other scholars insist on the obvious: prophets are often also "seers" and have visions (Andersen and Freedman 2000, 124). Prophetic visions increase in significance as the prophetic writings evolve toward apocalyptic literature (see Grabbe 2003).

If it was not a vision, then precisely how a "word of the LORD" comes to a prophet is the subject of extensive speculation. Many commentators have contributed to the argument that the word "coming to" Micah indicates that he is no diviner or magician. Micah does not control the act of receiving the word: God does! Such a perspective could be challenged, however, when we come to the recent debates about whether the book of Micah includes incantations (see below on 5:5b–6 [4b–5]), but the general point is not thereby lost.

There is simply no clear indication from the prophetic literature to clarify whether prophets *routinely* claimed to literally hear a voice and see visions, or if these "words" are the result of meditation, prayer, or the occurrence of strikingly new ideas attributed to outside inspiration (cf. 1 Sam 3; Acts 9:1–9). The question always calls for speculation, but I argue that any idea of inspiration involves the necessity of a willful involvement of human persons who are open to a relationship to God.

---

1. On the possible significance of this term in relation to prophecy, see Petersen (1981, 68).

The twelve shorter prophetic books are also not the same in terms of the time references provided. Hosea is the most extensive, naming Uzziah (783–742), Jotham (742–735), Ahaz (735–727 [715?]), and Hezekiah (727 [715?]–687 B.C.E.) of Judah, and Jeroboam of Israel, while Joel has no time reference at all. Amos refers to only one king of Judah, Uzziah, and to Jeroboam of Israel. Jonah names no king. Uzziah is considered among the strongest of Judah's rulers, although he himself died of leprosy, and his son Jotham was coregent until his death. It does seem odd that Uzziah is not mentioned in Micah; Andersen and Freedman speculate that this omission may be important in dating the book (2000, 111). Others simply suppose that Micah was later than Isaiah, Amos, or Hosea. We are undoubtedly safe to suppose an era of activity for Micah inclusive of 742 at the earliest (the death of Uzziah, although Jotham began as coregent ca. 759) and 687 at the latest (the death of Hezekiah). As for the end of Micah's period of activity, however, much depends on whether one can find clear references to the siege of Jerusalem around 701. Most commentators do not believe that this had happened as yet (at least in the "genuine" Micah passages), because the condemnations of Zion/Jerusalem in the book describe circumstances that did not actually take place (at least not in the ways Micah seems to suggest). Therefore many readers of Micah do not suppose that his period of active proclamation continued far into the reign of Hezekiah. What makes this more difficult, however, is the inherent lack of precision in poetic forms of discourse, where Micah need not be taken quite so literally in order to be appreciated or understood.

Finally, I read Mic 1:1 to state that Micah "saw" this word "against" Samaria *and* Jerusalem. It is frequently argued that "Samaria" is an addition, because of the rarity of a prophet addressing both northern and southern kingdoms. However, given Micah's rage against both capital cities, this is certainly not an inevitable conclusion. Furthermore, although the condemnation of Samaria and Jerusalem is divided in the text (1:6 for Samaria, 3:12 for Jerusalem), there is little reason to doubt that Micah has angry words for both cities. Indeed, his attack against *both* examples of central powers that exploit the countryside and surrounding agricultural villages supports my picture of Micah as a rural populist leader. Micah has an obvious interest in mitigating the aggressiveness of rulers toward the other kingdom (north vs. south), something that is not unprecedented among other tribal leaders speaking against the policies of the central regime (2 Chr 28).

Micah 1:2–7 Call to Court: Accusations against the Capital Cities

2 Listen,[a] all of the peoples;[b]
  be attentive,[c] land, and all that is in it![d]
The Lord YHWH approaches you[e] to give witness,
  the Lord from his holy temple.[f]

Call to Court: Accusations against the Capital Cities 49

3 Attention! The LORD comes out from his place,
   and he comes down^g and treads^h upon the sacred placesⁱ of the earth.
4 And the mountains will melt under him,
   and the valleys will split open like wax^j before the fire,
   like waters pouring down a slope.^k
5 All this for the rebellion of Jacob,
   and for the sins of the house of Israel.^l
   "Who"^m is the rebellion of Jacob? Is it not Samaria?
   And "who" is a high placeⁿ of Judah? Is it not Jerusalem?
6 And I will make Samaria a heap^o of the field,
   places^p for planting a vineyard.
   And I will throw her^q stones into the valley;
   and I will uncover^r her foundations.^s
7 And all her images will be crushed,
   and all her prostitutes' fees will be burned in the fire,^t
   and all her idols I will make desolate.
   Since^u she gathered [. . . ?]^v like a prostitute's payment,
   as a prostitute's payment they will return.

a. H. Utzschneider (2005, 34) points out that 1:2 connects with 5:15 (14), forming an "inclusio" for this entire section of the book.

b. The subject "peoples" is accompanied by the term "all of them" (*kullām*) in the third person instead of the expected second-person "all of you." This is only the first of many examples of an apparent mismatch of number and gender in Micah. One could attempt to reproduce "Listen, peoples, all of them" and suggest that we are dealing with oral style and poetic license here. One can well imagine a speaker addressing a crowd in this manner, implying that he is not speaking about the people immediately in front of him. Ben Zvi proposes an intentional ambiguity here rather than a grammatical mistake (1998).

c. The common term used in the command to "listen" at the beginning of v. 2 (the imperative plural of *šāmaʿ*) is combined here in parallel with the next phrase using *qāšab*, often translated as "heed" or "pay attention!" (Job 13:6; Pss 5:2; 55:2, notably Isa 28:23). Andersen and Freedman make note of the parallel poetic pattern: "Listen (you) peoples—all of them; Pay attention (you) earth—and her fullness!" (2000, 151). For "be attentive," the LXX uses a form of *prosechō*, the same term used in the LXX where Pharaoh speaks to Moses, "*Be sure* that you do not see my face again!" (Exod 10:28 S-C), and used in law codes to insert a command to attentiveness (Exod 23:21; 34:11; frequently in Deuteronomy, e.g., 4:9, 23; 6:12; 8:11; 11:16; 12:13, 19, 23, 30).

d. Many accept the LXX ("and all that is in it"), so Hillers (1984, 16), although Andersen and Freedman try to preserve Hebrew with "Earth, and her fullness" (2000, 132). Mays has "all who are in it" (1976, 39).

e. C. Shaw (1993, 32) wants to translate "against you," but McKane says that suggestions along this line are not convincing (1998, 26). However, Ben Zvi suggests that the ambiguity between "with" and "against" is quite intentional, as an "attention getter" (1998, 106). Given the context, I suggest "approach" to capture the sequence of action (cf. *GKC* 379).

f. Stansell (1988, 12–13) points out that vv. 2 and 3 are not consistent: one deals with the temple, the other with a "place"; v. 2 is legal in tenor, while v. 3 is a theophany; the call in v. 2 is to "hear," while the action is to be "viewed" in vv. 3–4. As opposed to those who would thus omit v. 2, others choose to omit all or part of v. 3 for the same reasons (e.g., McKane 1998, 29; Utzschneider 2005, 34).

g. Clifford argues against the notion that God coming "down" suggests a later image, noting that Ugaritic motifs of the Holy Mountain are already found in the 2nd millennium B.C.E. (1972, 144).

h. "Tread" (*dārak*) has clear military overtones (cf. Deut 33:29; Pss 60:12; 108:13). Wolff, however, wants to omit this second verb, which appears in a similar case in Amos 4:13; 1QpMic and some Gk. manuscripts support his supposition (1990, 41). Hillers, on the other hand, points out that the Qumran fragment is not clear and that most versions support both verbs (1984, 17). The action is consistent with Micah's agricultural motifs.

i. "High places" (*bāmôtê*, corrected from *bāmŏtê*) of the earth. It is significant to note, however, that Haran argues for *bāmôt* = "backs": God treads on the "backs" of the earth. Haran compares this to Amos 4:13 (Haran 1985, 19). This may refer to the mountains as the humped back of the primordial creature (Dever 2005, 92). However, "backs" might be a historical reference, but "sacred places" makes more sense in line with v. 5. The omission of Israel altogether, suggested by many who think Micah would hardly have addressed both kingdoms, is not supported in any texts (Wolff 1990, 43).

j. The only other places referring to wax in this form are in the Psalms, where the writers portray a heart, people, or mountains as "melting like wax" (*dônag*; Pss 22:14 [15]; 68:2 [3]; 97:5). In the LXX, the image of mountains melting is also picked up in Jdt 16:15, as well as in apocalyptic literature; see, e.g., *1 Enoch* 1.6.

k. "Slope," after Andersen and Freedman (2000, 160, 166), who wonder whether the image suggests landslides from God stepping on the "high places" or mountains.

l. *BHS* calls for the removal of "house of Israel" and suggests that "Judah" should have appeared here to maintain parallelism with the following condemnations. The Gk., however, supports MT.

m. The interrogative is somewhat unexpectedly "who" (*mî*) rather than "what" (*mâ*). Andersen and Freedman suggest that the cities are being personified (2000, 172–73), or perhaps the leaders of the places, but in any case, they find it hard to believe that this is not intentional.

n. The LXX changes this to "sin of," rather than "high place of," undoubtedly to bring it into conformity with the previous sentence about Samaria (Jones 1995, 108–10). With NRSV, I change to a singular form here: "high place" rather than plural "places."

o. The term 'î (here singular, but plural in 3:12) is translated in the LXX as *opōrophylakion* = a "worker's hut" of the field, which also appears in Isa 1:8, where the reference also suggests the modest structure of a temporary agricultural worker's dwelling, destined to fall and thus like a city destined to fall (esp. in war).

p. "Fields" is possible, but Wagenaar argues that the term is "hillsides," which parallels the mention of "mountain" in the judgment of Jerusalem in 3:12 (1996).

Call to Court: Accusations against the Capital Cities 51

q. The feminine is important to notice here, given the typical feminine form for cities. Whether "stripping *her*" is an allusion to abuse of females in Israelite society, see comments below.

r. The root for "uncover" (*gālâ*) may be suggestive. From the same root comes *gōlâ* = "exile," which may be associated with the treatment of prisoners of war. For a full exposition of this association of captivity with "stripping" prisoners of war in Mesopotamian practice; see Smith-Christopher 2002c, 141–58.

s. "Foundation" (*yĕsôd*), often of "base" of an altar in cultic practice (Lev 4:7, 18, 25, 30, 34) but also used to designate the extreme of destruction—e.g., Ps 137:7 ("down to its foundation").

t. The definite article, although lacking in Greek, suggests a fire known to the listeners, that is, an image that is familiar in oracles of judgment.

u. Reading the term *kî* in combination with the prepositional *min*, together as "on account of," simplifying to "since" (cf. *GKC* 378).

v. Many commentators supply the missing object of the verb (e.g., "them"), but a rhetorical absence of an object, thus implying only the "fees," is possible.

[2a] This section begins with a striking command to the "peoples," indeed, *all* peoples, to listen, followed by an equally striking command directed to the land/earth.[2] Notably, this opening phrase is also found in 1 Kgs 22:28, where it is the final phrase punctuating a warning given by Micaiah ben Imlah. The parallel underlines the importance of what is said in the warning. With the addition of a call to earth ("land"), there is similarity to Isa 1:2–3. The second term of command (*qāšab*) is often combined with references to the ear, or ears, of God (Pss 10:17; 86:6; 130:2). The same two terms are seen in combination in other poetic contexts, such as Pss 17:1; 61:1 (2 MT). The terms are known in prophetic literature as well. Isaiah features the same call to both hear and "heed"/"pay attention" in Isa 21:7; 28:23. Perhaps the most striking similarities in the prophets, however, are those few occasions where people are called upon to hear as well as earth or heaven (see Isa 34:1; 49:1; Jer 6:19).

The earth itself is being addressed as a euphemism in parallel to "the peoples" who are addressed in the first phrase (cf. Deut 4:26; 30:19, where heaven and earth are called as witnesses). Psalm 89:37 even calls on the moon as a witness. Ezekiel preaches *to* mountains and valleys (Ezek 35–36). It is as if all of creation can be a witness to the workings of God, which reminds one of the growing significance of astrological speculations in later apocalyptic literature, especially in *Enoch*. Micah 6:16 has a similar "double address" to place ("you" = "city," 6:9)

---

2. Andersen and Freedman suggest that the importance of "peoples" in this section mitigates the impression that gods are being addressed (2000, 148). McKane agrees that "all the people of the earth" is the intention, particularly the Gentile world (1998, 27), while Wolff is equally insistent that Micah would not have addressed the entire world (1990, 51).

and people: a threat directed against a place and then a parallel notion directed against the "inhabitants."

Coming as it does from a resident of the "frontier lands" (or "badlands") between Judah and Philistia, near a major trade route northward (the Via Maris = Sea Road), it is not entirely surprising that Micah might reckon that his words have significance for many peoples. The later portions of Micah show strong awareness of the attention of other peoples, almost an ongoing dialogue with other peoples, whether they are mere onlookers, or active enemies (e.g., 4:1–5, 11; 5:8–9; 7:8–10). This is further suggested by the otherwise awkward third-person plural in the address of 1:2: "you peoples" followed by "all of them." If we picture a prophet standing before a group of people locally but with his eyes toward the western horizon (Philistia), or the north (the route to Mesopotamia as well as Samaria), or east to the hills (Jerusalem), these changes of number are not entirely unreasonable. We suffer, of course, from having to read what was undoubtedly an impressive *oral* performance, complete with physical gestures that would likely have made the references clearer.

[2b] God is going to be a witness against the people, but God is acting as both prosecutor and, in the following verses, judge and even executioner! The term "witness" is certainly a very important aspect of the Israelite judicial system. False witnesses were considered especially heinous (Exod 20:16//Deut 5:20; also Prov 6:19; 12:17; 14:5, 25; 19:5, 9, 28; 21:28; 24:28), and multiple witnesses were essential to capital cases, a ruling apparently intended to put a curb on vigilante violence (Num 35:30; Deut 19). Ben Zvi suggests an intentional blurring of the meaning of "against you," or "with you," or "among you," so that the events could be considered more universal in scope (1998, 105–8).

The parallel phrase that God is coming from God's "holy temple" refers undoubtedly to a variety of images: God "coming down" from high and lofty places (Exod 3:8; Num 11:17). In prophetic literature, God's "coming down" is seen on occasion as an image of judgment, as if anything that moves God to actually *visit* is the result of intolerable behavior (so Isa 31:4 and the call in 64:1; cf. Ps 144:5, and possibly the unexpected appearance of God in Job!). That God is to be sought "in his temple," meaning both earthly *and* heavenly abode, is clear in many images (e.g., Pss 11:4; 18:6).

[3a] The opening phrase relates to God's coming from the holy temple, God's "place" in the following phrase, in order to "tread upon the sacred places." The term "tread" is frequently used in reference to the defeat of enemies: Deut 33:29c; Pss 44:5; 60:12; 108:13. Furthermore, in prophetic literature the imagery of treading grapes to make wine and the other image of "treading" enemies is explicitly combined (e.g., Jer 25:30; cf. Joel 3:13 [4:13]). Isaiah refers to God's use of the Assyrians ("rod of my anger," 10:5–13) in a context not dissimilar to an implied use of the invading Assyrians here in Micah. Thus God is called

Call to Court: Accusations against the Capital Cities

to battle, but surely not against the mountains (contra Andersen and Freedman 2000, 137). The significance of referring to God's "war" as opposed to human war is rich satire and political commentary: see Paul's use of "spiritual warfare" (Eph 6) and the "war" of Jesus against evil (Rev 19). Clearly this is a theophany: there is no suggestion (yet) that God intends to use other armies to do God's bidding; only God appears here. The specifics of the battle come later!

The phrases in 1:2b and 3a are clearly linked: judgment is combined with theophany. Furthermore, the term for "holy places" can be used of *all* holy places. It is not hard to interpret Micah's condemnation of all holy places, Judean, Israelite, as well as pagan. In fact, the generic condemnation is more fitting with Micah's general message as well as similar condemnations of specifically Israelite sacral practices in Isa 1:11–17; Amos 5:21–24, and the only somewhat milder condemnation in Hos 6:6 (see Cohen 1979). The punishment of the capital cities and their sacred centers is anticipated here, culminating in 1:6 and 3:12.

Stansell argues helpfully that Micah has "radically reversed" the usual object of a theophany (1988, 23, 34), using it to announce judgment rather than the expected salvation (in contrast to Isa 30:28, 31; 29:6–7; 31:4–5).

[4] The initial impression from reading this passage is that the imagery seems confused. Surely "melting mountains" (cf. Ps 97:5) ought to be combined with "fire," and the "split valleys" with the gushing of water (as in Deut 8:7 and implied in Isa 41:18), but the poetic expressions are likely to be intended. We are certainly dealing here with "atmosphere": the solemnity of God's actually appearing is accompanied by catastrophic events. The very next book, Nahum, also begins with a similar theophany, where comparable catastrophic events are also announced (1:5). However, the term for "melt" is more often used of warriors or others who are frightened and lose their strength (Josh 2:11; 2 Sam 17:10; Isa 13:7; Ezek 21:7, 15). If, then, part of the image is drawn from the "primordial battle" of ancient Near Eastern creation mythology, we ought not to lose the implication that the "mountains" (as part of the "enemy") lose heart; that is, the powers of this world cannot stand before the power of God.

Similarly, the term for the waters "gushing" or "bursting" in the valleys also has interesting associations. The term is often rendered in English as "split," as especially in the dividing of the Reed Sea in the exodus events (Exod 14; so also Ps 78:13), and the earth "split open" for the waters to rise in the flood accounts in Gen 7:11. However, it can also be used to speak of "breaches" in city walls (2 Kgs 25:4; Jer 39:2); notice the particularly close association with the entire context in Hab 3:8–13.

> Was your wrath against the rivers, O LORD?
>   Or your anger against the rivers,
>   or your rage against the sea,

>   when you drove your horses,
>   your chariots to victory?
>   You brandished your naked bow,
>   sated were the arrows at your command.   *Selah*
>   You split the earth with rivers.
>   The mountains saw you, and writhed;
>   a torrent of water swept by;
>   the deep gave forth its voice.
>   The sun raised high its hands;
>   the moon stood still in its exalted place,
>   at the light of your arrows speeding by,
>   at the gleam of your flashing spear.
>   In fury you trod the earth,
>   in anger you trampled nations.
>   You came forth to save your people,
>   to save your anointed.
>   You crushed the head of the wicked house,
>   laying it bare from foundation to roof.   *Selah*

Sweeney suggests that the image of melting mountains may refer to flooding in the Shephelah, a phenomenon with which Micah would surely have been familiar (2001a, 350). Melting wax, he also suggests, may suggest the flames of war. In any case, not to be missed is the interesting implication of imagining Micah standing in his lowland village, gesturing toward the hills and the capital city, as he delivers searing condemnation (with a gesture that would explain the otherwise odd use of "all of them" in v. 2, as noted above). While many commentators insist that Micah is already in Jerusalem, locating him in his own lowland home communities intensifies that oral impact of referring to "melting mountains" and judgment on "all of them."

[5] In parallel, the two terms for unacceptable behavior, "rebellion" (*pešaʿ*) and "sin" (*ḥaṭṭāʾâ*), create an interesting combination. The first term can certainly be used in a social or political sense (2 Kgs 1:1; 3:5; cf. Wolff 1990, 56). Isaiah uses this notion of "rebels" in same combination (Isa 1:28, "rebels and sinners"; cf. 66:24). The fact that it can be used for political rebellion, however, gives caution against always translating it with mundane terms like "sin" or "iniquity." The concept is clearly the sins of a group of people. The English word "sin" personalizes and privatizes the concept more than the Hebrew term appears to allow.

The second term, used in relation to "the house of Israel," has clear cultic associations and is used heavily in Levitical law (esp. throughout Lev 4–5). It is used in combination with a more common term (*ʿāwōn*) in Isa 5:18. The cultic term is perhaps better captured with an English term like "corruption" or "pollution."

However, the two terms here in Micah are used occasionally in parallel form in other contexts (Pss 25:7; 32:1). Significantly, the two terms are used together in Jacob's plea to Laban to explain his mistakes ("What is my offense? What

Call to Court: Accusations against the Capital Cities

is my sin?" Gen 31:36; cf. 50:17). The term is used in relation to the sin of idolatry (Exod 32:30; 34:7; cf. Lev 16:16), and notably in the Prayer of Solomon in 1 Kgs 8, which becomes part of the tradition of the Penitential Prayer in postexilic literature (v. 50, "Forgive your people who have sinned against you, and all their transgressions that they have committed against you"). It is precarious business to try to identify the particular behavior solely on the basis of the terms used. We must base such judgments on the rest of the book's message.

Jerusalem is called "a high place of Judah." High places were typically mentioned as locations for religious shrines (1 Sam 9–10 KJV, RSV) and appear to be neutral terms until 1 Kgs 3:3, where Solomon is condemned for introducing foreign religious cults into his kingdom. From this time onward, there is a consistency to the use of *bāmôt* to refer to pagan, and thus unacceptable, shrines (1 Kgs 11:7; 12:31–32; 13:2, 32). Not coincidentally, then, the term appears frequently in Josiah's reform campaign, reflecting the Deuteronomistic concern to portray Josiah's reforms as restoring the righteousness of David (2 Kgs 23:5, 8, 9, 13, 15, 19, 20).

[6] Having God say, "I will make/set Samaria," combines two divine roles or images: powerful creator and powerful judge. What God can make as "good" (e.g., justice in Isa 28:17), God can also make into "ruin" and desolation. The term used here is quite common (*śîm*); it is used to refer to "creating," "making," or "setting up" something. In the prophetic literature it often refers to God's act of carrying out forceful judgment by transforming something into ruin or a wasteland, a kind of "de-creation."[3] At times it appears that the means by which this uncreation will take place is direct destruction by God, but often it is clear that God will use a foreign army to do the actual demolition.

In a vein similar to Micah, Jeremiah proclaims that Jerusalem will be "transformed" into a wasteland (6:8). Indeed, the fearsome ability of God to "make" desolation is a striking matter in poetry (Ps 46:8); God's creative power can transform for good or punish and destroy (Ps 107:33, 35). The people's sin can also "transform" with a negative impact; the people's sin makes God's land into an "abomination" (Jer 2:7).

Samaria will be a "heap/rubble"[4] in the field. The unusual term (*'î*) appears in the plural in Ps 79:1b, as also in Mic 3:12. In a similar context of threat, the

---

3. So, e.g., in Isa 14:23 the city of Babylon will be put under judgment, and the city will be "turned into" a place for owls (*qippōd* or "porcupines"?) and pools of water ("swampland," NIV). Jeremiah refers to towns being made into wastelands from warfare (Jer 4:7; cf. 10:22); God "makes/changes" a city to "a ruin" (Isa 25:2).

4. The threat to reduce cities or important buildings to "ruins" is often noticed in the Hebrew Bible, but usually employing only one of two terms: *ḥorbâ* (Isa 44:26; 52:9; 61:4; Ezek 13:4; 26:20; 35:4; Mal 1:4; Ezra 9:9; Neh 2:17; Pss 9:6 [7]; 109:10) or *šammâ/šĕmāmâ* (Josh 8:28; Isa 24:12; Jer 4:7; 9:11). Is it tempting to speculate that Micah chooses this rarer term because of its association with the destruction of the village of Ai (Josh 8:28)?

term is also used in a parallel passage in Isa 17:1 with reference to Damascus, and it is presumed in the threat pronounced in 1 Kgs 9:8:

> This house will become a heap of ruins;[5] everyone passing by it will be astonished, and will hiss; and they will say, "Why has the LORD done such a thing to this land and to this house?"

The Greek translators, however, present Mic 1:6 as saying that the greatness of the city will be reduced to "a hut for field-workers," rather than mere "ruins." The same Greek term is also used for telling of other destructions (Ps 79:1 [78:1 LXX], for the Jerusalem temple; more lit., Isa 1:8). True to Isaiah's frequent use of agricultural metaphors, the image is used again in the Greek version of Isa 24:20. Other observations are relevant here, especially with regard to the prominence of agricultural motifs. Following McKane's analysis of the Greek terminology, one may wonder if the idea might be that the *useless* elite structures (from Micah's perspective) are replaced by at least an *agriculturally useful* field-workers' hut (McKane 1998, 114–15). This raises a further important question about the judgment on Samaria and the completion of the judgment on the two cities at 3:12.

It is critical that the judgments on the two capital cities be read carefully. The Greek translation picks up on the subtleties of this passage, an example of a very early "interpretation" as well as translation of the Hebrew. The two activities, plowing/sowing "fields" (as in Mic 3:12) and planting "vineyards" (as in 1:6), are often used together to signify cultivated lands, both in law (Exod 22:5; Lev 25:3–4) and in narrative (Num 20:17; 21:22), and even in proverbial wisdom, where the wife is praised when she appears to do all the work (cf. Prov 24:30; 31:10–31, esp. v. 16)! *Precisely these two activities* related to judgments on the capital cities are suggested by the tools made from weapons in 4:1–5: *plowshares* for plowing Jerusalem and *vine clippers* for the vineyards of Samaria (see comments on 4:1–5 and the Excursus at 3:12).

The term for a place of planting (*maṭṭāʿ*) is repeatedly used in the prophetic literature for an action of God (in Isa 60:21 the righteous are "the shoot that I have planted"; Isa 61:3 compares "oaks of righteousness" to "the planting of the LORD"; and in Ezek 34:29 God will provide "a place of planting" [S-C]). Here, too, God's action results in planting, implying that God's removal of Samaria makes the land potentially useful as a "vineyard." Among the more interesting prophetic references to a vineyard (occasionally paired with "field," as in Prov 24:30; 31:16) is Isaiah's Song of the Vineyard in Isa 5:1–7 (alluded to strongly in 27:2–3). These associations of "vines" with "people" may well

---

5. In this passage, it is presumed that in the reading *ʿelyôn* = "height/high" (which is, however, supported by LXX), the *ayin* and the *lamed* have been mistakenly switched, and the amended reading is supported by Aquila's Greek, the Old Latin, and Old Syriac (Gray 1970, 236).

suggest that Mic 1:6 is implying that God will initiate a "replanting" of a vineyard, in other words, cultivate a people more acceptable to God. So there may be at least two different ways to read the symbolism of this passage. Either God intends to start over by replanting Samaria, or Micah the prophet-farmer sees this passage as God's judgment on Samaria that results in local farmers being able to use the land for something useful, a vineyard, rather than a hovel for the rich and powerful.[6] Agricultural metaphors, however, are easily compatible with the annual task of replanting, since it involves the destruction of plowing to prepare for the new harvest.

Notice the strange image of "pouring stones" (cf. NRSV). The verb, already appearing in Mic 1:4, is used for the disturbing image of "giving over" (lit., "pouring") children to the sword in Jer 18:21 and Edomites against Judeans in Ezek 35:5, perhaps suggesting the act of shoving things over walls during a siege; but in this case, it gives the impression that God is clearing the hilltop of Samaria by removing the buildings. Thus the notion of "rebuilding" suggested by the previous phrase is clearer: there will be no rebuilding but rather a reuse of the land. As in Isa 5, where God as the vine-grower cleared the field of stones (v. 2), here God clears Samaria of stones so that the vineyard can be planted.

The passage speaks of exposing the "foundations." A similar phrase appears in Ezek 13:14, and Cush will suffer having their "foundations" torn down in 30:4. The term is often used of the altar's base in Leviticus (ch. 4), yet in some contexts it means foundations of walls and city (Ps 137:7). In this case, "stones" quite literally represent the building blocks of civilization and buildings, and clearing the stones for agriculture means clearing away the vestiges of the city itself.

Excursus 3: Feminist Analysis of Micah 1:6 and Beyond

Much more can be said, however, about the verb used here: *gālâ*, "uncover." There have been serious discussions about the sexualized connotations of "exposing foundations" in reference to cities always referred to in the feminine gender. Certainly the verbal root *glh* is used for the euphemism "uncover" to mean sexual intercourse (esp. Lev 18 and 20; Deut 22:30 [23:1]; 27:20; so Ruth 3:4, 7). It can also be used generally of "revealed" (Deut 29:29 [28]; 1 Sam 3:7, 21; Ps 98:2; Isa 53:1; etc.), yet even then may sometimes also have sexual connotations (e.g., Michel's disgust with David's behavior in 2 Sam 6:20). Readers of Micah have often suggested that the language implies a kind of sexualized punishment: "She will be exposed," suggesting that "Lady Samaria" will be humiliated or even raped. This perspective is unfortunately still maintained by recent scholars, including Andersen and Freedman: "Stripping and exposure to public disgrace were fitting punishment for a wife whose infidelity took this form" (2000, 178).

---

6. Andersen and Freedman (2000, 177) also pick up the implication that the city will be returned to "intentional" agriculture (Isa 5:7; Ezek 31:4), but this is contrasted with total destruction (Isa 7).

From the 1990s a serious body of literature[7] suggests that sexualized punishment is a particularly troublesome aspect of prophetic language in the Bible, assuming that God is actually threatening to "rape" Jerusalem (and sometimes other cities) by "exposing her," especially in texts like Hos 2:3 ("I will strip her naked and expose her") or Isa 47:3 ("Your nakedness shall be uncovered"). A working assumption by many historians is that these passages somehow refer to a known practice in the actual treatment of Hebrew women, perhaps those caught in adultery, by publicly stripping them. Even if not based on an actual practice, it was argued that this was the "pornographic image" suggested by prophetic texts of sexualized judgment. Carroll has written trenchantly of such passages: "These allegories of Jerusalem, Samaria, and Sodom as members of the same family and as daughters/sisters/wives/mothers heavily involved in prostitution with Egypt and Assyria (synonyms of imperial power) sound at best like the ravings of a driveling lunatic and if they were not found in pages of 'sacred scripture' they would be dismissed instantly by most modern readers as pornography (im)pure and (un)simple!" (1996, 68).

Clearly the pastoral, much less the textual and historical, implications of this debate are worthy of consideration. As Patton writes, "If God is allowed to abuse his 'wives,' human husbands will see a sanction for physical abuse of their own wives" (2000, 225). In her monograph *Battered Love*, Weems generalizes about this prophetic use of female imagery: "Perhaps more than any other material in the Bible, the portraits of women's sexuality drawn by Israel's prophets have contributed to the overall impression one gets from the Bible that women's sexuality is deviant, evil, and dangerous" (1995, 5).

With specific reference to Micah, Runions writes of the "Damsel in Distress" motif, where one seems to see "the image of the suffering penitent woman, rescued and led by male figures into a glorious future of domination" (2001, 198). But is "uncovering foundations" (as well as the references to "prostitute's payment" in Mic 1:7 and connotations in 4:11) a misogynist motif suggesting violence against women? Is this how we are also to read the villages and cities (always referred to in feminine gender) and their humiliation in the rest of Mic 1? These are important issues.

First, all modern readers of the Bible ought to identify this as objectionable imagery. Biblical patriarchy, especially with violence (and violent attitudes), is not to be somehow "approved," much less defended, by an uncritical reading of Scripture. Furthermore, there is a clear motif of feminizing the enemy and the defeated in the Bible, and in ancient Near Eastern literature generally (see, e.g., Isa 19:16; Jer 50:37; 51:30). With this in mind, however, I still suggest that there is another way of reading this graphic imagery of "stripping" and "uncovering."

The root word for the term "exposing" (*glh*) is the same root used for the common term to denote "exile/captivity" and "exiles/captives" (beginning with 2 Sam 15:19 in reference to Ittai the Gittite), deportees (2 Kgs 15:29; 16:9; 17:6, 11, 23), and Babylonian exiles throughout (2 Kgs 24:14, 15; 25:11, 21; Ezra 2:1; Esth 2:6; Jer 24:1; 27:20; 29:1, 4, 7, 14). This indicates an association between these conceptual fields of the root *glh*, that is, a relationship between "exile" and "stripped/exposed"—presuming that this was

---

7. Much of the literature relates more closely to studies in Ezekiel, but this is only because Ezekiel uses the disturbing imagery more fully. Most of the literature also touches on similar passages in Hosea, Micah, and others. I review much of the debate and cite the extensive literature in Smith-Christopher 2002c.

Feminist Analysis of Micah 1:6 and Beyond

a common practice for the treatment of captured enemy soldiers who were led away as "exiles." In fact, precisely this practice is widely attested, especially in Assyrian warfare iconography. The POWs are pictured, often stripped, on the surviving metal door braces from Balawat, now in the British Museum. A particularly good example, much closer to Micah's own "home," are the impaled and naked defenders of Lachish on the Nineveh reliefs.[8] These reliefs prominently feature nude prisoners being led away with their arms tied behind their backs. Finally, however, texts such as Isa 20 further support this argument, because in this text the prophet strips himself *in order to symbolize being a POW* (vv. 3–4). We need not stray far from Micah, however, since this will arise in discussing the significance of the very next section (1:8).

The critical point is that "stripping" is most certainly a reference to the treatment of [male] POWs and exiles, not an image drawn from some alleged Israelite practice against indicted women! Thus perhaps we have fallen prey to a misreading of the practice of Hebrew references to cities in the feminine gender. When prophets speak of "exposing" or "stripping" in the context of destruction or conquest of cities, it seems rather clear that they are referring to the practice by conquering armies, who then led away prisoners who have been stripped to both humiliate and pacify them. There may be further sexualized implications to the language (and still objectionable implications), but I am hesitant to affirm the frequent argument that rape or public exposure and humiliation of Hebrew women is the direct implication of all these texts. That "she" (speaking of "Lady Jerusalem" or "Lady Samaria"—phrases that bring out the feminine gender in references to these locations) will be "stripped" or "uncovered" is a euphemism for conquest and the status of POWs. It is ironically the *males* of the conquered city who are actually stripped. The language of war is certainly sexualized, but not because of some undocumented ritual of publicly stripping Israelite women allegedly referred to by prophetic discourse about stripping.[9] This does not entirely remove the offensive use of female imagery, as in prostitution, but it does question whether this imagery draws on actual practices in ancient Israel, or is rather part of the rhetorical "shock" of prophetic language. That the prophets use shocking rhetoric bordering on the inappropriate (either then or now) is consistent with a rhetorical style. In such matters, we must read historical texts critically, fearlessly pointing out where modern readers are free to criticize ancient as well as modern attitudes of oppression and suppression, with a clear acknowledgment of how we, too, may utter inappropriate language in the heat of anger, anguish, or crisis. Finally, however, we keep in mind Micah's concern expressed against the specific violence against women in 2:9.

---

8. Cf. Yadin 1963, 396–97; *ANEP* 124–25. Reliefs from the Palace of Sargon, Khorsabad (721–705 B.C.E.), feature executed opponents who have been stripped (Yadin 1963, 420–21). Enemies are often depicted with minimal or no clothing, as in the Palette of King Narmer (Yadin 1963, 124), either to indicate submission, humiliation, or their having been stripped as defeated.

9. As Day has clarified, there is no textual basis for such a presumed practice of publicly stripping and humiliating adulterous women other than the prophetic passages themselves that are presumed to refer to it (2000, 244). Day argues that the punishment of "Jerusalem" is a metaphor for breaking the covenant, not for adultery, which was punished in the law by stoning (Ezek 16:40). She points out that there is *nothing in the Mosaic law about public humiliation and stripping as a punishment for adultery or prostitution*.

[7] The term for "images" or "idols" (sg. *pāsîl*) is used in similar fashion in Jer 51:52 and of foreign images in Deut 7:5, 25, paralleled largely in Deut 12:3 with a cacophony of accusations and language of idolatry: "Break down their altars, smash their pillars, burn their sacred poles with fire, and hew down the idols of their gods, and thus blot out their name from their places" (in the prophetic literature: Isa 21:9; 30:22; cf. Jer 50:38; 51:47, 52). This is not, however, the more common term for "idols."[10] Nevertheless, it is hard to be precise about the vocabulary of idolatry; the Greek versions use a variety of terms to translate these various Hebrew terms rather inconsistently.

The term for "prostitute's payment" is clearly attested. Not surprisingly, given the specific attack on cult practices in the Josianic reforms (2 Kgs 23:7), Deut 23:18 states that money used in sexual transactions is tainted and not to be used in transactions associated with the temple. This passage in Deuteronomy seems particularly noteworthy in the light of Isa 23:17–18, which compares "prostitute's wages" with international trade in reference to Tyre. What is curious about the Isaiah passage, however, is the fact that these "wages" will then become "holy" to God (i.e., dedicated to God). Here we perhaps see prophetic poetic license because the symbolism of "prostitutes' fees" is not acceptable as a literal reference to real prostitution, as in Deuteronomy. The term is clearly associated with prostitution as symbol in Ezek 16:31, 34, 41; Hos 9:1, and so it would appear in Mic 1:7 as well. The Greek term used in Mic 1:7 also appears in Ezek 16, suggesting that the Greek translators saw the significant connection of imagery in these two passages. However, we are not finished with the imagery of the prostitute's fee, as the verse continues.

"I will lay waste," "I will transform . . . to desolation." Here again is the theme of "de-creation." The threat to transform that which is built up by humans—the city or a civilization—into a desolate wasteland is repeated here. God threatens to drive out the newly arriving Israelites in Lev 26:33. Land being "desolate" as punishment is a common theme in prophetic literature (Isa 6:11; 17:9; 64:10, reversed as a blessing in 62:4; Jer 4:27; 6:8; 10:22; 12:10–11; 49:33; Ezek 6:14; 12:20; 14:15–16; 15:8; against Egypt in Ezek 29:10, 12; against Egypt and Edom in Joel 3:19 [4:19]; also against Edom in Mal 1:3).

The phrases could read "They were gathered as prostitutes' wages" and "They will return to be prostitutes' wages," but this is awkward. I have read the term "return" (*šûb*) as a reference to the wages themselves. Perhaps some light can be shed on this from the use of the same two terms for "gather" and "return" in Jeremiah:

---

10. Much more common is *'ĕlîlîm*, used, e.g., in Lev 26:1; Ps 97:7; frequently in Isa 2:8, 18, 20; and as a parallel term to *pāsîl* in Isa 10:10; of Egypt in 19:1, 3; 31:7; cf. Ezek 30:13). Ezekiel prefers *gillûlîm* (e.g., 6:4, 5, 6; 20:8, 16, 18; 23:7, 30, 37, 39), while *'ăṣabbîm*, usually in plural form, can be seen in later Psalms (106:36, 38; and esp. see 115:4; 135:15). This term is also used with *pāsîl*, as in Isa 48:5.

The Initial Lament with Warning

> See, I am going to bring them from the land of the north, and *gather* them from the farthest parts of the earth, among them the blind and the lame, those with child and those in labor, together; a great company, they shall *return* here. (31:8, emphasis added)

Here "gathered" and "return" are the same two terms used in this awkward phrase about prostitutes' wages in Mic 1:7. Can these be read in a manner that makes a clearer impression? The Greek doesn't help. The first term is *synagō*, which is usually, but not exclusively, used of gathering people (Gen 29:22; Josh 24:1; yet Joseph gathered food in Gen 41:48–49). The second term, *systrephō*, can be used to refer to a conspiratorial gathering, "aligned against," as in 1 Kgs 16:9, 16; 2 Kgs 9:14; 10:9; yet in Prov 30:4 the same two terms are rendered by the NRSV as "gathered" and "wrapped up."

Mays was surely onto something in suggesting that, since relations with pagan nations are sometimes likened to "prostituting," Micah is here condemning political alliances that have morally corrupted Samaria and Judah. Thus "perhaps what is meant in v. 7b is that the idols have been acquired and established in securing relations with other nations, and will be broken up and carried away by [some]one" (1976, 48).

If one of the main issues that Micah addresses is financial greed and corruption, then the imagery of collecting "fees" for foreign "affairs" (taking full advantage of the double entendre in English) is entirely consistent with his criticism of the central powers. We can be distracted by the reference to idolatry and suspect that the "fees" have to do only with religious infidelity and that this is therefore an in-house debate among Hebrews about their religious practices. As we have seen, however, the use of the imagery of prostitution can be either the worship of foreign gods or the abuse of money/commodities, especially in foreign transactions by the central power. The latter is far more consistent with the message of Micah. He has attacked the capital cities not because they are centers of worship only—after all, this is before the centralization of worship during the reforms of Josiah in 640–609 B.C.E.! In Micah's day, worship was local *as well as* national (i.e., in Jerusalem). Micah's focus on the central cities is far more suggestive of the *political* corruption in the use of commodities through taxation—they are "prostitute's fees," and Micah suggests that they should "return"—to the people, most likely.

Micah 1:8–9 The Initial Lament with Warning

8 Because of this,[a] I[b] will mourn[c] and wail;[d]
   I will walk barefoot[e] and naked.
I will grieve like jackals,[f]
   and mourn like daughters of owls.[g]

9 Because she is weakened from her [war] wounds,[h]
   it has come to Judah—
an assault[i] on the gate of my people,
   to Jerusalem!

a. The phrase ʿal-zōʾt indicates the completion of a previous thought and points to the consequences. Andersen and Freedman also note that it echoes "all this" in v. 5 (2000, 189).

b. The LXX has "she" throughout, but Mur. 88 supports MT.

c. To lament or mourn (sāpad) is to mourn for death (e.g., Gen 23:2; 50:10; 1 Sam 25:1//28:3; Jer 16:4–6). The problem, however, is that the term is also used in the final phrase, where the act presumably also refers to a sound. Thus the comparison with an animal makes sense.

d. The term yālal, "wailing," can express all manner of sadness or grief at destruction and loss. J. Cha (1996, 25) notes the same two terms linked in Jer 4:8.

e. To go barefoot (šôlāl) is not well attested (cf. Job 12:17, 19), but this is also the understanding of the Greek.

f. Tan = "jackal"? Identification of specific animals in the Hebrew Bible is often quite uncertain (see comments). We are only slightly helped by the context: here animals are associated with the wild, not amenable to close human habitation, and presumably make a sound referred to here.

g. The difficulty of identifying the specific species is especially problematic in this case (yaʿănâ = "owl"?); some versions render this as "ostrich" (NJB) or "owls" (NRSV). The presumption that the sound was key led the Greek to render "daughters of Sirens" (McKane 1998, 38).

h. Also possible is "injuries" from warfare or even "casualties." See comments. Shaw reads "illnesses" (1993, 33), and Cha (1996, 127) notes the verbal association with Jer 15:18.

i. The term nāgaʿ has a very diverse use. It connotes "disease" in Levitical discussions of illness (Lev 13) and the last "plague" in Exod 11:1, but it more clearly refers to a violent assault in Deut 17:8; 21:5. The Greek translation plēgē ("plague" or "mortal wound") reappears prominently in later use in Revelation (13:3, 12).

[8a] The phrase opens with the causal conjunctive phrase "because of this." After extensive analysis, Renaud argues that the phrase always refers to previous material.[11] The lament thus relates to what has already been announced. Further, however, this verse begins an interlude that deals with emotive reactions to the judgments outlined in the previous verses. Andersen and Freedman notice the proper sequence being followed in these sections: "theophany, indictment, punishment, and lamentation" (2000, 187).

---

11. Many others have followed this interpretation (as indicated by Renaud 1977, 38–40; followed by Shaw 1993, 38; Hillers 1984, 23; Naʾaman 1995, 516–17).

The Initial Lament with Warning

What is involved in this destruction—however angrily Micah may have delivered the judgment—is also cause for sadness over the suffering involved. This gives pause to any who would read Micah as only enraged with "righteous indignation," an attitude rarely accompanied by sympathy. On the contrary, Micah can be understood to announce events with a certain empathy for those suffering the results of punishment, even if justified by reprehensible behavior, according to the prophet's view.

More significant is the debate about who the "I" is in these two verses of mourning. Andersen and Freedman insist that this is God (2000, 191) and compare the text to Hos 11:8–9, while Utzschneider is just as insistent that it is the prophet in light of Isa 20 (2005, 39). God is portrayed as empathetic with the suffering of people (Ezekiel) and even foreign people (Jonah). There is a rich theological tradition in Jewish, Christian, and Islamic theology about the pain and suffering of God (Kitamori 1965; Moltmann 1974; Fretheim 1984; Heschel 2007; Ayoub 1978). As important as this tradition is, we must not be so distracted by the significant notion of "God lamenting" that we overlook the fact that this idea is still suggestive of the attitude of the writer/speaker of Micah, who is conveying the image. Indeed, we are still dealing with the (probably originally oral) message of Micah himself, even when placed "in the mind of God." Is Micah *serious* about the need for lament, or is he engaged in the rhetoric of taunt and ridicule? When we examine the call to mourn in other prophetic texts, something other than sadness suggests itself, as in Isa 23:1, "Wail, O ships of Tarshish, for your fortress is destroyed"; Jer 48:20, "Moab is disgraced. . . . Wail and cry out!" (NIV). This can even reach what appears to be a mocking empathy, particularly nasty in the final phrase of Jer 51:8: "Babylon will suddenly fall and be broken. Wail over her! *Get balm for her pain; perhaps she can be healed*" (NIV, emphasis added). Finally, similar to Micah, even when the punishment seems deserved in the prophet's eyes, the call to mourn is present: Zeph 1:11, "Wail, you who live in the market district; all your merchants will be wiped out, all who trade with silver will be ruined" (NIV).

There is a clear difference in spirit among the books of the Twelve on precisely this point. Obadiah, bitterly denouncing Edom for apparently assisting the Babylonian invasion of Judah, contains no hint of remorse or mourning; Nahum sheds no tears for Nineveh (3:7). Nevertheless, it is hard to deny a radically different spirit in Jonah. Is Micah (or God, in Micah's rhetorical perspective) genuinely sad, or further emphasizing the seriousness of the matter?

Related to this, the term for "lament" or "mourn" (*sāpad*) indicates mourning for death (see textual note). In her review of mourning practices in the ancient Near East, Pham states:

> Mourning rites of the ancient Near East are closely related to the rites of supplication or lamentation. . . . They include loud weeping (usually aided by professional

wailing women), the tearing of clothes and donning of sackcloth, sitting or lying on the dirt, gashing the body, strewing dirt on the head, fasting, abstaining from anointing with oil. There are also some variant actions with regard to the hair and beard. (1999, 23)

Thus here in Micah we are not surprised with the mention of wailing (*yālal*), which is associated with all manner of sadness or expression of grief at destruction and loss. The call to "wail" for the fate of those who turn against God is frequent in the prophets, and we see other actions associated with this, as in Isa 13:6; Jer 4:8 ("Put on sackcloth, lament [*sāpad*]"); Ezek 21:12 ("Cry out, . . . beat your breast" [NIV]). Wailing is also used to describe reactions to devastation and conquest, including the prophetic call to foreigners to mourn their loss (Isa 15:3, "Everyone wails and melts in tears").

Going barefoot is not widely attested in the Hebrew Bible, but to be symbolically naked certainly is. What is important to point out, however, is that "going naked" does not seem to be a common Israelite practice associated with mourning or lamentation. I have called attention to a common treatment of prisoners of war in Assyrian and probably Babylonian practices on conquest (see comments on vv. 6–7; Smith-Christopher 2002c). Yet nakedness is normally also considered an invitation to a moral response since being naked shows need of assistance, and already in Ezekiel and Isaiah the notion of giving clothing to the naked is associated with acts of doing justice (e.g., Ezek 18:16; Isa 58:7).

The prophet Isaiah's sign-act of going "naked" in Isa 20:3 is often spoken of as a reference to the inevitability of being stripped like POWs (Jacobs 2001, 107; Smith-Christopher 2002c). An equally significant passage found in 2 Chronicles, representing the reversal of a battle against Judeans, is particularly important in this regard:

Then those who were mentioned by name got up and took the captives, and with the booty they clothed all that were naked among them; they clothed them, gave them sandals, provided them with food and drink, and anointed them; and carrying all the feeble among them on donkeys, they brought them to their kindred at Jericho. (2 Chr 28:15)

Punishment directed at "Lady Babylon" in Isaiah includes the same imagery: "Your nakedness shall be uncovered, and your shame shall be seen. I will take vengeance, and I will spare no one" (Isa 47:3).[12] With the stripping of POWs in mind, the following passages read differently:

---

12. With regard to Isa 47, Vanderhooft writes: "She will be exposed and defiled, images that very likely involve application to Babylon of practices directed toward captives in Mesopotamian military expeditions" (1999, 181–82; cf. Sweeney 2001a, 353).

The Initial Lament with Warning 65

> Jerusalem sinned grievously,
> > so she has become a mockery;
> all who honored her despise her,
> > for they have seen her nakedness;
> she herself groans,
> > and turns her face away.
> > > (Lam 1:8)

> I am against you,
> > says the LORD of hosts,
> > and will lift up your skirts over your face;
> and I will let nations look on your nakedness
> > and kingdoms on your shame.
> > > (Nah 3:5)

> He leads counselors away stripped,
> > and makes fools of judges.
> > > (Job 12:17)

> He leads priests away stripped,
> > and overthrows the mighty.
> > > (Job 12:19)

The "humiliation" of "Jerusalem" as female must be directly connected to the ideology and practice of Assyrian and Babylonian warfare, which sought to humiliate the armies and any resistance.

[8b] The animal similes used in this passage are striking. Important parallel imagery, using the same terms as in Mic 1:8, are found in both Job 30:29 ("I am a brother of jackals, and a companion of ostriches"; cf. Isa 34:13; 43:20) and with slight variation in Lam 4:3 ("Even the jackals offer the breast and nurse their young, but my people has become cruel, like the ostriches in the wilderness").

We need not be sidetracked by identifying the specific species. The wilderness bird is known for haunting sounds, and Andersen and Freedman suggest (with others) a species of owl, not ostrich (2000, 194). The notion of wild animals inhabiting a site that was once a human settlement is common in curse literature and prophetic warnings of destruction and desolation (e.g., Ps 44:19; Isa 13:22; 35:7; Ezek 13:4). Jeremiah features a similar threat to the capital of the Hebrews in terms probably influenced by Micah; thus Jer 9:11, "I will make Jerusalem a heap of ruins, a lair of jackals; and I will make the towns of Judah a desolation, without inhabitant" (so also 10:22; of Hazor in 49:33; of Babylon in 51:37; and of Edom in Mal 1:3).

Finally, v. 8, with its references to animals, relates to the final verse in this chapter, with its similar reference to another wilderness bird, the eagle. The animal references form a set of bookends that surround a series of warnings against cities and peoples. For those inclined to take scissors to the book of Micah, this may suggest an insertion of vv. 10–15 between vv. 9 and 16. However, as we shall see, the reference to "exile" may suggest otherwise in v. 16.

[9] The term for an "incurable" wound, or a wound that makes weak, is not common in the Hebrew Bible. The NRSV of 2 Sam 12:15 reports a child becoming "very ill." Job 34:6 is often cited to refer to an "incurable" or "mortal" wound. Two prophets use the term to describe a day of grief or pain. Isaiah writes of a "day of grief and incurable pain" (17:11), while Jeremiah refers to a "severe" or "fatal" day (17:16). Perhaps one should read "fatal" in the light of Isa 17:11.

This is similar to the use of terms in Jer 15:18. Here too the term for the "wound" (*makkâ*) is used of "plagues" or "afflictions" in warnings such as Lev 26:21; God strikes a severe "plague" in Num 11:33. In Deut 28:59 it is used three times, each time with a different modification: "Then the LORD will overwhelm both you and your offspring with severe and lasting afflictions and grievous and lasting maladies" (cf. v. 61). But the passage can be read: "YHWH will overwhelm you with afflictions—severe afflictions—*great* afflictions." Here too Mic 1:9 suggests a crescendo, with the three-step use of the preposition ʿad, "up to," "as far as." What "has come to Judah" reaches "the gate of my people," and even "to Jerusalem." If God is portrayed as speaking, the "gate of my people" is probably a parallel to Jerusalem; but if Micah is speaking, he could mean his own town: "It comes to Judah generally, indeed to my own hometown, and even to the capital, Jerusalem!"

Yet finally, the term *makkâ* can be rendered in many contexts as "casualties," or injuries and losses specifically from warfare. Thus it is not unusual to have the term modified with "large" or "great" (e.g., *makkâ gĕdôlâ*), especially in regard to the *military* victories described in Josh 10:10, 20; Judg 11:33; 15:8; and quite commonly in the Deuteronomistic History in describing various military victories against Israelites and enemies alike: against Israelites in 1 Sam 4:10; against Beth Shemesh in 1 Sam 6:19; against Philistines in 1 Sam 14:30; 1 Kgs 20:21, "heavy losses" (NIV) or "great slaughter" (NRSV). Also notice the "great slaughter" in the infamous passage of Esth 9:5 (S-C). This use can shed further light on the term used in combination with "illness": Jer 10:19; 14:17; 19:8, the "wounds" of a city. The same terms as in Mic 1:9 turn up in Jer 30:12; for Edom's "wounds" in 49:17; and in the same phrase against Babylon in 50:13 (cf. Nah 3:19 against Assyria). Survived "wounds" are noted in Zech 13:6. Thus "casualties" and "wounds" of a city suggest that the military associations with this term in Mic 1:9 cannot be dismissed. Runions also recognizes the "double entendre" intended by the use of "incurable" and "plagues": both sickness and warfare are implied (2001, 125).

What is coming to Judah, "the gate," and Jerusalem? Armies, perhaps as punishment, but the threat is very real. The images of bodily injuries, frequently with "sickness/illness," profoundly suggest the personal impact of the disasters that Micah speaks of. The metaphorical use of "wounds" suggests punishment and warfare. Verses 8–9 are arguably the laments of those weary from war.

More can be said. If the introductory phrase in v. 8 ("because of this") refers to the punishment of Samaria, then what Samaria was punished for will "infect" Judah, and Jerusalem herself, according to v. 9. What has led to Samaria's punishments will now threaten Jerusalem. Samaria's sacrilege is viewed as gathering the wages of a prostitute, which could be either the money gathered from pagan temples (?) *or the financing of a revolt against Assyria.* Either pagan religiosity or economic injustice or both are here said to threaten Jerusalem with infection.

Contemporary Christian faith and practice, especially a faith and practice informed by deeply held convictions about social justice and peacemaking, always belong in a context of lamentation rather than triumphalism. Surely one of the most abhorrent aspects of some recent Western conservative preaching has been this element of almost relishing, if not explicitly promoting, the suffering of those with whom one has serious disagreements. Self-proclaimed prophets invariably give away their lack of qualifications for the prophetic task by failing to include themselves in humanities' failures of judgment and compassion. Micah and Jeremiah, who follows in Micah's tradition, derive little joy from the truths they proclaim or the powers and interests they challenge. Challenging human dependence on force and violence involves looking into some of the darkest fears and shocking failures of the human enterprise. Not for nothing does Jesus proclaim that those who take up the sword risk that their goals, and their lives, will suffer from the very weapons they brandish (Matt 26:52). Jesus' warning powerfully rebukes modern military claims about "unintended" or "unforeseen" destruction and suffering in war, the so-called collateral damage.

Micah 1:10–16 The Impact of the Policies of Destruction

10 In Gath, don't tell [it]![a]
  Do not weep at all![b]
In Beth-Leaphrah[c]
  I roll myself[d] in dust.
11 Pass by[e] (for you),[f] resident of Shaphir,
  naked, ashamed.[g]
She did not come out,
  resident of Zanaan.[h]
A lamentation, Beth-HaEtzel,[i]
  He will take from you his place to stand.
12 Thus she will wait[j] for well-being,[k]
  resident of Bitterness.[l]

And evil will come down from^m YHWH,ⁿ
to the gate of Jerusalem.
13 Bind° chariot to steed,
resident of Lachish.^p
It^q is the first offering to the daughter of Zion.^r
Thus it was in you that the rebellions of Israel were found!^s
14 Therefore^t you will give territories^u near^v Moresheth-Gath.^w
The dwellings of Achzib will be a deception^x to the kings of Israel.
15 What is more, I will bring the conqueror^y to you,
resident of Moreshah;^z
and to Adullam will come
the glory of Israel.^{aa}
16 Shear away—cut away the heirs^{bb} of your luxuries.^{cc}
"Expand"^{dd} your baldness as an eagle!^{ee}
because they have been exiled^{ff} from you!

a. Cf. 2 Sam 1:20. Wolff (1990, 43) accepts the Greek, "Do not boast," which is surely as much an interpretation as translation.

b. The infinitive absolute *bākô* means, lit., "weeping." There is great pressure to amend with a place-name here, to match the brief previous phrase about Gath (which certainly would make sense), but no satisfactory geographical solutions have been offered (e.g., "Akko" is too far away to make any historical or geographical sense; most do not accept the attempt of the Greek to read a place-name "Akim"). Others argue that one place-name belongs in each presumed "verse" of the passage, but this is not always helpful. McKane (1998, 40) is not convinced. Hillers (1984, 25) suggests that it is crowding the passage with too many place-names, and in any case a place-name does not fix the grammatical problems.

c. Naʾaman suggests the possibility of reading "in the house of no dust" (1995, 519).

d. The term *hitpallāšitî* appears to be in the first person, but is typically amended to *hitpallāšî*, thus feminine second-person imperative, involving the removal of the penultimate "*t*." This is supported by a slightly different spelling in Mur. 88 (so Wolff 1990, 43). If we are presuming an oral performance, however, one could argue for allowing the first person to remain as an effective rhetorical move. Andersen and Freedman reject the identification as first person and suggest that it is an archaic perfect form (2000, 218). Is there a wordplay on "Philistine" here? (Sweeney 2001a, 355). Cha (1996, 126) notes the similarity with Jer 6:26.

e. In the MT, the imperative is in feminine singular.

f. The singular verb is followed by *lākem* = "to you [pl.]" or "for yourselves" (cf. 1 Sam 17:8, "choose for yourselves"). Either the first term in singular or the second term in plural is usually changed, with the majority changing the first to plural for consistency: e.g., "You all pass by the resident of Saphir." Andersen and Freedman suggest two different audiences being addressed. The easiest solution would be to simply remove "for you"! But cf. Deut 31:19 (MT, KJV) "for you," that is, for your instruction. Hillers (1984, 26) approves of older suggestions of reading this as "They will blow the

The Impact of the Policies of Destruction

trumpet for you," thus phonetically establishing the wordplay "Shofer" and "Shaphir," but without much enthusiasm for the grammatical changes required by such a reading.

g. There is no conjunction in the Hebrew. Could it have been read dramatically, perhaps with a pause between these two descriptions of the "resident of Shaphir"? Runions proposes, "Nakedness, shame, will not go out" or "The inhabitant of Shaphir is nakedness, shame" (2001, 128–29).

h. Note the wordplay in *yāṣĕ'â* ("come out") and *ṣa'ănān* (Zaanan). Utzschneider (2005, 45) notes association with Jer 6:25.

i. The term *'ēṣel* normally means "beside," "at the side of," but this does not help much. For the reading "House of no shade," originally suggested by von Soden (so Andersen and Freedman 2000, 209), see Na'aman (1995), who pointedly suggests that this is a play on Assyrian promises (2 Kings 18:31) that deportees will sit under their own vine and fig tree, or under the shade of the king!

j. For *kî-ḥālâ*, which could be read as referring to *ḥîl* = "writhe," "pangs" (cf. Exod 15:14), or perhaps read as *yaḥēl*, "wait" as in "wait on the Lord," sometimes translated "hope" (Ps 130:7), achieved by taking the *yod* from *kî* (cf. Wolff 1990, 40).

k. Cf. Deut 30:9. Hillers cleverly suggests, "She will wait for sweetness," as a play on "bitterness" (1984, 24).

l. Reading *mārôt* as feminine plural of *mar*.

m. In *mē'ēt yhwh*, the *'ēt* is almost always read here as the sign of the accusative, in this case, the name of God. But it is tempting to consider whether *'ēt* = "plowshare" is meant here as well: thus "the plow of God." The term is used in the famous "swords to plowshares" passage of Mic 4:3, and 1 Sam 13:20 speaks of Israelites having to "go down" to Philistia to sharpen any *'ēt* = "plow."

n. God can bring "evil" (*rā'*), as in Isa 45:7.

o. For *rĕtōm* ("harness" or "bind") probably read, as *BHS* suggests, *rātôm*, imperative, so as to address Lachish (Andersen and Freedman 2000, 227). The Greek chooses to speak of "sounds" of chariots and steeds. Hillers simply suggests, "Hitch the horses to the chariot" (1984, 24).

p. The wordplay is *rekeš* ("steed") and *lākîš* ("Lachish"). It could also be "cart to horse," suggesting a triple wordplay: chariots as war vehicles, but horse-carts as vehicles for exploiting resources. Carts are portrayed carrying the material of POWs in the Lachish reliefs in the British Museum.

q. Literally, "she," but it remains difficult to see why.

r. Also possible: "She being the beginning of sin to the daughter of Zion," so the Quaker translator, Anthony Purver (1764). Andersen and Freedman (2000, 229) suggest the possibility of a goddess cult referenced in this phrase, but see comments below.

s. Wolff (1990, 50) argues that the whole of v. 13b was added.

t. The use of *lākēn* ("therefore") may indicate a change from vv. 10–13 to 14–15.

u. The meaning of *šillûḥîm* is debated, but it is used as a "wedding gift" from Pharaoh to his daughter when Solomon is married to her (1 Kgs 9:16). The gift, however, was the devastated city of Gezer. The Greek reads *exapostellomenous* ("those sent out = emissaries," e.g., "diplomats"?). The Greek translation "inheritance" presumes a participial form of *yāraš*, perhaps even presuming another wordplay on the town name "Moresheth." See comments. McKane (1998, 49) notes that Kimchi already suggested "land grants."

v. The preposition 'al surely means more than the much simpler *lamed* preposition "to" Moresheth-Gath. Mays (1976, 49) removes it altogether; Hillers (1984, 24) preserves simply "to."

w. Sweeney (2001a, 356) proposes many more wordplays than most others have recognized, including "betrothed" for Moresheth and "divorce" for Gath.

x. The wordplay is *'akzîb lĕ'akzāb*. Hillers reads "dry watercourse" (1984, 24); Mays, taking the term more lit., translates "failing brook" (1976, 49). "Deception" is suggested to be the implication of a spring that was expected to give water but does not.

y. Gk. "inheritors." Mays (1976, 49) follows the Greek with "heir."

z. Here the wordplay is clearer: *yôšebet mārēšâ*.

aa. This line contains two wordplays in a row: *'ad-'ădullām* and *yābô' kĕbôd*.

bb. Reading "heirs" as the intended sense of "sons of." Cha (1996, 126) notes the similarity with the action of cutting hair in Jer 7:29, in the sense of mourning. The accidental similarity of "heir" and "hair" in English adds to enjoying an English rendering!

cc. Or perhaps the common phrase "children of privilege" is appropriate here.

dd. The term is often used of expanding territory, as in Deut 19:8.

ee. Or "vulture"? So Shaw (1993, 36).

ff. They have been "exiled" (*gālû*). The root *glh* can mean "stripped" as well as "exiled." Thus "They will be *stripped* from you" also makes good sense.

This rhetorical sequence is perhaps the most troublesome of the entire book of Micah. Andersen and Freedman are undoubtedly correct in reading this section as an oral performance that may have given rise to difficulties in reproducing the "event" in print: "in broken sobs the prophet allows the names of the various towns to trigger associated words and ideas. . . . They catch the mood of terror, outrage, helplessness, tragedy" (2000, 206). This suggestion of an intentionally dramatic presentation has been taken up more seriously by Utzschneider in his recent commentary (2005).

Certainly there is a kind of cadence conveyed in these threats, with wordplays and rhythmic speech. The two phrases "Tell it not in Gath" and "In weeping, do not weep" are similar wordplays, picking up similar sounds in the beginning and the end of each phrase. The cleverness of the Hebrew is missed without attempting an artificial explanation of the sounds, as with "tell" (*taggîdû*) and the place-name *gat*, "Bet Leaphrah" (*bêt lĕ'aprâ*) combined with "dust" (*'āpār*). I have tried to make note of these in transliteration in the textual notes (above).

Identifying this as "oral performance," however, does not mean that all of the passages are going to be transparently clear. There are surely many allusions to ideas, prejudices, or opinions about local political realities and regional struggles that we may never fully comprehend—some of which may even include made-up locations in the Shephelah simply to express the idea of local villages and their issues of concern (e.g., Maroth = Bitterness? Beth-Etzel? Beth-Leaphrah = "House of Dust"?) or even local nicknames lost to history.

The Impact of the Policies of Destruction

It is frequently pointed out that some of these place-names (certainly a few, others less certain) appear in Josh 15:33–47, which consists of a list of towns in the "lowlands" = Shephelah. On this basis, Robinson suggests that, for example, Samir and Ophrah (1 Chr 4:14) are probably Saphir and Aphra; Joktheel of Josh 15:38 is probably original for Beth-HaEtzel; Maroth is possibly Jarmuth (Josh 15:35) or Maarath (Josh 15:59); and Baka, if a place (*bākô*, instead of reading "weeping"), is in assonance with "Do not weep" (*'al-tibkû*) (1954, 133). Finally, Robinson notes that Isa 10:27b–32 has similar wordplays, and others have suggested a direct relationship between the Isaiah passage and Mic 1:10–16:

> On that day his burden will be removed from your shoulder, and his yoke will be destroyed from your neck.
> He has gone up from Rimmon,
>   he has come to Aiath;
> he has passed through Migron,
>   at Michmash he stores his baggage;
> they have crossed over the pass,
>   at Geba they lodge for the night;
> Ramah trembles,
>   Gibeah of Saul has fled.
> Cry aloud, O daughter Gallim!
>   Listen, O Laishah!
>   Answer her, O Anathoth!
> Madmenah is in flight,
>   the inhabitants of Gebim flee for safety.
> This very day he will halt at Nob,
>   he will shake his fist at the mount of daughter Zion,
>   the hill of Jerusalem.
> Look, the Sovereign, the LORD of hosts,
>   will lop the boughs with terrifying power;
> the tallest trees will be cut down,
>   and the lofty will be brought low.
> (Isa 10:27–33)

Although Jerusalem is the final destination of both sequences, the use of this list is controversial, and some of the attempts to bring Micah into harmony with this list seem forced and may effectively take away from the oral performance intended by Micah!

There have been many attempts to read the list as some path of destruction by invading Assyrian armies, and specifically Sennacherib's campaign of 701 B.C.E. This specific conjecture runs into difficulties because the towns (even if they could all be identified) do not appear to form a logical direction of deployment. But granted the difficulty, there is still serious reason to question

Andersen and Freedman's claim that "there is very little language that suggests military activity" (2000, 211).

Much of the language of the sequence is that of mourning and lamentation (rolling in dust and weeping in v. 10), but there are clear references to military and political instability as well: naked residents (POWs, v. 11), loss of territory ("place to stand," v. 11), evil coming "to the *gate* of Jerusalem" (v. 12; gates were the most vulnerable parts of city walls because the wood was susceptible to burning), chariots and horses at the known fortress city of Lachish (v. 13), loss of territories (v. 14), "the conqueror" (v. 15), and loss of life or exiling of the young (v. 16). It is hardly a forced interpretation to suggest that military actions are very much behind a good deal of the imagery in this section. As even Andersen and Freedman concede, the imagery suggests that "some kind of military disaster had evidently overtaken them (or is predicted for them)" (2000, 205). I consider it reasonable to continue associating this passage with Sennacherib's campaigns, despite the controversies surrounding that identification. In the end, that Micah refers to a military reprisal against Jerusalem's policies is more important than being certain *which* campaign might be referenced in history. Even if Micah's words predate the campaign of 701, as a lowlander he would know the most logical path of any incursion toward Jerusalem, and thus his general allusions to villages in the general direction that Sennacherib's armies actually took are not really an impressive act of prophecy!

[10] Gath is clearly the Philistine town that was occasionally under Judean control (see introduction). The phrase that appears here is similar to 2 Sam 1:20, and some have suggested a borrowing from that location, or an oral tradition regarding the same stories of past dealings with Gath. Gath appears frequently in the Historical Books in descriptions of conflicts with Philistia and was the home of "Goliath" (1 Sam 17), a story that surely expresses the classic context of a frontier town between disputed Judean and Philistine territories. This suggests the reason why the phrase was borrowed from 2 Sam 1:20, or from the oral traditions around David that informed both literary uses in Samuel and Micah, highlighting the rivalry between Gath and nearby Moresheth. This passage begins the sequence that follows, and I suggest that it is to be read somewhat differently from what follows. The sequence speaks of instability and trouble in the Judean towns of the Shephelah, and Micah warns the rival, Gath, not to be overjoyed about these troubles as they might have been at the death of Saul and Jonathan. Thus the lament is not necessarily for Gath, as if Gath were presently under Judean control, but rather a warning to the residents of Gath. Indeed, even if under Judean control, the Philistine residents surely would see instability as an opportunity to throw off their Judean masters (and gain favor with the Assyrians)!

The Impact of the Policies of Destruction 73

Ophrah, possibly the reference intended here, is mentioned infrequently as a place-name, mostly as a location in the story of Gideon (Judg 6:11, 24; 8:27, 32; 9:5), but Andersen and Freedman are surely correct to dismiss this identification as "out of the question" because it would be much too far from Micah's hometown and the immediate area. The Greek associates Ophrah with "Ephrath/Ephrata," thus near Bethlehem (Gen 35:19; 48:7; Ruth 1:2; 4:11), and it is used heavily in inserted comments in the LXX tradition, but this suffers from the same geographical problem.

The issue here is mourning. Rolling in dust, more often putting dust on one's head (Josh 7:6; Job 2:12), are signs of anguish. If Micah intends a fictional local town, the message could well be that the local villages have reason to mourn.

[11] The command to pass over, or through, is directed at the "inhabitants" of Shaphir. Again the English cannot capture the sounds of "inhabitants" (yôšebet) and the town (šāpîr). Many translations presume "horn" should be supplied here: "Sound the horn [šôpār], Shaphir!"[13] But as is, the command amounts to saying, "Be unsettled, settled ones." That this action, whether "passing by" or "being unsettled," is to be done in "nakedness and shame" is awkward. In Ezekiel, the same term is used as "*naked* and bare" in one of the most troubling passages of misogynist metaphor against Jerusalem (Ezek 16:7, 22, 39; cf. 23:29). In Hab 3:9, God "uncovers" his bow in the great battle of creation. In any case, to "pass by," thus engaging in movement, in nakedness and shame strongly suggests prisoners of war being led away, as previously proposed, since suffering from Assyrian conquest appears to be the chief punishment in Micah's rhetoric.

The residents of Zaanan are not to "come out" (lō' yāṣĕ'â); the verb sounds similar to "Zaanan" (ṣa'ănān). Again, the strange sentence can be interpreted enough to suggest movement of people, as in the first line with regard to Shaphir. I thus infer that we are still on the subject of the movement of peoples amid the instability of warfare. This links with the final thought in this verse as well.

Although a place is called Azal in Zech 14:5, yet the last phrase, "Beth-HaEtzel, He will take from you his place to stand," is built less on sounds as perhaps on meaning. It is not obvious how to understand this wordplay. Thus many commentators have tried to radically alter the reading of this passage. However, maintaining the general theme of military violence in the region, we suggest the sense of Micah's intended pun. The common meaning of 'ēṣel as simply "next to" or "adjacent to" (e.g., Gen 41:3; Lev 6:10 [3]) suggests the possibility that bêt hā'ēṣel (lit., "house in the vicinity"?) may then mean, "Your place will be taken." However, since the much more common term qārôb ("near") is used in general discussions of a location near to something, perhaps it is not too much to notice that the term 'ēṣel is often used for something "standing" or

---

13. Andersen and Freedman speak of the shophar being "smuggled" into the text (2000, 213)!

"placed" near a cult image or royal symbol (e.g., Lev 1:16; 10:12; Deut 16:21; 1 Kgs 2:29; 2 Kgs 12:9; Ezek 9:2; 1 Sam 5:2; ironically "next to" a stone named Ezel [*ʾēṣel*] in 1 Sam 20:19; lions next to a throne in 1 Kgs 10:19//2 Chr 9:18, and similarly Ezek 1:15 and 10:6, 9). In each of these examples, the term seems to suggest "standing near" in a kind of regal pose, which in English is perhaps captured by saying that it is intentionally "*placed* near." Then the idea of having your "place to stand taken away" makes sense for a town named "The House Standing/Placed Near."

We can summarize our tentative suggestions: Residents of Shaphir and Zaanan are threatened with some form of forced movement, and Beth-HaEtzel is threatened with loss of possession or territory, all similar results of suffering attack and warfare.

[12] The Hebrew term *mōrat*, related to *mārôt* from the root *mrr*, can connote "bitterness" (cf. Gen 26:35; 1 Sam 1:10; Prov 14:10). Thus the phrase in Micah implies, "Residents of Bitterness are sick for good." The second phrase in v. 12 says that God will bring down "evil" (*rāʿ*) "to the gate of Jerusalem." The apparent sign of the accusative (*mēʾēt*) followed by "YHWH" can also be read to be God's "plow" (cf. Hos 10:11, where God imposes farmwork on Israel and Judah) approaching the gate of Jerusalem. In any case, that God brings "evil"[14] right to the "gate" of a city is a clear military reference.

During sieges, the city gates, being made of something moveable like wood (Isa 24:12), are especially vulnerable. To "possess the gates" is thus a reference to the most likely place for a city to fall. In Gen 22:17, the patriarch Abraham is promised that his "offspring shall possess the gate of their enemies" (cf. 24:60). Famously, the city gate was also the place of judicial discussion among the elders (Deut 21:19; Josh 20:4; Job 29:7; hence the call for justice at the gate in Prov 22:22).

Verse 12, then, ends with Jerusalem, the center of power in Judah. It declares that God is bringing "evil" right to the gate, which appears to be a culmination of the events described up to this point. All of this suggests that God is initiating events that the townspeople of the Shephelah will have reason to deeply regret and indeed mourn!

[13] The residents of Lachish are told to harness chariots to steeds/horses. Such horses for war (1 Kgs 4:28 [5:8]) imply coming battles and a need for fear and preparation for war (Esth 8:10, 14). The fact that God will remove horses and chariots (Mic 5:10) strongly suggests, however, that the tradition behind the book of Micah is not sympathetic to the need for such weaponry.

---

14. Hagstrom points out an interesting sequence in the use of the term *rāʿ* in chs. 1–3, noting its first use in 1:12, then again in 2:1, 3; 3:2; and finally in 3:11 for this section. This underscores "the correspondence between sin and punishment" (1988, 58).

The Impact of the Policies of Destruction

A "beginning of sin" (NRSV) is somewhat awkward for a term that is often translated the "first" or "best" (*rē'šît*), as in "the best of first fruits" in ceremonial contexts (Exod 23:19; 34:26; Lev 23:10; Deut 26:10; see also Lev 2:12; Deut 18:4; "best land" in Deut 33:21 and Ezek 48:14; the "best" of the devoted things in 1 Sam 15:21). Psalm 78:51 uses the term in parallel with "first fruits" (cf. Ps 105:36). Jeremiah 2:3 brings this implication of "first fruits" closer to the prophetic textual traditions of Micah, as also does Ezek 20:40. Amos 6:1 refers to the "first ones" or "highest authorities" of the nations. Hence I suggest: "First fruits as a sin offering were brought to the house of Zion" or perhaps even "Sinful first fruits were brought to the house of Zion." The term for sin is thus read as a modifier of the "first fruits."

In "you" (Judah?) were found crimes similar to Samaria. The sole use of "crimes" or "offenses" in the Torah appears in Gen 31:36, when Jacob asks Laban, "What is my crime?" (NIV). The term appears in Job, in parallel with "sins/transgressions" (Job 7:21; 13:23; 14:17; 31:33; as also Pss 32:5; 39:8 [9]). In prophetic literature, perhaps most famously, the term is the choice for "sins" of the nations in Amos's series of "Oracles against the Nations" (1:3, 6, 9, 11, 13; 2:1, 4, 6). The two terms used for sin reappear in Mic 6:7, one of the most famous passages in all of the prophetic literature (see comments).

Chariots are a massive expense for central powers of the ancient Near East. In the context of our suggestion that Micah is a rural elder enraged about the massive tribute being levied by the central powers to produce their weaponry, the notion that the fortress of Lachish is "a beginning of sin" is a powerful statement. For Micah, Lachish's massive fortifications and possibly also its chariot forces thus illustrate military obsessions that were characteristic of the far more bellicose northern kingdom, Israel. The sentiment, in short, makes a great deal of sense to a man who wishes that he and his fellow farmers could beat swords back into plowshares. The message is clear for moderns, who today surely should blush, if not recoil in horror, at the massive expenditures for war when so many starve.

[14] In this verse we return to wordplay and rhetorical devices. In the opening phrase, the Hebrew listener would focus on the consonantal sounds of *shin* and *mem*, then *mem* and *shin*. The key term used here, "parting gift" (*šillûḥîm*), is not common in Scripture, but a particularly striking example is found in 1 Kgs 9:16. I have thus chosen "territories" to express what I consider to be Micah's intent here.

The town name Achzib appears to be less than complimentary since it means "deceptive" (Jer 15:18 refers to "deceptive waters" [S-C]), and in this case the wordplay is entirely obvious. The town itself is referred to in Joshua and Judges, apparently near the coast (Josh 15:44; 19:29; Judg 1:31). In Joshua it is mentioned in the same vicinity as Mareshah. If we are speaking here of land grants given to the northern kingdom (Israel), then Andersen and Freedman strongly suggest that Mic 2:1–5 may be referring to the same incident of Jerusalem having to cede territory in some kind of agreement, such as the "marriage" implied in the "dowry" (2000, 233). On the other hand, 2 Kgs 16:3 blames Ahaz for acting like the kings of Israel, which further supports the notion that relations with Israel, or acting like Israel, is the issue at hand here.

[15] The opening phrase plays on the sounds of "conqueror" and "residents" and perhaps even the location "Mareshah." In Josh 15:44, Achzib (mentioned in the previous verse in Micah) is followed by a reference to Mareshah. This place-name is not frequently attested in the Bible. A later tradition suggests another prophet from Mareshah (2 Chr 20:37). The site, now identified with Tel Sandakhannah (and between Maresheth and Lachish) became very important in the Hellenistic period, where there are considerable ruins and rich archaeological finds, but only a few LMLK stamps from layers previous to the Hellenistic period (Iron Age IIC; see Kloner 1996, 524).

The root *yrš* is often used for "taking possession" or "conquering" (e.g., Exod 15:9; 34:24; Lev 20:24; throughout Deuteronomy and Joshua). Ironically, and in close relation to images in Micah, Isaiah speaks of wilderness animals "conquering" or "taking possession" of former lands and cities (Isa 34:11).

Adullam is also not mentioned frequently in the Hebrew Bible. It appears most often in early Deuteronomistic Historical sources (Josh 12:15; 15:35), and in a reference to the "cave" of Adullam in the early stories of David (1 Sam 22:1; 2 Sam 23:13). Nehemiah 11:30 mentions Adullam with "Zanoah," suggesting that it was a large-enough settlement to identify by name in the context of referring to smaller settlements in the immediate area. The LXX, however, oddly replaces "Eglon" with "Adullam" in Josh 10, where it appears as the kingdom of one of the kings in a list of central sites with Jarmuth, Lachish, Jerusalem, and Hebron (Josh 10:3, 5, 23) and then as one of the conquered cities (Josh 10:34, 37). Judges 3, however, names Eglon as the king of Moab. A site identified tentatively as Eglon appears on the Shephelah, inland from Ashkelon and Gaza, and south and east from the site identified as Adullam, but there continues to be controversy regarding the identification. One problem is raised by the discussion in 1 Sam 22, where David retreats to the cave of Adullam and then proceeds to leave family members in safety with the king of Moab in vv. 3–4. If the identification of Adullam is far from the border with Moab, this story presents some geographical difficulties. Perhaps this is one reason why the LXX associates one "Eglon" with Moab and another "Eglon" with the place-name Adullam in Josh 10.

The phrase "glory of Israel," as Mays notes (1976, 58–59), is among a series of uses of the term "glory of PN [place-name]," which suggests prestige, economic success, and power of a particular location (e.g., "glory of Moab" in Isa 16:14; "glory of Lebanon" in 35:2; 60:13; "glory of Kedar" in 21:16; a large population is called the "glory" of a king in Prov 14:28). Most commentaries observe the assonance of sounds in keeping with the wordplays of this entire section. Yet there is a possibility that this reference goes beyond simply the coincidence of sounds of "unto," "toward" (*'ad*), and "Adullam." Is it possible that the phrase "glory of Israel" coming to "Adullam" refers to David's retreat in 1 Sam 22, when he was on the run from Philistines and Saul? If so, the prophet may be referring to the "glory of Israel" having to be "on the run," as David once was—another sign of impending troubles. It is not a direct reference to the king of Israel, especially since David (or later kings) is never called "the glory of Israel."[15] But the imagery need not be that literal: the "glory" of Israel must retreat as David once had to do, and this would be enough to make the point, especially if "Adullam" commonly called up memories of the tradition of David. Precisely this may be established by the fact that the Maccabean literature, certainly a Hellenistic-era attempt to revive the glories of the Davidic state, suggests that Judas goes to Adullum to "regroup" in much the same way that David is said to have done (2 Macc 12:38).

[16] In many ways, v. 16 marks a return to vv. 8–9. One clear similarity is the use of animal simile. Yet it also contains a sense of judgment and perhaps loss of territory and personnel, and thus is logically placed in this sequence. "Shave and shear yourselves," rendered by the NRSV as "Make yourselves bald," seems an apt phrase here. Most often in the Bible, the verb *gāzaz* is used of shearing sheep (Gen 31:19; 38:12; 1 Sam 25:2; Isa 53:7; Jer 7:29, undoubtedly influenced by Micah, where mourning also goes with the imperative: "Shear yourselves!"). The image "bald as an eagle" raises problems of which species we are talking about; thus the replacement often proposed is "vulture," which has a featherless head. While Prov 30:17 certainly suggests vultures, such a use of this particular species would probably meet some modern resistance if it replaces "eagle" in such famous passages as Exod 19:4, where God liberates Israel "on eagles' wings"; or Isa 40:31 (NIV), where God lets them "soar on wings like eagles" in their return from exile. On the other hand, the ambiguity of the species does allow for some interesting exegetical possibilities when, for example, "vulture" replaces "eagle" in the famous exilic-era warning in Deut 28:49, "YHWH will bring a nation from far away, from the end of the earth, to swoop down on you like an eagle [or vulture?], a nation whose language you do not understand" (similarly Jer 48:40). That vultures normally feed *on the dead* makes the change of species even more challenging.

An old suggestion is notable here. Gregory the Great (540–604 C.E.) argued that an eagle loses feathers all over its body rather than a person who is bald only on the head, thus the reference is to a nation losing all its people (Ferreiro

---

15. Cf. 1 Sam 15:29, "Glory of Israel" = YHWH, but note 2 Sam 21:17, "the lamp of Israel" = David; cf. Ps 132:17.

2003, 152). According to Gregory, the "balding head" of the capital cities is a euphemism for the "planting" and "plowing" of the hilltop cities (Samaria and Jerusalem) named in 1:6 and 3:12.

The reference to "sons" and "luxuries" is certainly awkward. The literal use of "sons of your luxuries," however, may suggest more than merely pampered children. After all, the same term "luxuries" is used in 2:9 to refer to precious houses, supporting the idea that the advantages of the privileged classes are referred to here, not merely spoiled children. Proverbs 19:10 ("It is not fitting for a fool to live in luxury") gives us a classist attitude of the upper echelons of Judean society and exemplifies precisely the class that Micah despises with his comments. Thus "children of privilege" may capture Micah's rhetoric more effectively. The way the term is handled by the Greek translators suggests that we read the term this way; *tryphera* recalls a similar use in Isa 47:1, 8 in reference to Babylon's "daughters" (47:1) losing their privileges:

> Now therefore hear this, you lover of *pleasures*,
>   who sit securely,
> who say in your heart,
>   "I am, and there is no one besides me;
> I shall not sit as a widow
>   or know the loss of children."
>
>   (Isa 47:8)

Indeed, Susanna is called a woman of "refinement" or "privilege," using the same term (1:31 LXX).

The children of privilege have "gone from you," into exile. This could certainly be a reference to 722 B.C.E., the deportation of the northern tribes' upper classes under the Assyrians, but some are tempted to see a reference to Babylon here (Andersen and Freedman 2000, 238).

In this section, and in the entire book, Micah addresses issues that he knows are of intense interest to the residents of the lowlands. Yet it does not take much effort to notice that while *sympathy* is expressed for the fate of most of the villages, *anger* is directed at Lachish, "the beginning of sin," the foremost town that Judean kings have fortified as the military defense of the road to Jerusalem.

Even if the common interpretation of this section is no longer confidently held—that this section represents the devastated path of Sennacherib's destructive march to Jerusalem in 702–701 B.C.E.—there is no doubt that this is the direction that attacking armies would logically take (southward along the coast, and then eastward up the valleys to Jerusalem). Furthermore, the control and conquest of Lachish is certainly portrayed in Assyrian reliefs from Nineveh as central to Sennacherib's campaign. If this sequence (in Mic 1) does not relate directly to Sennacherib's campaign, it could certainly come from

The Oppression of the Ruling Elite

any time before that in Micah's era, with Lachish being the site of preparations for war and Micah anticipating the result for his fellow lowlanders in the nearby villages.

Reading Micah involves listening to the cries against the "peripheral damage," "unintended casualties," the "civilian losses," and all the other euphemisms modern media use to mention, always in passing, the suffering of noncombatants in modern warfare. But Micah is surely equally concerned for the suffering *of the combatants*—young men from the villages—and not only "collateral damage." Preventing noncombatant death is supposed to be one of the primary criteria in Christian theology for a "just war." The modern notion of "double effect" (what we primarily intend, yet what also happens) attempts to maintain a semblance of morality in accepting such horrific losses. The book of Micah, however, stands with the peripheral, the unintended, and the doubly affected noncombatants as well as the soldiers themselves. If the sentiment is "swords into plowshares," then Micah clearly can also be understood to desire "soldiers into farmers"! Overemphasizing Micah's alleged loyalty to Jerusalem only perpetuates this easy dismissal of "peripheral damage" in Judah. In an age of governments that carefully "manage perception," carefully wording all public references to include great "sacrifice" and "patriotism," Micah's blunt assessment of human and physical damage is patriotically "incorrect."

If these words do not come after Sennacherib's campaign, then they represent what Micah anticipates as Jerusalem prepares for conflict. Micah, therefore, is not caught up in nationalist bravado used to rouse history's masses for battle. He knows what is coming and tries to warn others. There is no higher calling for modern Christian prophetic preaching than standing against all idolatrous patriotism and violent nationalism.

Micah 2:1–5 The Oppression of the Ruling Elite

1 A Warning![a]
[About[b]] those who plan[c] wickedness
    and acts[d] of evil on their beds.[e]
At morning's light they carry it out,
    because they are powerful.[f]
2 They desire fields, and so steal them!
    Houses, and so they carry them away![g]
They oppress[h] a citizen[i] and his household,
    a man and his just portion [inheritance].[j]
3 Therefore,[k] YHWH says this:[l]
Now![m] I plan[n] against this tribe
    an evil that you will not lift[o] from your necks.

And you will not walk exaltedly,
   because it will be a time of evil.ᵖ
4 In that day a sayingᑫ about you will be lifted up,ʳ
   and it will be a grave lament,ˢ
saying: "We are completely devastated;ᵗ
   the property of my people is altered.
How will it be carried back to me?
   Our fields will be parceled out to an apostate."ᵘ
5 Therefore you will have nobody to cast a line
   at the apportionment in the assembly of YHWH.

a. The term *hôy*, undoubtedly a spoken sound intended to increase drama, is often rendered "alas," but here the drama emphasizes the gravity of the point being made and thus it means "Warning!"

b. Implied term supplied.

c. Many have suggested "conspire."

d. The typical phrase *pōʿălê ʾāwen*, "evildoers" (14 times in Psalms, e.g., 5:5 [6]; 6:8 [9]; 14:4; 28:3) is split in Mic 2:1 between two phrases: "thinkers" of evil (*ʾāwen*) and "doers" of wickedness/evil (*rāʿ*).

e. The two participles "thinkers of evil" and "doers of evil" are then followed by "on their beds." This has encouraged many to translate "doers" as "acts of evil," that is, continuing the "planning" of the first participle.

f. The phrase speaks of "power to their hands [*yādām*]." For strength of rulers or armies, see Dan 3:15, in which Nebuchadnezzar asks, "Who . . . will deliver you from my hands?" In Neh 9:24, the Canaanites are given "into their hands." Political power is the point. McKane refers to "Might is right" as the essence of the saying, the ability to act like a god (1998, 60).

g. The common verb *nāśāʾ* simply means to "carry, lift up." Micah is either being ironic—dwellings cannot simply be "carried away"—or he is referring to the actual destruction of dwellings under expropriation of land.

h. The verb *ʿāšaq* is the basic term for economic exploitation and oppression in biblical use. See comments below.

i. The term *geber* generally means "young, strong man," but here it suggests a man with basic rights, a full-fledged member of the people of Israel. Note the parallel use of simply "a man" (*ʾîš*).

j. The term *naḥălâ* refers to the equal portion of each tribal member that in Levitical law is inalienable. McKane (1998, 61) refers to a state where the "foundations of society are being shaken."

k. Here *lākēn*, "therefore," is often taken to be a signifier of a shift in the prose, but this follows as the result of the previous accusations.

l. This is the famous "messenger formula" common throughout the prophets.

m. The term *hinnēh* is famously rendered "behold" in KJV English.

n. The verb *ḥāšab* is also used of those who "plan" in v. 1.

o. The term *mûš* usually means "take away," but the use of "necks" suggests that a yoke is implied—a common term for foreign oppression (e.g., Jer 28).

The Oppression of the Ruling Elite   81

p. The second time *rā'â* ("evil") is used in this verse; it is the same term used for the planners' acts in v. 1.

q. A "saying," a "byword," "satire," or a "taunt"—all have been used to translate *māšāl*. The English terms have different shades of meaning; it could simply be an awareness that others will talk about this event, either in horror or in mocking anger.

r. Again, the simple verb *nāśā'* ("carry" or "take up"), possibly playing on its use throughout this section, but it is a very common term.

s. This is the first of two phrases built with two forms of the same word—lit., "with a lamentable lamenting."

t. Repeating the same term in the Hebrew colloquialism, "devastating devastation."

u. As is often suggested, those who are spared from disaster (i.e., the remnant; cf. Isa 10:21–22) are those who will "return" (*šûb*). The participle from this root could be rendered "apostate" ("those who turn away," as Andersen and Freedman translate [2000, 286], suggesting perhaps territory given over to Assyrian conquerors), but it can also refer to those who will eventually return.

[1] The mood of the book of Micah shifts significantly in the second chapter. From lamentation and the anguished recital of warnings to his fellow lowland villagers, the mood changes to angry denunciation directed at those whom the prophet considers responsible for the suffering that will come if present policies and practices are not changed. The prophet's anger is especially incited by what he perceives as the calculated cruelty and exploitation, "planned wickedness," and the exploitive violence done to outlying villagers, safely away from the eyes of the greedy elite whose policies enact such anguish. Thus the prophet pits God's "plans" against the evil "plans" of the elite. In the tradition of the God of the Torah, who hears the cries of the oppressed (e.g., Gen 21:17; Exod 2:23–24; 22:27), the prophet narrates God's response.

As attested in the Hebrew Bible, a limited variety of phrases refer to "doing evil," such as the phrase *la'ăśôt hāra'* ("to do evil [in the sight of YHWH]"; 2 Kgs 17:17; cf. Eccl 8:11, 12) and "do wickedness" (*'ăśôt reša'*; e.g., Prov 16:12). More troubling, however, are those who "plot" or "plan" to do evil (Prov 24:8, "Whoever plans to do evil will be called a mischief-maker"). In the prophets, however, there is a marked increase in condemnation against "doers of evil," featuring the same terms we find in Mic 2:1. Isaiah 1:4 speaks of people "heavy with wickedness" (*'āwōn*; S-C). One way of referring to the opposite behavior that is desired is to "cease" to do evil and/or "do good" (Isa 1:16–17). The reader might be forgiven for considering these phrases somewhat mundane, but the thought is no less profound for its simplicity: there is wrong and right, and the prophet is concerned to clarify the importance of this difference. The assumption is that all know what these two categories are; the call is to live it out.

The evil ones are condemned not for sins of omission: they are condemned for knowing full well what they are doing and indeed carefully planning it! More broadly, "think," "conceive," and "regard" are normal translations of the

Hebrew verbal root ḥāšab. It is translated with a striking variety of nuances in English, however. In Gen 50:20, for example, Joseph explains his good fortune to his brothers: "Even though you *intended* to do harm to me, God *intended* it for good." But in Ps 144:3, "What are ... mortals that you *think* of them?" Ritual objects are described in Exod 26:1, 31 and 28:6 as made "skillfully" (NRSV), or to use a modern parlance, "with focused attention." On the other hand, and closer to our concern here, is the suggestion to "devise" or "plan" (2 Sam 14:13–14). In Psalms, we hear more often of the "schemes" of the evil ones (Pss 10:2; 21:11; 35:4; 36:4, "plot mischief while on their beds"; 52:2 [4]; 140:2, 4 [3, 5]). In the prophets, the verb is often used either in disclosing the conspiracy of the powerful to maintain their privilege, status, and wealth and to silence criticism (Jer 11:19; 18:18; so also Ezek 11:2; 38:10; Zech 7:10; 8:17), or in accusing those who are scheming against God (Hos 7:15; Nah 1:9).[16] Many have noticed that Micah reverses the standard phrase "plan evil" (Gen 50:20; Hos 7:15; Mic 2:3), or "doers of iniquity" (Andersen and Freedman 2000, 261).

The acts occur "in the morning," that is, "at first opportunity." If they have been plotting "on their beds" (cf. Ps 36:4), morning is the time to act on the plots! This contrasts with the Psalms, which represent the morning as most often a time of rejoicing and a sign of hope (e.g., 30:5; 46:5; 59:16; 65:8; 90:5, 14; 92:2; 130:6; 139:9; 143:8). Although this may simply be figurative, since poets often speak of the morning giving fresh hope and perspective, it may also refer to early morning prayers and sacrifices (Ps 88:13; 1 Chr 16:40; 2 Kgs 16:15; 1 Sam 1:19; Ezek 46:13, 14; Amos 4:4). There is also a suggestion of judgments in the morning (Zeph 3:5; Jer 21:12). Thus the notion of carrying out *evil* in the morning may be all the more significant if the morning is normally to be considered a time of hope, a time of just judgment, a time of prayerful sacrifice to God. Isaiah 5:11 also speaks of wasteful sloth in the morning by the wealthy: "Ah, you who rise early in the morning in pursuit of strong drink" (cf. 5:22; the repeated association of the privileged elite with strong drink in Amos 2:8, 12; 5:11; 6:6, "drink wine by the bowlful!" [NIV]).

The rich believe that this behavior is well within their power, or literally, "by my hand." There is a parallel use of ʼēl as "power" rather than as a reference to God in Gen 31:29, "It is in my power to do you harm." Some traditions of the LXX try to work with ʼēl as a reference to God. Although awkward, it may suggest the "power" exercised by those not humbled by the presence of God: "They do not remove their hand before God." Perhaps what is intended is the thought that they do not care about God's watchful eye for injustice (similar in thought to Wis 17:2). Certainly the powerful can boast of the power of their "hand" or of enemies being delivered "into my hand" (e.g., Isa 43:13; 1 Sam 17:46; 24:11; 2 Kgs 21:14; Dan 3:15 [Aramaic]). The idiom conveys the claim that the poor

---

16. Willis speaks of "dreaming about" the greedy acts (1969a).

are "in the hand" of the powerful. As McKane aptly describes, "Their fist is their god = might makes right" (1998, 59–60).

[2] To covet houses and fields echoes the accusations of Isa 5:8:

> Ah, you who join house to house,
>> who add field to field,
> until there is room for no one but you,
>> and you are left to live alone in the midst of the land!

Something that is "coveted" (ḥāmad) is desirable "to the eye" or "to the sight" (Gen 2:9; 3:6). Joshua 7:21 speaks of Achan "coveting" spoils that belong to God. The term is used in the final commandment of the Decalogue against wishing to take that which belongs to others, including fields (Exod 20:17; Deut 5:21). Thus, in legal language, "fields" are often paired with other indications of personal possessions (also as late as Neh 5:3, 11; so Jer 32:15; see also Mark 10:30 par.). So Jeremiah's threat (Jer 6:12) of the Babylonian conquest: "Their houses shall be turned over to others, their fields and wives together; for I will stretch out my hand against the inhabitants of the land, says the LORD" (cf. Lam 5:2).

The use of the verb "carry away" suggests actually uprooting or destroying the buildings of the people. Andersen and Freedman object, stating that there is "no suggestion in the text itself that the mechanism for the expropriation of these estates was foreclosure on the indebted by their creditors, the old story of rich versus poor" (2000, 274). However, the tribal property *is* the topic here! Micah's angry denunciation makes the point! Even if the people are allowed to continue to work their land as debt slaves (effectively sharecroppers), this is a violation of the spirit of the Mosaic laws of distributive justice as implied in the legal traditions of the naḥălâ (tribal allotment). Micah's use of the verb "carry away" (nś') is still suggestive. The people undoubtedly stayed in the area even if not continuing to work "their" land, as all of the profits now go to the new landlord (see introduction above).

The use of the term naḥălâ at the end of the verse (e.g., "inheritance" or tribally apportioned territory) raises the stakes considerably. This term refers not merely to property of any kind, but precisely to ancestral property that, according to the Mosaic law codes, was an inherent right of possession for families, to be divided among descendants but always maintained in the family and the tribe.

Although Israel, as a people, is frequently referred to as the "inheritance" of God (thus Isa 19:25; Jer 2:7; Mic 7:18), readers need to keep the economic policy of land distribution in mind. It is notoriously difficult to be precise about the practice as reported in the laws of Jubilee (Lev 25), but the tradition is that all tribal families have an allotment of land, with the exception of the priestly families, who are to be supported by the financial tithes of the people (Num 18; Deut 18).

Deuteronomy 4:20–21 uses the term *naḥălâ* to suggest that the land is God's own "possession" and presented to the people by God's choice (cf. Jer 12:15). Accordingly, the Deuteronomistic Historian presents the idyllic picture of equal distribution of land at the time of the conquest (or revolution!) (Josh 11:23; later chapters describe the distribution, with people traveling to their allotted area [Judg 2:6]; cf. Neh 11:20, an idyllic "restoration" similar to Ezek 45).

One of the most important aspects of the use of *naḥălâ* = "inheritance" is that it is property held by virtue of God's intended distribution! Thus one thinks of the protests of Palestinian farmers and landowners in conflict with early twentieth-century Israeli settlers when the latter presented deeds of sale from absentee Ottoman-era landlords. The Palestinians responded (and still respond) with equally vociferous defense of their "ancestral properties," which for them had the force of law *by tradition*. Similarly, the astonishment of Native Americans, Indigenous Aboriginal Australians, and the Maori of New Zealand (a full list would be depressingly long), when presented with "deeds of sale" issued by a government hardly acknowledged by their own tradition and sense of legality and justice. In some cases of biblical use, therefore, *naḥălâ* needs to be understood as "the just portion" or "legitimate distribution" of God's land. Micah's accusation recalls Ahab's injustice in 1 Kgs 21: the stealing of property from the common people without actual rights. The prophets acknowledge a religiously based sense of justice in land distribution, irrespective of the machinations of legalities engineered by the powerful. To "covet" these fields means that Micah sneers at the notion that such land transactions are in any sense legitimate (Robinson 1954, 133).[17]

Wolff speculates that the issue may well be the forced quartering of soldiers in these villages, putting a severe strain on local resources (1990, 78). McKane, however, is not convinced that this is the only issue here: "We are not to suppose that the homesteads and fields were surrendered to a show of physical force" (1997, 10).[18]

Yet there is little ambiguity in the use of the verb *'āšaq* ("oppress") in Mic 2:2. It is the key term in the Hebrew Bible for economic exploitation and

---

17. Robinson compares with Isa 5, but with the difference that he thinks Micah himself has experienced this oppression and loss of land.

18. Furthermore, McKane is impressed with medieval rabbinic traditions suggesting that the oppression is at the hands of fellow Judeans, but under conditions of "economic change" (McKane 1998, 59–74). However, McKane's argument severely weakens Micah's objections by simply saying that those who benefit from economic change should "take into consideration the amount of social damage and dislocation which their measures cause" (1998, 63). The powerful have always answered with a weak response such as: "Of course, we will" as they proceed to do just as they please in defense of "progress" and "growth," the latter sounding so much more responsible and inevitable than "greed," much less "tearing the skin off my people." The Maori, e.g., are only too familiar with the abuse of the Treaty of Waitangi (1840) to justify continued plunder, similar to "treaties" with Native Americans that were promptly ignored.

The Oppression of the Ruling Elite

oppression. In the legal texts, it is used to refer to underpaid workers (or not paid at all: Lev 6:2, 4 [5:21, 23]; 19:13; Deut 24:14). Deuteronomy 28:33 uses the term to warn what foreign nations will do to the Israelites if they disobey God's laws. The Psalms also use ʿāšaq to warn specifically of economic oppression (Pss 62:10 [11]; 72:4). It is also used in the Prophets (Jer 7:6, "If you do not oppress the alien, the orphan, and the widow"; Amos 4:1, the elite who "oppress the poor, who crush the needy"; perhaps best summarized by Hos 12:7, "A trader, in whose hands are false balances, he loves to oppress"). Whatever the precise nature of the new economic arrangements forced upon the *geber* and the *ʾîš*, the one being singled out in this passage is the head of household. The force of Micah's speech is that these are citizens with full rights in the Mosaic ideal system of distribution (Wagenaar 2001, 66), and the prophet will turn his attention to the rest of his family soon enough (2:9).

[3] In answer to the "plan" or "scheming" of the powerful, Micah announces that God is doing God's own kind of "scheming." That God also "schemes" or "has a plan" to counter the evil inclinations of humans is not a common notion, but it is a theme found in Jeremiah (18:11; 29:11; also Lam 2:8) and may be a notion influenced in this later work by Micah's own understanding of God's own "plans" to counter human "plans." Again, it is not difficult to appreciate the pointed oral performance of Micah in telling his people that God has a "counter-conspiracy" in mind (so Dempsey 1999, 120–23).

The image of the neck is probably not a reference to an expression of power by putting the foot on a neck of conquered fallen soldiers (Josh 10:24) but rather the image of a yoke. The image of the yoke "on a neck" to express political subordination is also common in Jeremiah, but is found in many other locations as well (Gen 27:40; Isa 10:27; 52:2; Deut 28:48; Jer 27:2, 8, 11, 12; 30:8; Lam 5:5).

The translation in NRSV to walk "haughtily" or "exaltedly" derives from the root term "height," and thus the same root term appears in the phrase "to be raised up" and "be exalted" in Pss 21:13 (14); 57:5, 11 (6, 12); 108:5 (6). Perhaps "You will not walk in an exalted manner" is more precise, if less elegant.

This will be an "evil time" (so Amos 5:13). The Greek term *ponēros*, often used to translate "evil" or merely "bad" from the Hebrew (thus "good and evil" in Gen 2:9, 17), also certainly turns up in cases of specific economic trouble (Prov 11:15), wickedness, miserliness (Eccl 4:8; cf. Neh 13:17, suggesting greed), and most notably in a series of advices offered by Sirach (14:5, 8, 10). Although it would be going too far to suggest a technical nuance of "miserly" or specifically "greedy" for such a general term, it is noteworthy that a specifically economic evil is most certainly part of the field of meaning and ought not to be homogenized into a generic sense by using the more banal English terms: "bad" or "evil," rather than "greedy." Pastors are only too familiar with the dangers of being too specific about "evil." Micah hardly exhibits such fear.

The "plan" of God is against this "tribe" (*mišpāḥâ*). While it has often been suggested as an "inept gloss" (Andersen and Freedman 2000, 275–76), Wagenaar objects that it simply means that the accusation is expanded. "Tribe" "may refer to a pre-exilic local institution which was responsible for the administration of justice and redistribution of community property" and thus ought not to be ejected (2001, 64).[19] Micah's use continues to suggest biting sarcasm here, however. The distribution system of the land *was according to tribes and clans*. Thus Micah calls this group of greedy elite a "tribe," setting themselves over against the legitimate tribes and clans and their rightful expectations of land distribution.

[4] The phrase "on that day," while occasionally used as dramatic effect in the recounting of a story (e.g., Josh 4:14; 6:15; 10:28; 1 Sam 14:24), often helps to announce a specific circumstance accompanying a warning: "on the occasion that . . ." (e.g., Deut 31:18; 1 Sam 3:12; 1 Kgs 22:25). This is especially prominent in the Prophets, where the phrase points to an oracle of the future, most notably in Isaiah (e.g., 2:17, 20; 4:2; 7:18, 20, 21, 23; 10:20, 27), Jeremiah (4:9; 30:8; 39:17), Ezekiel (24:26, 27; 30:9; 38:10, 14, 18–19), Hosea (1:5; 2:16, 18), Amos (8:9; 9:11), Obadiah (8), Zephaniah (1:9, 10; 3:11, 16), Haggai (2:23). Indeed, it appears to increase in Zechariah in its move toward apocalyptic use in the later chapters (e.g., 2:11; 3:10; 9:16; cf. 12:3, 4, 6, 8, 9, 11; 13:1, 2, 4; 14:4, 6, 8, 9). The catchphrase seems to have become clearly associated with apocalyptic speculation in the New Testament (e.g., Matt 7:22; Luke 10:12; 17:31).

A *māšāl* = "proverb" (Gk. *parabolē*), "saying," or "byword" (NRSV, "taunt song") is used occasionally in the Deuteronomic History (see Deut 28:37; but cf. 1 Sam 24:13 [14]; see also Ps 44:14 [15]; Prov 1:6). Habakkuk 2:6 challenges:

Shall not everyone taunt such people and, with mocking riddles, say about them,
 "Alas for you who heap up what is not your own!"
 How long will you load yourselves with goods taken in pledge?

What is particularly notable, however, is the extensive use of this idea of "proverbs" and "sayings" being debated and discussed among the exiles, as in Ezekiel (12:22; 16:44; 17:2; 18:2, 3; 20:49 [21:5]; 24:3). Even the Deuteronomy text mentioned above is a clear exilic reference (28:37). Among POWs resettled in Babylon, rumor and dark humor (judging from the tales of Daniel) were common (Smith-Christopher 2002b, 163–88). It was a matter of concern to Ezekiel, who clearly saw some of these rumors and grumblings to indicate serious problems among some of the resettled Judeans. Its presence here in Micah may be an editorial addition, but also it possibly reflects the sense of

---

19. Mays suggests that the phrase must refer to the entire people (1976, 64).

being "watched," engendered by the pressures of imperial Assyrian presence and the debates generated among smaller states about what to do in the context of such pressures. More widely, however, the Hebrew Bible shows signs of communities being concerned with what others think of them (Exod 32:12). The force of this passage, too, seems be a threat of humiliation in the eyes of others. Some anthropologists have argued that in communities where social control consists heavily of "honor and shame," the presence of threats of humiliation are particularly powerful (Péristiany 1966; Laniak 1998; Stiebert 2002; see Excursus at Mic 4:11, "Being Watched").

It is difficult to recognize, without pausing for a moment of reflection, that there is a sadly rich vocabulary of lamentation and mourning in the Hebrew Bible, including terms normally translated "mourn" (*'ābal* in Isa 3:26; 19:8), "dirge/lament" (*qînâ* in 2 Sam 1:17; Jer 7:29; Ezek 26:17; 28:12), a call to "howl" (*yālal*) or "lament" (*sāpad* in Jer 4:8; 16:6, and the cognate noun *mispēd*, a "wailing," in Jer 48:38) or "house of mourning" (*bêt marzēaḥ* in Jer 16:5). The term used in Micah (*nāhâ*, "lament"), however, is not nearly as common. To be called to wail, sing a dirge, or give lamentation, is expressed also in Amos:

> Therefore thus says YHWH, the God of hosts, the Lord:
> In all the squares there shall be wailing;
> and in all the streets they shall say, "Alas! alas!"
> They shall call the farmers to mourning,
> and those skilled in lamentation, to wailing.
>
> (5:16)

Jeremiah calls for a dirge/lamentation, using also the same term as here in Micah with regard to God "ruining" (*šādad*)[20] the people in Jer 9:19 [18]: "For a sound of wailing is heard from Zion: 'How we are ruined! [*'êk šuddādnû*]'" (cf. 31:15).

The notion of land being "parceled out" (*ḥālaq*, the same term as in Mic 2:4) to conquering enemies is evident in Amos 7:17, "Your land shall be parceled out by [measuring] line." Finally, the notion that the land will be parceled out to "captors" (so NRSV) is a bit of a stretch for the terms used here in Hebrew and Greek. The notion that fields will be distributed among "those who have turned away" (from the root *šûb*), presumably "the faithless" (so in the Greek with *apostrephō* [lit., "apostates"]), is not so easy to associate with foreigners. The Greek term can be used in the sense of "rejected" (Hos 8:3) and of God's anger not "turning away" (Isa 9:12, 17 [11, 16]). The Hebrew term is used often only in Jeremiah to express "faithless children" (*bānîm šôbābîm*) or faithless "daughter" (Jer 3:14, 22; 31:22; 49:4). Andersen and Freedman continue to use "apostate" in their suggested translation, but also recognize the difficulty

---

20. Here *šdd* means "measure out for sale" (Cathcart and Jeppesen 1988, 194–95).

of assigning this term to Assyrians or other foreigners. Thus they suggest the possibility that some of the violence in the context for Micah's war-weariness is precisely the civil wars between the northern and southern kingdoms (Israel and Judah), both of which are addressed in the book as it now reads (2000, 286–87). A striking alternative, however, is that Micah is calling the wealthy Judeans "apostates" for violating the Mosiac laws of equal distribution.

The term for "dividing" or "portioning out" (*ḥālaq*) is often used in the context of dividing plunder or spoils of battle (Josh 22:8), in the Prophets as warning (Isa 9:3 [2]; 17:14; 33:23; 53:12), in apocalyptic promise (Zech 14:1), but also "scattered" among the nations (Lam 4:16). Joel 3:2 (4:2) speaks of the nations under judgment because they have scattered (from *pizzar*) the people and "divided up" (from *ḥālaq*) the lands of God's people, the latter closely resembling the notion here in Micah. The double use of the term in Mic 2:4 is ironic and humiliating, once again an example of Mican wordplay:

| nĕšaddunû ḥēleq | our portions ruined |
| śādênû yĕḥallēq | our fields parceled out [as spoil] |

Andersen and Freedman see nine occasions of "my people" in the book of Micah, and six of those nine are found in divine speech (2:8, 9; 3:5; 6:3, 5, 16). However, they do not believe that God is speaking here in 2:4 because of the "difficulty of understanding the rest of the speech as Yahweh's" (2000, 285; but Pixley argues that this is a call for peasants to rise up! [1991, 59–60]).

The entire series of discussions about distributing land, however, is considered by Wolff to be a redactor's interpretation, exilic references perhaps inspired by allotments of land in the book of Joshua (ch. 14, and chs. 18–20). In terms of scattering people, however, Wolff proposes: "Perhaps Micah actually saw the troops stationed in the fortified cities departing for the prisons of Assyria" (1990, 79–80).[21]

[5] Micah speaks of the occasion when there is nobody to "throw" or "cast" the "cord/line/rope." The term for "line/rope" (*ḥebel*) can be used in different contexts with considerably different meanings, depending on slight variations in the vowel sounds yet using the same root consonants. It can be vocalized as "region" (Deut 3:4, 13), and as "pledge" or "collateral" in legal language (e.g., Exod 22:25; Deut 24:6; cf. Job 22:6; 24:3; Prov 20:16; Ezek 18:12). However, here in Mic 2:5 we find reference to a line, cord, or rope (as "ropes" in Josh 2:15; "cords" in Esth 1:6; cf. Ezek 27:24). Such "ropes" are compared to fetters in Job 36:8 and to another term for "ropes" (*'ăbōt*, pl. *'ăbōtôt*) in Hos 11:4. There

---

21. McKane does not believe this is a case of physical eviction by the abuse of law, and he cites Kimchi and Ibn Ezra as rabbinic authorities who already saw sharecropping slavery in these losses of land (1998, 61).

are also images such as "ropes of death" (Ps 18:4, 5 [5, 6]) and "cords of the wicked" (Ps 119:61). Jeremiah was let down into, and brought out of, a cistern with ropes (Jer 38:11–13). Isaiah 5:18 is especially helpful in context of ropes on animal carts.

For our purpose, more specifically, Ps 16:6 refers to "boundary lines" (ḥăbālîm) and the notion of apportioning land, perhaps literally measuring out boundaries with a line, as suggested in Ps 78:55 in the context of "apportioning" one's "inheritance" (běḥebel naḥălâ; so also Ps 105:11). The combination of this brief series of passages along with Mic 2:4 suggests the loss of the ability to divide and apportion land. The implication is that this is caused by foreigners' conquest, leading to Micah's people losing their God-given right to make land transactions and decisions by assembly. One result of suffering conquest will be their inability to divide land according to familial and tribal needs—undoubtedly an important part of the survival of small agricultural villages of the lowlands.[22] Confiscation of tribal lands, whether in ancient Israel, or more recent Native American, Aboriginal Australian, and New Zealand Maori, is always about more than simply land use—it is also the disruption of a communally based economic system that allows a group to watch over, and participate in, the distribution of resources for a large body of people.

It does not take a profoundly detailed analysis to discern the point of 2:1–5. Micah, speaking for his fellow farming villagers, speaks of the terrible disruption of their lives as a result of the scheming of the wealthy elite as they attempt to not only solidify their own economic power, but position themselves to benefit from Jerusalem's resistance against Assyria. The wealthy are typically militant patriots. As the opening decades of the twenty-first century reveal, people all over the world are becoming increasingly aware of the devastating consequences for the average worker, the student, and the poor when the elite "scheme." Taunting, one of the only weapons left to the angry poor, will be transformed from grumbling to ecstatic joy at the judgment that is coming. Those who have schemed to take away their land will lament at their fate when their riches are taken from them by the hand of God. It is hardly a matter of wonder that Christians in the developing world find such prophetic words of judgment, as in this passage, just as comforting as those in the developed world find them troubling. The Epistle of James carries a similar warning against coddling the rich among Christian communities

---

22. In his summary of vv. 1–5, Ben Zvi claims that it is not possible to be precise about the historical circumstances of the "evil" being described in this section. It has been intentionally "defamiliarized" so that it can be reread and reapplied to later generations (1999). One presumes, however, that Ben Zvi would not object to the overview on social-justice issues from Micah proposed by Dempsey (1994, 272–76) as long as we do not claim to know the eighth century in great detail.

of faith; in chapter 5 it presents as shocking a "taunt song" as you will find anywhere in Scripture, including Micah!

Micah 2:6–7 Micah Anticipates His Opponents' Objections

6 "Don't drivel on!"
—so they will drivel on!
They[a] won't preach of such things:
  "Humiliations[b] will not overtake us."[c]
7 "Can this be said[d] about the house of Jacob?
  Does the spirit of God fall short?
Are these his acts?
  Aren't my words[e] for the good
  of those who walk[f] with the upright?"

a. The verb is in the third person but is often changed to a command in the second person. It depends on the presumption of who is speaking at this point.

b. The term is plural. "Humiliations" suggests the political impact of these "insults."

c. Wolff, however, reads, "The reproach does not apply (to us)" (1990, 68). The verb *sûg*, which has caused headaches among translators, is used in Deut 19:14 and 27:17 to refer to "displacing" boundary stones (cf. Prov 22:28; 23:10). Wagenaar suggests, "The reproaches do not cease!" (2001, 77).

d. *He'āmûr*, with the interrogative marker prefixed to a verb of speech ("said"), is often emended to *he'ārûr*, "accursed," rendering: "Can the house of Jacob be accursed?" The two letters that must be exchanged to achieve this, however, do not resemble each other in appearance, which in my view would allow more latitude for this emendation (Andersen and Freedman 2000, 309).

e. Hillers (1984, 34) amends the first person to third person, referring to God. The debate over who is speaking here, and to whom the reference is directed, is a central discussion of these two verses. See comments.

f. To "walk" uprightly or "with" the upright. The translation offered preserves the use of the Hebrew to "walk" (*hālak*) as part of the common Hebrew idiom (cf. Mic 6:8).

[6] These two verses clearly deal with Micah's conflicts with the prophets who vehemently oppose Micah's message. To speak of "rival prophets" here (as many commentators do, usually comparing rivalries between prophets such as Jeremiah versus Hananiah in Jer 28, and Micaiah ben Imlah in 1 Kgs 22) presumes that Micah, at the time his words were remembered and set to writing, was himself considered a prophet, which is a continued source of debate (see introduction). Possibly Micah simply opposed the general prophetic caste of his time, but this does not necessarily imply that he thought of himself as a prophet. In any case, Micah's rather vicious attack on *these* advisers (whether considered prophets or not) is further indication of his opposition to the advice provided to the central leadership. As already noticed, the short story of Micaiah ben Imlah

also deals with this issue of military policy, and Jeremiah's public debate with Hananiah, clearly a prophet who sided with Zedekiah's hopes for a revolution against Babylonian control, also deals with military policy.

One of the most important terms introduced in these two verses, continuing in the sections to follow, is used by Micah for the "preaching" of the prophets he opposes: *nāṭap*. It is used when Ezekiel is called to "preach" (21:2, 7), and closer to Micah, Amos also is commanded not to preach "against the house of Isaac" (7:16). The term occurs twice here and again in Mic 2:11. It is a somewhat odd term since it can also be read as "drip" (in the context of wine or honey; Prov 5:3). So the NJB offers the clever translation: "'Do not drivel,' they drivel, 'do not drivel like this!'" Here I have adopted "drivel," although Andersen and Freedman object to the implied negative connotation, not found, for example, in Ezekiel (2000, 303). However, I think it is hardly used as simply a synonym for common preaching or speaking, and in the context of Micah it fits well as the kind of satirical slur he clearly tends to favor. Mays uses "preach," which Hillers approves of, commenting that "preach" can have a negative as well as neutral connotation in English (Mays 1976, 66; Hillers 1984, 34–35). Stansell's English rendering of Wolff's discussion even suggests "slobber," an even more colorful way for Micah to be saying that they "utter nonsense" (1988, 81)!

The verb "overtake" (from *sûg*) is third-person masculine singular, whereas the following word is feminine plural (*kĕlimmôt*), usually rendered "insults/ disgraces." Translators normally "fix" the verb so that the final term is what will not "overtake" us, meaning insults or humiliations. Thus in the previous phrase "these things" must refer back to the social injustices outlined in vv. 1–5 (Andersen and Freedman 2000, 302).

This is not the only way to read the line. A third-person reference would fit in the context of an oral presentation given to a listening (and likely sympathetic, even if occasionally shocked) crowd. Micah would then be referring to what these false advisers themselves refuse to confront and deal with. In fact, their refusal to tell the truth will be the subject of Micah's continued accusations in this section.

The term for "insults" or "disgraces," however, is far more common (*kĕlimmôt*) and often paired with "shame" (*bōšet*), thus Ps 44:15 (16), "All day long my *disgrace* is before me, and *shame* has covered my face" (cf. pairing of two terms in Isa 30:3; Jer 3:25). The term is taken up heavily in Ezekiel (16:52, 54, 63; 32:24, 25, 30; 34:29) and, again, with strong awareness of the potential insults from other nations (36:6, 7, 15; 39:26). On this awareness of other nations, see Excursus at 4:11.

The basic disagreement between Micah and his opponents seems clear. Prophets often clash about whether a particular policy will be disastrous or advantageous for the people as a whole (Jer 28 is the classic example). The missing element in this debate (at least up to this point) is the people who actually have the authority to act on these prophets' advice. They will make their appearance in the next chapter. It is interesting, then, that Micah begins his diatribe with an attack on the advisers and then moves to focus on the power center itself. This suggests that, for Micah, policy should be rooted in the experience and discernment of God's leading, not merely in power. To critique policy, one begins by critiquing the theological foundations that the policy is built upon. This is certainly an enduring message that too often goes unheeded, especially in Western tradition.

[7] The phrase rendered "Is the LORD's patience exhausted?" (NRSV) is a bit awkward as an image, but it is found in other locations where it is translated slightly differently. The operant term *qāṣar* is commonly used to speak of "reaping" (Lev 23:10, 22) and thus is used to speak of something being "cut short" as well. Other examples provide interesting comparisons. Numbers 11:23 asks whether "the power of the YHWH is limited." Job asks: "Why shouldn't my spirit be cut short?" (Job 21:4 S-C). The image of reaping serves the writing prophets well: Isa 37:27 speaks of those whose strength is "shorn" (e.g., cut like grass), and God's hand is not "too short to save" (Isa 59:1). Haak has strongly suggested that the term should be understood "Is God *impotent*?" (1982), a stronger implication.

The question seems to be whether God is angry with the behavior of the central leadership and thus is about to punish them, or whether their policies and actions have God's approval. This would be the only question that prophets would be expected to answer, not whether the policies "work." However, a related question is whether God has actually been active in the events that have transpired thus far, and this depends a great deal on the dating of these verses. If this is written under the threat of Assyria, then the question may well be whether these threats are God's doing. On the other hand, the questions could apply to Micah's own message: Is Micah's message really God's doing?

God's words are good especially for those who "walk uprightly." The phrase occurs elsewhere to speak of acting in accordance with the laws and statutes of Moses:

> Those who walk uprightly fear the LORD,
>   but one who is devious in conduct despises him.
>   (Prov 14:2)

The widely used term *yāšār*, "straight" or "correct(ly)," is often used in the phrase "walk (or do) uprightly" in the eyes/sight of God, especially in Deuteronomic usage ("Do what is right and good in the sight of YHWH," Deut 6:18; so also 12:25, 28; 13:18; 21:9). The phrase is used of those who act justly, as opposed to the foolish, in Proverbs (e.g., 11:3, 5, 6, 11). The term *yāšār* is rarely

Micah Anticipates His Opponents' Objections

used in the Prophets, yet it does occur (Jer 34:15) and is used in Micah relatively frequently (also in 3:9; 7:2, 4). Perhaps most famously, Isa 40:3 refers to making a "straight . . . highway" in the wilderness, and God makes the "paths straight" for Cyrus (45:13), but this has a rather different suggestion than its use in Micah.

The real question about v. 7, however, is *who* is speaking about "*my* words"? Many commentators change this to a third-person speaker, "his words," presuming a reference other than Micah or his opponents. Is the question in reference to Micah's own (previous) words? Certainly not God's words, but it could very well be that these are the false prophets claiming that they are doing the right thing! After all, "words" being "good" has an interesting association with the debacle at Shechem after the death of Solomon. According to 1 Kgs 12:7, Rehoboam is counseled to speak "good words" (*dĕbārîm ṭôbîm*) to the people, but he choses arrogance instead, leading to the break of the ten tribes from the house of David. Alternatively, Wolff is certain that "my words" begins Micah's reply, but it is unclear why Micah's (prophetic?) opponents could not themselves be citing the tradition to defend their confidence in God's protection. In fact, it makes more sense that Micah's opponents passionately argue that their viewpoint is moral, just, and based on tradition. Mays, for example, argues that vv. 6–7 offer a summary of the opponents' views, and v. 8 begins Micah's angry reply (1976, 68–69).

Either way the point is fairly clear. If Micah is speaking, then the words of Micah are considered provocative and challenging to those they confront—but Micah asks whether his warnings shouldn't be good news to those who seek to do the right thing! If the "false prophets" are speaking, then they are claiming to be in the right.

The dialogue captured in vv. 6–7 highlights one of the most disturbing realities that the people of faith face in the Western world: both sides of social and political debates cite religious language. Jesus is made to defend both war and peace, both pro-business capitalism and pro-labor socialism. What is clear in the twenty-first century, as much as it was clear for the book of Micah, is that theological language is most often the slave of social and economic presuppositions rather than acting as the driving inspiration. Biblical studies is only irrelevant to social and political policy when it follows as an afterthought to policy decisions, or merely decorates policy speeches, rather than *driving and inspiring* debates of policy. If the latter, then the prophetic emphasis on justice for the poor, and Jesus' equally strong emphasis on compassion (echoed by his brother in the Epistle of James) would surely lead to a criticism as trenchant as Micah's for all modern Samarias and Jerusalems.

Finally, however, Mic 2 stands as a bitter denunciation of history's warmongers, whose praise of gallantry irresponsibly (and conveniently) omits the horrendous suffering of soldiers and civilians. Witness the careful government and media control of televised suffering from war, including returning caskets, since the horrendous nightly visions that Americans saw on their televisions during the Vietnam War. We still hear ever-louder calls for more weaponry and military spending while even veterans' health care is ignored lest the public see the suffering of war's survivors. Micah denounces the lies of war, in his time and in our own.

Micah 2:8–13 Micah Condemns the Judean Military Elite and Denounces Their Prophetic Supporters in Judah

8 In the past,[a] my people rose up[b] against an enemy,
  [but] you stripped from them[c] a cloak of peace,[d]
because of[e] those who violate[f] the security
  [of] the ones returning[g] from war![h]
9 You drive the women of my people from their precious homes,[i]
  and from the children you take my glory forever!
10 Rise up! Go! Because this is not a place of rest;
  because there will be a ruinous corruption and painful destruction.
11 If a man, one who walks (in) a spirit[j] and deceptively lies:
  "I will 'drivel out'[k] [preach] to you[l]
for wine and for strong drink . . . ,"
  that would be a "preacher of drivel"[m] for this people![n]
12 I will surely gather Jacob, all of you,
  I will surely assemble a remnant of Israel together.
And I will make you like a flock in Bozrah,[o]
  as a herd in the midst of a pasture,
  making a great noise from a people.[p]
13 The one who breaks[q] through will go up before them;
  they[r] will break through, passing over[s] a gate.
They will go out of it;
  their king will pass before them,
  and God will be their head.[t]

    a. It is widely presumed that the Hebrew word (wĕ'etmûl) at the beginning of this verse is corrupt and ought to read, "But you . . . !" This involves splitting the word into a second-person reference and using the remaining letter to form the preposition "against" for the following reference, "my people." Thus the common translation, "But it is you who rise against my people as enemies" (Hillers 1984, 34); or "But you! Against my people you arise as enemy" (Mays 1976, 67). I propose, however, that it makes sense to read these harsh verses in the manner I have translated, especially in context with the following verses.
    b. Emending the collective singular (yĕqômēm), "he rose up," to plural (yāqûmû).

c. On the force of the Mosaic tradition against taking cloaks from the poor (Exod 22; Deut 24), Hillers reads "From the laborer you strip his cloak" (1984, 34).

d. I am suggesting a wordplay on the word "outer garment" and "peace." In fact, two terms used for robe or garment are similar: *śimlâ* = "garment" (cf. Gen 9:23; Exod 12:34) and *śalmâ* = "garment" (cf. Exod 22:9 [8]). If one shifts the sound of the first letter from a *sin* to *shin* (admittedly rare, but not unheard of), there is a possible *šalmâ* = "peaceable." However, if an actual change to a term suggestive of "peace" is proposed here, then Hillers, among others, wants an emendation to a plural phrase here, agreeing with others who propose "from the peaceful ones," *mēʿal šalmîm* (Hillers 1984, 35; cf. Andersen and Freedman 2000, 319). Certainly such wordplays are consistent with Micah's style. A similar, albeit somewhat awkward, reading is in Mays 1976, 67, "From the peaceful their cloak you strip."

e. Reading the preposition *mem* as causative (*GKC* 383).

f. Reading the participle as "transgressors" (*'ōbrîm*); cf. Jer 34:18.

g. The participle is difficult here: *šûbê* followed by *milḥāmâ* = "war" is often read to refer to those who "turn aside" from war, although "returning from" would pick up on the opening phrase referring to past conflicts, meaning those who come home from wars they have been called upon to fight in the past. Andersen and Freedman suggest "from" war is implied from an earlier use of the partitive *mem* = "from" doing double duty in the previous phrase and this phrase (2000, 319).

h. The Greek does not help us much, instead launching into a quite different interpretive rendering: "His skin they flayed to take away hope, the conflict of war"[23] (cf. Andersen and Freedman 2000, 295), although perhaps the LXX is intending something like "take away hope *by/in* the conflict of war," in which case the LXX reading can be construed to be quite sympathetic to our reading of this passage.

i. In this case, simply rearranging the phrase order for easier English reading.

j. Cf. the phrase about Joshua, *'îš 'ăšer-rûaḥ bô* (Num 27:18); Jer 5:13, "wind."

k. The ironic use of "drip" for "preach" continues here; cf. Mic 2:6.

l. *BHS* proposes changing the second-person address from singular (*lěkā*) to plural (*lākem*).

m. Adding "preacher" to achieve the full sense of the participle, lit., "a driveler" = *maṭṭîp*.

n. Cha insists that this is not "my people" (1996, 61).

o. Sometimes amended to read *baṣṣîrâ* ("in sheepfold"), although *BHS* suggests *baṣṣîrâ*.

p. Wagenaar has argued for a reading "from Edom," rather than "from a person," and thus reads the end of v. 12 as the beginning of the thought in v. 13, "From Edom the breaker went up before them" (Wagenaar 2000, 538). His intriguing argument suggests that the issue is a liberation of captives in Edom, which was noted for slave trading in this time period (cf. Amos 1:6, 9, 11).

q. The substantive participle is awkward in English: "the breacher," so often rendered as an attacker or "conqueror," is assumed to be an Assyrian ruler. Brin, among others, argues that the "breaker" could be God, in the act of initiating an exile (1989, 123–24).

---

23. Cf. *NETS*: "contrary to his peace they stripped off his skin, to remove hope in the crushing of war"

r. *BHS* suggests third-person singular here, reading *ûpāraṣ* rather than *pārṣû*, "they."

s. Andersen and Freedman suggest third singular (*wayyaʿăbōr*) for MT's *wayyaʿăbōrû*. In fact, *BHS* suggests *yaʿabrû* ("they will pass over") in MT. Alternatively, the *waw* can be read as the pronominal suffix for "it" (i.e., the gate). The LXX preserves the plural form throughout this phrase, referring consistently to "they."

t. Reading *běrōʾšām*, "at head/front of them."

[8] This is one of the most controversial verses in a book full of very controversial verses! In terms of the preferred translation, a great deal depends on the assumptions of the translator with regard to what is going on, because major changes in the *implication* of these sentences can be achieved by very minor emendations. At times I have sided with common emendations, yet in this section I am making a few bold suggestions. This is based, clearly, on my reading of Micah as a populist antiwar lowlander, angry at Jerusalem's militant nationalist theology. Thus in this passage is a considerable discussion about violence and warfare. All of my suggested emendations, therefore, are based on the assumption that this is an important subject of concern in these verses, and that any change that contributes to an understanding of this theme is worthy of serious consideration.

With regard to v. 8, it is widely presumed that the first word (*wĕʾetmûl*) is corrupt and ought to read "But you" (see textual notes). This also requires changes to the verb "rise up" to fit the number as well. Although this certainly results in a sensible change, it is also possible to retain the reference to the past. For example, the Hebrew, as written, might be rendered, "formerly," or "in times past," or even "recently," but that would then miss an opening address referring to "you." Andersen and Freedman are not entirely convinced of the changes to get a second-person plural address and therefore try to leave in some form of a reference to the past (2000, 315–17); Hillers and Mays both prefer the commonly adopted emendation. Further, however, Andersen and Freedman recognize that there may be an inclusio formed from a reference to the past at the beginning of v. 8 and "forever" at the end of v. 9 (2000, 314).

The problems, however, do not end there. Making sense of the phrase in any precise form is difficult, but in general we understand the idea. Andersen and Freedman helpfully summarize a number of attempts to render the phrase (2000, 295–96), to which I add two more recent attempts:

But an enemy arises against My people. (NJPS)
But since long past my people rise up as an enemy. (Wagenaar 2001, 61)

The call to "rise up" is quite often associated with a call to military action, including those calls to God to "rise up" against enemies (e.g., Pss 3:7; 7:6; 9:19; 10:12; Isa 14:22; 28:21; Jer 49:14, 28, with God calling humans to battle!). As stated, the clear references to war in this section assure us that this association is intended.

I am proposing a change from singular to plural (*yěqômēm* to *yāqûmû*) so that the reference is to "those" who rose up, rather than to a singular "he rose up" (see Andersen and Freedman 2000, 314). This suggestion dramatically changes the implications of this verse. Micah is pointing out that his people have responded to calls to muster the young men for war in the past, as if to say, "We have responded loyally in the past . . . *but* . . . ." Much depends on the partitive sense that I am suggesting here: Micah is about to contrast the present with the past. He acknowledges the military occasions in the past, but now he is war-weary, tired of calling his people to muster yet again, and tired of making sacrifices yet again. Micah insists that it is too much! Wolff is not far from this in suggesting that the issue is the forced quartering of Judean troops in the lowland villages, and he identifies these Judean troops as being called "an enemy" (1990, 82).

Like the texts accusing the greedy privileged who steal even the outer garment of the poor (as in Amos 2:8; declared illegal in Exod 22:26 [25]; Deut 24:12–13), Micah bitterly condemns those who call for war again and again, a call directed against the peaceful. In this case the "outer garment" could be a wordplay on "cloak of peace," but my arguments do not depend on this particular proposed wordplay.

What we have, then, are clear references to "an enemy" and a possible play on the word "outer garment" (*śalmâ*) and "peace" (*šālôm*), the two words distinguished mainly by the *sin* and *shin*.[24] Certainly Micah has proved to be fond of wordplays throughout this work. Further, as Alfaro rightly observes (1989, 30), "The rich whom Micah has in mind here are those merciless creditors who take away the clothing of the poor, casting aside the basic norms of the Covenant (cf. Exod 22:26–27)."[25]

Shaw has rightly objected that the imagery here may not refer to the clothing of the poor in the Mosaic law at all, and he points out that stripping a cloak off someone does not suggest handing it over. The act seems to be more violent in Mic 2:8, and Shaw implies that the people being attacked here have turned away from war (1993, 79–81).

This image is followed by two awkward participial forms at the end of the verse, which may make sense when read as accusations about the suffering of people. I want to also acknowledge that my tendency in translating this passage as an attack on war, and preparations for war, is very much in the spirit of the

---

24. Andersen and Freedman (2000, 319) discuss Sellin's suggestion that an emendation to *šělēmîm* ("peaceful," as in Gen 34:21) is be read here. Waltke (2007, 109) renders: "rich robes from the tunics from those that pass by without a care." But this surely misses the point, as well as the Mosaic tradition with regard to the cloaks of the poor.

25. Wolff (1990, 83) suggests that this is further violence against the villagers by quartered troops, although it is unclear if he means Judeans or Assyrians. But if Micah is referring to the Mosaic law re the cloaks of the poor, then that implicates Judean troops, those to whom Mosaic law should have applied!

eighteenth-century Quaker Bible translator Anthony Purver,[26] whose translation reads as follows:

> Whereas lately my people rose up for an enemy
>   You pulled off the cloak from the garment it was on,
> From such as were passing by securely
>   *Turning away from war.*
>   (Purver 1764, 2:303, emphasis added)

Even so, most readings of these last two participle forms are not radically different in implication from my proposed translation. They suggest that Micah is actually speaking of his fellow villagers, people who are "passing by" in security (innocently living their lives, or as Judges 18:7, "quiet and unsuspecting" [NRSV]) and not thinking of warfare. Andersen and Freedman speak of people actually *returning from* war (2000, 320).

Solomon's reign was regarded as an age of "security" and "peace" (1 Kgs 4:25 [5:5]). On more than one occasion, the book of Micah evokes memories of that past ideal as contrasting with the present. But we will have occasion to wonder if Micah is also quoting, with rich irony, the Rabshakeh's promise of vine and fig tree for everyone, in 2 Kgs 18:31 (see comments on 4:1–5).

Who are these people from whom a cloak was taken? McKane suggests "unsuspecting travelers" and writes, "The travelers are not expecting trouble (they are not armed to the teeth), for they have taken an aversion to war—they have renounced war" (1998, 85). McKane's interesting comments, however, raise more questions. Travelers? Why have travelers "renounced war"? Possibly refugees? Those who are deserting from duty? Such precision would require more confidence about the actual time of the comment—just before the Assyrian attack on Jerusalem of 701 B.C.E.? Before the Babylonian siege of 597 or 587? As early as Tiglath-Pileser III's campaigns of 734? In the absence of chronological precision, however, we can still presume that Micah is referring to his own people of the lowlands, those who repeatedly suffer the brunt of mustering, preparations, and taxation, those who beat their precious farming tools into weapons, in preparation for any level of mounting resistance to Assyrian or Babylonian forces. The "cloak" image, in any case, is undoubtedly inspired by the prohibitions against exploiting the poor, combined with a possible wordplay on "shalom." After all, the cloak is the last piece of collateral that the poor can offer against a loan, according to the Mosaic tradition, and other prophets have condemned the abuse of this

---

26. Anthony Purver's Bible was (and is) the only full translation of a Bible ever done by a Quaker. Although never reprinted after the 1764 first edition, it is available as a free ebook (2011). Thomas Jefferson had a copy in his library, but one hopes it was not the New Testament edition to which he took his scissors!

system (Amos 2:8). Thus Micah mentions cloaks as one today might refer to giving "the shirt off the back" in order to make the same point. While Wolff and others suggest that it is outsiders who are taking cloaks from the peaceful, it is more likely the military mustering of Micah's fellow lowlanders that involves "taking their cloaks." Through forced military service, the security of Micah's fellow villagers is violated. So Miller renders: "But you rise against my peoples as an enemy; you strip the robe from the peaceful, from those who pass by trustingly with no thought of war" (1982, 14–15). Most impressive is Rogerson's rendering:

> But you rise up as an enemy against my people
> You strip the garment from him who desires peace
> From those who live securely and turn away from war. (2010, 97)

The force of Micah's accusations against the Jerusalem elite is in regard to their misguided preparations for warfare. I seriously considered the possibility that the participle commonly rendered "those who turn from war" might actually refer to those who "stripped the robe" from the people—and thus part of a further accusation against leaders—calling them "restorers of war," or even "warmongers." Also calling them "violators of security" accuses those who attack the people's well-being. The angry denunciation is precisely because the war defended as "God's will" and "good for us all" is transparently intended to benefit the Jerusalem elite. This is the essence of Micah's populist criticism. Micah would surely approve of the title to Dorothee Soelle's book *The Arms Race Kills Even without War* (1983). Radical Labor movements' opposition to warfare, strongly suggestive of Micah's attitude, has always been based far more on the economic consequences rather than on only a religious or philosophical opposition to killing (see introduction).

There is another solution to this imagery of removing cloaks, however, that seems to have escaped virtually all previous comment on this difficult passage. We have already mentioned the fact that male POWs were stripped naked when captured by Babylonian and Assyrian forces. Since this is undoubtedly a well-known fate for captured soldiers, Micah may also be referring to the fate of male soldiers who answer the muster and will be stripped by the conquering armies (for discussion of the ancient military use of stripping POWs, see Smith-Christopher 2002c). This has the potential of being the most striking interpretation of all because it portrays Micah stating that Jerusalem's warmongering will make peaceful farmers into POWs. In short, the king's war policies will "strip the robes" from the farmer-soldiers.

[9] Our reading of Micah's accusations is supported by the continued tone of accusation in v. 9. The further implication of what the central leadership is doing has impact not only on the mustered soldiers themselves but also

on their families. So the accusations of v. 8 continue! The men's cloaks are stripped from them (as they are led away as POWs?); likewise now the women are driven from their homes (because the husband is a casualty, or at least preoccupied with warfare?), and the children suffer. Surely Waltke (2007, 118) is missing the point to read in this passage an indication that the people are not poor: "Micah does not represent the people as economically poor. He represents the men as stalwart landowners (2:2), their homes as delightful (2:9) and their children as displaying a glory (2:9b)." But this passage has the prophet emphasizing what common villagers value as opposed to the palaces of the rich! Yet even these humble homes are threatened. Andersen and Freedman are more in line with the spirit of this angry passage by pointing out that ancient Near Eastern epic literature often speaks of the glories of war, but "it is otherwise in the Hebrew Bible, especially in the prophets. The horrors of war are reported; the atrocities of war are condemned. This is a prominent theme of Amos's oracles against all the nations in the region" (2000, 320).

What war means for the common people, even those wars brought about by God as punishment, is frightfully clear for all the families involved:

> I will gather all the nations against Jerusalem to battle, and the city shall be taken and the houses looted and the women raped; half the city shall go into exile, but the rest of the people shall not be cut off from the city. (Zech 14:2)

In our passage, Micah states that the women are being "driven out." To be "driven out" is a common term, beginning already with Adam and Eve being "driven out" of Eden (Gen 3:24). God "drove out" nations to plant Israel in the land (Josh 24:12, 18; Judg 6:9; Ps 80:8 [9 MT], often in the context of the entry into the land). Hosea 9:15 repeats God's threats to "drive out" the people because of their sin, likely a sense of "reversing" God's driving out the original inhabitants at the time of Joshua.

The "luxurious" homes of the women seems awkward and suggests disapproval of their lifestyle (cf. Prov 19:10). But reading "precious" (cf. Mic 1:16) renders a different picture. The homes are certainly "luxuries" to the poor, even the poor man's "castle," as the old saying goes (cf. Andersen and Freedman 2000, 321). As for the children, they always suffer from preparations and conduct of warfare. The description of conquest in Nah 3:10 is suggestive:

> Yet she became an exile,
>   she went into captivity;
> even her infants were dashed in pieces
>   at the head of every street;
> lots were cast for her nobles,
>   all her dignitaries were bound in fetters.

Also in Isa 13:16, "Their infants will be dashed to pieces before their eyes; their houses will be plundered, and their wives ravished." Indeed, most often the mention of children is found in the context of lamenting their fate in times of crisis (e.g., Lam 1:5; 2:11, 19; 4:4).

Here children are said to carry the "majesty" or "glory" of God. God's "majesty" is referred to with regard to humanity in Ps 8:5 (6; "glory" and "majesty" [NASB]) as well as numerous times in Isaiah (2:10, 19; 53:2), but nowhere other than Mic 2:9 is this "majesty" of God used in explicit reference to children, unless the loss of royal families is alluded to in Lam 1:6. Indeed, there is the further possibility that the term usually translated "luxurious" in describing homes of the women is a corruption of a term that actually applies to children, since it occurs just before "from children/youth." If so, the phrase about the majesty of God being taken forever would stand alone as a separate comment. More likely, Micah is being ironic: the "luxurious" homes of the common people and the "glory" of their children contrast starkly to the actual luxuries of the wealthy elite and the "glories" of their own children. Again, even the laborer's home is his castle.

[10] Some have aligned the call to "rise up" with v. 6, but to the contrary I count this as a call in line with v. 8! Instead of "rising up" against an enemy, Micah calls the people to "rise up" and *go*! Refuse! This is no place of rest! If Micah is addressing his fellow villagers who happen to be in Jerusalem, then the implication of this "rise up" and "go!" is far-reaching indeed! Revolt! Refuse to participate in this! Micah's call would be an ancient Green Corn Rebellion like the Oklahoma farmers in 1917 who prepared to march on Washington (D.C.) and refuse to participate in war (see introduction)! In this case, Micah is calling for the same revolt against the war plans of the central leadership that we have documented in 2 Chr 28:12–15, as well as the opposition to mustering for war by the prophet Shemaiah (1 Kgs 12:21–24), among others.

Furthermore, we know that false prophets offer the comforting words that the people have found a place of rest (cf. Isa 28:11–12). "Rest" is stated as "peace" in the Solomonic prayer of 1 Kgs 8:56, and Solomon is known as the "man of peace" (*'îš měnûḥâ*, 1 Chr 22:9). More generally, the promise (however false reliance on it can occasionally be) is based on the inheritance promised to the Israelites as a land of "rest." Deuteronomy 12:9 refers to those who should not stay in Transjordan, because it is not the place of rest promised to the people: "You have not yet come into the rest and the possession that YHWH your God is giving you" (12:9). More generally, Isaiah speaks of the land as the resting place as well: "My people will abide in a peaceful habitation, in secure dwellings, and in quiet resting places" (32:18).

Strikingly, although Psalm 132 refers to the temple as God's "resting place" (vv. 8, 14) even after the destruction of the temple, a postexilic text in Isaiah challenges the notion of Jerusalem, and the temple, as a singularly special place:

Thus says YHWH:
"Heaven is my throne and the earth is my footstool;
what is the house that you would build for me,
   and what is my resting place?"
                                               (66:1)

Instead of their city being a special place, a place of rest and peace, Micah accuses the warmongers of a corruption that will bring destruction. Amos likewise refers to a land of exile by using the cultic term "unclean" (often in Levitical laws, as in Lev 5:2; 7:21; 11:6; 27:11):

Therefore thus says YHWH:
"Your wife shall become a prostitute in the city,
   and your sons and your daughters shall fall by the sword,
   and your land shall be parceled out by line;
you yourself shall die in an unclean land,
   and Israel shall surely go into exile away from its land."
                                               (7:17)

Once more, notice the same series of images we have in Micah: wives and children followed by reference to place. In Micah we have the clear declaration that if Jerusalem is to be a place of rest in the ideal age (i.e., Solomonic age), then the prophet declares that this vision is a bitter irony now. Thus Stansell (following Ehrlich) reads v. 10: "For the gain of the slightest thing you pledge with a ruinous pledge" (1988, 125). The fifth stanza of the "The Internationale" (from the Russian) begins:

    Enough of clouding our minds in the haze of war
      On the behalf of kings!
    War to the tyrants! Peace to the people!
      Go on strike, sons of the army!

We can only imagine the bitter disappointment of the Russian people that their hopes, like Micah's, were dashed by ongoing history.

[11] And who is held responsible for this deception and these crimes of excessive greed and warmongering? Micah has already attacked the false prophets, and here he returns to this theme: their words are not to be trusted! Once again the image of "dripping" = "preaching" ("drivel," as creatively rendered by NJB) is taken up, but with biting satire: Micah speaks of their "liquid words" inspired by other liquids!

The terms here, typically, are quite awkward, and most readers have tried to read them as a sensible phrase. Thus "a man" is often seen to be modified by the strange appearance of the simple noun "spirit," leading to "a man of a spirit" (the article is not present), that is, a prophet. The awkwardness may, however, be read as Micah's sarcastic avoidance of speaking of the person as a true prophet, a genuine "man of the spirit," which Micah himself will claim (3:8)!

This person "deceives." The term *šeqer* = "falsehood/false witness" (e.g., Exod 20:16; Ps 27:12; Prov 6:19) not only relates to the famous commandment, but also recurs in many contexts of trials and legal proceedings (so Prov 12:17).[27] Significantly, the concept of a "lying spirit" (*rûaḥ šeqer*) is mentioned in the story of a spirit volunteering to God to deceive the kings of Israel and Judah, and even Micaiah, at first, following that example (1 Kgs 22:15, 17, 22–23). The implication is clear: the prophets working for the central leadership are liars. Micah accuses them of preaching whatever they are paid to preach. One thinks of paid "consultants" in the ubiquitous "think tanks" of industry, or the political "policy experts," who can always be depended upon to cite studies, statistics, or polls to back up the policies of their paymasters who create the lucrative "research institute" positions in the first place. Micah accuses them of precisely this kind of corruption.

"Wine and strong drink" are commonly phrased together (Num 6:3; Judg 13:4, 7; 1 Sam 1:15) and are associated with the lifestyle of the wealthy, who seek these pleasures so much that they are willing to oppress the people to get them. "You who rise early in the morning in pursuit of strong drink, who linger in the evening to be inflamed by wine" (Isa 5:11). Isaiah 28:7 shares Micah's accusations about even the leaders seeking to indulge themselves in such luxuries:

> These also reel with wine and stagger with strong drink;
> the priest and the prophet reel with strong drink,
>   they are confused with wine,
>   they stagger with strong drink;
> they err in vision,
>   they stumble in giving judgment.
> (Isa 28:7; cf. 56:12)

The biting satire of Micah's reference to prophets who "drivel" = "preach" continues. We have already seen Micah's use of the unusual term for "preach" (*nāṭap*, which can mean "dripping," as with honey or strong drink; see on 2:6), but it is not unusual in other prophetic sources as well, such as in Ezek 20:46 (21:2); 21:2 (7). Yet the use of this term can also be construed as satirical in Amos 7:16, where the prophet refers to others who urge him (Amos) to preach with less accusation: "You say, 'Do not prophesy against Israel, and do not preach [*nāṭap*] against the house of Isaac.'" Micah's ironic accusation is that such a corrupt prophet would be an appropriate "preacher for this people."

---

27. Cha notes a similar use of the root *šqr* in Jer 5:31 and Mic 2:11 (1996, 127).

"This people" surely is directed at those who would listen (as well as provide the payment) for drunken prophets such as these. Here Wolff pointedly remarks that Micah's reference to drinking is a "favorite theme of officers and soldiers—alcoholic drinks for every taste!" (1990, 84).

Promise of Salvation or Warning of Exile (vv. 12–13)?

[12] It is widely held that vv. 12–13 are an interlude of salvation—thus typically thought to be inserted at a later time. There is no doubt that the concept of being "gathered up" and compared to "sheep" are themes that appear in postexilic texts of salvation and restoration after the devastations of 596/587 B.C.E.[28] Similar images of being "gathered" and assembled appear in Mic 4:6. Themes of gathering are frequent in late prophetic speech: Isa 43:5; 54:7; Jer 29:14; Ezek 11:17; cf. 20:34, 41; 36:24; Zeph 3:20.

If it is supposed, however, that Mic 2:12–13 is not from the prophet but rather articulates another false hope from the prophetic "preachers of lies," then it is possible to read these passages as continuing a dialogue between Micah and his opponents.[29] Mays, on the other hand, mildly suggests the possibility that these are not salvation oracles at all, or at least may be "salvation" oracles that are somewhat backhanded (1976, 75–76). What he suggests is that these are indeed later insertions from the Babylonian period, but that v. 13 refers to God actually doing the "breaching" of the walls and leading the people. In other words, the punishment of Jerusalem is God's doing, and salvation will follow God's punishment of Jerusalem. Preserving the usual reading of plural forms (i.e., "*They* will pass by, . . . *they* will be led out past a gate," etc.) further supports this. There is no doubt that this adequately summarizes Jeremiah's theology of God's punishment, with restoration only to follow. Jeremiah's theology is that the people themselves brought on the attack ("We brought this on ourselves"), and therefore Jeremiah's counsel of nonresistance to Babylonian control is likely a view shared by a significant community led by Gedaliah at Mizpah (see Lipschitz 2005, 87–88).

McKane reports that there was already debate on these verses in medieval rabbinic commentary; Kimchi suggests v. 12 is a preparation for exile, while Rashi argues that it is a sign of hope and that v. 13 refers to Zedekiah (1998, 88). Van der Woude suggests that vv. 12–13 are yet another occasion of the confident nationalist theology of Micah's opponents (1969), while Sweeney

---

28. So Andersen and Freedman write that this passage is "rightly suspected of being an oracle from that later period, added to update Micah at a time when the judgments he spoke about were complete and a new future had to be faced" (2000, 332).

29. Van der Woude points out that ch. 3 starts with "But I said," and 2:11 may be read to introduce these words as false prophecy (1969, 257).

argues that the image of sheep outside of their pens hardly conveys an image of security (2001a, 366). Allen, on the other hand, is just as confident that these verses are from Micah, not from opponents, and that they refer to salvation (1976, 242).

The reference to Bozrah in v. 12 may mean the capital of Edom, and thus possibly people who are being gathered from Edom. Certainly the Edomites were accused of slave trading in Amos (1:6, 9, 11), so in this case a redemption *from* Edom would make good historical sense. Edom also represents the direction of salvation, from trans-Jordan into the promised land, but Andersen and Freedman do not comment on the bitter tradition of condemning Edom in prophetic literature (2000, 339–40). Were some of the POWs rounded up by the Assyrians and offered to Edom, which could sell them to merchants on the King's Highway? Micah may then refer to their liberation, which would make good sense of the "bursting through gates" imagery in the following verse.

Finally, this gathering in v. 12 is accompanied by a great "resound" or "uproar," which recalls the "sound" of Israel: "When the ark of the covenant of the LORD came into the camp, all Israel gave a mighty shout, so that the earth resounded" (1 Sam 4:5; cf. 1 Kgs 1:45).

It is difficult to argue with the general consensus that v. 12 is an insertion from the exilic era, although it could possibly be argued that it is an early example of the theme that later becomes a veritable wave in the exilic prophets Ezekiel and Jeremiah. Brin, however, argues persuasively that it is possible to see vv. 12–13 as God having initiated an exile: God is leading the "breacher" or "breaker" (a foreign ruler?) to carry out the deportation of Jerusalem (1989). God as the author of punishing events is a major theme in the prophets, in both the eighth and the sixth centuries. This is not to say, however, that v. 13 easily goes with v. 12.

[13] God can scatter and gather! Deuteronomy and Leviticus warn of just this (Deut 28:64; Lev 26:33). The exilic prophets speak of God scattering as well as gathering (Jer 13:24; Ezek 5:10; 22:15; including foreigners, Jer 49:5). On the other hand, Wagenaar argues that this passage is a positive indication of God leading the people out of exile and thus is an exilic-period passage. He notes, for example, that the verb "to go up" is not typically used for *leaving* Jerusalem (2001, 236). So, noticing similarities of thought in Ezek 11:17; 34:11–19, as well as in Jer 23:1–4 and even Deutero-Isaiah (52:12), Wagenaar dates this to the sixth century (238–40).

There is no difficulty in reading God as the author of "breaching walls" as well as scattering the Hebrew people. God can also be praised for "bursting out" against enemies. Consider the folk etiology supplied in 2 Sam 5:20 for the place known as "Baal-perazim": "YHWH has burst forth against my enemies before me, like a bursting flood." But this can just as easily be turned against Israel (cf. Ps 89:40). In Isaiah's famous metaphor of the vineyard, punishment is described as God's smashing the orchard: "I will break down its wall, and it shall be trampled down" (5:5; see Ps 80:12 [13] for a similar agricultural image; Isa 30:13 clarifies that the people's sins invite breaches in a wall).

Perhaps most importantly, Amos (4:3) angrily condemns the privilege of the wealthy living in walled cities by declaring that God will breach walls (or at least allow them to be breached): "Through breaches in the wall you shall leave, each one straight ahead."

When read in the spirit of Amos, therefore, Mic 2:13 can mean God's assault on Jerusalem! It is a description, in the manner of Jeremiah, of what will happen if present circumstances and practices continue, perhaps an idea that deeply inspires Jeremiah's later theological assessments. It can just as easily come from that period, inspired by Jeremiah. However, that is not absolutely certain—and we already have clearly established that Jeremiah certainly "read" Micah (Jer 26:18).

Sweeney, too, reads both these passages as expressing judgment:

> The passage out of a gate represents the loss of security as the gate of a city is generally the strongest features of its defenses. . . . [The words] . . . convey the image of a decimated people led out from the security of their stronghold to the uncertainty and danger of the wilderness or open pasture. (2004, 320)

In the light of his views about dialogue in the book of Micah, van der Woude wonders if 2:12–13 is from the false prophets, answered by Micah in 3:1. It is an interesting possibility, but that would involve reading this passage as suggesting false hope (1969, 257). As we have seen, this is not the only way to interpret 2:12–13.

I have raised another possibility. If "Bozrah" refers to the Edomite city (rather than amended to simply mean "sheepfold"; Andersen and Freedman 2000, 339), then we can learn from Micah's contemporary Amos, who refers to Edomite slavery. If the Edomites are trading slaves, then POWs would be an obvious source for them (Paul 1991, 56–57). Furthermore, if an Assyrian collection of POWs is used even partially to reward Edomite loyalty (for Assyrian interest in Edom, see Liverani 2014, 410), then Micah may be referring to an impending liberation of these Judean POWs from Edomite captivity.

Finally, to speak of God "at their head" is to use royal language (2 Chr 20:27; cf. Ezra 5:10). The form "at the head of them" (*bĕrō'šām*) is typical of later Hebrew formulations. It could, after all, be a positive word of hope that interrupts the negative judgment both before and after, and now indicates a later phrase. It is equally possible that Micah warns what God has in mind as the social result of Judah trying to violently oppose the Assyrian regime on their terms: military opposition. It is, in short, the wrong kind of opposition.

When Peter foolishly presumes to take up arms against Rome, Jesus warns him with words that disarmed his followers forever: "Put your sword back into its place; for all who take the sword will perish by the sword" (Matt 26:52). Although we are used to arguing that Jesus intends a moral argument against all violence, his life and teaching are more likely to be read, like Micah, to say, "This is not the kind of resistance I call you to." The common mistake in reading Jesus, as well as Micah, is to believe that opposition to violent resistance means opposition to *all* resistance. This is wooden thinking, morally irresponsible, and the typical self-serving argument of militarized minds[30] (as well as the mistake of oppressors), which cannot imagine or understand the power of alternative forms of nonviolent resistance.[31]

Micah 3:1–4 Micah Accuses the Political and Military Leadership of Economic Cannibalism

1 And I said, "Listen,
heads of Jacob[a] and commanders[b] of the house of Israel!
   Shouldn't you know what justice is?[c]
2 Haters of Good! Lovers of Evil!
   You who rob[d] their skins off them,[e]
   and their flesh from their bones!"
3 [Like meat][f] they[g] eat [the][h] flesh of my people,
   and rip skin from their bones!
They break up and spread[i] their bones in the pot
   as meat[j] for the cooking cauldron.
4 Then they will call to YHWH,[k]
   but he will not answer them;
And he will hide his face from them in that case [on that occasion][l]
   because they have done evil[m] by their actions.

    a. Biddle discusses a possible confusion of the use of "Jacob" and "Israel" in Micah. Here, Jacob and Israel seem to refer to Judah, while in 1:5 they refer to the north as "Jacob" and the south as "Jerusalem/Judah." He suggests that an "earlier" version of Micah was addressed to two different capitals, but later the terms came to refer to the exilic community, who saw themselves as the remnant of all Israel (2000).
    b. On *qāṣîn*, cf. Josh 10:24, *qěṣînê 'anšê hammilḥāmâ* ("commanders of the men of war"). McKane (1998, 99) observes that these are military leaders but presumes that both offices ("heads" and "commanders") are intended to be in parallel and objects to the tendency to make these specific to the judiciary. He further compares Micah's choice of an older term to Isaiah's preference for *haśśārîm* (21:5) and cleverly wonders whether

---

30. On the militarization of cultural norms, including moral arguments, see Denton-Borhaug 2010.
31. Excellent help on these issues is provided by York and Barringer 2012.

Micah intends to suggest satirically that "leaders are not what they used to be" (102). Sweeney (2001a, 369) also presumes military leadership here.

c. On not knowing, cf. Jer 5:4 and 8:7.

d. Lit., "robbers [of their skins]."

e. Lit., "from *on* them." The phrase does not mean simply "take away from them," which it would be without the use of the preposition *'al*. The image, therefore, is more grisly with the preposition, e.g., "skinning them." The image recalls Assyrian practice (Bleibtreu, 1991).

f. Agreeing with LXX, "as flesh." See L. Allen 1973, 71.

g. Maintaining the third-person verbs throughout.

h. The definite article is not present in Hebrew but is in the LXX.

i. Is stirring implied?

j. "As meat" is widely accepted. McKane (1998, 98) has "flesh for the pot."

k. Wolff (1990, 91) cites Ps 56:9 (10) for the implication of calling on God for deliverance.

l. Rendering *bāʿēt hahî* as "in that case," rather than common "time." More lit., "when that happens." Wolff (1990, 91) omits this phrase entirely; see also McKane 1998, 98.

m. The verb is "do evil," *rāʿaʿ*; cf. the noun/adj. *rāʿâ*.

[1] The initial call to "listen" has received an inordinate amount of attention among scholars. It is often taken to signal the beginning of a new "section" of the book, since it appears here, earlier at 1:2, and again later at 6:2 (other occurrences are explained as not necessarily indicating major sections at 3:9; 5:15 [14 MT]; and 6:9). However, these calls to attention, to "listen" also signal a particularly strong turn in Micah's rhetoric: at precisely the point when those who most need to hear the word would rather turn away, the text calls the "hearer" (and reader) to be attentive to what follows.

The opening clause, "And I said," is often read to connect what follows with what has gone before. Other prophets were speaking at the end of Mic 2, and now we read Micah's response. Yet it is quite unusual for the prophet to speak as himself, that is, *in his own voice* to those listening to him. Most often when prophets speak in their own voice, they are communicating directly to God in conversation (e.g., Jer 1:6, 11, 13; 14:13; Ezek 4:14) and not with fellow Israelites, to whom they normally speak as messengers of God's word. But the third-person reference to God in v. 4 shows that this is possibly an angry word from Micah himself, who does not necessarily claim that it is God who is speaking. It reminds the Christian reader of the striking places in Paul's Epistles where the apostle (or Deutero-Paul) draws attention to his own view, writing in his own hand, which is a moment of intimacy with the person behind the message (1 Cor 16:21; 2 Cor 10:1; Gal 5:2; Col 4:18; 2 Thess 3:17).

Furthermore, and perhaps more significantly, no other prophet speaks directly to the "heads" and "rulers" of the people in this manner! Isaiah addresses the "house of David" in somewhat similar terms (7:13), and Jer 5:21 is written as a message from God, as is clarified in the very next verse (v. 22). Micah, however, makes no such clarification in this series of phrases.

Whoever they are, these leaders are responsible to "know justice." It is a rare term used for "leaders," but Isaiah does refer (in a very negative manner) to such "leaders/rulers" who abandon Jerusalem (?) in a time of need (Isa 22:1–4), and even more negatively to "leaders/rulers" of Sodom and Gomorrah (1:10). "House of Israel," on the other hand, is a common term for addressing people as a whole, appearing in many prophetic texts (Isa 5:7; 14:2; 46:3; Jer 2:4 and 18× more; 82× in Ezekiel; and late in Zech 8:13).

The "leaders" (lit., "heads") of Jacob are addressed, and then the *qĕṣînîm*, "commanders." Andersen and Freedman, as well as Wolff (1990, 97–98), notice the military associations of this term in the Deuteronomistic History (Josh 10:24; Judg 11:6, 11; I add Prov 6:7; contra Andersen and Freedman, Isa 22:3 does suggest military officers), but then they suggest, "In Isaiah and Micah, *qāṣîn* does not seem to retain the military connotations it has in Joshua and Judges" (2000, 349). Given the heavy military themes that so pervade the book of Micah, I maintain that military associations are precisely what Micah intends to convey here.

[2–3] The speech changes from address in the second person (you!) to third person until the end of v. 4. This change seems strange to some but may be explained by oral technique.[32] To "hate good" and "love evil" is a reversal of the norm that is surely familiar from Micah's contemporaries: Isa 5:20 ("Ah, you who call evil good and good evil, who put darkness for light and light for darkness, who put bitter for sweet and sweet for bitter!"), implied in Amos's statement (5:15) of how it should be with judges ("Hate evil and love good, and establish justice in the gate"), and noted in Ps 52:3 (5; "You love evil more than good").

The term used for "hate" is not common but is often associated with the actions of enemies (esp. in the Psalms: e.g., 25:19; 35:19; 38:19 [20]; 41:7 [8], of enemies in the community; 69:4 [5]). The theme of "hating evil" is especially notable in the Wisdom literature, which emphasizes that wise rulers are those who "hate" evil or "hate" the doing of evil in various forms, as in Prov 15:27 ("Those who hate bribes will live") and 28:16 ("A ruler . . . who hates unjust gain will enjoy a long life."). Finally, Isa 61:8 speaks of the injustice that God "hates" ("For I YHWH love justice, I hate *robbery* [the term also used in Mic 3:2] and wrongdoing"). When we recognize the prevailing wisdom association with this reference, then it is hard to miss the implication that these are the upper classes,

---

32. Andersen and Freedman (2000, 368) are perplexed by changes in address in Micah: "you," then "them." But if Micah is being quoted, then he could be speaking to an audience but changing the addressee easily and abruptly, as if to say, "And tell them—wait, I will tell them myself! Hey YOU!'" One can imagine a protestor outside a government building talking *about* the officials inside, then turning to address "them" directly in a rhetorical flourish.

the educated ones whom Micah presumes would know better! Wisdom literature has often been associated with the wealthier classes, considering some of the advice in Proverbs, for example, that are hardly relevant for the poor, agricultural workers (e.g., on lending money, as in Prov 11:15).

The frightful image of physically maiming the people has an unmistakable double meaning. The term that is used, translated "tear" (*gāzal*) also has a clear economic meaning when translated as "robbed," and a number of examples make the point (with emphasis added): "When any of you sin and commit a trespass against YHWH by deceiving a neighbor in a matter of a deposit or a pledge, or by *robbery*, or if you have defrauded a neighbor . . ." (Lev 6:2). In addition, "You shall not defraud your neighbor; you shall not steal; and you shall not keep for yourself the wages of a laborer until morning" (Lev 19:13; cf. Deut 28:29). "There are those who *snatch* the orphan child from the breast, and take as a pledge the infant of the poor" (Job 24:9). "You, [O LORD,] deliver . . . the weak and needy from *those who despoil them*" (Ps 35:10). "Put no confidence in extortion, and set no vain hopes on *robbery*" (Ps 62:10 [11]). "Do not *rob* the poor because they are poor, or crush the afflicted at the gate" (Prov 22:22; cf. 28:24; Isa 10:2). Jeremiah 21:12 equates justice with delivering the "robbed" "from the hand of the oppressor." "The people of the land have practiced extortion and committed *robbery*; they have oppressed the poor and needy, and have extorted from the alien without redress" (Ezek 22:29). "'What a weariness this is,' you say, and you sniff at me, says YHWH of hosts. You bring *what has been taken by violence* or is lame or sick, and this you bring as your offering! Shall I accept that from your hand? says YHWH" (Mal 1:13).

More direct is the parallel from Proverbs:

> There are those whose teeth are swords,
>   whose teeth are knives,
> to devour the poor from off the earth,
>   the needy from among mortals.
>   (30:14)

In these passages Micah uses the imagery of cannibalism to speak of robbery and economic exploitation of the populace, Micah's fellow villagers; this is "economic cannibalism," according to Wolff (1990, 100). Extended discussions of the possibility that Micah alludes to actual human sacrifice is, I argue, an unnecessary diversion.[33]

On the other hand, the horror of the image of cannibalism (as opposed to human sacrifice) should not be taken lightly. Some of the curse formulas of Leviticus include such a threat in 26:29, "You shall eat the flesh of your sons,

---

33. Sweeney agrees (2001a, 370), citing 2 Kgs 6:28–29 for cannibalism while the city is besieged.

Micah Accuses the Political and Military Leadership

and you shall eat the flesh of your daughters" (cf. Ps 27:2; Zech 11:9). Furthermore, cannibalism associated with conditions of siege warfare is probably to be considered part of the curse formulas as well:

> I will make them eat the flesh of their sons and the flesh of their daughters, and all shall eat the flesh of their neighbors in the siege, and in the distress with which their enemies and those who seek their life afflict them. (Jer 19:9; cf. Isa 49:26)

We are justified in raising the central question of militarism once again. The curse formulas threatening cannibalism thus refer to the horrible conditions of siege (cf. the Rabshakeh's speech in Isa 36:12//2 Kgs 18:27). Andersen and Freedman also call attention to the fact that "flaying" prisoners of war is a known threat in Neo-Assyrian propaganda from precisely the time of Micah (2000, 353; cf. Bleibtreu, 1991).

"Economic cannibalism" is familiar as a common metaphor in modern American slang referring to an objectionably high price as demanding "an arm and a leg." Yet Micah's context for using this imagery is much darker. In view of the fact that siege warfare was the most common form of battle at this time, a shocking double meaning is likely present here: like cannibals the elite "rob" the poor, and in conditions of siege (it was the elite who lived in the walled cities) they may well end up dining on the poor! I therefore consider Andersen and Freedman's long discussions of the possibility that human sacrifice is behind the imagery in 3:3 to be distracting, however interesting it is as a topic of discussion in Israelite and ancient Near Eastern practice and however relevant it may be for a full grasp of the image in Mic 6:7, if not here in 3:3 (Andersen and Freedman 2000, 354–55).

There is another interesting possibility, however, suggested in a study by Warren (2014), who refers to the priestly ceremonial meal (*zebaḥ*) that involves boiling sacrificial animal flesh (Lev 6:28 [6:21]). After Josiah's reforms, it was limited to the Jerusalem temple (Lev 17). Warren argues that Micah's use of this temple ritual in chapter 3 inspired Ezekiel's use in Ezek 11 and 24 (2014, 503). The point for us, however, is the Jerusalem temple reference. If this is the source of Micah's imagery, then it is an even more powerful criticism of the Jerusalem elite (including the priests!) and their economic oppression: instead of a holy meal of sacrificial animals, the priesthood "boils" the people in the cauldron!

[4] To "call out" or "cry out" (*zāʿaq*) in reference to crying out *to God* is a classic reference to that first important "cry out" to God in Exod 2:23. But by the time of Micah, however, the reference could be to other textual traditions where the people have "called" upon God (e.g., Ps 107:13, 19). Isaiah speaks of cities that "cry out" in distress (Isa 14:31; 15:4, 5) and even promises God's response in better times (30:19).

The notion of God "answering" the "cry" is also typical of biblical rhetoric. God "answers" the cry of the oppressed (Isa 41:17; 49:8; 58:9). An important implication, however, is that God's intention to answer is measured by the justice of the cause in question. In Micah, those calling are those who believe they have a just cause: they are crying from the threat of Assyrian domination (or as others have argued, from the threat of northern pressure to join an anti-Assyrian coalition) in hope that God will answer. Here, Micah states, there is only silence. It is a notion found in some of the prophets that God refuses the prayers of the unjust, as in the striking implication of Amos 5:21–24 and perhaps part of the implication of Jesus' famous teaching about settling issues between people before approaching God (Matt 5:23–24).

In Micah, God's silence is the result of the leaders "doing wicked deeds" or "deeds of wickedness." This becomes a stock phrase in prophetic rhetoric, as seems clear from Jeremiah's drawing upon Micah, Hosea, and Isaiah's use (Isa 1:16; Hos 9:15; Jer 4:4; 23:22; 25:5; 26:3; 44:22). Zechariah 1:4 indicates that the phrase was already known to be an older and familiar notion among earlier prophets. Alternatively, God's "deeds" are remembered as great (Pss 77:12; 78:7).

The LXX chooses, however, to use a somewhat loaded term to express the "deeds," the root term *epitēdeuma* rather than the more common *ergon* for simple "acts." Again the LXX translates *and interprets* the possible significance of this. In many cases, *epitēdeuma* refers to actions committed by foreigners, thus suggesting idolatry. After many uses of the more common term *ergon* in the laws, Deut 28:20 LXX uses *epitēdeuma* only in the context of the curses, again suggesting not simply objectionable but also "detestable" actions. The term does not appear in Isaiah at all, but does so in Hosea (LXX: 9:15; 12:3) and becomes more common in the sixth-century prophets, used about twenty-five times in Jeremiah and Ezekiel.[34]

That God will "hide" from the people (and thus not be reached by prayers or pleading) is a notion also appearing in Isaiah, who nonetheless affirms his faith in the God who is, at present, hiding from the evil ways of the Judeans ("I will wait for the LORD, who is hiding his face from the house of Jacob, and I will hope in him" [8:17]). It appears, however, that this poetic sense of God's "hiding" may come from classic lament themes. Thus the sense of abandonment is expressed in some of the lament psalms (e.g., 13:1; 27:9; 30:7; 44:24; 88:14 [15]; 89:46; 102:2; 104:29; 143:7; but responding to the poor in 22:24, 26). The Greek term *apostrephō* has the suggestion of "turning away" or

---

34. Hutton proposes an interesting resolution to the question of who "they" are who cry out to God in this passage. By arguing that those who cannibalize the people are the Babylonians (dating the text later), those who pray to be spared will be refused (1987), in keeping with Jeremiah's theology of punishment.

Against the Corrupt Prophetic Advisers

"withdrawing" and thus is used elsewhere in the LXX for God's "turning back" God's own anger (Isa 14:27); famously in Jonah, the Assyrians hope that God will "turn away from" God's anger (Jonah 3:9 KJV)).

This section therefore associates the suffering of the poor with their actually being "eaten away" by leaders, accompanied by corrupt prophets who support the calls for war. Questioning the wisdom of resisting the Assyrian forces clearly raises the question "Wouldn't we be better off resisting to the last person?" as well as other more patriotic appeals for God's assistance. Then, as now, the militant calls to gloriously "die to the last man" fall predominantly on the poor, that is, Micah's fellow lowlanders. But Micah goes even further: in answer to those who would point to the oppressive behavior claimed in Assyria's own propaganda, Micah angrily retorts, "*We are already suffering the horrific treatment that Assyria is famous for—and it is from our own leaders!*" To this, Micah will go on to say, the prophetic advisers of war have no answer.

Micah 3:5–8 Against the Corrupt Prophetic Advisers

5 The Lord says this[a] against[b] the prophets,
   the ones who lead[c] my people astray,
      the ones who, with mouthfuls in their teeth, cry "Peace!"[d]
But when nothing is given for their mouths,
   they sanctify[e] a war!
6 Therefore, it will be a night for you with no vision,
   Darkness[f] for you, with no revelation.
The sun will dawn upon the prophets,
   but it will be dark upon them that day!
7 The seers will be humiliated;
   the interpreters of signs will be shamed.[g]
They will wrap themselves up to their moustache,
   because there is no answer (from)[h] God.[i]
8 However, I[j] am full of strength,[k]
   the spirit of YHWH,[l] and justice,
and (with) the power to declare to Jacob his rebellion,
   and to Israel his sin.

a. For arguments that this opening phrase should be omitted, see discussion in McKane (1998, 104). In fact, he comments generally that vv. 5–8 are "formless."

b. The preposition *'al* is read oppositionally here. Given the context of Micah's previous condemnation of the prophets, "against" makes the best sense.

c. The participle "leaders astray" (*hammat'îm*) must be split for sense in English. Note the possible sound-play here: *hammat'îm* immediately follows *hannĕbî'îm*!

d. Cha draws attention to the important and unique parallels in Jer 6:14–15 to these verses, suggesting the influence of Micah (1996, 72–73).

e. The verb is *qādaš*, "make holy." Also quite possible, noting the meaning of "pontificate" (speaking with presumed religious authority), one could suggest that they "pontificate in favor of war!"

f. Vocalizing as "darkness," *ḥăšēkâ*, rather than "it is dark" (*ḥoškâ*); see McKane 1998, 106.

g. Cha, in his arguments about the influence of Micah on Jeremiah, points out that the term *bôš* is used of shame for prophets only in Micah and Jer 6:15; 8:12 (1996, 128).

h. "From" is implied but does not appear in the text.

i. The LXX does not read "God," but rather "for them," presumably reading *'ălēhem* instead of *'ĕlōhîm*.

j. *'ānōkî* is an elaborate term for "I" rather than simply *'ănî*.

k. Wolff, along with others, reads "courage" (1990, 90). McKane notes that Ibn Ezra already saw this as a contrast to rulers mentioned in 3:1 (1998, 103–5).

l. Some would delete "spirit of God," but this seems to fit with Micah's argument. See McKane (1998, 108).

[5] Micah returns to another searing attack on the prophetic advisers of the ruling elite in Jerusalem. The key concept here is being "misled" or "led astray" by advisers and leaders. Isaiah rails against the same corruption, using the same term (*tā'â*, in Isa 3:12; 9:16 [15 MT]). Indeed, Isa 28:7 also speaks of corruption of prophets, adding "drinking" to Micah's accusations of eating:

> These also reel with wine
>   and stagger with strong drink;
> the priest and the prophet reel with strong drink,
>   they are confused with wine,
>   they stagger with strong drink;
> they err in vision,
>   they stumble in giving judgment.

Jeremiah repeats the accusations against those who are supposed to be trusted advisers, clarifying what is implied in Micah: God is against those "who lead my people astray by their lies and their recklessness, when I did not send them or appoint them" (23:32). Later psalms also speak of "straying" from the commandments of God (e.g., Pss 119:110, 176; cf. Prov 10:17; 12:16; 14:22; 21:16).

These accusations against the prophets are rich with suggested meaning. The English usually tries to convey the sense of "something to eat," but the Hebrew is more literal in suggesting that they have "bites in their mouths." However, while the term used for "bite" (*hannōškîm*) can certainly mean "bite" (as in a snakebite, thus Gen 49:17; Num 21:6, 8; Prov 23:32), more often the term is used for collecting interest on loans. Thus it appears in the vehemently anti-interest laws of Moses and is used in the context of bitter condemnation of greed even into the postexilic period (Exod 22:25 [24]; Lev 25:36; Deut 23:20–21; Ps 15:5; Ezek 18:8, 13, 17; Hab 2:7). The language, therefore, is not unlike

Against the Corrupt Prophetic Advisers

the famous phrase from Shakespeare's *Merchant of Venice* (1596–98), which became a colloquialism that refers to any collections by bankers or tax collectors as requesting their "pound of flesh." In the context of Micah's bitter condemnation of prophets-for-hire, the double entendre is definitely a sharp weapon. As long as they are "paid" or "fed," they proclaim peace, but without their "bite" (I have suggested "mouthful," which still doesn't quite connote "money" as it should), they "sanctify" war (Andersen and Freedman cite Hab 2:7 [2000, 362]). The threat that is implied is also powerful: if you do not pay now in cash, you will pay later with your lives!

The final phrase is, once again, more suggestive in Hebrew than in Greek. The LXX states that prophets "raise up" (*egeirō*) for war, while the Hebrew speaks of religiously sanctioning (*wĕqiddĕšû*) war by using the term for "holy" (Exod 3:5), "made it [seventh day] *holy*" (Gen 2:3), or "sanctify" (Exod 19:10; Lev 20:7). The term thus draws on one of the presumed tasks of the major prophets: to indicate to the king propitious times for battle, or to announce God's military intentions. As von Rad (in 1951, German first edition) points out in his study *Holy War in Ancient Israel* (1991, 41–48), the act of "sanctifying" soldiers for battle is a common motif for wars "called" at the behest of God (typically through prophets or oracles from priests): Josh 7:13 and Isa 13:3 refer to "sanctified warriors" (cf. NRSV, KJV); Jer 6:4, "Sanctify yourselves for war!" (S-C); Joel 3:9 (4:9), "Consecrate for war" (ESV). In her study of war in the Hebrew Bible, Niditch points to the frequent use of "purity" and "sanctification" language in association with some (but certainly not all) theologies of warfare present in the Hebrew biblical tradition (1993, 29–30, 78–89). The Hebrew Bible generally shows that wars, when fought at God's behest, must be announced by an authoritative source, typically by a prophet or a priest. God must be consulted. This was, as Kang points out, a requirement for warfare throughout the ancient Near East: "The war starts with the divine consultation to seek the divine will through the accepted methods like omens, oracles or others by the priests. Whenever a military campaign was planned, the divine will was sought by the various divine consultation methods, and with a favorable divine answer the military action began" (1989, 109).

Thus Micah's accusation becomes all the more serious. He claims that calls to war may be based not at all on real national crises, and certainly not always based on the call of God, but rather on the "appetites" (literally and figuratively) of the prophets and others who profit from warfare. Micah's deep suspicion is that this pious methodology of sending Judeans to war is subject to serious financial corruption. Ezekiel, in a later era, has similar suspicions about such false prophecy (13:16).

The wording of the Hebrew is that the prophets declare war "on" the people who do not feed them. It is not necessary, however, to insist that this rules out the prophets theologically endorsing *actual* wars in which Micah's fellow villagers must send their sons to fight.[35] But just as easily, the "war" could be any number of other kinds of calamities "sent by God" if the prophets are insulted or ill fed. Moreover, this powerful accusation gives further support to our earlier translation of Micah accusing leaders of harassing villagers to muster and fight when these villagers wish to "turn away from war" (thus Mic 2:8) and go back to their farms (Mic 4). The financial strains of warfare are weighing heavily on the backs of the village farmers whom Micah represents and drive this true prophet (3:8) to question whether such wars are truly God's will or merely profiteering by the elite (see Wagenaar's translation and discussion in 2001, 105, 115).

[6] The two-phrase condemnation is powerful, literally: "It will be night to you [lākem].... It will be darkness to you." The term for "vision" has an unusual deployment in the Hebrew Bible. It is not particularly widespread, since it is not typical for prophets to be described as those who have "visions," rather than being men and women to whom "the word of YHWH" has come, which they pass on as a messenger. This is not to say, however, that the term "vision" is never used. Proverbs famously speaks of the important guiding power of visions from God that assist in keeping the law (29:18 KJV).

Most of the prophetic works begin with the standard phrase, "The word of YHWH as given to/revealed to PN." But three prophetic introductory lines speak of visions. Most significantly, the primary one appears in Isa 1:1, but also in shorter books: Obad 1 and Nah 1:1. Hosea speaks of God "multiplying visions" (12:10), yet mentioning that in the context of bringing judgment. It is striking how often "visions" are spoken of in negative contexts and are paired with divination. Thus Jeremiah features two bitter denunciations of prophetic corruption that strongly echo Micah: Jer 14:14, "The prophets are prophesying lies in my name; I did not send them"; and 23:16, "Do not listen to the words of the prophets who prophesy to you; they are deluding you." Jeremiah's contemporary in Babylon, Ezekiel, also speaks of the absence of guidance in dark days (12:24). Even more directly echoing Micah, Ezekiel speaks of prophets who falsely prophesy *success*, *well-being*, and *peace* (13:16, all of which are possible readings of šālōm). The lack of such visions can also be an indication of disaster (Lam 2:9).

The term for "revelation" (or "divination") is also used to speak of a "diviner," a qōsēm (Isa 3:2; Zech 10:2); thus the root term is used to speak of divination, and usually of the forbidden variety (e.g., Deut 18:10, 14; 1 Sam 6:2; Isa 44:25). In short, what we have is a general condemnation from Micah, cast in vocabulary that speaks of the typical work of prophets: divining, seeing visions, reporting God's intentions. For Micah, these are no longer reliable sources! Furthermore,

---

35. Although I do not agree, Wolff (1990, 103) wonders if these are "personal" wars, not referring to actual fighting. See also Rudolph (1975, 71), who cites Ps 120:7.

Against the Corrupt Prophetic Advisers

Andersen and Freedman notably object to any translation conceding that these prophets once had valid visions: in their view, one should not read Mic 3:6 as saying, "There will be no *more* visions for you."[36]

The root term *qādar* is often used in contrast to light, perhaps anticipating the use of darkness in later apocalyptic language (thus Joel 2:10, "The sun and the moon are darkened"; see also 3:15). The noun form of this term can be translated "afflicted" or "those who mourn" (Job 5:11) or even "sunless gloom" (Job 30:28; cf. Pss 38:6; 42:9; Jer 14:2). The LXX translates with the more common term *dysetai*, used of the sun going down (Gen 28:11) but also of God's miraculous changing of the natural movement of the sun to darken it (Amos 8:9; Joel 2:10; 3:15 [4:15], as noted above).

Micah describes the fate of corrupt prophets as silent darkness. There is no doubt whose fate he is describing: "against the prophets" and "on them" is repeated throughout, clarifying that he is speaking about the prophets. We do not need to look far to see the contemporary equivalent to the prophetic advisers to the ancient kings.[37] One need only witness the proliferation of "institutes" and "think tanks," all with innocent-sounding names but nonetheless established and well funded in order to promote particular and narrow social or political ideologies in contemporary American political practice. On the demand of their paymasters, they provide "studies" that amount to another argument for their particular privileges, academically repackaged in ever more complex "statistics." "Scientists" report that tobacco is not addicting, labs "report" on the safety of their paymaster's products in the pharmaceutical companies, and war is good for the economy, though death is, of course, unfortunate "collateral damage" of the policy. Well-paid "institutes" conveniently deny climate change for their industrial paymasters. Micah's targets have multiplied immeasurably in modern society. Perhaps the modern equivalent of Micah's threat of "silence" and "night" from God is a refusal to trust the paid "reports," leading to a disbelieving silence from the people!

[7] The result of this dark silence from God will be the shame of the prophets. Micah implies that they will come to understand why all is silent, or perhaps more likely, when they are disgraced as they are exposed in their lies and are ashamed. The two terms used are "shame" and "disgrace" (thus *bôš* and *ḥāpēr*). The first term seems often better rendered as "embarrass," while the second term is often translated by "humiliate" (Job 6:20; 19:3; Pss 6:10; 22:5; 44:7;

---

36. Andersen and Freedman ask, "Is it likely that Micah would make such a concession to the false prophets?" (2000, 374).

37. There seems to be no shortage of pastoral support for war. R. H. Abrams's 1933 classic, *Preachers Present Arms* (reprinted 1969), documented religious leaders' unflinching support for the military, lending their blessings to the growing threat that Eisenhower would later warn about in America, namely the development of a dangerous "military-industrial complex" (Jan. 17, 1961). Perhaps Micah warns us of a similar "Prophetic-Priestly Complex" among the Jerusalem elite.

Prov 14:35). However, one can only delineate unique meanings with difficulty. The two terms are used together quite frequently in Psalms (e.g., 35:4, 26; 40:14 [15]; 70:2 [3]; 71:24; 83:17 [18]; cf. Prov 19:26). More significantly, perhaps, is the use of the two terms in Isaiah (1:29). Notice especially the same terminology in Isa 24:23, which uses many of the same images we find in these passages of Micah:

> Then the moon will be abashed,
>   and the sun ashamed;
> for YHWH of hosts will reign
>   on Mount Zion and in Jerusalem,
> and before his elders he will manifest his glory.

As Cha (1996, 128–30) points out, Jeremiah deploys these images in judgment oracles against both Judah (15:9, including sun and moon going down) and then in the later chapters of Oracles against the Nations, against Babylon (50:12), and against other prophets opposing him (6:14–15).

The LXX chooses to heighten Micah's anger. In Greek, words constructed with the prefix *kata-* are typically and strongly negative, and the Greek version of Mic 3:7 introduces a third term in the verse, suggesting three judgments, rather than two in Hebrew:

A	*kataischynō*	to be put to shame
B	*katagelaō*	to be disgraced
C	*katalaleō*	to be slandered

Thus, in the LXX, (A) seers will be put to shame, (B) diviners will be disgraced, and (C) they will all be "slandered/humiliated" because "they will not be heard" (presumably by God, but not explicitly stated in the LXX as it is in the Hebrew). After the term for "shame," the second term suggests the stronger sense even of "laughingstock" (*katagelaō*, as used in Gen 38:23; Ps 25:2, enemies who "gloat"; Prov 17:5; cf. Job 30:1 and elsewhere in Job, as one might expect. Jesus, similarly, is mocked in Matt 9:24//Luke 8:53). Finally, the prophets will be "slandered," using the Greek term often translated as "speak against" God and Moses (Num 21:5), and in reference to those who "speak lies against me" (Hos 7:13). According to Jer 2:26, shame comes to those who are caught in their lies and injustice.

As a result of this shame and humiliation, they will cover up to their "upper lip," or "moustache." The term *śāpām* is not common, but it does appear in discussions of purity in Leviticus: the leper must cover the "upper lip" and declare oneself to be "unclean" (13:45). Since the term is not used frequently in the Bible, one wonders if Micah is suggesting that they cover their embarrassment as one would hide from debilitating physical illness and their resulting deformities. Ezekiel 24:17, 22 similarly implies covering the mouth as part of dressing for mourning. The general idea, suggest many commentators, is that in shame they will cover themselves completely, up to their nose.[38]

There is no "answer" (perhaps "response"; cf. Prov 15:1) from God. The Greek renders as "They will not be heard," or literally, "There will not be an audience," using a phrase similar to that in Prov 21:13.

[8] Micah contrasts his status against those he has revealed to be frauds: "I am full . . . of the spirit of YHWH, and justice, and power" (some read "courage"). Isaiah speaks of a time when Jerusalem was "filled with justice" (1:21 S-C), but angrily condemns towns that are "full of silver and gold" and "full of horses" and "full of idols" (2:7–8 S-C). Jeremiah, too, speaks of being "full" of the wrath of God (6:11). The writer of Luke–Acts picks up on this Micah-like sense of being "full" of the Spirit (Luke 4:1; Acts 6:3, 5; 11:24). Wagenaar, however, cautions that this notion of being "full of the spirit" is language typical of the exilic period (Ezek 11:5, 24; 37:1), and that the rest of v. 8 suggests that Micah's older diatribe leveled against a few select Judean leaders has been expanded in a later edition of Micah to be directed to "Israel" (2001, 248–56).

The Hebrew term for "justice," *mišpāṭ*, is used over four hundred times in the Hebrew Bible. Yet having a "spirit" of justice is rare, though appearing in Isaiah, including one of the famous Servant Songs: Isa 28:6, "a spirit of justice to the one who sits in judgment" (cf. 42:1)

To speak of "greatness," "strength," or "power" (*gĕbûrâ*) is more typical of political language, suggesting royal "valor" (e.g., 1 Kgs 15:23; 16:5, 27; 22:45 [46]; 2 Kgs 13:12, in explicit reference to Joash's military victories; cf. Ps 80:2 [3]). The term is especially associated with virtues of military accomplishment, as in referring to the divine warrior (Pss 20:6; 21:13), being "clothed" or "girded" with strength (Ps 65:6 [7]), soldiers (Isa 28:6), Assyrian military power (Isa 36:5), Babylonian might (Jer 51:30). This military association is not exclusive, however. Typically of the wisdom tradition, Prov 8:14 suggests that wisdom is powerful, rather than military strength, as stated explicitly in Eccl 9:16. Isaiah 11:2 speaks in messianic terms of the one whose power is in counsel and wisdom (cf. Isa 30:15). This contrast between Micah's "power" and the elite's power is important for the prophet, and he will return to this notion in 7:16, when the nations will be ashamed *despite* their military power.

Micah addresses north and south: toward "Jacob," Micah aims the accusation of "rebellion" (*pešaʿ*), and to Israel, "sin" (*ḥaṭṭāʾt*). The two terms

---

38. Andersen and Freedman (2000, 375) offer the idea that the verb is always used for clothing of different kinds. Here the use of moustache means "to wrap oneself in a robe right up to the moustache, leaving only nose and eyes visible."

are occasionally used together for rhetorical emphasis, thus "crime" and "sin/fault" (Gen 50:17; Exod 34:7; Lev 16:16, 21; Josh 24:19; 1 Kgs 8:50; Job 13:23; Ps 32:1. Isaiah frequently uses the two terms together as well, as in 43:25, 27; 53:12; 58:1; 59:12; cf. Jer 33:8). In fact, the former term is used in 2 Kgs 1:1; 3:5 refers to the "revolt" of Moab, while 2 Kgs 8:20 refers to the "revolt" of Edom, both suggesting that this term can have a political/social connotation.

There have been some discussions about whether Micah sees himself as a prophet in contrast to false prophets, or whether he attacks the prophetic movement as entirely corrupt and then contrasts his ability to see the truth clearly. Carroll, for example (in a widely cited study), wonders if Micah is to be considered a prophet at all, given the strong contrast implied in the phrase "but as for me!" in v. 8 (1992, 74–84). Micah's anguish is our own: Does money and privilege always corrupt the ability to see clearly? Is truth simply the tune called for by those who pay the piper?

When modern churches (and their universities!) employ unexamined "management techniques" and uncritically use "marketing strategies" drawn from business models, do we risk the corruption exposed centuries ago by Micah? As this commentary is being written, we in the post-Christian West are experiencing an unprecedented internationalized capitalization of virtually all aspects of society, and faith and education are most certainly included. Information has become a digitalized commodity susceptible to market forces in ways unimaginable by previous writers on Micah, even a few decades ago. Now we must ask: How are we to reclaim the critical abilities to assess what we are told, read, or hear? Is trust now a relic of the past? It appears that forming communities of accountability within and among the peoples of faith is a direct implication of meditating on Micah's anger. One might well begin with Jesus' strong caution against taking examples from the surrounding societies:

> But Jesus called them to him and said, "You know that the rulers of the Gentiles lord it over them, and their great ones are tyrants over them. It will not be so among you; but whoever wishes to be great among you must be your servant, and whoever wishes to be first among you must be your slave; just as the Son of Man came not to be served but to serve, and to give his life a ransom for many." (Matt 20:25–28)

Yoder famously labels this call from Jesus "revolutionary subordination": the way of God's kingdom in relationships among the believers who rightly ignore the status and class symbols of the surrounding world (1994, 162–92). In a world where the only ones who are "answerable" are those who are taken to court, Jesus calls us to be answerable to one another regularly.

Micah 3:9–12 Micah Warns the Central Leadership of Coming Judgment

9 Listen to this, rulers of the house of Jacob,
    and commanders of the house of Israel,
you who abhor[a] justice,
    and make crooked all that is straight!
10 You who build Zion in bloodshed,
    and Jerusalem in injustice,
11 Leaders who make judgments—for a bribe,
    priests who teach—for hire,
prophets who divine messages[b]—for silver,
who lean on God, and say,
    "Surely God is among us!
    Evil will not come upon us!"
12 Therefore, because of you,[c]
Zion will be plowed as a field,
    and Jerusalem will be a heap of stones,[d]
And the mountain of the house
    will be woodland "high places."[e]

a. Participle plural (*hamăta'ăbîm*), awkward in English with the definite article.

b. Prophets who "divine" (*qāsam*). McKane wonders if this use is pejorative (1998, 113).

c. The use of the term *biglalkem* is difficult. Typically this is read as "because of you" (cf. Deut 1:37), with the announced punishment following.

d. Either referring to the former dwellings of the city simply abandoned, or gathered up in heaps so that the land can be worked. The latter makes more sense in context.

e. "Forest" or "woodland" follows immediately, without conjunction, after "high places." I suspect that the grammar comes from reproducing an oral delivery. McKane also sees the wordplay in reading *bāmôt* (1998, 115). I suspect further irony from Micah here, using "high places" as a normal term for sacred places, but now "wooded" (i.e., abandoned and returning to natural growth, or else available for agriculture and orcharding [e.g., vines and fig trees!]).

[9] Now Micah turns his attention back to the leaders themselves, using the same phrase as in 3:1: the "heads" of Jacob and military leaders of Israel. The common term "heads of" frequently refers to leaders in very generic terms. The second term, also used for "leaders" of Israel, is not so common. It has military connotations in Josh 10:24 and Judg 11:6, but Isaiah uses it in tandem with "heads" or "leaders," as well in his address to the political and communal leaders (so, ironically, "leaders" of Sodom in 1:10; then 3:6 may suggest local leadership). Protests among modern commentators that the term is not

necessarily "military" in Micah, however, once again neglect the prominence of the military theme throughout this book.

The term used for "abhor" (justice, in this case) is quite strong, used of those under the curse of the ban in Deut 7:26; God "abhors" even those who were once the "inheritance," the ancestral possession of God (Ps 106:40). More closely paralleling Micah, however, is the assertion of Amos that some people "despise" or abhor those who stand for justice and truth "in the gate" (Amos 5:10).

According to Micah, all that is "straight" is made crooked (for the term "straight" or "right," so in Deut 6:18; cf. 12:28; God's ways are "right," Pss 19:8; 25:8, "right and good"; paired with "true" in 111:8). The term is heavily used in the wisdom tradition to speak of the honest or upright (e.g., Prov 2:7, 13, 21; 11:3, 5, 6, 11; 14:9, 11, 12), and "straight paths" and "roads" are used in Isaiah (26:7; 40:3; 45:2, 13). This sense of "direction" is particular clear in Hos 14:9 (10): "For the ways of YHWH are right, and the upright walk in them, but transgressors stumble in them." In contrast, ways that are "twisted" or "crooked" are also cited in the wisdom tradition (Prov 2:15; 10:9; 28:6). Similar to Micah, Isa 59:8 contrasts peacefulness and justice with crooked or twisted paths: "The way of peace they do not know, and there is no justice in their paths. Their roads they have made crooked; no one who walks in them knows peace."

[10] To "build in blood" is an unforgettable image. Here is a strong echo of the same thought and accusation in Hab 2:12, "Alas for you who build a town by bloodshed, and found a city on iniquity!" Isaiah 1:15 refers to the peoples whose "hands are full of blood," while Isa 4:4 points to the "bloodstains of Jerusalem." The righteous are those who stop their ears from hearing plans that involve bloodshed (Isa 33:15; cf. 59:3). Those who do evil "rush to shed innocent blood" (Isa 59:7). Lamentations 4:13 lists shedding blood in Jerusalem among the sins for which the exile is just punishment. Ezekiel refers to Jerusalem as "this city of bloodshed" (Ezek 22:2 NIV; cf. Nah 3:1).

Once again, I argue that Andersen and Freedman's extended references to human sacrifice are a distraction from the "bloodshed" that is more obviously of concern to Micah: bloodshed in warfare (2000, 382). Wolff famously argues that the specific bloodshed Micah has in mind is the abuse of overworked laborers, perhaps those employed in Hezekiah's expansions and vast military preparations (2 Chr 32:27–29; Wolff 1990, 105–7; Sweeney concurs [2001a, 374]), and wonders whether the qĕṣînîm (Mic 3:9) are to be understood as "overseers." McKane chooses to emphasize the attitude of the financiers and planners and eloquently comments: "It is the megalomania of those who build or acquire property ruthlessly without regard to the social damage which they inflict and the trail of human suffering which they leave in their wake. The possession of power, access to wealth, the thirst for prestige and self-advertisement, has changed them into monsters emptied of moral sense" (1998, 112).

The parallel phrase claims that Jerusalem is built with "injustice" (see Pss 58:2 [3]; 64:6 [7]). Proverbs 22:8 refers to sowing injustice. Malachi 2:6 contrasts this form of injustice with leaders who promote peace and justice. Hosea suggests that political leaders are involved in this particular kind of injustice because they believe that their military power will protect them from the consequences:

> You have plowed wickedness,
>   you have reaped injustice,
>   you have eaten the fruit of lies.
> Because you have trusted in your power
>   and in the multitude of your warriors . . .
>   (10:13)

The LXX uses *adikia* to speak of the injustice of Jerusalem; the term is first used in the Greek translation of Genesis to speak of the "lawlessness" of the earth, which brought on the flood (6:11, 13). Psalm 11:5 speaks of a "lover of violence." The Greek translator uses these terms again in Mic 7:18, 19 to speak of guilt and iniquities.

Jacobs summarizes that the terms point "to harsh and cruel measures—forced labor, heavy taxation and bloodshed—by which the building of the city was accomplished" (2001, 137). The founder of the Quakers, George Fox (b. 1624), once felt moved by the Spirit to walk in the city streets and proclaim, "Woe to the bloody city of Lichfield!" In his journals he states that he later wondered why the Spirit would lead him to condemn a city where, it was true, many had died in recent wars, but no more than other English towns. Later he discovered that many Christians were martyred there during the Roman occupation of Britain! Fox, as always a colorful character, may give an insight into what it might have been like to hear Micah speak of a city built with bloodshed.

[11] We are not left in doubt as to the political nature of Micah's accusations. To "build a city with blood" involves carefully planned injustice and perversions of God's intentions. Again, there are three kinds of leadership included in the accusation:

1. The leaders make judgments for bribes (clearly those with authority over legal matters, including the king).
2. The priests offer an answer depending on payments (including presumably the interpreting of signs such as casting lots).
3. The prophets see visions that facilitate the silver given to them.

Accusations of taking bribes have an important history in the Old Testament. The first four occasions of the term "bribe" in the Torah are in laws forbidding the corruption of taking bribes for legal decisions (Exod 23:8; Deut 10:17;

16:19; 27:25). That such bribes were common in statecraft is clear in the historical works (1 Kgs 15:19; 2 Kgs 16:8; cf. Prov 17:8; 17:23). Bribes are associated with interest on loans (Ps 15:5) and were seen by the prophets as a cause for injustice:

> Your princes are rebels and companions of thieves.
> Everyone loves a bribe and runs after gifts.
> They do not defend the orphan,
>   and the widow's cause does not come before them.
>   (Isa 1:23)

Thus the one who "waves away a bribe" (NRSV) is an exemplar of righteousness (Isa 33:15). Ezekiel compares bribes to the price for a prostitute (16:33, perhaps following Deut 23:19), but also makes the same association of bribery with injustice and bloodshed: "In you, they take bribes to shed blood; you take both advance interest and accrued interest, and make gain of your neighbors by extortion; and you have forgotten me, says the Lord YHWH" (Ezek 22:12).

The priests will "teach" (*yārâ*, as in Deut 33:10; Ezek 44:23) for "payment" (the Hebrew suggests also "price": Isa 55:1; cf. Jer 15:13). The LXX reads more directly: "wages" or "reward" (Gen 15:1; 29:15; 30:32; so "wages" in Zech 8:10; Isa 23:18 speaks of "merchandise . . . wages . . . profits").

Finally, the prophets will see visions "for silver." The Hebrew term can also mean "money" more generically, but the rhetoric of Micah seems sharper when the substance is translated literally—similar to those who cite "thirty pieces of silver" as far more suggestive and powerful than "money." The audacity of claiming to be acting under God's direction by saying, "God is with us," is likely to be derived by the writer of Micah (if not the prophet himself) from the episode of the so-called murmuring in the desert in Exodus, where nearly the same phrase is used: "The Israelites quarreled and tested YHWH, saying, 'Is YHWH among us or not?'" (17:7).

[12] As a result of the accusations enumerated above, Zion will be plowed as a field. The translation is difficult. One of the opening terms, *biglalkem*, is usually rendered "Because of you" (Andersen and Freedman 2000, 380). This translation, in parallel to Deut 1:37, certainly follows the logic of Micah's previous accusations.

In parallel with "plowing Zion" is the following phrase about Jerusalem being turned into a "ruin" (see Ps 79:1). The Greek term means "shed," as in the makeshift buildings thrown up in fields for workers to find cover (so Isa 1:8; 24:20). Clearly the Greek presumes an agricultural setting for both the images of judgment in Mic 3:12: Jerusalem will be useful again, fulfilling a radical farmer's dream of a proper judgment against urban waste.

The Judgments against Samaria and Jerusalem

There is a popular emendation suggesting that the hill of Zion will be a place for "wild animals" to wander. While it is quite true that this is a common image of abandonment in the Hebrew Bible (see Hos 2:12 [14]; cf. Ps 50:10; Isa 13:19–21; Zeph 2:13–15), this emendation contradicts the usefulness of the land, which I consider to be one of Micah's most significant satirical suggestions. At least part of the former location will be plowed!

Wolff does not believe that the Hebrew term *śādēh* can be taken as useful land, but concedes that the Temple Mount is only one part of the city. On the contrary, however, I point out that there is a consistent imagery in Micah of plowing and vine-dressing in the punishments of Samaria (1:6) and Jerusalem (3:12), which links with the famous pilgrimage to Zion in the very next passage (4:1–5). Agriculture is Micah's definition of usefulness. Stansell's discussion is helpful here: contrasting Mic 2:1–2 and Isa 5:8, he observes that Isaiah and Micah have "quite different expectations of the future; for Micah the Judean peasants will again care for the land; for Isaiah the land will be devastated, the inhabitants removed." He concludes, "The Judean peasants will have their expropriated land restored to them; hence it is with them, whom Micah calls 'my people,' that any future existence is to be found" (1988; 131–35).[39]

Shaw compares the threat to Jerusalem with ancient treaties, as in an Esarhaddon treaty that threatens: "May Shamash plow up your cities and districts with an iron plow" (1993, 113, citing *ANET* 529). Shaw follows this by making the fascinating suggestion that Micah may be referring to a treaty that Jerusalem is breaking by attempting to resist Assyria!

Excursus 4: The Judgments against Samaria and Jerusalem

Many commentators have noticed the difficulty with the phrase "and the mountain of the house a wooded height" (NRSV), but Hillers's work on this passage is particularly helpful. He recounts previous suggestions that propose reading "wild animals" here, as a near parallel to 5:8 (7 MT) might suggest ("among the animals of the forest"), thereby reading in 3:12 *běhēmôt* ("animals") rather than *bāmôt* ("high places") (1984, 47).

If this correction is accepted, Hillers then suggests that this would be a further example of the theme of animals present among the ruins of a former city as part of a classic threat. The Bible uses this threat of animals wandering among ruins as a part of a threat or curse. While Isa 34:11–17 (the curse against Edom) may be the fullest form of this, other examples can be cited:

> But the hawk and the hedgehog shall possess it;
>   the owl and the raven shall live in it. . . .

---

39. Stansell concludes these comparisons by noting the parallel with Jeremiah, while Isaiah's belief in the inviolability of Zion sounds much closer to Jeremiah's opponent, Hananiah (Jer 28)!

It shall be the haunt of jackals, an abode for ostriches.
Wildcats shall meet with hyenas. . . .
There shall the owl nest and lay
and hatch and brood in its shadow;
there too the buzzards shall gather,
each one with its mate.
(Isa 34:11, 13–15)

Also Isa 5:17, "Then the lambs shall graze as in their pasture, fatlings and kids shall feed among the ruins" (cf. Jer 9:11; 51:37). Hillers's important 1964 study of treaty curses helpfully explains the relation of these treaty curses to some of the details of prophetic oracles. He further reports that one can find examples of threats in the Sefire Treaty texts that include the threat that one's ruined house will become a dwelling place for animals (Sefire Stela I A 32–33), which he relates to passages such as Mic 3:12 (1964, 45–54).

With regard to these prophetic passages, however, one wonders whether there is a significant difference between Isa 5:17, where the ruins are productive land for *domesticated* animals, as opposed to Jer 9:11 and 51:37, where the land is wild and useless, a home for *dangerous* animals. The difference between the two may hold the key to an argument that the treaty curses relate more to the Jeremiah passages than the Isaiah passage, and by extension the Micah passages we are presently considering. In fact, the commentary literature reflects an ambiguity about the images in Mic 1:6 and 3:12: are the cities to be wasteland or agricultural land?

I could go further in summarizing previous work; here I simply identify two common interpretive strategies with regard to these threats that I believe are worth questioning. The first approach has been the attempt to connect Micah's threats with known events of Assyrian imperialism in the West, as if Micah is speaking of threats to Jerusalem and Samaria from invading Assyrian armies. This would obviously "internationalize" the interpretation and lead to detailed discussions of the dating of Micah. Ben Zvi points out that readers of Micah tend to agree that the references or allusions made by the textually inscribed speaker to events such as the destruction of the city or town are directly and unequivocally related, at least in the original text, to actual, particular, historical events that happened either shortly before or soon after the composition of the text (2000, 25).

McKane (1998, 19–20) and Andersen and Freedman illustrate precisely this tendency. For example, in their summary discussion of Mic 3:12, the oracle against Jerusalem, Andersen and Freedman's entire discussion is focused on the various historical suggestions for dating the passage, and they conclude their entire analysis by despairing of the possibility of historical precision (2000, 388–91). However, I agree with Ben Zvi (and others) and suggest that seeking precise historical associations with Assyrian troop movements may not be the most productive direction to take on understanding the aesthetics of violence in these passages. Furthermore, to emphasize the similarity with treaty curses is only a variant of the interest in the details of the historical threat. Both the actual Assyrian invasions, or the threats in treaty curses, suggest to modern interpreters that the cities will be reduced to useless wastelands. But that is not what the text in Micah actually implies.

The problem with either of these directions of interpretation is not that they are not suggestive—which they are—but rather that they can distract from the possibility that

The Judgments against Samaria and Jerusalem

Micah is speaking on behalf of an internal, subordinated group within Judean society. Micah is not merely speaking about an Assyrian attack or simply speaking on behalf of a judgmental God threatening all Judeans and Samarians. Furthermore, Micah is not using capital cities as a symbol of the entire population, including even himself (which seems implied in Smith's brief analysis [1984, 35]). If Micah's implied threats are toward the interests of a particular group, the urban elite, then speaking of ruins does not necessarily mean that the land is henceforth useless and abandoned, like Romans plowing salt into the fields around Carthage to render the land a useless ruin. In short, we must ask, Useless *to whom*? Thus I dispute the view of Wolff, who argues that 3:12 implies a threat to turn the city into useless land (1990, 108). Wolff proposes that Micah's use of the term "field" is to be compared to Gen 27:3, as a wilderness for hunting. Yet why he restricts the term "field" in this way is not clear when the same term also has very common associations with agriculturally productive "fields" (e.g., Exod 22:5 [4]; Num 16:14; Prov 24:30).

The fascinating arguments of D. N. Premnath (2003) help us develop the idea that the *specific images* used by Micah tend to suggest a social and political context that relates closely to the internal social-class structures of eighth-century Israelite and Judean society. I suggest that if we disengage from a focused attention to the specifics of the threat, perhaps we can listen more carefully to the angry imagery. Finally, however, we will soon take up the connection between the "peace passage" (4:1–5) and the threats against both the capital cities.

In the end, Micah implies that a city built on blood will not be allowed to stand. The city that is "built" in the opening verses (3:9–10) becomes a "ruin" in the final verses (3:11–12). To point out, as does Mays (1976, 92), that Jerusalem has never become a ruin to this day, risks reading Micah too literally and perhaps a bit hastily. First, we now realize that the destruction of Jerusalem in 587 B.C.E. must not be minimized: parts of the city most certainly would have been a "ruin" (Lipschitz 2005, 70–90). Nor should we forget to appreciate that even if Jerusalem survived the earlier Assyrian siege of 701 B.C.E., dozens of nearby villages certainly did not (including many of Micah's near neighbors, especially around Lachish).

In reading Micah's imagery of plowing Jerusalem so literally in 3:12, there is a risk of concluding that it could not possibly be compatible with the picture of Jerusalem in 4:1–5, or even be written by the same person (even though 4:3 does refer to plowing as well!). We certainly do not normally read Micah's imagery about cannibalism in 3:1–3 with the same level of literalism! Perhaps we should allow the poet his license throughout; if not, we risk arbitrarily revoking it only on those occasions that suit a complex redactional theory. That the same Jerusalem could be "plowed" in 3:12 and yet still be the site of an international gathering of nations to arbitrate differences in 4:1–5 requires no less suspension of historical care in reading, or critical sensibility, than does our appreciation of the meaning of "tearing skin off people" in 3:1–3.

Finally, even if Micah's warning was not literally carried out, the warning itself carries a powerful message filled with fascinating implications for capital cities needing to serve their people. One immediately thinks of the ubiquity with which modern states, especially those of the developing world, pour millions (at times including aid funds) into state mansions and palaces while their populations starve. But is the "Christian" West innocent of such lavish spending on its symbols of power and permanence? Agrarian protest movements attest otherwise.

Gerard Winstanley's seventeenth-century English Digger Movement refused to recognize the loss of common lands by instructing his radical Christian followers to literally dig up formerly common lands to reappropriate them for the people. The great Maori Prophet Te Whiti (1830–1907; the "Wh" requires an *F* sound) instructed his followers to nonviolently, but systematically, dig up the wooden survey stakes of European land speculators trying to expropriate indigenous lands in New Zealand (Elsmore 1989, 211–24). Bissett (1999), Burbank (1976), and Schwartz (1976) helpfully document a history of such agrarian protests in the United States as well. As for the excessive spending on monumental architecture, the simplicity of the early Quaker meetinghouses was an intentional architectural and moral criticism against the opulence of the state church's spending, a witness that Friends themselves too often forgot in the flush of financial successes after the industrial revolution. The continued struggle of modern labor movements reminds us of the consequences of cities "built in blood." In many developed nations, the supply of illegal and/or underpaid labor results in cities literally built in bloodshed and protected by the "volunteer" armies composed of the unemployed. Micah's words continue to ring in our ears.

Micah 4:1–5 Micah's Vision of the Economy of Peace

1 It will happen at the end of these days:[a]
the mountain of the house of YHWH[b] will be established
   as the "leader"[c] of the mountains,
lifted up over the hills.
   The peoples will stream[d] up to it!
2 Many nations will walk and say,
"Come! We will go up to the mountain of YHWH,
   and to the house of the God of Jacob,
and he will teach us his ways,[e]
   so that we may walk in his paths."
Because torah will go out from Zion,
   and the word of YHWH from Jerusalem.
3 And he will enact decisions between the many peoples,
   and reprimand[f] the many peoples even far away.[g]

They will hammer their swords into plows,
   and their spears into vineyard shears.
A nation will not lift up a sword[h] against a nation,
   and they will no longer train for war.[i]
4 A man will dwell under his vine[j] and his fig tree,
   and will no longer fear,[k]
because the mouth of YHWH of Armies has insisted.[l]
5 Because all the peoples walk,
   each man in the name of his god,
but we will walk in the name of YHWH
   our God for all time.

   a. Sedlmeier proposes that the phrase be understood as suggesting a time when all of God's initiated plans come to fruition (1998). See comments below.

   b. Wagenaar (2001, 271) claims that this phrase appears only in 2 Chr 33:15, suggesting a late text. This must be balanced against the common references to "mountain of God" in Exodus, which could easily have been adapted as a later reference to the temple, even as early as the eighth century. Willis notes a variety of near parallels to parts of this phrase in many psalms, particularly Pss 68:16 and 78:68 (1997, 296–97).

   c. The term $rō'š$ was rendered "rulers" in Mic 3:9. By preserving this, I am suggesting another wordplay. Willis (1997, 298–99) calls attention to a similar motif in Ps 48, where the mountain is raised and is "the joy of the whole earth" (esp. v. 2).

   d. The verb $nāhărû$ is clearly related to $nāhār$, "river." See Hillers 1984, 49. Wagenaar suggests it is only used with reference to peoples in Jer 51:44, thus arguing that it is a late term (2001, 271). Willis, however, points out that the "flowing river" in reference to Zion is a common motif in the Psalms (1997, 299) and adds in regard to Ps 46:4 and Isa 8:6 that "the figure here may be based on the actual existence of a canal which brought the waters of the Gihon spring along the eastern slope of the city down toward the south." But the term may have been suggested from other, and older, analogies. One might point out that Prov 5:16 uses the term "scattered" (used most frequently of people, so, e.g., Gen 11:8) to refer to water, suggesting a parallel use of a similar term, one that can compare the movement of water to the "flowing" of people.

   e. The LXX changes the emphasis to "they will show us"; thus the Israelites become the teachers of torah, as discussed by McKane (1998, 123).

   f. On $wĕhôkîaḥ$, cf. 2 Kgs 19:4, where God will "dispute" the words of the Assyrian military spokesperson in the time of Hezekiah (cf. Isa 11:4).

   g. Hillers (1984, 50) disputes with those who suggest that this line ought to be removed by arguing that it is hardly a "gloss" since it does not explain anything.

   h. Wagenaar (2001, 271) suggests that a similar use of "lifting swords" and "learning war" appears only in 1 Chr 5:18, befitting his later date for this passage. Yet 1 Chr 5:18 is less impressive as a parallel than it seems. Again, earlier suggestions about "learning war" (e.g., 2 Sam 22:35) could well indicate older sources.

   i. Andersen and Freedman suggest, "and they will never train for war again" (2000, 396).

j. Specifically a "grapevine"? See Wolff 1990, 112.

k. Cha (1996, 14–15) proposes that this line be compared to the "ironic" expression of Jer 7:33, where animals are not frightened away.

l. My use of the literal "YHWH of Armies" is in agreement with the observation by Sweeney (2001a, 380) that this "motivation clause" emphasizes YHWH's role in enforcing the arrangement. Isaiah does not have this feature.

[1] "In days to come" (NRSV) suggests the near future, when the mountain of the house of God is "established" (*nākôn*, used of primeval creation; see Clifford 1972) as the highest of the mountains (the term is translated in NJB as "confirmed" in Deut 13:14 [15]; 17:4; cf. NRSV, "establish" in Pss 51:10 [12]; 65:6 [7]; cf. NJB, "made secure" in Isa 9:7 [6]; 16:5).

The following phrase speaks of "raising" the hill. The term (*nāśā'*) is normally used for "lifted" (KJV: 1 Sam 6:13, "lifted up their eyes"; cf. Zech 1:18 [2:1]; 2:1 [5]). The LXX suggests that the mountain will "soar up above the hills" (cf. Obad 4; Ezek 10:16–17, 19).

The tendency in commentary literature, and in the accompanying theological comments based on this famous phrase, has been to cast this passage safely into the distant future so that it has little ethical force in the present. Hillers, for example, states that the future orientation of the opening lines identifies this vision as "the mysterious, mythical transformation of political and even geological conditions" (1964, 50).

Recently Becking has challenged this tendency on the basis of Akkadian analogies and suggests understanding Micah's phrase as follows: "In the near future a turn in the sense of a decisive change will take place" (2002a). Similarly, Miscall observes that the "future" intended in the phrase "in the days to come" is not an "isolated future" but an actual anticipated one (1993, 14). Sweeney argues that the Hebrew implies simply "the future," while it is really the LXX that casts the sentiment into the *distant* future (2001a, 378). Finally, this phrase does not suggest, "Wouldn't it be nice someday if . . . ?" Andersen and Freedman rightly protest: "It is more precise than 'days to come' (NJB, REB). Here it marks the time of fulfillment of the Creator's intentions and purposes for the world" (2000, 401). If these events cannot be stored safely on the shelf marked "Impossible Dreams," then what is being proposed here?

Questions must be raised about a widespread tendency to present the destruction-of-weapons motif in Mic 4 (and Isa 2) as "utopian" or as a "peasant ideal" (so Marrs 1999, 199 n. 46). The images of beating swords into plowshares and not learning about war can be *made more unrealistic* by exaggerating the future tense. The future can be emphasized to such a degree that it becomes more fantasy than vision, a false hope as opposed to a real hope or even a moral statement that could guide contemporary action! Thus Micah's proposal is turned effectively into a sentimental greeting card ("much celebrated for its utopic content" [Runions 2001, 151]), accompanied perhaps by an appropriately angelic choral film score. Talmon argues (already in 1971) that Mic 4:4 was added to the original oracle precisely to make the previous thought more "realistic," thus undercutting the utopian sense of the original saying.

It is possible to read the image far more radically. The "mythical" nature of Micah's proposal is perhaps lost on (for example) the Doukhobors, the Russian-Canadian Christian sect who deeply inspired Tolstoy in Russia before they immigrated into Canada, who to this day celebrate their faith by an actual bonfire created by piling up whatever weapons they can pull together! So Schultz, for example, believes that the context in Micah stresses turning from war as a central theme of the book and declares that when the present regime is overcome, this vision may well prevail (1999, 305). Thus he argues that Mic 4:5 is the *application* of vv. 1–3. Ben Zvi also understands the ideal future as having serious "contemporary" implications: "Images of an ideal future are significant indicators of the horizon of thoughts, dreams, desires, fears, and self-understanding of the community in which they develop" (2000, 88). Sedlmeier proposes that Mic 4:1 refers to the fulfillment of God's initiated plans, thus reading the opening phrase as referring to the "end" of the events unfolding at the present time (1998, 76–77). In any case, the notion of reading the future tense to suggest "merely a utopia" continues to be rejected by the Quakers, Mennonites, and Church of the Brethren, who still struggle for disarmament and diplomacy as the modern ethical implications of listening to what God intends "in the days to come." For further discussion, see the Excursus below.

The final phrase of the first verse is perhaps the most arresting: the "peoples" will "stream" (flow as does water, the term derived from *nāhār*, river, as in Gen 2:10, 13; Ps 24:2 ["flowing waters," S-C]; cf. Ps 78:16). The idea that people and goods will "flow" toward Jerusalem is also common in other examples of the thematic procession of the nations thence: Isa 60:5, "The wealth of the nations shall come to you"; 66:12, "I will extend prosperity to her like a river, and the wealth of the nations like an overflowing stream" (cf. Jer 31:12). But Andersen and Freedman (2000, 403) claim that this term (from *nāhār*) is only used of *people* "flowing" toward worship (e.g., Jer 51:44). The LXX conveys the further sense of peoples "hurrying" to Zion. This is particularly intriguing, given the fact that the only other occasion of precisely this form of the Greek term appears in the adjacent book (Nah 2:5). Likely Micah intends an inward "flow" of people *in contrast* to an outward "flow" of captured prisoners and expropriated goods (thus counting against the incoming "wealth" of Isa 60:5).

There surely is great irony in the mountain becoming a "leader" or a "peak" among other mountains, immediately after it has been plowed like a field in 3:12! But there is no suggestion here that the city has somehow been reassembled as an administrative center in some future time, despite the prevailing assumption that there is to be a conceptual (and perhaps even chronological) break between 3:12 and 4:1–5. Wolff declares that this passage "stands in antithesis to the fearsome judgment prophesied in 3:12" (1990, 117), and McKane repeats the famous observation of Wellhausen that 4:1–5 is a "Band-Aid" on the wound of 3:12 (1998, 117). Jeppesen observes: "Even if one takes a long pause for breath between Mic 3:12 and 4:1, the change in outlook for the future is surprising; it is like moving suddenly from night to day—and that is, of course, one of the reasons why scholars declined to read the two texts together" (1999, 209).

I am aware that I am challenging the weight of opinion by suggesting that this assumed "break" between the notions of 3:12 and 4:1–5 is false. I argue that Jerusalem is being *redefined* by the prophet: it is no longer the administrative center for Judah and thus the hovel of greed that Micah believes it has become. Rather, it is now an *international* center. The contrast between the former Jerusalem that was plowed under (according to 3:12) is that this new "Zion" is an international (and agrarian!) center for peacemaking, not the center of conspiracies for war by a Judean elite. That Jerusalem in the twenty-first century is being unreasonably claimed by many in one nation as exclusively for themselves, rather than allowing a second people to also locate their capital there, seems a sad refusal to be guided by this famous internationalist vision. I insist that we not lose sight of the connection between (1) planting vines and plowing fields in 1:6 and 3:12, and (2) vine shears and plows in 4:1–5.

[2] The "many nations" (*gôyīm rabbîm*) will go up, and they will say "Let's go!" (Pss 34:11 [12]; 46:8 [9]; 66:5, 16). The call to "come" or "let us go" is always positive in the Psalms, except for 83:4 (5), where foreign nations call for Jerusalem's destruction. Nevertheless, in the famous Peace Prophecy (here in Mic 4:2), these same foreigners hurry to learn from God! If translated "come," rather than "let us go," the call suggests that some who are on the way are calling on others to join them, which is closer to the famous sentiment in Zech 8:20–23. The matter of choice seems critical to an understanding of what is being expressed by Micah in this passage as a whole; choice is often missed by those who argue that this passage represents Judah in a military victory over its enemies (even if miraculously accomplished by God). In this spurious view, these enemies supposedly cower before the victorious Judeans on the mountain of Zion. Micah 4:1–5, however, portrays foreigners apparently *wanting* to go to Zion to learn the ways of God's peace! In stark contrast to the many times this passage has been compared to a more *negative* thematic procession of the nations (i.e., by comparing only two examples, such as Isa 49 and Isa 60, where there is a note of threat against foreign nations), we insist that it is far more plausible to read it in combination with the equally important *positive* thematic procession, such as Zech 8. There simply is no singular thematic procession of the nations: there are *two different versions* of it. Given our argument that Micah has serious differences with Isaiah, there are serious grounds for questioning the frequent comparison to the Isaiah passages!

Micah's Vision of the Economy of Peace 133

The "mountain of Yahweh" and the "house of the God of Jacob" seem to be a clear reference to the temple. Micah's angry sentiment in 3:12 does not necessarily suggest, it seems, that the temple (or some place of meeting) is no longer standing in Jerusalem, or else we must contend with Micah "predicting" a destruction and rebuilding of the temple many generations before Jeremiah's famous sermon in Jer 7. More interesting is what follows in Mic 4, suggesting that one may be 'set' in God's ways, or even 'established according to' God's ways. The same phrase occurs in Judg 13:8, "Teach us what we are to do." Further, they are invited to walk in his "paths" (cf. "path of life" [Pss 16:11]; "Teach me your paths" [25:4]; the "paths" of YHWH as "steadfast love and faithfulness" [25:10]; "path" of integrity [27:11] in contrast to "deceptive paths" [119:128]; "path of the righteous" [Isa 26:7]; "path" of God's justice [26:8]).

The Greek translations seem to like the notion of following God's "paths." In Isaiah, the LXX uses a term for "path" (*hodos*) over 65 times, far more often than the Hebrew term (only about 8×). At times this can be particularly suggestive: the Greek version has Isaiah speak of "paths" that God will make for the many peoples coming from far away (Isa 49:11). Upon his realization of God's power, Nebuchadnezzar proclaims that God's "paths" are just (Dan 4:37). Thus the LXX suggests that knowing the "paths" of God is something that is possible for the many peoples of the nations and, according to Daniel, even for enemies.

The peoples will then know "torah/teaching" and the "word of God." Thus Isaiah often speaks of the teaching/torah in parallel with justice (51:4). In times of crisis, Lamentations speaks of sadness that "torah" (NRSV: "guidance") is not heard from leaders, nor visions from prophets (2:9), and Zeph 3:4 speaks of priests doing "violence to torah" (S-C; cf. Hag 2:11). Use of the term "torah" here emphasizes that peace is *God's* intended status for humanity.

The "word of YHWH" (*dĕbar-yhwh*) "first" comes to Abraham through a vision (Gen 15:1, 4), but mainly through prophets (1 Kgs 22:5, 19, 28; 2 Kgs 7:1; 9:36). The phrase is common in the introduction to the prophetic books (e.g., Isa 1:10; Jer 1:2, and throughout Jeremiah and Ezekiel; Hos 1:1; Joel 1:1; Zeph 1:1; Hag 1:1; Zech 1:1).

The Peace Prophecy (Mic 4:1–5) is also consistent with the prophetic critique of ritual worship (e.g., Isa 1:10–17; Amos 5:21–25; Jer 7; esp. Mic 6:6–8): the function of the mountain of God is to teach about behavior and promote justice. This is precisely what many of the prophets believed was neglected in the rituals of sacrifice. The same sentiment is echoed by James with regard to the injustices of hypocritical worship among early Christians (Jas 2) and arguably intended by Jesus when he combines Jer 7:11 and Isa 56:7 in the famous Cleansing of the Temple (Luke 19:45–48//Matt 21:12–13). Micah declares Jerusalem a place for learning more than a place for ritual sacrifice (cf. Mic 6:8!).

[3] To "judge between" is a common-enough phrase in calling for fairness: "May YHWH judge between you and me!" (Gen 16:5; cf. 31:53; Num 35:24;

Deut 1:16; 1 Sam 24:12, 15 [13, 16]. In Isa 5:3, the divine winemaker calls on the people to "judge" God's case between God and his sown fields. Likewise Ezek 34:17 undoubtedly inspired Jesus' parable of the Sheep and the Goats (Matt 25:31–46). The nations being referred to here in Mic 4:3 can be "far away" (Joel 3:8 [4:8]; see also Isa 5:26; 59:11). The phrase ʿad-rāḥôq, in reference to the many peoples "far away," is dropped in Isaiah, and some suggest that the version in Isaiah is thus a "simplification" (Andersen and Freedman 2000, 401). While the reference to Hebrews who are "far" (or "near") in Solomon's dedication prayer (1 Kgs 8:46) suggests exiles, here the "nations" (gôyīm) clearly include foreign peoples.

To "reprimand" (others have suggested "decree" or "reprove," ykḥ in Hiphil) can also be used "between" people (Gen 31:37). Leviticus speaks of "reproving" or "disputing" (arbitrate or negotiate?) with neighbors so that hatred does not build up (Lev 19:17). The term is used heavily in Job, where 5:17 speaks of God's "discipline," and 9:33 (NJB) uses "arbiter" (cf. Isa 29:21; the "man who teaches justice at the city gate" in Amos 5:10 NJB). Job 13:15 and 15:3 speaks of making a "defense." Psalms 6:1 [2] and 38:1 [2] ask God to "correct" or "discipline" without anger. Psalm 50:21 suggests a legal "charge," but there are decided differences in rendering this term (see Ps 94:10 as "punish" in NJB, but "chastise" in NRSV). Therefore the verb ykḥ cannot be said in all cases to be negative and thus inevitably punishing. In many cases, the intent is to *prevent punishment by warning of the consequences of inaction*. Isaiah 1:18 suggests "negotiate" or "debate" (cf. the familiar "reason together" from KJV). Often ykḥ is paired with "judge," špṭ (as Mic 4:3 and also in Isa 11:4): God will righteously "judge the poor" and "decide with equity for the meek." I have chosen "reprimand" because I suggest that virtually all universalist sentiments in the Hebrew Bible (e.g., Jonah) include an element of reprimand for the unjust behavior of foreign nations, even as they are accepted as potentially among those forgiven by the God of Israel. Even Jonah does not include a blanket amnesty, without repentance and recognition of the sins of violence and warfare (Jonah 3:8; cf. Isa 19:22).

The sentiment seems clear: nations would want a judge and arbitrator. Social justice requires the ability to appeal to an authority who listens to all sides of the story and decides what is in the best interests of peace and justice for all. The idea that "many nations" would have to be *forced* to seek arbitration and justice is a notion one would gain from listening only to the elite, who would lose power and influence. As usual, the wealthy are the ultranationalists. Most of the population, those who supply the foot soldiers, would readily welcome peace talks.

The people who gather are to "beat" (kātat) their swords (KJV). "Sword" (ḥereb) is the standard term for weapon in the Hebrew Bible. There is no basis for suggesting that it is unique or special: it is the generic term. The verb kātat is notably used of "crushing" idols, such as the golden calf (Deut 9:21; cf. 2 Kgs 18:4; 2 Chr 34:7; Mic 1:7), but often functions as a hyperbole of warfare (2 Chr 15:6; Ps 89:23 [24]; Isa 24:12; Zech 11:6). Both uses of the term are suggestive in this context: the weapons themselves are to be treated as idols and "defeated," beaten up, as though in warfare.

The term for a "plow" (*'ēt*), on the other hand, is rare. Despite translating a different Hebrew term (*môrag*) in 1 Chr 21:23, the LXX presumed that "threshing sledge" (NRSV) must also be a plow and uses the same term as Mic 4:3 (cf. Sir 38:25). The classic comparative passage is the reference to the monopoly on iron by the Philistines in 1 Sam 13:20–21.

> So all the Israelites went down to the Philistines to sharpen their plowshares, mattocks, axes, or sickles. The charge was two-thirds of a shekel for the plowshares and for the mattocks, and one-third of a shekel for sharpening the axes and for setting the goads.

"Spears" (sg. *ḥănît*) are also mentioned far less prominently in the Hebrew text than swords. Nahum 3:3 provides a near example of descriptions of battle as using swords and spears ("Horsemen charging, flashing sword and glittering spear"). Notably, however, "spears" also appear among weapons to be banished in times of peace: "He makes wars cease . . . and shatters the spear" (Ps 46:9). These spears become, traditionally, "pruninghooks" (KJV, for *mazmērôt*), seen only elsewhere in Isa 18:5 ("He will cut off the shoots with pruning hooks, and the spreading branches he will hew away"). In Mic 4:3 the LXX names the same tool (*drepanon*, also in the parallels Isa 2:4 and Joel 3:10 [4:10]) for pruning as used for harvest, presuming a "sickle" in Jer 50:16 (and Joel 3:13 [4:13]) despite the use of a different implement in the Hebrew (*maggāl*) in these same two verses.

Perhaps precision with regard to the instrument is not finally necessary; we clearly understand the agricultural context. I have suggested "vineyard shears" based on my reading of the agricultural activity as noted in Isa 18:5, but more significantly also based on the two agricultural "punishments" in Mic 1:6 (Samaria into vineyards) and 3:12 (Jerusalem into a plowed field). Are the two images in Mic 4:3b—plowing and implements of war—related because similar blacksmithing skills are being referred to here? The Hebrew root *ḥārāš*, "engraver, metalworker, smith" (Isa 41:7), is clearly to be understood in some sense of cutting since it is also used of plowing—engraving into the earth, so to speak (Judg 14:18; 1 Sam 8:12; 1 Kgs 19:19, Elisha plowing).

Nations will not "lift up against a nation" the sword (the swords that earlier were refashioned; here is the same term for sword). The term for "lift up" (*nāśā'*) is the same as the "lifting" of the hill of Zion above the mountains (Mic 4:1).

Finally, the people will not "learn" (or "teach") war any longer. To "teach" or to "learn" about God is the intent of the law (e.g., Deut 4:1, 5, 10, 14; 5:1), but in this case Micah refers to the tradition of "training for war." Thus Judges tries to explain the persistent existence of the Canaanites as a way for Israel to "learn war" (Judg 3:1–2), and 2 Sam 22:35 (where Ps 18 is translocated) speaks of

David as being "trained for war" by God (cf. 1 Chr 5:18, those "trained for war"; Song 3:8, "trained in war"). Here in Mic 4:3, among the people not training for war any longer are the Israelites themselves. Thus I strongly dispute Andersen and Freedman's observation that "this state of affairs will eventuate, not when all nations join the confederacy on the same basis as the tribes of Israel, but when they have been subjugated by victorious Zion" (2000, 408). This flies in the face of Micah's consistent antimilitarist stand, beginning with a bitter condemnation of the fortress of Lachish as the "beginning of sin" (1:13 NRSV) and continuing here with an emphasis not on conquest but on disputing, debating, and resolving conflicts—like elders in villages do! Furthermore, the exclusive reference to the *negative* thematic procession of nations consistently neglects any motivation on the part of the conquered, while the positive thematic procession (arguably more relevant here) focuses precisely on their *willing participation* (e.g., Zech 8, consistently and too conveniently ignored in this debate).

God's threats notwithstanding, it is a strange myopia that conveniently overlooks the fact that Micah, throughout this work, places his fellow Judeans under the same demanding gaze of God, an eye of judgment that is here also directed toward all other nations! Wolff (1990, 121–22) clarifies the importance of seeing differences between various texts foretelling a procession of the nations to Jerusalem. He observes that the people are portrayed as freely gathering in Mic 4, not "summoned" as in Isa 49. Furthermore, it is the *people* who destroy their own weapons, not God (as God does in Ps 76).

Many modern commentators follow Erlich's 1908 suggestion that the basic tradition of nations recognizing Zion is quite old and draws from the Zion/ temple theology of Ps 48, echoed in Isa 28 (see Rudolph 1975, 75–81). Thus some suggested that Isaiah the prophet was himself the author of the sentiment in Isa 2:2–4, which was taken up in Micah, and that this idea was simply an aspect of the prophet's beliefs about the coming significance and international importance of the temple on Mount Zion. Even foreigners, so Isaiah seems to be saying, will come to recognize Zion's significance. Micah 4:1–4 is thus merely a redacted insertion, based on Isaiah.

Wolff, however, reasserts the idea that Mic 4:1–4 and Isa 2:2–4 represent a synthesis of ideas not anticipated by older Zion material in either Ps 48 or Isa 1–39, notions much more likely the products of postexilic speculation about God's role in wider world affairs after 587 B.C.E. World peace, for example, was not an element of Ps 48, nor was the direct participation of foreigners. Thus Wolff renews Wellhausen's inclination to see the peaceful sentiment as a later addition (1992). But I urge, Not so fast!

[4] This is the unique continuation in the Micah version of the great Peace Prophecy that differentiates it from Isa 2. The notion of "sitting under" a vine and fig tree is a farmer's ideal (or with Marrs, a word for the "despairing poor of the countryside" [1999, 187]). Of course, agricultural abundance is one of the promises for the land given by God (Deut 8:8, "a land of wheat and barley, of vines and fig trees and pomegranates, a land of olive trees and honey"). Indeed, the Israelites themselves are often called the "planting" of God, famously in Isa 5 (whence it appears to have deeply influenced early Christian thought, as in John 15 and Rom 11; see also Isa. 61:3; 1QS 8.5) yet also in Ps 80:8 ("You brought a vine out of Egypt; you drove out the nations and planted it") and Hos 10:1; it also is taken up in late seventh- and sixth-century prophets in Jer 2:21 and notably of a branch replanted in exile in Ezek 17. In Jer 24, the other image of "figs" is applied to the Israelite people as well (cf. Hos 9:10). In Jotham's Fable (Judg 9) the vine immediately follows the conversation with the fig tree, and the two images appear in love poetry as well (Song 2:13). In positive form, sitting with one's vine and fig tree is used often enough to suggest a theme of peace, as in 1 Kgs 4:25 [5:5], "During Solomon's lifetime Judah and Israel lived in safety, from Dan even to Beer-sheba, all of them under their vines and fig trees" (cf. Joel 2:22; Zech 3:10; 8:12; in LXX, 1 Macc 14:12).

Perhaps most significantly, however, the promise of a "vine and fig tree" was proposed to the surrendering Israelites as a benefit of Assyrian occupation in the Rabshakeh's speech: "Then every one of you will eat from your own vine and your own fig tree, and drink water from your own cistern" (2 Kgs 18:31// Isa 36:16). Conversely, the absence of the vine and fig tree reflects the theme of punishment (Ps 105:33; Isa 34:4; Jer 5:17; Hos 2:12 [14]; cf. 9:10; Joel 1:7). Hence here is an unavoidable hint that Micah may be directly citing the Rabshakeh's promise—and thus may indicate that *Micah proposes to accept the offer!* According to 2 Kgs 18:13–16, Hezekiah does just that, and history's judgment may well be that it was the wiser choice, avoiding massive suffering for his people. Zedekiah, in Jeremiah's day, did not accept terms of surrender, and Jerusalem paid a horrific price. Notice that the more nationalist, pro-Davidic Isaiah text entirely omits Hezekiah's payment to Sennacherib. To accuse all calls for negotiation to prevent war to be "selling out," "unpatriotic," or "appeasement" is the counsel of fools (or military contractors). The classic doctrine of the "just war" demands that *all* other means to settle dispute must be pursued prior to conflict—an aspect of that ancient concept typically forgotten or ignored.

To "tremble" (*ḥārad*, Mic 4:4) is often used of people's "fear" before God (Exod 19:16; 1 Sam 4:13; Isa 66:2, 5; and later, in Ezra 9:4; 10:3, where Blenkinsopp cleverly refers to postexilic "quakers" [1988, 178]). More often, the term is used of the terror of warfare. Thus it can be used of "panic" among enemy soldiers or cities under threat (Judg 8:12; 1 Sam 14:15; 2 Sam 17:2; Ezek 30:9; Isa 19:16, of God's miraculous warfare; cf. Isa 41:5; Amos 3:6; Zech 1:21 [2:4]). In 1 Sam 16:4, the people of Bethlehem are "trembling" and asking if Samuel comes in peace (cf. 1 Sam 21:1 [2]). All the more important, then, is the theme of peacefulness described as a state where there is no such terror, and no one will make them afraid, as in Lev 26:6, "And I will grant peace in the land, and you shall lie down, and no one shall make you afraid; I will remove dangerous animals from the land, and no sword shall go through your land" (cf. Job 11:19; Jer 30:10 and 46:27; Ezek 34:28; 39:26; Zeph 3:13).

The idea that "the LORD . . . has spoken" (4:4 NRSV), a phrase referring to the power of God, or the notion that a thing is determined because of God's "stamp of approval," is common, beginning with the law itself (Exod 19:8; Lev 10:11; Num 15:22). The prophets appeal to their authority based on what "God has spoken" (Isa 1:2; 21:17; 22:25; 24:3; 25:8; Jer 23:35; 27:13; 48:8, Joel 3:8 [4:8]; Amos 3:1; Obad 18; Ezekiel speaks against the false use of this claim in 22:28). In the context of the trial theme in Mic 1 and 6, another legal statement from God as authority fits well in this context.

Here, where Micah is declaring his opposition to the violence of warfare and its devastating economic implications for his fellow farmers, this is the one and only place Micah chooses to use the appellation "YHWH Sabaoth" (ṣĕbāʾôt), "YHWH of Armies," used so heavily in Isaiah and other prophets.[40]

[5] Micah refers to acting "in the name" of a deity. That the phrase can refer to authority is suggested by representatives who speak "in the name of David" (1 Sam 25:9; cf. Esth 8:8). In reference to the authority of God, the phrase occurs occasionally. Deuteronomy mentions Levites ministering "in the name" of God (18:7) and later speaks of prophets speaking "in the name" of God, or of other gods (Deut 18:20, 22; cf. 1 Chr 21:19; Jer 26:9, 20; Zech 13:3; cf. Matt 23:39; Luke 21:8); and 1 Kgs 18:32 refers to building an altar "in the name of the LORD" (cf. Ps 20:5). Of the authority to speak "in the name of God" or "the LORD," see 2 Kgs 2:24 (cf. Pss 118:10; 124:8). Finally, Neh 13:25 contains the phrase in the context of an oath.

Does this presume some kind of *affirmation* of peoples walking in the name of their gods? If so, this would be unprecedented (contra Deut 18:20, 22), and it seems unlikely.[41] More likely, it is an identification of the current state of the world and a further reassurance of God's presence as something that leads to the peace spoken of in the passage as a whole. On the other hand, Mic 4:3 speaks of negotiations between nations and says nothing of a mass "conversion" to the ways of God. That these other nations continue to walk in their own ways but not threaten Israel is a hopeful image.

Utzschneider also wants to insist, with others, that v. 5 is not a description of some kind of universal "conversion" of the people (2005, 93). McKane comments on the significance of v. 5 in Micah's version: it was used to "calm the

---

40. Andersen and Freedman (2000, 410–13) continue their insistence on the military meaning of 4:1–5 by arguing that an association with Ps 2 suggests Israel's dominance of the world. I insist that ideology can drive the choice of "comparable passages" and again ask, Why not cite Zech 8?

41. Nevertheless, note Wagenaar 2001, 141, "The difference in conduct of Israel and the peoples, nevertheless, seems to warrant a concessive interpretation."

flames" of vv. 1–4. Thus, he reasons, v. 5 was added "by someone who was skeptical about the description of the ideal future which it contained, or even viewed it with hostility, and who contrasted the utopian portrayal with the realities of the present which contradict it" (1998, 126).

As for the theme of "walking," Schultz has noticed a functional similarity in the placement of the swords-into-plowshares imagery in both the Micah and Isaiah contexts. Both follow negative judgments and end with different thoughts, which nonetheless refer to "walking":[42] Isaiah has an invitation to "walk in the light of YHWH" and Micah contains a reference to Israel walking with their God while other nations follow their own paths (1999, 296–97). Again, we are reminded of Micah's call to "walk" in the ways of God at 6:7–8.

Furthermore, affirmation that God will reign "forever and ever" derives from the law (Exod 15:18; cf. Pss 45:6, 17; 48:14; 145:1–2; etc.). Sometimes the reign of God is associated with absence of other nations (Pss 9:5; 10:16). Prophets promise God's blessings and presence "forever and ever" (Jer 7:7; Dan 7:18). The phrase appears to become increasingly popular in late Judaism and early Christianity, especially as an assertion of the power and dominion of God, and thus with political overtones, likely in contrast to the claims of eternity in common imperial propaganda[43] (so 1 Esd 8:85; 4 Macc 18:24; Tob 13:17; and heavily in the Epistles: Gal 1:5; Eph 3:21; Phil 4:20; 1 Tim 1:17; Heb 1:8; 1 Pet 4:11; 5:11; and in Rev 1:6, 18; 4:9, 10; 5:13; 7:12). In sum, the "eternal" reign of God can be interpreted tyrannically (the humiliation or destruction of enemies), or as the rule of a liberating and compassionate ruler (e.g., Ezek 34).

Wagenaar states that Mic 4:5 is a "liturgical" element (cf. Isa 2:5), suggesting a congregational response. He argues that this entire sequence is a late addition to Micah and Isaiah (2001, 263). Just as assertive, however, is Willis's arguments that this famous passage, if removed from Isaiah and Micah and placed in the Psalms, would pass as a Zion Psalm. Thus he aligns with opinions that this is an older motif cited by the actual prophets Isaiah or Micah (1997).

Excursus 5: The Peace Passage: Reading Micah 4:1–5 in "Contexts"

Modern Context

Micah 4:1–5 is quite possibly the most dramatic antiwar sentiment expressed in the entire Hebrew Bible. The ramifications of establishing what is intended here can be

---

42. The metaphor of "walking" (i.e., a way of living) is a theme linking the whole of Micah, not only in the famous peace passage here but also in commands to not "walk exaltedly" in 2:3 and to walk mindfully in 6:8 ("humbly" in NRSV).

43. So Nebuchadnezzar II, "may my offspring rule forever . . ." (*ANET*, 307).

seen not only in understanding later rabbinic antiwar sentiments (e.g., Rabbi Yoḥanan ben Zakkai's opposition to the Jewish Revolt of 66–70 C.E.; see Neusner 1962, 104–28; cf. Genot-Bismuth 1980; Eisen 2011, 65–110) but also Christian pacifist sentiments as well (Yoder 1994). The debate over a scriptural "basis" for a faithful opposition to human lethal violence is one of the most central ethical debates in Christian history. Thus it seems hardly surprising to discover that if anyone should take Mic 4:1–5 too seriously, if hammers of peace actually start striking on the anvils of weaponry, the mood can turn decidedly ugly. Having a clear sense of this famous passage, then, can be serious business indeed. It is hard to deny that reading this passage "in context" begins by considering modern contexts. But what "contexts" are we speaking of? Surely we must consider modern contexts as well as ancient contexts: both of them can deeply color our views of the meaning of this passage. The passage plays heavily in modern political debate.

For example, when defending his unprecedented peacetime military buildup in the final quarter of the twentieth century, President Ronald Reagan glibly dismissed this biblical passage as having no moral force—indeed, calling it "weakness." "'We have tried turning our swords into plowshares, hoping others would follow,' the President said, referring to the biblical dictum for peace. 'Well, our days of weakness are over. Our military forces are back on their feet and standing tall'" ("Military of U.S. 'Standing Tall,' Reagan Asserts," *New York Times*, December 13, 1983, A1).

The Reagan-era military buildup, however, faced serious opposition in using the very same passage! Among the most striking modern "contexts" for understanding this passage is that provided by the Catholic activists Philip and Fr. Daniel Berrigan, S.J. These two, along with six compatriots, nonviolently trespassed onto the grounds of the General Electric Nuclear Missile construction buildings in King of Prussia, Pennsylvania. While there, they took hammers to nuclear warhead nose cones and poured blood onto documents and files, attempting, in their own words, to fulfill the words of the prophecy about turning swords into plowshares. The action riveted the attention of the nation, especially given the religious convictions of the members of the so-called Plowshares 8 (W. Robbins, "Trial of Berrigans and 6 Recalls Antiwar Activism of 60's," *NYT*, February 27, 1981, A10; idem, "Judge Bars 4 Defense Witnesses in Berrigan's Trial," *NYT*, March 5, 1981, A18; idem, "Berrigans and Six Are Convicted in Attack on Missiles," *NYT*, March 7, 1981, 9; see sympathetic commentary on the case by R. J. Lifton, "Norristown, Pa., 1981: The Plowshares 8," *NYT*, March 28, 1981, 23).

The famous passage became equally controversial in Germany in the same decade: Christian activists from both sides of the Berlin Wall used the passage as their motto of opposition to preparations for war on both sides! Buttons featuring "swords into plowshares" became an unofficial insignia of the East German movement (John Tagliabue, "4,000 East Germans Dispute Official Defense Policy," *NYT*, February 15, 1982, A3; idem, "East Germany Sizes Up Its Antimilitarist Groups," *NYT*, July 6, 1982, A2, reporting that the badges "have become fashionable"). Soon it was reported that East German government officials were becoming irritated with the ubiquity of the swords/plowshares motif; Klaus Gysi, the East German State Secretary for Church Affairs, was quoted as saying that the badges with their "swords/plowshares" motif "were being misused and were undermining military service in East Germany" ("East German Pastors Protest Ban on Pacifist Badges," *NYT*, April 12, 1982, A3).

Modern "contexts" clearly raise more questions than answers about the original sentiment intended by this famous passage. But it soon becomes clear that debates about the ancient "context" are equally partisan! How one constructs a "context" by citing other biblical texts is often a measure of one's political sympathies.

Ancient Context

In his work on verbal parallels in the prophetic literature, Schultz observes that Isa 2 and Mic 4 constitute "the most extensive verbal parallel within the prophetic corpus" (1999, 290) and that 51 of the 61 words in Isa 2:2–4 are paralleled in Mic 4:1–3. It is virtually impossible to analyze either occasion of this passage without referring to the parallel passage. Yet lengthy reviews have not resulted in a consensus view of the relationship of the two passages. Modern commentaries routinely refer with gratitude to the detailed analysis in Wildberger's (1991) and McKane's (1998) commentaries, which helpfully summarize much of the history of commentary on the famous passages and their possible relationship. In these two passages, the arguments about the source of the imagery can be categorized as follows:

1. Isaiah borrows from Micah.
2. Micah borrows from Isaiah.
3. Both cite a previous author.
4. Both cite a well-known aphorism or proverb, which would neatly explain why Joel (3:10 [4:10]) chooses to reverse it while not requiring that the writer of Joel be familiar with its use in Isaiah or Micah.
5. It is a later insertion in both locations, whose *Sitz im Leben* is to be located in the postexilic period and influenced by the more "universalist" ethos of Deutero-Isaiah or even Zech 8:20–23 (Sweeney 2001b).

However, does the comparison with Isa 2 overly determine the reading strategies for Mic 4? Sweeney, for example, believes that Mic 4 and Isa 2 are both based on a "liturgical composition" of the postexilic period, originally written in the context of rebuilding the temple circa 520 B.C.E. (2000, 377). The Isaiah context of the peace sentiment follows punishment (as suggested by Isa 2:6–22) and invites the audience to join the other nations in recognizing the sovereignty of God on Zion. The Micah context, however, includes the thought that the nations remain separate in identity and even religion (4:5) but is also to be read in a context, according to Sweeney (378), pointing to "the role of the Davidic king in punishing the nations that have oppressed Israel (Mic 5:1–8), and . . . describing Yahweh's destruction of weapons and idols of the nations (Mic. 5:9–14)." Sweeney then argues that the Isaiah context presents the pilgrimage to Zion as a direct result of the nations' desires for peace. In contrast, the Micah context, he argues, emphasizes YHWH's sovereignty, suggesting that God's role is assertive and forceful in bringing about the world peace that is envisioned (380).

Is Micah more militant toward "the nations" than Isaiah, as Uffenheimer argues (1984, 7–21)? There is a strong tradition of interpretation that constructs an ancient "context" in such a way that it *denies that either passage—Isa 2 or Mic 4—is really about peace at all*. It may be positive for the Judeans, so this view states, but it really describes the military defeat of all Judah's enemies. This interpretation, however, is typically based on comparing the peace passage with other *Isaiah* texts rather than Micah texts, as well as based on selecting the most *negative* and violent themed passages on the procession of nations, all the while dismissing the peaceful procession passages that could have also been cited. So, argues Hobbs, any peacefulness to be found in any other comparative prophetic text must be toned down by the *overwhelmingly "violent nature" of the Isaiah passages* (1989, 221). However, it is clear that privileging the violent images and the more violent texts in such comparative analyses means that the imagery of "beating swords into plowshares" becomes subsumed under the supposed "normative violence" of other Hebrew texts. Despite the common accusation that only peaceniks tend to read this passage as proposing a policy of peace, it is entirely clear that part of the force of using carefully selected "comparative texts" is driven by the ideologies of the interpreter: one can find comparative texts to back up one's inclination, peaceful *or* violent! A great deal depends on the texts one selects to "compare" with either Isa 2:2–4 (or 2–5) or Mic 4:1–5. If Isaiah's context is different from Micah's, perhaps we ought to read Mic 4:1–5 primarily in the context of Micah, because reading this passage in the wider context of Micah significantly changes the potential relationship between 3:12 and the "peace vision" of Mic 4. Let us set aside the problem of whether Mic 4:1–3 is an intrusion into the book, such as the objection that 4:1–3 flatly contradicts 3:12 (which I do not accept). Micah 3:12, however, is not the only significant passage in the context of Mic 4.

Micah 4:1–3, read in conjunction with vv. 4–5, suggests a strong sentiment of peace. For example, McKane's discussion of the interpretive tradition surrounding v. 5 and its relation to the previous material is instructive. Rudolph, he notes, believes that v. 5 *contradicts* vv. 1–4—the heathen nations will not receive instruction in Zion. So McKane: "The division between Israel and the nations, between idolatry and true religion, is eternal" (1998, 120). He observes: "Verse 5 . . . is a rejoinder to Mic. 4:1–4 by someone who was skeptical about the description of the ideal future which it contained, or even viewed it with hostility, and who contrasted the Utopian portrayal with the realities of the present which contradicted it" (1998, 126).

Wolff, on the other hand, viewed v. 5 not as a contradiction but as a "cool appreciation of the nature of the present" (1990, 121). Hillers believed v. 5 to be a congregational response to vv. 1–4, not a contradiction of it (1984, 50–52). Limburg, similar to Brueggemann's recent suggestions, is more sanguine about the final verses of Isa 2:2–4 and Mic 4:5—*both* refer to "walking" in the way of YHWH, and thus the presentation of peace is concluded by calls to act in such a way that the vision is actualized: "The hearers will be challenged to work for the realization of that vision, to 'walk' toward it" (1988, 181). Clearly, there are strong voices on both sides of the issue of whether Mic 4:5 contradicts, or agrees with, the peaceful-sounding sentiments in Mic 4.

What about going beyond vv. 4–5 to achieve a wider "context"? Clearly this also depends on *which* passages in Micah one chooses as a "context" for "properly reading" 4:1–3. Continuing to read the passage from v. 1 to v. 10 does not significantly change the impression of a peaceful sentiment. However, if one insists that 4:11–13 provide

The Peace Passage: Reading Micah 4:1–5 in "Contexts"

an additional clarification of vv. 1–3, then the sentiment is clearly far less peaceful and can thus be read in the context of Israel's dominance. If one can argue that the whole of Mic 4 forms a conceptual whole, then the peaceful interpretation may be in trouble. But not according to all readers of Micah. Many accept van der Woude's arguments that the last few verses are actually *the words of Micah's nationalist opponents* (1969, 248–51). Furthermore, Wolff claims that the "war" envisioned in vv. 11–13 is not actual warfare but God's miraculous intervention, not a significant departure from the sentiment of vv. 1–5 (1990, 119–23).

Sweeney's analysis of Mic 4 further highlights the problem and reaches beyond 4:1–3 for "essential" contexts: "The syntactical joins (*sic*) at Mic 4:1 and Mic 5:1 [5:2 NRSV] bind the material in Mic 3:1–5:14 [3:1–5:15 NRSV] together" (2001a, 367). Quite interesting, however, is the following sentence: "The call to attention in Mic 6:1 marks the beginning of an entirely *new* unit within the book of Micah," and thus chapters 6–7 are eliminated from Micah's interpretive "context." In this case, Mic 4:1–3 is read by Sweeney as part and parcel of a "Micah-inspired hope" (in Mic 3–5 as a whole) that "a new monarch in Israel from Bethlehem signals the restoration of (presumably) Davidic kingship and an era of peace and security for Israel" (368). Yet Miscall objects, stating that the royal era is not an era of a *human* king (1993, 26). How much wider can the search for a proper context expand?

Moving beyond Micah

What if one moves the borders of an "essential context" even more widely? Recent work on Mic 4:1–5 raises the stakes yet again by insisting on a reading within the context of the entire collection of the Twelve Prophets as a unitary literary product. Consider Sweeney's work on the context of Micah *among the Twelve Prophets*, finally redacted as a literary unit. Given the work on the Twelve Prophets as a literary whole, the Micah passage can also be read in the context of other prophetic writings, and this brings us to the problem of relating Mic 4:1–3 to the famous "contrary passage" in Joel 3:10 (4:10 MT).

Limburg argues that Joel 3:10, even if chronologically later than Mic 4 and Isa 2, should not be construed as an intentional reversal of Mic 4 and Isa 2. Instead, Joel 3 (4) should be viewed as the example of a long-established tradition of a call to arms, which Limburg compares to texts such as Jer 46:3–4; 51:11; and Isa 21:5. The Joel passage, therefore, may be in a work that is later than either Micah or Isaiah but actually reflects a much-older sentiment, as Limburg argues: "Such calls are indeed ancient, and this one could have been passed on for centuries until it found written expression in Joel. This would mean that the promise that one day nations would 'beat their swords into plowshares' would be a reversal of a well-known wartime slogan" (1988, 182).

McKane similarly argues that the Joel passage is part of a "declaration of war, a call to arms and rearmament, to a switch of production and a refashioning of ploughshares into swords and pruning-hooks into spears . . . it is likely that the author of Mic. 4:3 (Isa. 2:4) had this in mind and that it triggered his description of the reverse process of disarmament as a prelude to universal peace" (1998, 124).

Let us set aside for the moment Wolff's important argument (1992) that Joel 3:10 is *not* a contrary, and thus more violent, sentiment in intentional contrast to Mic 4:1–3, and presume that it is. One might then argue, in agreement with Sweeney, that Joel 3:10 knows Mic 4//Isa 2, but that the writer of Joel believes that, quoting Sweeney, "this is clearly no time for peace, but a time for war" (2001a, 182). Here is a direct example of how widening the contextual borders to the Twelve Prophets as a whole changes the equation yet again—for why would Joel *reverse* the imagery in a context of promoting or announcing warfare, if the imagery in Mic 4 *was already understood as a violent image*? Would it not make more sense to argue that the writer of Joel 3:10 wants to reverse the imagery precisely because the writer of Joel appears to disagree with a *peaceful sentiment* in Mic 4 and/or Isa 2, and thus wishes to express a more belligerent image? In short, we are back to a *peaceful* interpretation of Mic 4:1–3.

My point is this: one starts with an apparent peaceful sentiment in reading Mic 4:1–3 in isolation. Next one adds passages "in the context" of Micah, which can suggest that the sentiment is not peaceful at all. Then, if one reads wider in Micah (e.g., beyond ch. 4), it seems possible that the peaceful sentiment is consistent with Micah's suspicions of Jerusalem and forced preparations for war. Once again, however, if one goes even further and adds Joel to the relevant "context," we seem to be back to a conclusion that Mic 4:1–3 *was* perceived as peaceful after all, and indeed, *too* peaceful for the later writer of Joel 3:10; otherwise, why "reverse" it? Is there a way to read passages in an appropriate methodologically determined "context" that is not a suspicious attempt to use carefully selected "contextual passages" to push the reader toward a specific reading?

Wagenaar, who has extensively reviewed the German-language debates about the use (and suggested reversals) of the *Volkerkampf* and *Volkerwallfahrt* themes, concludes: "Both the peaceful pilgrimage of the nations and the conversion of their arms into agricultural tools in the *Volkerwallfahrt* in Mic 4:1–3//Isa 2:2–4 constitute the reversal of the *Volkerkampf* motif from the hymns of Zion in Pss 46:5–7 + 10; 48:4–6; 76:3–7 and the prophecies of Joel 4:1–3 [3:1–3 NRSV]; 4:9–12 [3:9–11]; Mic 4:11–13; Zech 12:2–9; 14:1–3; 14:12–15" (2001, 267).

Thus far in this commentary, I have highlighted the textual evidence of a profound critique of Jerusalem's military policies in Micah—an *agrarian antiwar motif*. Micah contains a critique of Jerusalem's military policies as destructive to outlying lowlanders and villagers such as Micah's Moresheth and its neighbors in the Shephelah. If Micah is understood to be *serious* about beating swords into plowshares—resisting the constant mustering of war because it is seen as yet another example of how the wealthy elite "eat the poor" and cheat them of their livelihood—then not only does Mic 4:1–5 fit within a wider, more radical social message of the book as a whole; it also presents a challenge to the constant appeal to Isaiah as the only relevant text simply because of the parallel use of words. Jeremiah presents a more dramatic "parallel" because this later prophet's social and religious opposition to military resistance against Babylon more fully represents a social criticism of the elite very similar to what we have found in Micah. The fact that Micah is actually *cited* in the book of Jeremiah to support Jeremiah's preaching is even more indicative of a perceived similarity of their messages! Beating swords into plowshares, when read as part of a bitter sociopolitical agenda against the Jerusalem elite, no longer remains in the realm of "utopian sentiments" and is restored to its proper place within a "People's History" of Judah, representing some of the sentiments of the subordinated classes as revealed in their spokespersons, such as Micah and later Jeremiah.

Building a New Society out of Crisis

What is clear in our reading of Micah, however, is that the imagery of the peaceful sentiments is critically important: weapons turned into farming tools, reflecting the protests of Judah's agricultural sector. In the words of the early twenty-first-century American movement, "Farms Not Arms"! By transforming our reading of Mic 4:1–5 from a "pacifist sentiment" (which it is not) to an agrarian antiwar protest (which it is), we restore the angry voice to Micah the Moresheti and further come to realize that there were other perspectives in Judah, especially those different from the royalist/nationalist voice of Isaiah of Jerusalem!

Micah 4:6–10 Building a New Society out of Crisis

6 In that day, YHWH says,
    I will bring together the lame;[a]
the ones who were cast out I will gather up,
    those whom I afflicted with evil.[b]
7 I will establish the lame as a remnant,
    the cast-off as a mighty nation.
And YHWH[c] will reign over them,
    on the Mountain of Zion,
    from now and forever more.
8 And you, Tower of the Flock,[d]
    Mound of the daughter[e] of Zion,[f]
To you shall come the former dominion,
    Sovereignty[g] to the daughter of Jerusalem.[h]
9 Now,[i] why do you cry out?[j]
    Is there no king with you?[k]
Has your counselor[l] perished,
    because severe anguish has seized you,
like a woman in labor?
10 Writhe and burst forth, daughter of Zion,
    as a woman giving birth,
because you shall go out of a city,
    and dwell in the field;
    you will be brought into[m] Babylon.[n]
There you will be delivered;
    there YHWH will redeem[o] you,
    from the hand of your enemies!

    a. "One who limps," writes Hillers (1984, 54), comparing Zeph 3:19.
    b. The verb is $rā'a'$, meaning "harmed" or "afflicted"; cf. Num 16:15. Wolff reads "harshly treated" (1990, 112).
    c. Hillers (1984, 54) rejects changing this to a first-person reference rather than a third-person reference to "Yahweh." Wolff (1990, 115) argues that the third person in

the final lines of this verse suggests an addition. McKane concurs, calling the addition a "liturgical response" (1998, 130).

d. Some transliterate the Hebrew in the translation, presuming a specific place-name: *migdal-ʿēder*.

e. "Daughter" is omitted by many commentators.

f. Sweeney (2001a, 383) has a complex theory concerning the significance of *migdal-ʿēder* in reference to the Jacob traditions. True, the "lame" or "limp" in v. 6 was related by Wolff (1990, 123) to Jacob (Gen 32:31 [32]). It may be a stretch, however, to suggest that these place-names are intended to "suggest" the Jacob stories in much the same way that the Bethlehem references are to "suggest" David.

g. Jones (1995, 103–4) notes that the LXX inserts "from Babylon" here, most likely influenced by 4:10. Perhaps the LXX translator understood v. 8 to be a promise of a return.

h. Wolff (1990, 125) and others have wondered whether the image suggests flocks grazing in the vicinity of the destroyed Jerusalem after 587 B.C.E.

i. Sweeney (2001a, 383–85) and others notice the contrast between passages that indicate a "now" time (*ʿattâ*, 4:9, 11; 5:1 [4:14]), as opposed to those indicating a future time ("it will come to pass," *wĕhāhâ*, 5:5, 7, 10 [4, 6, 9]).

j. The verb *rûaʿ*. Runions (2001, 242) observes that the term is usually a depiction of military and jubilation cries and does not normally have a connotation of panic or pain. Birth cries are often read negatively, however, but this is not required by the use of the term (cf. Num 10:7; etc.).

k. Hillers (1984, 58–59) wonders if this is to be read as a taunt (they do have a king), but Micah is taunting them by asking them why they act like they do not have one. Others read that God is intended to be the king implied here (cf. Jer 8:19).

l. McKane (1998, 139) wants to read plural, "counselors," which would require a mere *yod* before the final *kaph*.

m. Runions (2001, 244) points out that the term is not "from" Babylon but "in" Babylon—suggesting that the deliverance will take place there.

n. Babylon is usually taken as a sign of a later insertion; so Hillers 1984, 59. Rudolph (1975, 87) suggests that originally the reference was to Assyria. McKane (1998, 136) points out that if Babylon is removed, the passage as a whole could well refer to the siege of 701 B.C.E. Allen (1976, 246), however, disagrees that a reference to Babylon must be a sixth-century reference, citing 2 Kgs 17:24; 20:12–18 in reference to Hezekiah's reception of Merodach Baladan. Thus references to Babylon could well be in Micah's traditional late eighth-century period.

o. Here *gāʾal*, "to redeem"; Mays (1976, 106) points out the prominence of this term in Deutero-Isaiah, further suggesting a later insertion in combination with the reference to Babylon.

[6] The passage begins with two set phrases, "in that day" (*bayyôm hahûʾ*) and "YHWH says" (*nĕʾum-yhwh*), which contrast sharply to indications of "now" in vv. 4, 9, 11; 5:1 [4:14]. Beginning with the time reference "that day" might suggest that the writer wishes to continue describing the "future time" announced at the beginning of the previous passage (4:1). This is possible, but

there are a number of time indicators in this passage, and these are often seen as either editorial markers of additions to the text (see, famously, a comparative text in the whole of Isa 19, with many such suggested alternative time markers in the prose additions toward the end) or, at least, separate ideas being added one upon the other.

Micah has already spoken of God's "gathering" of the survivors (2:12). Yet this particular manner of speaking, referring to the "lame" and "outcast," is a theme found elsewhere, notably in Zeph 3:19 ("I will deal with all your oppressors at that time. And I will save the lame and gather the outcast, and I will change their shame into praise and renown in all the earth"). "The lame" (*haṣṣōlēʿâ*) can refer to those who are afflicted or suffer a setback (Ps 35:15; Jer 20:10; see Olyan 2008 on "disability" in the Hebrew Bible). A few try to draw some connections to the Jacob tradition (Gen 32:31 [32], "limping"). Wolff (1990, 123) wonders if the community addressed by passages in Micah somehow emotionally or spiritually identifies with the "wound" of Jacob (at this stage, however, Wolff presumes an address to the later Babylonian exilic community because of the references to Babylon).

God's actions in "gathering" can either be fearful, as in "gathering the nations" to punish Israel (Zech 14:2) or, in later use, a gathering of the people of Israel after dispersal, thus Isa 11:12: "He will raise a signal for the nations, and will assemble the outcasts of Israel, and gather the dispersed of Judah from the four corners of the earth" (cf. Isa 49:5; Ezek 11:17; Jer 32:37).[44]

Excursus 6: The "Lame" in the Greek Version

The LXX's translation of the "lame" goes further than the Hebrew, using "broken/ crushed" (*syntribō*). The term has a strong military association, like the "shattering" of trees (Exod 9:25); God is a "shattering" warrior (Exod 15:3) who thus "shatters" the adversaries (15:7; cf. 1 Macc 3:22, 23; Ps 10:15 [9:36 LXX]); God "shatters" doors of bronze (Ps 107 [106 LXX]:16; Amos 1:5). Against enemies, national and otherwise, see Nah 1:13; Isa 10:33; ch. 14; Jer 28:2. Of defeat, see Ezek 6:4, 6; specifically of Jerusalem's defeat by Babylon, see Ezek 26:2; etc.). Deuteronomy speaks of "shattering" idols (7:5); likewise the Babylonian idols are "shattered" on the ground (Isa 21:9); as a curse for defeat, see Jer 17:18, "Destroy them with double destruction!" Psalm 105 (104 LXX):33 states that God, in the plagues against Egypt, "shattered the trees of their country." But in rich irony, God's peace "shatters" weapons (Ps 46:9 [46:10 MT; 45:10 LXX]; cf. Ps 76:3 [76:4 MT; 75:4 LXX]); Hos 2:18 (20 LXX, MT) speaks of an age of peace when God declares, "I will abolish [lit., "shatter"] the bow, the sword, and war from the land." Finally, in a manner reminiscent of the Islamic concept of the "inward Jihad," the term can be turned inward, describing the "shattered" spirit/heart (Ps 51:17

---

44. The term for "gather" here suggests a military muster, perhaps gathering up remnants of defeated armies (cf. Andersen and Freedman 2000, 433).

[19 MT; 50:19 LXX]; Isa 57:15; 66:2). This theme is picked up in later Hellenistic literature, as in the Prayer of Azariah 16–17a: "Yet with a contrite heart and a humble spirit may we be accepted, as though it were with burnt offerings of rams and bulls."

It seems, then, that Mic 4:6 LXX makes the connection between defeat and God's "punishment" of the Hebrew peoples, a theme quite central to the postexilic penitential prayer traditions of Dan 9; Ezra 9; Neh 9; and Baruch. In short, *we* are the "lame"—and given the Greek associations with destruction in war, we can appropriately call up the image of disabled veterans of previous conflicts.

In Mic 4:6, the term for "stray" (*nādaḥ*) can be used in a number of different contexts, such as of "straying" animals (Deut 22:1), but also those "strewed" abroad, such as "outcasts" in Isa 16:3, even those cast out by God, as in exile: Deut 30:1, 4. Notice Ps 147:2, "YHWH builds up Jerusalem; he gathers the outcasts of Israel" (cf. Isa 56:8; Jer 8:3; 16:15; 23:2). See also Jer 30:17, "For I will restore health to you, . . . because they have called you an outcast" (cf. Isa 11:12; see "banished" in 2 Sam 14:13; 2 Chr 13:9; Neh 1:9).

The phrase referring to people being "treated harshly" harkens back to the exodus event (Exod 5:22–23; Num 20:15; Deut 26:6). Even God admits to "treating harshly" in Zech 8:14, and Moses complains to God about being "treated harshly" (Num 11:11). But Deuteronomy also speaks of treating the poor "harshly" (15:9, 10), suggesting that such action emulates the Egyptian mistreatment of the Israelite slaves. However, Wagenaar proposes that this phrase does not read "evil," that is, "affliction" from God, but rather God's shepherding, "so that I may shepherd them," citing Jer 25:6, 29; 31:38; Zeph 1:12; Zech 8:14 (2001, 144). A major question is whether Micah the prophet ever offers such words of hope for a regathering of the defeated. Andersen and Freedman protest the frequent resort to postexilic dating of these sentiments: "Micah was concerned for the victims of the eighth-century wars, of which he was a witness. It is arbitrary, indeed dogmatic, to assert that he had no message of hope for them" (2000, 435).

To refer to a gathering of the lame, a restoration of the afflicted, is once again an opportunity to consider the different possibilities for reading this passage. Recent work in biblical studies has focused on the imagery of the "disabled" in dialogue with "disability studies" (e.g., Avalos, Melcher, and Schipper 2007; Moss and Schipper 2011; Yong 2011). Melcher, for example, identifies the restoration of the lame and the outcasts as a theme seen in a few late prophetic texts (Jer 31:8; Zeph 3:19; Melcher 2007, 122–23; cf. Yong 2011, 134, who specifically notes the Micah reference). Certainly the imagery is read in these prophetic texts as a promise of restoration for the community as a whole: those who previously suffered (under Assyrian and/or Babylonian domination) will be restored to some semblance of power or independence. On the other hand, the "lame," those who are injured, could just as easily be read as those who have suffered *at the hands of fellow Judeans*. If this is the case, then gathering a community of

Building a New Society out of Crisis

the lame is tantamount to proclaiming a new community, built from the rejected of the previous community (cf. Matt 11:5//Luke 7:22; Matt 21:14), those who suffered under the privileged and the powerful. In short, it is important to be cautious about reading Micah as invariably restoring the previous elite to power (or their sons), when he otherwise attacks and criticizes their unjust behavior so severely. This is an especially dangerous reading strategy if the "lame" indeed refer to the injured and disabled *veterans of warfare*, those who have suffered from previous musterings for wars, especially if they cannot now fully engage in the farming that is so central to Micah's notion of well-being and justice.

[7] The notion of the surviving "remnant" is a biblical concept that has inspired a significant secondary literature, beginning especially with the initial work of Gerhard F. Hasel (1974). However, read from a social perspective, the most obvious setting for a "remnant" concept would be among survivors of disaster; if located in Micah's time, that would involve the Assyrian invasions, but if due to a later editing, would clearly allude to Babylonian devastation and exile in the early sixth century B.C.E.

The "first" occasion (canonically, not chronologically) for the use of the concept of "remnant" is itself most likely a product of the Babylonian exile, contained as it is in the edited story of Joseph, who declares, "God sent me before you to preserve for you a remnant on earth, and to keep alive for you many survivors" (Gen 45:7). The concept is particularly evident in the theology associated with the book of Isaiah (yet cf. Amos 5:15; and in the later generation of prophetic works such as Jeremiah and Ezekiel). This is acknowledged also in the parts of the Isaiah tradition appearing in the historical works: 2 Kgs 19:31//Isa 37:32, "For from Jerusalem a remnant shall go out, and from Mount Zion a band of survivors. The zeal of YHWH of hosts will do this." Also, see Jer 23:3, "Then I myself will gather the remnant of my flock out of all the lands where I have driven them, and I will bring them back to their fold, and they shall be fruitful and multiply" (cf. 31:7). The concept was particularly used to refer to the group left behind with Gedaliah (Jer 40:11, 15; 42:2); many texts refer to "remnant of Judah/Israel/the people" (e.g., Jer 42:15, 19; 43:5; 44:7, 12, 14; Ezek 11:13; Zeph 2:9; 3:13; Hag 1:12, 14; Zech 8:6, 11, 12). In any case, any talk of a "remnant" either means the totality of those who are left alive, or the "genuine" or "righteous" portion of those among the people. The latter suggests partisan conflicts about the nature of the true community. Micah has already shown himself to be such a partisan!

The concept of a "mighty" or "strong" (*'āṣûm*) nation draws heavily from Deuteronomic tradition. The same notion appears when God threatens to destroy the Israelites and make a "mighty nation" from some other group (Deut 9:14). Deuteronomy 26:5 repeats God's *previous* promise that Israel would become a "mighty nation," a status threatened by Israel's own sin. Consequently the late portions of Isaiah pick up on God's postexilic promise to revive a "mighty nation" in terms quite reminiscent of Micah, but here the promise is to the "little" (*qāṭōn*) and the "insignificant" (*ṣāʿîr*): "The least of them shall become a clan, and the smallest one a mighty nation; I am YHWH; in its time I will accomplish it quickly" (Isa 60:22). That the adjective (*ʿāṣûm*) is often associated with military strength is clear from Joel 1:6 and 2:5.

God, of course, is frequently praised as "king" (e.g., Ps 95:3), a king that will reign "forever" (Jer 10:10; Ps 9:7; cf. Ps 10:16). Once again, it appears that uses of the term "forever" may be drawn from political propaganda; thus Micah (and others who proclaim God as king over any human) contrasts this with the claims of imperial rulers.

Not only the frequency of the term "Zion" but also references to "forever," as in the full form in Micah ("from now and forevermore"), logically belong to the tradition of singing and praise:

> Blessed be the name of YHWH
>   from this time on and forevermore.
>   (Ps 113:2)

> But we will bless YHWH
>   from this time on and forevermore.
> Praise YHWH!
>   (115:18)

> YHWH will keep your going out and your coming in
>   from this time on and forevermore.
>   (121:8)

> As the mountains surround Jerusalem,
>   so YHWH surrounds his people,
>   from this time on and forevermore.
>   (125:2)

> O Israel, hope in YHWH
>   from this time on and forevermore.
>   (131:3)

This use has led McKane to propose that these final lines of the verse (in the third person) are part of a "liturgical response" (1998, 130). But the second most numerous use of "Zion" in poetic imagery and praise is in Isaiah (cf. 33:5). Furthermore, "Zion" appears seven times thus far in Micah (up to 4:10).

That something would last "into eternity" is a sign of power and strength. Here Micah's message could be read as an important reassurance to the people

Building a New Society out of Crisis   151

in the light of an end to one kind of Israel and the beginning of another. The former days, dominance from Jerusalem and the royalty, are over; now God will gather those who have suffered from their policies and reign over them directly—forever.

[8] Zion is here referred to as "Tower of the Flock" (cf. Gen 35:21). Micah has already used the notion of Israel as a flock of sheep (2:12), which also appears in prophetic literature (cf. Joel 1:18; Isa 40:11; Jer 13:17; 31:10; Ezek 34:12; cf. Ps 78:52). The term used by Micah here, however, is not the typical term for "flock" (either of goats or sheep). The LXX renders this with the generic term used many times (*poimnion*), but Wagenaar is convinced that the reference in Hebrew is to a place, "Migdal-Eder" in the vicinity of Bethlehem (Gen 35:21), and the notion that it is a part of Jerusalem where flocks once roamed seems "too elaborate to be convincing" (2001, 148, citing Wolff 1990, 123).

Notably, "the hill" of the daughter of Zion is difficult. One other citation allows the possibility of a "dark/dry place" (so the LXX appears to presume), that is, a place for animals (Isa 32:14). References to "daughter of Zion" in other prophetic works appear to use the feminine term to refer to one who is abandoned, perhaps rhetorically increasing the sadness by using the image of a young, abandoned woman, such as in Isa 1:8; 10:32 (cf. 37:22; 52:2; picked up by Jer 4:31; 6:2, 23; the lament over "daughter Zion" in Lam 2).

In Micah studies, Runions (2001) is the most articulate critic of inferences often drawn from the use of feminized Jerusalem as "daughter Zion." Here we may find the assumption of the abandoned woman "saved" by the heroic male depiction of God. But, Runions protests, there is often far too much "weakness" associated with feminine biblical imagery, especially in the light of the following section, where Runions reads the possibility of feminine warrior-god imagery.

Zion is promised the former "sovereignty." The Hebrew term *mamlākâ* used for "sovereignty" or "rule" is not common (just over 15×), referring only occasionally to the rule of Israelite kings (1 Kgs 9:19), but appears in Psalms to refer to the "rule" or "dominion" of God (103:22; 114:2; 145:13). It is significant, however, that as time passes and the Israelites live under foreign imperial rule, concern with issues of "dominion" and "rule" rises dramatically; increasing use of the Greek term *exousia* is a telling measure of this (esp. Daniel in LXX; notably in Matt 10; Luke 20; and esp. Revelation). The "reign" of God is thus opposed to the "reign" or "sovereignty" or "dominion" of foreign rulers. This sentiment seems clearly at the heart of this increased use of the term in later texts such as Daniel, and it is arguable that already in the Assyrian and Babylonian crises concerns about "dominion" and "reign" become significant. In short, who is really "in charge" here? The bluster of the foreign empires? Or God? The assurances of a restored people in vv. 6–7 act as a compassionate reassurance in the face of the claims of the Assyrian and later Babylonian (and Persian, Greek,

Roman!) Empires that God is, in fact, "in charge." Compare this to Jesus' daring talk of "the kingdom of God" in the face of the Roman Empire (Matt 6:10; Mark 12:17; John 18:36–37).

The most interesting change in the LXX, however, is the inclusion of the phrase "*from* Babylon," suggesting that the "rule" will transfer from Babylon to Jerusalem. Hillers (1984, 56) suggests that this is a later interpolation (after 587 B.C.E.), promising that the Davidic line, captive in Babylon, will be returned to Jerusalem. What is interesting, however, is the perception of a proposed later editor that the issue of "rule" certainly does raise issues of imperial control, and therefore Babylon comes to mind rather easily. Hence adding "Babylon" (in LXX) may represent one of the earliest "commentaries" on Micah!

Finally, "daughter of Jerusalem" is used here as a parallel phrase to "daughter of Zion" (cf. 2 Kgs 19:21; Isa 37:22; Zeph 3:14; Zech 9:9; Matt 21:5; John 12:15).

[9] "Daughter of Zion" and "daughter of Jerusalem" are both associated with "shouts," which connects vv. 8 and 9 (are Zech 9:9 and Zeph 3:14 both influenced by Micah?). This form of the phrase to "cry out" is associated *not* with pain of birth but rather with "battle cries" (Num 10:7, 9; Josh 6:5, 10, 16, 20; 1 Sam 4:5; Pss 41:11 [12] NJPS; 60:6 [8]; Jer 50:15; God's own battle cry in Isa 42:13), but it can also be used for "shouts" of joy (Pss 65:13 [14]; 66:1; 81:1; 95:1; cf. Isa 16:10). With Runions (2001), I agree that it is thus misleading to regard the female imagery of the city of Jerusalem as a sign of weakness or submission.

As we have noticed, van der Woude argues for a considerable amount of dialogue between Micah and false prophets. He suggests that these false prophets were constantly giving assurance of God's protection, and therefore the "king" mentioned here is actually a reference to God protecting Jerusalem! Thus Mic 4:9 may be precisely echoing the false prophets' claim in 3:11 that "God is surely with us!" In short, 4:9 is a word from the false prophets, filled with false hope (1969, 250).

Micah appears to taunt the leadership about the absence of good counselors. He has already bitterly condemned the prophets (ch. 2), so the question "Has your counselor perished?" seems an appropriately sneering comment from our farmer-prophet. The term for "counselor" (from the verb *yāʿaṣ*; see Exod 18:19; Num 24:14; 1 Kgs 1:12; in participial form, 2 Sam 15:12 [Ahithophel]). The ideal of a counselor and (receiving) counseling appears in the Wisdom tradition:

> Where there is no guidance, a nation falls,
>   but in an abundance of counselors there is safety.
>   (Prov 11:14)

> Without counsel, plans go wrong,
>   but with many advisers they succeed.
>   (15:22)

Building a New Society out of Crisis

> For by wise guidance you can wage your war,
> and in abundance of counselors there is victory.
> (24:6; cf. 13:10)

Isaiah 1:26 suggests that the return of counselors is indication of the success of Israel's future, and the ideal coming ruler will be a "counselor" and a man of peace (9:6). However, Isaiah returns to the theme of God's disappointment that there are no wise counselors among the people ready to receive God's word (41:28). Ezekiel refers to wicked "schemers" who give bad counsel (11:2). God is a wise counselor, in contrast to the foolish counselors of the nations (Isa 19:11–12).

Furthermore, the counselors have apparently "perished." It is unlikely, however, that Micah refers to the actual death of such counselors. More likely what has perished is wise counsel! Isaiah refers to the "perishing" of wisdom (29:14), and Ezekiel to the "perishing" of instruction (7:26; cf. Jer 7:28).

As for being seized by "anguish" or "pangs" of labor, see the same phrase in Jer 6:24 (cf. 50:43). Otherwise the image of pain associated with a woman in labor is common enough in prophetic warnings (Isa 13:8; 21:3; 42:14; Jer 4:31; 13:21; 22:23; and as a prophetic warning, 1 Thess 5:3).

In reference to this passage, Andersen and Freedman suggest that the language is not merely about the death of a particular king, but about the end of a dynasty, indeed the end of kingship itself. This "end," then, is seen as the basis for the language of catastrophe, since (under normal circumstances) the death of a particular king simply leads to another king (2000, 445).

[10] If this is a dialogue with a false prophet who speaks in v. 9, then Micah in v. 10 thunders forth a warning in reply! The prophet calls on the city, "daughter of Zion," to "writhe" (for the verb in various other contexts, see Pss 114:7; 29:8; Job 15:20). The term for "city" (*qiryâ*) is often set in parallel with the more common term for town or city (*'îr*), as in Isa 1:26; 22:2; 25:2; Jer 49:25. It is difficult, if not impossible, to discern a strong difference between the two terms, certainly not as explicitly implied in the English use of "town" (smaller) and "city" (much larger). Nevertheless, to be sent out of the city or town is to be sent "into the field," and this may simply be a contrast to living in the city, where the aristocracy ply their trade. But in Jeremiah 40–41, being "in the field" or "open country" is a place of escape from Babylonian devastation (40:7, 13; 41:8). Ezekiel 7:15 implies, however, that those trying to escape "in the open country" will *not* be spared.

From the fields they will be "rescued," indeed "liberated" (*nāṣal*). God "rescues" the Israelites from slavery (Exod 3:8; 6:6; 18:4, 8), but Egyptians were "despoiled" (12:36, ironically, the same root term!). God is praised as the one who rescues (e.g., Pss 18:1, 17 [2, 18]; 22:8 [9]; 31:15 [16]; 106:43; 143:9). In a controversial passage, Isaiah speaks of God's response to those in Egypt:

"He will send them a savior, and will defend and *deliver* them" (Isa 19:20). Furthermore, having "no one to rescue" is a frequent warning (Hos 2:10 [12]); 5:14; Zeph 1:18; Zech 11:6). But what is the context in Micah?

Notably, the Assyrian officer who shouts before the besieged city of Jerusalem repeatedly warns of no rescue (Isa 36:14, 15, 18, 19, 20; 37:11, 12), but Isaiah promises that God will indeed "deliver" the city (38:6) and in a later passage defiantly uses the same language to speak of God, rather than the Assyrian monarch: "I am God, and also henceforth I am He; there is no one who can deliver from my hand; I work and who can hinder it?" (43:13; cf. the Aramaic boast of Nebuchadnezzar in Dan 3:15). Finally, Jeremiah praises the God who "rescues/delivers" (1:19; 15:20; 20:13; 39:17).

In parallel with being "rescued," God will "redeem" (*gā'al*) Israel. The concept of the "redeemer," one who reclaims a lost or impoverished member of a family, is rooted in the Levitical tradition of family and tribal restorative justice (Lev 25 and 27, and illustrated in Ruth 3–4). That God is "redeemer" is praised in Pss 19:14 [15]; 69:18 [19]; 72:14; 74:2; 77:15 [16]; 78:35; 103:4; 106:10; 107:2. Deutero-Isaiah frequently uses this motif, praising God as the "redeemer" of Israel (41:14; 43:1) and especially in direct reference to Babylon: "Thus says YHWH, your Redeemer, the Holy One of Israel: For your sake I will send to Babylon and break down all the bars, and the shouting of the Chaldeans will be turned to lamentation" (Isa 43:14; cf. 44:6, 22, 23, 24; 47:4; 52:9).

To be delivered "from the hand (or clutches) of enemies" (1 Sam 4:3; 2 Sam 19:9 [10]; Ezra 8:31; Pss 18: title [1]; 71:4) appears rarely in the Prophets other than in the following passage, which seems to be derived from a knowledge of the Micah tradition: "I will deliver you out of the hand of the wicked, and redeem you from the grasp of the ruthless" (Jer 15:21).

Finally, the presence of Babylon in this verse is often cited as evidence of a postexilic addition to Micah, perhaps even the entirety of chapters 4–5. This has never achieved anything like a consensus, however. Not only could the single word "Babylon" easily appear here (rather than adding an entire section); the notion of an exile could also easily fit the entire Assyrian period as well (so van der Woude 1969, 252).

As we have seen, this entire section of the book of Micah offers assurance to the "lame," those who have suffered previously. Whatever the cause of their impairments or disabilities (military wounds?), the general notion is clear: those who have suffered will be redeemed. Furthermore, the "lame" will become the basis, the foundation, of a new Judah. Whether a later addition or from Micah himself, this passage is certainly not inconsistent with what has passed before regarding the agrarian prophet's suspicions. For Micah to give a message that the sufferers will be redeemed by God, and then turn to a tirade against Jerusalem—all this is entirely consistent for this prophet and for the book that bears

An Exilic-Era Insertion on Future Restoration

his name. In fact, if this passage comes from the sixth century B.C.E., it hardly changes a thing!

There is another possibility, however. If we remove the phrase about Babylon (an obvious addition from a sixth-century editor to "update" Micah's message with this single phrase), then another thought presents itself. If Micah calls for people to come out of Jerusalem and camp in the "field," is he inviting those sympathetic to his call for a nonviolent revolt to come out the villages and join him? The startling implication would be that God's "redemption" will come in the countryside, a redemption from the "enemies" in Jerusalem itself! Frankly, only the presence of "Babylon" detracts from this more radical reading of the passage. Certainly nothing has suggested much sympathy for Jerusalem up to this point.

That this book contains a political critique that radically challenges centralized power is clear not only from the "base" documents (e.g., Mic 1–3, which may or may not be the only genuine Micah material in the book), but also from the tone of the rest of the book and its later use. Jeremiah cites Micah in defense of his own equally searing criticisms of central authority as he prophesies amid threats of conquest by another imperial power (Jer 26:18).

Micah 4:11–5:1 An Exilic-Era Insertion on Future Restoration (4:11–14 MT)

11 Now, many nations[a] are assembled against you, saying,
   "Let us pollute her;[b] let our eyes gaze upon Zion."[c]
12 But they do not know the thoughts[d] of YHWH,
   and they do not discern his counsel.
   He gathers them as grain [on][e] the threshing floor.
13 Rise up and tread, daughter of Zion!
Because I will make your horns into iron,
   and make your hooves into bronze;
you will crush[f] many peoples,
   and I[g] will sanctify[h] to YHWH their profits,
   and their might to the Lord of all the earth!
5:1 [4:14 MT] Now muster, daughter of [a group of[i]] conscripts![j]
A siege is against us!
   With a rod they strike the cheek of the judge of Israel.

a. McKane (1998, 141) summarizes the argument that the "many nations" refers to Sennacherib and his allies.
b. Wolff (1990, 129): "Let her be polluted"; Mays (1976, 106): "Let her be desecrated."
c. Lit., "see Zion in our eyes."
d. "Designs" of YHWH (Hillers 1984, 60–61).

e. Implied. It could be read as "threshing-floor grain."

f. Many have commented on the fact that horns do not crush; hooves do.

g. Runions (2001, 243) notes the crux of who the "I" is, a person who sanctifies something to YHWH! She argues that the maker of the iron horns, then, can hardly be God.

h. Hillers (1984, 61) and others notice that this term connects to the ancient ḥrm = "Yahweh War" tradition of dedicating all living things to God.

i. The term is, lit., singular (like a "band") but suggests a group. To clarify, I have inserted this phrase. It is almost universally translated as a plural reference.

j. "Troops," says Wolff (1990, 129); so also Bryant (1978, 210–11); "daughter of troops," proposes Pannell (1988, 139). There is a strong tradition among commentators of reading the root *gdd* as "gash," and thus, e.g., McKane 1998, 147: "Now keep gashing yourself"; Mays 1976, 111: "Now gash yourself, daughter of marauders"; Hillers 1984, 62: "Now you are gashing yourself with gashes." Commentators typically refer to Canaanite practices as reported, esp. in 1 Kgs 18:28 ("and they gashed themselves" [S-C]). Yet Willis (with Bryant 1978) is on firm ground in noticing the military context of the passage and citing Syriac and Vulgate translations, which presume similar readings, as well as comparing this to other "daughter" references in Mic 4:8, 10, 13 (1968b, 534).

[11] There is considerable debate about the identity of the "many nations." Is this a reference to Sennacherib and his allies? Is it part of a later reference to Babylon and its allies, such as the Edomites (cf. Obadiah)? References to the "many nations" are always negative in Deuteronomy (7:1; 15:6; 28:12; cf. Ps 135:10). Yet "many nations" are also portrayed as watching Zion/Jerusalem, either astonished or wondering what is happening to Israel (e.g., Isa 52:15; Jer 22:8; Ezek 38:23). A survey of the use of the term in relevant texts also includes the astonishing claim that "many nations" will acknowledge the God of Israel (Zech 2:11).

Here the term "pollute/profane" (*ḥānēp*) is associated with ritual impurity, although it does not appear in Leviticus, where the more common term for "unclean" is *ṭāmē'* (for *ḥānēp*, see Num 35:33; Ps 106:38; Isa 24:5; 32:6; Jer 3:1, 9). This term is not rendered in the same manner in the Greek. The LXX chooses *epichairō*, which is then rendered "gloat," as in LXX of Ps 35:19, "Let not my lying enemies gloat over me" (cf. vv. 24, 26; Prov 17:5; Obad 12). Wisdom counsels against such gloating (Prov 24:17; cf. Sir 8:7).

The second term ("gaze") in Greek is *ephopraō*, to "focus one's sight upon" (cf. God "looked with favor" in Gen 4:4 NIV; God "looked upon" the Israelites in Exod 2:25; Pss 5:3; 92:11, "*My eyes have seen* the downfall of my enemies"). It is frequently used in circumstances very much like Micah, as in Ps 112:8, "Their hearts are steady, they will not be afraid; in the end they will look in triumph on their foes." Thus the Greek renders a sense of "gaze and gloat" without necessarily a sense of "profaned" or "polluted," as suggested by the Hebrew. The differences and similarities of these two terms suggest an opportunity, in Scripture, to consider the entire motif of "being watched."

Excursus 7: "Being Watched" in Micah and Biblical Literature

Feminist analysis has produced a considerable literature on the "male gaze," describing a male "point of view," generally intended to mean a presumed right to view females as objects of desire; this seems to derive from feminist analysis of visual media, hence the emphasis on the "gaze" (Mulvey 1999). The term "gaze," however, suggests other uses of the concept of the "gaze": the way in which others are seen, assessed, and evaluated. Studies of indigenous peoples in early photography also suggest quite literally the colonizer's "gaze" (Faris 2003; Lydon 2005; Graham-Stewart 2006). A "male gaze" is therefore alleged in wide-ranging social and historical analysis of both the production *and reading* of texts, and especially texts that lend themselves to being gendered in some profound sense (e.g., cities described as women, warriors who are afraid to be called "women"). In biblical studies, this interest includes a considerable discussion about the implications of the feminized Zion being "profaned" (esp. in the imagery of Jer 3, e.g., where Judah "waits for her lovers" in the desert). When biblical writers speak of how others "view" the people of Israel, such thinking might be illuminated by a consideration of the presumed gender bias of the "viewers" and the "viewed." In Mic 4:11, there appear to be gendered terms of abuse implied in foreign nations wishing to "gaze" upon a defeated and demoralized Hebrew people, whose circumstances are thus "feminized." "Defeat" is like being an abused woman, and there is even a hint of pleasure in the foreigner's "gaze" on Zion, the defeated woman. Runions (2001) challenges many of these presumptions in the reading of Mic 4, yet an approach that calls attention to the act of "viewing," "gazing," and the like is highly suggestive for the gendered context of both the production and reading of Mic 4 (among other biblical texts where similar dynamics are evident). Feminist scholars rightly ask if we, the modern reader, become complicit in the engendering of abuse by not raising critical questions about the use of such abusive language in these texts.

Related to this approach, I am also interested in reading this passage through the lens of social psychology, with the possibility that there may be even more evidence for dating this material in times of confronting imperial interests (Assyrian or Babylonian) based on a social-psychological tendency in the language itself. Inspired by the success of feminist insights into engendered imagery, I propose an "imperial gaze" that is also operating in the Micah material.

The term *ḥānēp*, to "profane" or "pollute," is translated as "godless" heavily in Job and Jeremiah and more as "profaned" in Isaiah (Isa 24:5, the earth is "polluted"); but I am particularly intrigued by the combination with the "seeing" or "gaze" of the nations in Mic 4:11 in addition to this talk of a *māšāl*, "taunt" (cf. Mic 2:4). The nations "gaze" on the "pollution" of Zion, and many commentators limit their comments to the alleged *religious* impact of the temple being destroyed. Yet surely this is related to shame and humiliation as well, not exclusively to *religious* ideas.

Although the feminine noun *ḥerpâ* ("shame/humiliation") does not appear in Mic 2:4 or 4:11, tracing the use of this term sheds further light on this notion of the "gaze of the nations," which lies at the heart of 2:4 and 4:11. The term has much wider use in the biblical texts than "profaned" or "godless" (*ḥānēp*). Sometimes "shame" seems to be a very personal phenomenon—as in the "shame" that Genesis mentions for a woman who is humiliated in not having a son or in being married to an inappropriate partner

(Gen 30:23; 34:14; echoed in Isa 4:1). But shame can also be communal, conferred upon an entire people, as in Josh 5:9 and 1 Sam 11:2 (Nahash wants to bring disgrace on Israel). Psalm 89 adds an element of "many nations" watching and taunting the Israelite peoples:

> All who pass by plunder him;
>   he has become the scorn of his neighbors. . . .
> Remember, O Lord, how your servant is taunted;
>   how I bear in my bosom the insults of the [many] peoples.
>   (89:41, 50 [42, 51])

Here the emphasis is on taunts and derision from "many peoples" (*kol-rabbîm 'ammîm*). Isaiah 25:8 has YHWH promising to take his people's shame and disgrace "away from all the earth." In Jer 24:9 YHWH tells some who did not go into exile that he will make them a "disgrace, a byword, a taunt, and a curse in all the places where I shall drive them"; then 25:18 returns to this theme of the perspective of all the nations (cf. Jer 51:51). This change to being seen by "all" the nations becomes a prominent theme in Ezekiel (e.g., 5:14); echoing Jeremiah's list of humiliations, Ezekiel reports what YHWH says: "You shall be a mockery and a taunt, a warning and a horror, to the nations around you, when I execute judgments on you in anger and fury, and with furious punishments—I, YHWH, have spoken" (5:15).

This notion of being an object of scorn *to the nations* is palpable in Ezekiel, even in promises that this humiliation will end (22:4; 36:15, 30). In the postexilic tradition of the penitential prayer, this notion of being humiliated in the eyes of the nations turns up in Dan 9:16 and is repeated in Joel 2:17 and 19. Does social psychology shed any light on this trend toward a concern for being "watched" by the nations? In this regard, social psychology studies two interesting tendencies: (1) How does being watched impact personal performance? (2) What is the social effect of powerful structures like institutions or states using strategies of watching?

It can be argued that the very raison d'être of social psychology is to study the impact of others on the individual's behavior. It is hardly surprising, then, that one of the primary areas of investigation in the mid-twentieth century was the impact of "being watched" on individual behavior. One of the ways this is addressed in the literature is to speak of "social facilitation." A good part of this discussion is founded on the work of R. B. Zajonc (1965), who proposed that when subjects felt watched, simple tasks were more efficiently carried out, but complex tasks were not. There has been considerable discussion as to why the presence of others modifies behavior, but that it most certainly does is considered beyond question. One of the (pernicious) directions that this research takes is management theory (e.g., allegedly improving productivity by increasing supervision).

The second view is directly related to the steady march of the managerial state: the social analysis of "surveillance" in the modern state. Michel Foucault (1977) famously cited Jeremy Bentham's proposed prison design from 1791, known as the "panopticon," an "all-seeing" prison building. Bentham had proposed that this constant state of being observed would be therapeutic and restorative, but Foucault was interested in social attempts to increase control by ever more impressive and comprehensive notions of discipline and punishment. Similarly, Erving Goffman (1961) famously spoke of "total institutions," which attempt to exert complete control over individuals as part of their "treatment." In many writings associated with modern "Refugee Studies," aid workers speak of the heightened awareness of refugees in manipulating their image in the eyes of the powerful (Smith-Christopher 2002a, 78–81).

In the context of ancient history, however, Piro (2008) reflects on the possibility of seeing aspects of ancient architecture, such as palaces or temples built on high structures, as attempts to enact a sense of being "watched" by the empire and/or the imperial gods, or effectively as an ancient panopticon. The writer of Ezekiel, as part of his bizarre "call narrative," refers to "eyes all around" (1:18), and later in the book speaks of God revealing God's power to the "eyes of the nations" (36:23; 38:16). Exilic texts, then, arguably reveal an increased awareness of being watched by the nations. But does all this necessarily signal a postexilic context for these texts in Micah (such as 4:11)? Dubovský has written a detailed analysis of the many layers of Neo-Assyrian spying and intelligence services already in the time of Micah (2006).

The attention given in social psychology and cultural criticism to the study of "being watched" suggests that we should *expect* that biblical texts set during times of confronting imperial powers would exhibit a heightened awareness of being watched, and not only in the sixth century. Thus we can refer to "the imperial gaze" in Micah as well as in Ezekiel and other books.

In reference to the Neo-Assyrian Empire, Kuhrt writes of Assyrian awareness of people's perceptions of the royal power. She cites reliefs depicting the Assyrian kings reclining near the severed heads of enemies, as well as Assyrian inscriptions boasting of the dead rebels draped on their city walls, or rebellious rulers entrapped in cages with wild animals that are then suspended at the entrance to cities. The king, she writes,

> was awe-inspiring; the fear that filled his enemies was the terror of those knowing that they will be ruthlessly, but justly, punished. The royal power to inspire fear was visualized as a shining radiance, . . . a kind of halo that flashed forth from the royal face. . . . It made him fearsome to behold, and it could strike his enemies down, so that they fell to their knees before him, dazzled by the fearful glow. (1995, 516)

I argue that already in Micah at the time of Assyrian interference in Judah, there is a heightened sense of "being watched." This awareness of the imperial gaze thus begins already with Neo-Assyrian involvement, yet dramatically increases with Neo-Babylonian and especially Persian imperial control (Daniel, Esther, Ezra–Nehemiah).

[12] Continuing the theme of "the peoples," v. 12 continues to say that the nations do not know the "plans/thoughts" (*maḥšĕbôt*) of God. That God "frustrates" the plans of the nations with God's own plans is stated in Ps 33:10–11; Job 5:12. Jeremiah declares that God can plan for war (51:29) as well as for peace (29:11). Critical is the fact that the writer contrasts God's plans against the imperial plans of the other nations but does not contrast the plans of Jerusalem's royal elite against other nations. It is not "our" strength that will answer "their" strength.

God's "understanding" or "counsel" (*bîn*) is not known among the nations. As one might expect, the term is heavily used in the Wisdom writings and Psalms (e.g., Job 13:1; 18:2; 23:5; 26:14; 28:23; Pss 28:5; 92:6 [7]; Prov 18:15; 19:25; cf. Isa 5:21!).

God plans to bring the nations as "sheaves," a term that is rare (Jer 9:22 [21]; Amos 2:13; Zech 12:6). Here again is the agricultural motif. Possibly the writer intends this image to be entirely destructive, yet threshing is the process whereby the useless chaff is separated from the useful grain. A subtheme in Mic 4 is non-Judeans who are acceptable to God, and those who are not. Such sorting is an important element of judgment themes and becomes prominent in the New Testament and Christian tradition (Mark 4:1–9; Matt 25:31–46). But we have also been alert to the possibilities that Micah is suggesting differences between the Jerusalem elite and his own people. If "my people" are to be thought of as a "remnant" in Micah, then a sorting process is clearly a logical image to use. Is this so different from Jesus' famous judgment teaching where "sheep" and "goats" are separated (Matt 25:31–46)?

[13] The debate surrounding this verse is rich and fascinating, and the issues at stake are critical. First, notice that this passage is among those proposed by van der Woude to be arguments made by Micah's opponents (1969, 251). In other words, in the wake of Micah's accusations, a nationalist group is trying to reassure the crowds by asserting that God is on their side and that they will surely defeat the enemy. Certainly the appeal to sacral-war traditions, such as the dedication of spoils to God, suggests precisely such a military confidence in victory.

Mays calls this passage a "summons to war" (1976, 107). However, as with so many other identifications of genre and form, this "summons" is certainly adapted. The verb that follows the call to "rise up" is to "tread/trample," used of the agricultural work of threshing as well (Deut 25:4; cf. 2 Kgs 13:7; Job 39:15; Hos 10:11; Amos 1:3; Hab 3:12, "In fury you trod the earth, in anger you trampled nations").

Readers need to consider the many violent images used in this key verse. Horns are used as symbols of strength throughout the ancient Near East, not only in the Hebrew Bible, as in Ps 75:10, "Horns of the wicked I will cut off." More important, a horn symbolizes strength for a nation and thus a new king, as in Ps 132:17, "There I will cause a horn to sprout up for David." A horn signals the power of a nation generally, such as "the horn of Moab" (Jer 48:25). It becomes prominent imagery in apocalyptic texts as well (Dan 8; cf. Zech 1:18, 19, 21 [2:1, 2, 4]).

Similarly, the verb can speak of hooves, as in battle (Isa 5:28) and the sounds of battle horses (Jer 47:3; cf. Ezek 26:11). The hooves are to be made into bronze, a metal ubiquitous to warfare in the ancient Near East (2 Sam 22:35//Ps 18:34 [35]; Isa 45:2). The hooves will "pulverize" or "crush" many peoples. The term is also used in grinding idols to powder (e.g., 2 Kgs 23:6, 15; 2 Chr 15:16) but also of enemies (2 Sam 22:43; Isa 41:15).

Finally, following this destructive pounding is a "devoting" of profits to God. The term for "devote" [to YHWH], from the root ḥrm, is associated with the infamous genocidal "ban," heavily featured, for example, in the conquest narrative (e.g., Josh 2:10; 6:17, 21; 8:26; 10:35) and in God's judgment in the Prophets (Isa 34:2, 5; 37:11; 43:28). Jeremiah claims that God will "devote" the land of the Israelites to conquest (Jer 25:9; and then later 51:3, the destruction for Babylon). Zechariah, on the other hand, appears to reverse God's conquests in Zech 14:11, "People will make their homes there. The curse of destruction will be lifted; Jerusalem will be safe to live in" (S-C). What is here proclaimed "cursed," meaning "sanctified" to God, is the "plunder" of oppressive nations (beṣaʿ = "loot," "ill-gotten gains," "profit"; cf. Gen 37:26; Exod 18:21; Judg 5:19; Prov 1:19; 15:27; 28:16; Jer 6:13; 8:10; 22:17). In Ezek 22:12–13 the concept is perhaps most clear:

> In you, they take bribes to shed blood; you take both advance interest and accrued interest, and *make gain* [wattĕbaṣṣĕʿî] of your neighbors by extortion; and you have forgotten me, says the Lord YHWH. See, I strike my hands together at the *dishonest gain* [biṣʿēk] you have made, and at the blood that has been shed within you.

The related term in the final phrase of Mic 4:13, used in parallel with beṣaʿ, is ḥêlām. This term can be translated with emphasis on power and ability, or "possessions" (Gen 34:29; Num 31:9, "and all their *goods* as booty"; Hab 2:9, "Alas for you who get *evil gain* for your houses"; or "wealth/possessions," Job 5:5; Ps 49:6, 10; Zeph 1:13). In the Deuteronomic tradition, the term's use shifts to ability (Deut 8:17, "the *power* to act like this" [NJB] and to a related term for "army" or "soldier," as in ḥayil).

"Lord of the whole earth" is similar to "God of the whole earth" (Isa 54:5). This form "Lord" of all the earth is rare in biblical Hebrew (Josh 3:11, 13; Ps 97:5; Zech 4:14; 6:5). The Greek form of the phrase, however, occurs in the later Judaic literature, thus Judith 2:5, which is clearly (and sarcastically) contrasted to imperial claims (cf. 11:1, 7).

This emphasis on the God of everything is to be compared (contrasted) with the Neo-Assyrian claim (later repeated in Babylonian and Persian propaganda) that the earthly ruler is ruler of the "four corners of the earth," a term that appears to come from third-millennium Mesopotamian propaganda and reappears in Mesopotamian royal inscriptions from that time onward (e.g., Cyrus Cylinder; see Hallo and Younger 2000, 315).

What is being suggested by these images in v. 13? Andersen and Freedman speak of a "mood" of salvation for Zion: "The mood of this unit is strangely different from that in the Book of Doom. Here Zion's sufferings are seen as undeserved. The treatment she has received from her enemies demands retribution that Zion herself will inflict upon them. As they did to her, she will do to them" (2000, 455).[45]

Similarly Jacobs, who suggests that God "brings nations to war and commands Israel to beat people into pieces with iron horns and bronze hooks, and by this means to subdue the nations, . . . in stark contrast to the future of peace in Zion where swords are beaten into plowshares" (2001, 152). A stark contrast indeed, *if* that is what is really being said here.

Runions, however, cites entirely different traditions behind this imagery, proposing that the classical Near Eastern female warrior deities are in view here, that "Lady Zion" is actually personified as Anath, the horned cow, perhaps through Ugaritic influence. The "hybrid image" depicts female Zion rising up in destructive force against her enemies. What we may have here, then, is an engendered vengeance passage! Lady Zion, as Anath (Ishtar, et al.), rises up with her classic horns of power against her enemies (2001, 238–49).

However, few commentators have assessed the connection between the imagery in v. 13 and the story of Micaiah ben Imlah, where his prophetic opponent uses the imagery of horns (the text says he makes metal horns for emphasis) to indicate nationalist strength: "Zedekiah son of Chenaanah made for himself horns of iron, and he said, "Thus says the LORD: With these you shall gore the Arameans until they are destroyed" (1 Kgs 22:11).

The connection strongly supports the suggestions that v. 13 represents a view other than Micah's own: a promise of Judean nationalist strength, against which Micah is preaching. The very next verse, indeed, may well represent Micah's scoffing response to such confidence in the "horns of power" proclaimed by alternative voices in Jerusalem.

[5:1 = 4:14 MT] The unusual key term in this verse is "muster" (*gādad*, rendered by NRSV as "band together" in Ps 94:21), but it can also be rendered "cut yourself," in Deut 14:1 or 1 Kgs 18:28 (associated with pagan worship in Jer 16:6; 41:5; 47:5). The following phrase, undoubtedly sarcastic, refers to "daughter of a group of raiders" (cf. Gen 49:19) or "marauders" (Jer 18:22) or even "bandits" (Hos 7:1). The idea seems to be a group mustered or "banded" together.

The passage then refers to a "siege" (*māṣôr*) laid against, presumably (but not necessarily), Jerusalem. The term is used for a city under siege in Ps 31:21 (22) and in Ezek 4:2, "Put siegeworks against it" (cf. Nah 3:14). In the LXX, the Greek uses *emphrassō*, "sealing up" or "blocking up" (2 Chr 32:3; Jdt 16:3; 1 Macc 2:36; Pss 63:11 [62:12 LXX]; 107 [106]:42; Zech 14:5; Lam 3:9; "blocked" mouths of lions in Dan 6:22 [23 Theodotion]).

---

45. Furthermore, Andersen and Freedman do not believe it is possible to be specific about the actual events "behind" this imagery (2000, 457). They point out that Judah survived Assyrian onslaughts in 734 and 701 B.C.E., but certainly did not turn and trounce Assyria!

Finally, the "judge" of Israel is struck with a "rod" or "staff," or even "scepter" (Pss 2:9; 23:4; 45:6 [7 MT]; 89:32 [33]; 125:3). In the Wisdom literature, the term refers to the discipline of a "rod" (Prov 13:24; 22:8, 15; 23:13, 14; 26:3; 29:15). In the Prophets, we find the "rod of the oppressor" (Isa 9:4 [3]; cf. Assyria as the "rod" of God's anger and violence in 10:5, 15, 24; 11:4), and notably Isa 14:5, "YHWH has broken the staff of the wicked, the *scepter* of rulers" (cf. 30:31, similar to Ezek 19:11, 14; Amos 1:5, 8; Zech 10:11).

Here in Micah, the rod/staff strikes the cheek of the leader. For a slap on the cheek, see 1 Kgs 22:24 (cf. Job 16:10); yet a slap can also signify being abused by captors or humiliated (Isa 50:6; Lam 3:30) or a way of insulting the enemies (Ps 3:7).

In fact, the poet of Lamentations, speaking of Jerusalem's humiliation by the Babylonians in 587 B.C.E., takes up several themes we perceive in Mic 5:1 (4:14 MT):

> YHWH is good to those who wait for him, to the soul that seeks him.
> It is good that one should wait quietly for the salvation of YHWH.
> It is good for one to bear the yoke in youth,
> to sit alone in silence when the Lord has imposed it,
> to put one's mouth to the dust (there may yet be hope),
> to give one's cheek to the smiter, and be filled with insults.
> For the Lord will not reject forever.
> Although he causes grief, he will have compassion
>   according to the abundance of his steadfast love;
> for he does not willingly afflict or grieve anyone.
> When all the prisoners of the land are crushed under foot,
> when human rights are perverted in the presence of the Most High,
> when one's case is subverted—does the Lord not see it?
>   (Lam 3:25–36)

Finally, the term used for the leader seems odd. The Hebrew reads "judge of Israel," while LXX renders "tribe of Israel." Ezekiel 18:30 has God claiming to be "judge" over Israel. As with many others, Andersen and Freedman insist that judge probably refers to the king mentioned in 4:9 (2000, 461). Hillers also seems impressed with the arguments insisting that judge = king, even though he does not believe we may ever be able to identify the historical event behind the reference here. He helpfully points to Ps 89:39–45 for a description, in general, of the treatment of Israelite rulers by invaders (1964, 63). Psalm 89 and Mic 5:1 (4:14) raise interesting questions about whether the Gospel writers have these passages in mind when describing not only the treatment of Jesus in the Passion Narrative, but also Jesus' own advice to "turn the other cheek," to accept humiliation as an alternative to warfare (Matt 5:39// Luke 6:29). Is such a move, like Lamentations, an appeal to God's assistance (thus Rom 12:17–19)?

The meaning and status of this particular verse is one of the most controversial in Micah. If opponents are being quoted, with their confident assertion of nationalist power in 4:11–13, then perhaps Micah is responding in 5:1 (4:14) with sneering sarcasm, as if to say, "If you think you are so powerful, then go ahead and muster your troops, daughter Zion!" This would then be followed by an assertion of how powerless they really are, because the result will be the "judge" of Israel being struck on the cheek. Micah surmises what will happen, perhaps at the hands of the Assyrians, if they continue their pointless resistance.

If opponents are *not* speaking in 4:13, then we are stuck with the classic problem in Mic 4:1–5:1 (ch. 4 MT) as a whole: a vision that begins with beating weapons into farming tools and then ends with a confident assertion of Zion's "iron-horned" power to repel enemies, but capped off with an assertion about the defeat of Israel's king! One solution frequently offered is to "trump" the peace sentiment at the beginning of Mic 4 by declaring that the "peace" is really Judah's conquest of enemies, hence in no contradiction with the belligerence of the end of chapter 4 (so Andersen and Freedman 2000, 457). But this is such a strained reading of 4:1–5, involving language so entirely incompatible with the sentiments of 4:13, that this is hardly an acceptable resolution to the matter. Neither, it seems, is the other common suggestion to simply assign different dates to the apparently conflicting sentiments so that peacefulness, or belligerence, simply apply to different circumstances.

Dialogue with his opponents is already a clear and undeniable aspect of the Micah literature (with van der Woude 1969). It is therefore no stretch that we have a continuation of some kind of dialogue at the end of Mic 4 (MT), whether quoting opponents directly or alluding to their false confidence, and this dialogue best explains the otherwise confusing conflict of ideas in 4:1–5:1 (ch. 4 MT).

Mays, on the other hand, seems confident that Micah himself is describing a righteous battle against Israel's enemies, made all the more righteous, he argues, because spoils are to be given to God rather than packed away in military and temple coffers: "Zion's war will not be simply another case of those military ventures which serve the self-interest of those who mount them" (1976, 110). Wagenaar believes that 4:11–13 was inserted later as an assertion of Zion's inviolability. He argues that the original form of this sequence of thoughts was 4:9–10 and then immediately 5:1 (4:14), with vv. 11–13 dating to the postexilic period (2001, 280–81).

However, the likely intentional allusion to the nationalist prophet Zedekiah against Micaiah ben Imlah in reference to the "horns" points even more clearly to a satire against Micah's opponents (1 Kgs 22:11). The result of Micah's opponents' policies, belligerence and mustering for war against Assyria, is that the "judge" (not "king") of Israel will be struck by the "rod" ("scepter") of the one who is now actually in power: the Assyrian ruler! According to Wessels,

The Ideal King

Micah believes that the current ruler will be punished by the Assyrians, and this reveals that "Micah has no hope for the current leadership and the city (Jerusalem) as the seat of power. In the future, a new leader with different qualities will emerge (by returning to Bethlehem to start again). Chapter 5:1–4a [MT] expresses this expectation in more detail" (1999, 633). Once again, I find myself in agreement with Wessels's reading of Micah.

Micah 5:2–5a The Ideal King (5:1–4a MT)

2 But you, Bethlehem of Ephrata,[a]
    little among the clans of Judah,[b]
From you he will come out to me,
    to be a ruler[c] in Israel.
His origins are from old,
    from former days in the past.[d]
3 Therefore he will give them over until the time
    when she who is giving birth will have a child,
and the remainder of his kindred[e] will return to the people of Israel.
4 He will stand and shepherd them with the strength of the LORD,
    in the majesty of the name of the LORD his God.
And they will settle, because it[f] [the Name] will be magnified,
    even to the ends of the earth.[g]
5a And this will be peace. . . .[h]

    a. There is considerable debate about the actual reference. The Greek, which reads "house of Ephrata," has led many to suspect that the mention of *leḥem* to derive "Bethlehem" was not original but a correction (see Hillers 1984, 64; cf. Mays 1976, 115). Bryant (1978, 220–21), relating the place-name to Ruth 4:11, suggests that the two communities were so close as to be associated together.

    b. Wolff (1990, 144) compares to Isa 60:21–22, while Pannell proposes: "Too small to be among the brigades of Judah" (1988, 139).

    c. Wolff (1990, 144–45) suggests that the term *môšēl* = "ruler" appears instead of the standard term for "king" (*melek*) because God is to be considered King.

    d. A reference to the Davidic line? Cf. Neh 12:46; Amos 9:11. Willis argues for returning to Bethlehem to restore a true Davidic heir (1968b, 535). See comments.

    e. Lit., "his brothers."

    f. The referent to "be magnified" (*yigdal*) need not be the one who is born, particularly given the tradition of God's "greatness."

    g. Wolff (1990, 146) insists that such a phrase is postexilic (cf. Isa 45:22; 52:10; Pss 22:27 [28]; 98:3).

    h. Others emphasize the identification of a person, so Wolff reads, "He will achieve peace" (1990, 130). Pannell similarly reads, "He will be one of peace" (1988, 140); and

Bryant, "And this one will be peace" (1978, 224). All these readings seem to be directly drawn from the text, as opposed to the translation given by Mays, who amends the latter part of the verse to read, "This shall be salvation from Assyria" (1976, 117).

[2] The commentaries devote a great deal of discussion to the relationship of this verse to the passage immediately preceding it and the following reference to Bethlehem. Wagenaar denies that there is a connection, suggesting that 5:1 (4:14) does not "introduce" the passage about Bethlehem, at least originally (2001, 291). Nevertheless, there are ways of reading this association that make good sense. Bryant, for example, sees a clearly established contrast set up: "In 4:14 [MT] the 'judge of Israel' is smitten, whereas the future ruler in 5:1ff will deliver the land. In the present time the ruler trusts in military might, but the king who is coming will trust in Yahweh" (1978, 214).

Ephrata is associated with Bethlehem (Gen 35:19, and a strange genealogy also connects the two location names in 1 Chr 4:4). The place is considered "small." The biblical tradition is that David comes from Bethlehem (1 Sam 16–17), and the New Testament also associates Ruth with the line of David (Matt 1:5). The book of Ruth is set in the vicinity of Bethlehem, thus associating the openness-to-the-foreigner attitude in Ruth (esp. when compared with harsh attitudes toward Moabites; see Deut 23:3; Ezra 9:1; Isa 25:10) with the royal line of David. In fact, Bethlehem is a location of *no* importance and figures *nowhere* else in the prophetic literature (the single side note in Jer 41:17 only makes the point). This raises interesting questions about how significant the association of Bethlehem with the royal line really was, since one might have expected at least a reference in the royal psalms, but there is none.

Furthermore, the reference to a *môšēl*, "ruler," is a somewhat rare term. Solomon is called such in 1 Kgs 4:21 (5:1); the promise of one who will "rule over Israel" (using the same phrase) is part of the famous covenant with David as restated in 2 Chr 7:18 (cf. Prov 29:26; Eccl 9:17; yet also God is ruler in Ps 89:9).

The thought that this ruler is "from old" is intriguing (cf. Ps 74:12). The Deuteronomistic Historian portrays international events as part of God's plans from "long ago" (2 Kgs 19:25). The poet speaks of memories of the past as "days of old" (Ps 77:5). Similarly, later passages in the book of Isaiah refer to thinking about history in this way (63:11). Is there a connection between this use of "ancient times" and the reference in Mic 7:20 ("in former days"), serving as an "inclusio" for the final section of the book? Certainly this passage (in Mic 5), like Isa 63:11, seems to be making a similar point to Mic 7:20, deriving a lesson from a consideration of history. One suspects, however, that this reference to "former days" in the context of going back to Bethlehem suggests that we are not speaking of restoring the existing line. Why talk about going to "former days" if you are not speaking of going back to beginnings?

The Ideal King

Here the use of "little" or "small" (*ṣāʿîr*) seems to mean significance instead of size. In other texts, it is used in reference to a younger brother (Gen 25:23), to a minor section of a tribal group (Isa 60:22), and to small in size and strength (Ps 119:141) or "insignificant," as in Gideon's complaint of his own status (Judg 6:15).

When the passage speaks of "the one" who is coming and then refers to the "days of old," it seems hard to avoid the impression that the Davidic line is being implied, even if it is not explicitly mentioned. Andersen and Freedman observe: "The language used in Mic 5:1 [MT] is in line with a theme that turns up throughout the Hebrew Bible, the theme of the unexpected exaltation of an unlikely person to public office, the irregular, indeed illegal (Deut 21:16), supplanting of a senior brother by his junior" (2000, 464–65). However, they are equally struck with the fact that David is not explicitly mentioned throughout this passage—an odd circumstance if everything was supposed to point to fulfilling the promise to the Davidic line (470). It has also been suggested that the reference to Bethlehem or Ephrata is a reference not to David specifically but rather to Jesse (1 Sam 17:12) The implication, then, is *starting over!* Go back to the beginning place and find another son: begin again. Such a view turns the standard interpretation of this passage on its head. Rather than an approving reference to the line of David, it is precisely the opposite: *a summary rejection of the line of David and a sentiment to go "back to the drawing board" on Judean kingship!* Pannell, for one, supposes that the premonarchic David—the shepherd and not the warrior—is appealed to here, and therefore this passage is consistent with Micah's antimilitary agenda (1988, 131–43). However, as sympathetic as I am to Pannell's argument, I think it is also quite possible that Micah implies a "starting over": go back to Bethlehem and find another line, one that will not resort to violence so easily. I am thus in agreement with the readings by Oberforcher (1995, 106–7) and Bryant (1978, 221), who suggest that the appeal is to a ruler who trusts in God rather than in military might.

Finally, however, mention must be made of the Dead Sea fragment of Mic 5:1–2 (sometimes associated with 4QXII^f; see introduction). Callaway states that this fragment contains a "startling" reading: "Out of you shall *not* come forth . . ." (2011, 88). One immediately suspects an anti-Jerusalem polemic typical of the Qumran writings from the late Second Temple period (300–100 B.C.E.), but it is not good to be hasty. Given the spirit of the rest of Micah, this alternative reading is not impossible: it would dramatically confirm the anti-Jerusalem, antimonarchical stand that we believe Micah has otherwise taken throughout the rest of the book of Micah.

[3] This last sentiment is supported by a strong emphasis on birth: Zion "giving birth" to a new king (cf. Andersen and Freedman 2000, 469). In the

final phrase, the reference to "those who are left" (*yeter*) suggests a significant group of "survivors" of a disaster, such as exile in the sixth century B.C.E. (or with Hillers, still in the Assyrian period after Sennacherib's invasion [1984, 66]), and therefore potentially those able to carry on the tradition. That it can be used in this significant manner is clear from its appearance as a parallel term to the more common terminology for "remnant" (from *šā'ar*), as in Isa 4:3. Thus Jeremiah's letter is addressed "to the remainder of the elders in exile" (*'el-yeter ziqnê*, Jer 29:1; cf. 39:9; Ezek 14:22; Zeph 2:9). Nonetheless, it is widely recognized as an awkward phrase; Hillers thinks that a proposal like "He who surpasses his brothers will rule" might make some sense (1984, 67), and thus he rejects the notion of a reference to "survivors" or "remainders" in the land.

If the implication is a "reunification" of north and south, there are similar promises elsewhere (2:12), but Micah may be referring to exiles rather than some reunification of the northern and southern kingdoms. One could compare the action of God having led the exiles out and then gathering them back in Ezek 39:28. The promise of God to "regather" those who are dispersed among the nations becomes a central theme in Isaiah, as well as in Micah, and then becomes even more common and developed in the later generations of prophets: Isa 43:5, "I will bring your offspring from the east, and from the west I will gather you"; 54:7, "For a brief moment I abandoned you, but with great compassion I will gather you"; Jer 23:3, "Then I myself will gather the remnant of my flock out of all the lands where I have driven them" (cf. Jer 29:14; 32:37; Ezek 11:17; 20:34; 34:13; 36:24; 37:21). Jeremiah's constant emphasis that it was God's action *in both directions* (God sent, God will gather back) is muted in Ezekiel, as it is in Zeph 3:19 and Zech 10:8. The promise can also become conditional (Neh 1:9). Finally, in some (late) texts, the promise seems to be expanded to include even the possibilities of non-Jews becoming "gathered" to the people of God (Isa 56:8; 66:20). If we are correct, then Micah's use of this idea may have helped to lay the groundwork for this rather extensive later use in the sixth-century prophets.

[4] The "he" who is to be born is now identified as the one who will "take his stand" and feed the flock of God. "To take a stand" is to assume a position or place of authority, as suggested in some uses of the phrase (Isa 3:13; 2 Sam 15:2), or "take a position" (Dan 11:3 KJV) and thus perhaps take a rightful place. Related to this, then, is the idea of being appointed as king and thus the "shepherd" of the people. This is a motif with rich imagery throughout the ancient Near East, and Israel is hardly exceptional (e.g., 2 Sam 5:2; Ps 78:70–72). Even a foreign ruler can be proclaimed "shepherd" of God's people, such as Cyrus in Isa 44:28. Furthermore, a prophetic motif of judgment is God's anger or disappointment with these same "shepherds" (Jer 23:2).

What is to be done about unacceptable leadership among Israelites? Two solutions are often presented by the prophets. Either a new shepherd, an ideal

The Ideal King

one, will be appointed (or born, as in Isaiah's promises about the continued line of David)—or God will change the terms of the agreement and take the job! God occasionally is also called "Shepherd" (e.g., Ps 80:1, "Shepherd of Israel," and the familiar Ps 23:1). The notion of God as Shepherd is particularly striking in Ezek 34, where God declares God's disgust with previous shepherds of God's sheep, announces that God will take back (v. 10) the sheep from the shepherds, and then, somewhat startlingly, declares, "I myself will be the shepherd of my sheep" (Ezek 34:15–16). Yet in the same chapter Ezekiel declares that a new "David" will be set over the sheep, in much the same way that Micah announces a replacement (vv. 23–24)! It seems that an editor, supporting a monarchy, wanted to back away from the implications of God actually ending the monarchy in violation of the promise to David! Despite this, Zech 11 also presents God declaring that God is finished trying to be the shepherd over a stubborn people and thus turns Israel over to an evil shepherd! The New Testament picks up the theme of the new Shepherd (see John 10; Rev 7:17). In other words, what I suspect Micah is hinting at—replacing the shepherd—becomes an explicit tradition in later prophets. Furthermore, I consider it likely that Jesus is seen not merely as a descendant from, but actually a corrective to, the violent and flawed David.

When God "takes over," the "strength" of God is thus celebrated (e.g., Pss 21:1, 13 [2, 14]; 28:7; 46:1 [2]; 59:9 [10]; Isa 12:2; Jer 16:19), as well as God's "majesty" (Isa 24:14) and the importance of the "name of YHWH" (e.g., Pss 7:17 [18]; 113:1–2; Isa 24:15; esp. "the Name" taking action [Isa 30:27; 59:19; cf. Joel 2:26]).

It seems perfectly reasonable, then, to associate the call of Micah for the "ideal king" by drawing on the phrase "to the ends of the earth." In Hannah's prayer, clearly associated with royalty in Israel, "The LORD will judge the ends of the earth" (1 Sam 2:10). Likewise, the exiles will be redeemed "from the ends of the earth" (Isa 41:9; 43:6). Most important, however, is Ps 72 and its description of the ideal king, who defends the weak and powerless, who rules "to the ends of the earth" (v. 8), but in whose rule all nations are also blessed (v. 17; cf. Ps 67). In Ps 98 God is judge of the whole earth, a theme clearly reminiscent of Micah's notions of God as judge (cf. Jer 25:31). Notably, then, the phrase also occurs in the praise of world peace under the ideal rule of the future godly king: "He will cut off the chariot from Ephraim and the war-horse from Jerusalem; and the battle bow shall be cut off, and he shall command peace to the nations; his dominion shall be from sea to sea, and from the River to the ends of the earth" (Zech 9:10).

Thus attention to "all the earth" or "to the ends of the earth" calls forth either judgment or more often a sense of world peace and harmony (Ps 22:27 [28]; Isa 45:22; Jer 16:19). The theme continues into Hellenistic Jewish tradition as well (e.g., Tob 13:11). Finally, the New Testament makes use of the universal theme "to the ends of the earth" (e.g., Acts 1:8; 13:47). Once again, it is important to see different traditions in the texts, especially the peaceful themes, without emphasis on the violent ones.

[5a] Finally, there is the strange clause "And this will be peace." Is this a concluding thought to be read after 5:2–4 (1–3 MT)? Or is this a thought intended to begin vv. 5–6 and following? It is often suggested that the phrase refers to Solomon, but Wagenaar recognizes the "independent adverb of place" and reads simply, "And there will be peace" (2001, 179–80). In order to suggest either possibility, either ending previous thoughts or beginning new ones, I have chosen to repeat it in both locations for the reader to consider both possibilities of association (see below). In any case, the ideal ruler is a person who brings about peace (Ps 85:8; Isa 9:6; 32:18; 52:7; 60:17).

The theme of coming peace is a major aspect of prophetic hope for the future: Jer 29:11, "Yes, I know what plans I have in mind for you, YHWH declares, plans for peace, not for disaster, to give you a future and a hope" (S-C); Jer 33:6 foretells a new order of peace; Ezek 34:25 expects "a covenant of peace" that banishes wild animals, similar to "peaceable kingdom" motifs in Isa 11:6; 65:25 (cf. Ezek 37:26). Zechariah 8:16 is clear: "These are the things that you shall do: Speak the truth to one another, render in your gates judgments that are true and make for peace."

I propose reading Micah as containing prophetic words of comfort to the weary, tired, and oppressed. What has been the source of this oppression? I have argued and still argue that the oppression comes from the military adventurism of the central authorities in Jerusalem, responding to perceived Assyrian threats with force rather than diplomacy. This fits Micah of the eighth century, yet it can equally fit the age of Jeremiah in the sixth century B.C.E., and for the same reasons! Micah, in exhaustion at what he sees as suicidal and dangerous policies of violent resistance, lashes out in response to the elite's rejection of Assyrian offers of truce that promise "vines and fig trees." We have noticed that the text of Micah includes the same ideal of "vines and fig trees" that were offered by the Assyrian officials; the prophet says, in effect, "Take the deal!" Similarly, in a later generation, Jeremiah clearly opposed Zedekiah's plans to resist Babylon. In both cases, nationalist readers of the Bible over the ages staunchly resist what appears to be a lack of patriotic fervor, but such fervor is typically the luxury of the elite (who have, of course, the most material privilege to lose). Clearly Micah shows no more love for Assyria than Jeremiah later shows toward Babylon. But that is not the point: the issue is choosing the best means of resistance and the best means to carry on with life. After all, Assyria and Babylon are temporary problems (as apocalyptic faith will later emphasize).

Workers and farmers often have their own means of resisting injustice, but it is a means that results in far less destruction and death for their own people.

A Curse and Warning against Assyria

To give to Caesar what is Caesar's is not an invitation to appeasement: it is a revolutionary call to pick your battles and not squander your resources and family to the wild machinations of an elite panicking at the imminent loss of their power, privilege, and authority. Micah's call for spiritual resistance by trusting in God's ultimate care reminds us of the Danish resistance to Nazi Germany; Gandhi and Abdul Ghaffer Khan's resistance to British oppression in India, Pakistan, and Afghanistan; Te Whiti's resistance to colonialists in New Zealand; and Correnderk's Aboriginal Australian resistance to displacement in Victoria, Australia. In short, it is what Jesus means by the second half of his radical teaching: "Give to God the things that are God's!" (Matt 22:21).

Micah's frustration (or that of the editor adding to Micah's tradition) finally leads to the suggestion that the best way forward is to start again. New leadership is required. While Isaiah reassuringly tells the Jerusalem elite that their line is secure, that a birth will continue the line, Micah is ready to start over again—a sentiment that would surely send a shudder throughout the houses of power in any capital.

Micah 5:5–6 A Curse and Warning against Assyria (5:4–5 MT)

5a And this will be peace. . . .[a]

5b When Ashur[b] comes into our land,
    and when he marches against our fortresses,
we shall rise up against him,
    seven shepherds and eight princes[c] of the land.[d]
6 They shall shepherd the land of Ashur with the sword,
    and the land of Nimrod,[e] with open gates.[f]
And he shall deliver from Ashur,
    because he [Ashur] came into our land,
    and because he [Ashur] stepped within our borders.

    a. Wolff (1990, 147) argues that this clause should be attached to v. 6b (5b MT), starting at "and he shall deliver," removing vv. 5b–6a (4b–5a) from this context as an insertion. McKane (1998, 164) simply reads, "This is the peace we shall have from Assyria." See comments above on 5:5a (4a).
    b. "Ashur" (Assyria) can be used as code for later regimes (Lam 5:6; Ezra 6:22; Zech 10:10). See Wolff 1990, 147.
    c. The LXX translates as "bites" (*dēgmata*). This presumes the Hebrew root *nāšak* rather than *nāsîk*. What this may mean in the LXX is explored briefly below.
    d. "Leaders of men" (so McKane 1998, 150, 164), but "generals" in Allen 1976, 347. Hillers (1984, 68) believes that the reference is specifically to Aram (*'ărām*) rather

than to *'ādām* ("man"), due to graphic confusion of one letter, and thus reads "eight Aramean chiefs."

e. Mays (1976, 120) argues that a reference to Nimrod evokes a general reference to ancient Near Eastern regimes (Gen 10:8).

f. Hagstrom accepts the emendation "with the drawn sword" rather than "in her gates" (1988, 71 n. 95).

[5a] As we have seen in the previous section, there is considerable discussion about the placement and the presumed context for reading the clause "And this will be peace." Andersen and Freedman wonder what "this" refers to. The previous scenario? Or what follows? Does the time of "peace" end the previous description, or does it introduce the following conquest (cf. Andersen and Freedman 2000, 472–73)?

If this is a reference to a person rather than to a period of time, it is important to repeat that the ideal ruler is a person who brings about peace (e.g., Isa 9:6; 32:18; 52:7; 60:17). Certainly, whether by person or by announcing a time, the theme of coming peace is a major aspect of prophetic hope for the future (Jer 29:11; 33:6; Ezek 34:25; 37:26; Zech 6:13; 8:16).

The description that someone will "raise up" something against another is also used in prophetic literature, usually in reference to siege works (cf. Isa 29:3; Ezek 26:8). But where one might expect battle implements, Micah instead declares that we will raise up "seven shepherds" and "eight princes" (of Aram?) against Assyria.

The identity and meaning of the "seven and eight" is a subject of considerable, and at times quite fascinating, debate. For example, it is possible that this is a satirical reference to the Assyrians having divided local areas of Palestine into seven (by some counts) *provinces*. If this is being said to the Assyrians, then it could be read as, in effect, "What you did to this region, will be done to you." My attempt at making sense of these verses stumbles on the perplexing numbers. Another possibility is that this is an example of "number parallelism" in Hebrew poetry, such as the well-known example in Amos 1–2, "three sins, and four sins."[46]

As to the specific numbers seven and eight, others have suggested a reference to David and his brothers: Jesse had "eight" sons (1 Sam 17:12). But note also that Moses was said to have defeated "seven kings" in the land (Josh 13:21; cf. Deut 7:1). The notion of "seven shepherds," however, may even derive from Persian-period insertions in Micah.[47] In the famous Persian letter in support of Ezra's mission to Jerusalem, the Persian monarch refers to "seven friends/ counselors" (Ezra 7:14//1 Esd 8:11; cf. Esth 1:14). It is likely that the Ezra text

---

46. So Sweeney 2001a, 390, citing Prov 30:18.
47. Contra Hillers 1984, 69.

refers to the tradition of the Persian "council of seven," which seems to have participated in the revolt that successfully enthroned Darius.[48] Thus, if this is the reference in mind in the Micah passage, perhaps the notion is that "Assyria" (meaning "Babylon") will be conquered by the Persians, thus commenting on the eventual fall of the Babylonian Empire.

The LXX is not much help, presuming "bites" as a misreading of the Hebrew term for "princes," which are similar-sounding terms. Yet one might speculate on the possible associations made by the Greek translators' rendering. The "bites" of insects, after all, are mentioned as part of the punishment received by indigenous nations of the promised land (bites of locusts and insects) when Joshua entered Canaan (so also Wis 16:9). And the only other use of the precise form of "princes" (*nĕsîkê*) is found in Josh 13:21, which refers to Moses' "defeat" of seven (!) kings/nations. In short, the LXX translator may have made some interesting leaps in logical association.[49]

Yet another reading comes from Cathcart's suggestion that we have an *incantation* here, a magical formula whereby Judah is protected from Assyrian attack. In two carefully argued articles, Cathcart identifies striking similarities between the numbers here and other parallel "incantations" in Ugaritic and other ancient Near Eastern magical practice (*CTU* V:3.1.3–4, "Seven lightnings; eight storehouses of thunder"; or the Aramaic incantation from Nippur, "By the seven bonds which are not loosened and the eight seals which are not broken"). Cathcart even cites a fourth-century-C.E. Mandaean amulet: "O sorceries of the seven fortresses, and of the eight cities" (1978, 42). Cathcart's reading of the opening of v. 5 (4 MT) supports his interpretation: "And this will be *protection* from the Assyrian," with the incantation following (1978, 39). Thus Cathcart suggests that the LXX reading, "biters of men," may well refer to Babylonian incantations where spirits are said to do precisely that![50] Wagenaar, for one, is impressed with Cathcart's ancient Near Eastern parallels and points out that if these terms are pronounced with the same consonants but different vowels, one can read "demons" or "evil spirits" (2001, 183–84).

Now, however, comes the test case: what about the invading imperial powers? Is there peace for them as well, or only vengeance and punishment? The first phrase, "when the Assyrian comes into our lands," is paralleled with "walks to our citadels/fortresses" (*'armôn*). Most translations favor the LXX translation, which has *chōra* ("countryside") in parallel with the Hebrew *'arṣēnû*, "our land" (Gk. *gēn hymōn*).

---

48. On this, see Herodotus, *Histories* 3.68–71, as discussed by Briant 2002, 128–37.
49. On the number seven in Ugaritic literature, see Kapelrud 1968.
50. Thus "biters of men," similar to Babylonian incantations where spirits were said to devour men. See also Wagenaar 2001, 185.

Who, however, is pronouncing this passage, incantation or not? Cathcart observes that if this is a magical formula, then perhaps it is condemned by Micah as an example of depending on "soothsaying" (cf. 5:12 [11]) and is therefore a quotation from Micah's opponents rather than a promise from Micah himself.

Wagenaar, again in agreement with Cathcart, states: "In view of these similarities between Mic 5:4b–5 and *CTU* I:119.26–36 and other Ancient Near Eastern incantations, . . . the conclusion that Mic 5:4b–5 does not list military but ritual and magic practices seems to be justified" (2001, 295). But Wagenaar is not convinced that this means the incantations were not considered legitimate and thus are to be assigned to "false prophets" (he cites Elisha's rituals in 2 Kgs 4:34).

It is possible, however, to read these passages another way. Pannell proposes that the raising of "seven and eight" human leaders is intended to be Micah's condemnation of the typical policy of Judean warfare, to try to outnumber the Assyrian armies. In contrast, Pannell (1988, 135–39) argues that Micah advocates the approach of a new leader whose method will be peaceful (entirely consistent with the sentiment of 4:1–5!). Similarly, Wessels argues that

> the contrasting statements in verse 4b and verses 1–4a respectively should not escape one's attention. Salvation and peace were promised through an act of Yahweh who will raise up a ruler. However, in verse 4b seven or eight chieftains will take matters into their own hands and they will determine the future through military action. (1999, 635–36)

Comparing the Keret Epic, Bryant suggests that the intention of this passage is not to "speculate about the numbers of leaders who will rule but to depict the conditions that the Messiah will bring" (1978, 216). That is to say, there will be plenty of leaders, a prolific royal family.[51]

[6] In keeping with the theme of "shepherding," the NJB gives a better rendering with "They will shepherd Assyria with the sword" than the NRSV, which misses the wordplay with "rule." Yet the second phrase, referring to Nimrod being ruled "at its entrances," is awkward. The Greek does not help ("in their trenches"?). Hillers (1984, 69) is unhappy with the Hebrew sense of one who will rule over the "entrances" (from *petaḥ*, so Ps 24:7, 9; Prov 8:34). Reading with Ps 55:21 [22], he proposes that Nimrod is defeated by a "dagger" or "sword" (from *pĕtîḥâ*; Hillers 1984, 68). Wagenaar (2001, 186) wants to read "smash" the land of Assyria with the sword (*rāʿaʿ* = "break/smash," rather than *rāʿâ* = "rule"; cf. Ps 2:9, "smash" with iron rod). Open gates, however, may well suggest peaceful rule, or at least an end to the violent rule of the Assyrian city.

---

51. Furthermore, Bryant dates this entire sequence, 4:14–5:5, to the time of Sennacherib's invasion, and thus firmly in Micah's time (1978, 217).

A Curse and Warning against Assyria

The sentiment would not be far removed from that of Jonah, where an Assyrian city repents of the violence of their hands. In this passage, a feared Assyrian city is ruled with open gates.

I have translated strictly according to the third-person singular verbs in v. 6b (5b MT). Thus the first "he" who delivers is God, while the second "he" who enters the land is a collective reference to the Assyrians. On the idea that God will "deliver," see such verses as Isa 19:20; 31:5; Pss 7:1 (2); 18: title, 17, 48 (1, 18, 49); 25:20; 31:15 (16).

The final phrase repeats the previous verse, with the exception of "borders" instead of "lands," yet many translators prefer to repeat the previous. However, consonant with Isaiah, one cannot ignore the importance of peace within "borders" (so Isa 60:18; Ps 147:14). In any case, we are by no means finished with the problems in these two verses. As Andersen and Freedman point out (2000, 473), in v. 4 (3 MT) YHWH saves; in vv. 5–6 (4–5) peace is won by the sword; in v. 4 (3) future dominion is to "the ends of earth," yet in v. 6 (5) "they" will rule the land of Assyria. What connects the individual in vv. 2–4 (1–3) and the shepherds in vv. 5–6 (4–5)? The promise that Israel and/or Judah would not only repel the Assyrian attack but also actually engage in a counterattack on Mesopotamian territories seems to Andersen and Freedman as "wishful fancy": "The language it uses conjures up memories of great moments (doubtless exaggerated) in the past, when one man could defeat a thousand, because Yahweh his God fought with him (Josh 23:10)" (2000, 480). Indeed, even in Isaiah and 2 Kings, the prophet does not claim that God will attack, but only that Assyrians will be turned back (e.g., Isa 37:29, 33–35).

The presumption of a dialogue between Micah and his opponents might help with this passage. If Cathcart is correct, that we have the suggestion of an incantation here, this would hardly accord with Micah's own condemnation of soothsaying in 5:12 (11). Furthermore, the intention of the incantation (if it is that) is not easily compatible with Micah's sentiments as expressed elsewhere in the book. Micah's refusal to endorse the nation's mustering against the Assyrians seems incompatible with a confident assertion that the Assyrians are hardly a threat and can be dealt with by a mere curse! Either Micah's confidence is based on the notion that such curses are more effective than military resistance (implying that Micah himself endorses the sentiment expressed in vv. 4–6 [3–5])—or this confidence is being asserted by Micah's opponents, who support mustering against Assyria with the assurance that Assyria is not ultimately a threat.

Attempts to render this passage as a clear contradiction to Micah's otherwise peaceful sentiment are forced. There is little basis here for a clear-cut call for military invasion. To the contrary, there is plenty to suggest that other sentiments are operating here: trust in God's protection, for example, as opposed to massive military preparations. Assyria is not destroyed but subdued and even has open gates. The enigmatic reference to the "shepherds" actually suggests a sentiment familiar with the Wisdom tradition: "By wise guidance you can wage your war, and in abundance of counselors there is victory" (Prov 24:6). If anything, Micah seems to sweep away the warning that always seems to be the challenge of generals: "What about the Assyrians?" Or cast more currently: "What about the Russians?" "What about the jihadists?" To all such, Micah responds, "What about God?"

There is another possibility worth mentioning. We have already established that Micah speaks with fiery rhetoric. Could these verses against Assyria be satire? Micah may well be baiting the Jerusalem elite by mocking their claims to mount up superior firepower to the Assyrians! It is as if Micah is asking, "With *what* shall we defeat the Assyrians? A few shepherds, perhaps seven or eight?" If Micah has just spoken of the one who rules by peace—he could very well be following this up with a mocking parody of those who would presume to defeat Assyria by military means.

Micah 5:7–15 Judah over (or among?) the Nations (5:6–14 MT)

7 And the remnant of Jacob will be
in the midst of the many peoples,
as a mist [dew][a] from YHWH,
    as showers on the vegetation [crops?],
which does not wait on a person,
    or hope[b] in the sons of the earth.
8 And the remnant of Jacob shall be
among the nations[c] and in the midst of the many peoples,
as a lion[d] among the beasts of the woods,
    as a young lion among the flocks of sheep,
which tramples and tears wherever he passes,
    with no deliverer.
9 You will[e] raise your hand upon your adversaries,
    and all your enemies will be cut off.[f]

10 In that day, says YHWH,
I will cut off your horses from among you,
    and I will destroy your chariots.
11 I will cut off the towns of your land,
    and throw down all your fortifications.
12 I will cut off sorcery from your hand,
    and divination will not happen among you.
13 I will cut off your idols and your pillars from among you,
and you will not bow down any longer to the work of your hands.

Judah over (or among?) the Nations 177

14 I will pull down your Asherahsg from among you,
and I will destroy your towns.ʰ
15 In anger and rage, I will take vengeance on the nationsⁱ
that do not listen.

   a. "Dew" = Isaac's blessing, so Wolff 1990, 155. Dew is "mysterious" (Job 38:28).
   b. See comments on the use of "hope" rather than "wait."
   c. Some manuscripts omit the phrase "among the nations," so that this opening phrase would then be precisely the same as the opening phrase in v. 7 (6).
   d. Wolff (1990, 157) famously contrasts the two "among the nations" in vv. 7 and 8 (6 and 7)—if not dew, then lion!
   e. Wolff (1990, 150) insists on the jussive form here.
   f. McKane (1998, 166) reads this as a "wish of the reader" or "prayer to Yahweh."
   g. Wolff (1990, 151, 159) wants to read this as "adversaries" in parallel to the second term used in v. 9 (8). Also, he argues, the root *nātaš* is always used in relation to people, thus connecting this sentiment to v. 15 (14) more effectively.
   h. Willis reads "idols" here, emending *'ārêkā* to *ṣārêkā* (1969c, 354). Jeppesen, however, counters that "cities" is entirely appropriate and may be connected to idolatry, that is, idols associated with specific cities (1984a).
   i. Many interpreters are troubled with "the nations" here. Among suggestions, McKane (1998, 173) reads "the proud," thus understanding a reference to *gē'îm* ("proud") rather than *haggôyīm*. This change, of course, has dramatic implications for who is being addressed by these threats.

[7] The phrase "many peoples" recalls the famous Peace Prophecy in 4:1–5. Here the "remnant of Jacob" is surrounded by the "many peoples." Thus they are hardly destroyed! One can trace a clear conflict over attitudes to "the nations." For example, the phrase recurs in 4:3 and later in 4:13; the latter verse is read by many as an "answer" to the Peace Prophecy. In fact, of the fifteen occasions of this phrase, four occur in Micah alone. Clearly we are dealing with an interest in what moderns would call "foreign affairs." For Micah and his fellow lowlanders, these affairs are obviously of very personal interest.

In 5:7 (6), the people are compared to dew. "Dew" is always a positive image (e.g., Gen 27:28, "May God give you of the dew of heaven"; Deut 32:2, "May my teaching drop like the rain, my speech condense like the dew"; Zech 8:12, "For there shall be a sowing of peace; the vine shall yield its fruit, the ground shall give its produce, and the skies shall give their dew; and I will cause the remnant of this people to possess all these things"). These lines in Micah remind us of the language of Ps 72 regarding the ideal king: the psalmist hopes for a king who is "like rain that falls on the mown grass, like showers that water the earth" (v. 6), and people blossom like "the grass of the field" (v. 16).

The final phrase speaks, somewhat awkwardly, of not having to "wait" on a person, using two different terms for "waiting": the first form of "wait" (*qāwâ* in Piel; cf. Ps 27:14), the second phrase reads "wait" (or "await," *yāḥal*; cf.

Pss 31:24 [25]; cf. Ps 38:15 [16]). These can be rendered in different ways, of course. In the first instance Wagenaar suggests, "Put their hope in a man"; and in the second, "nor depend upon mankind" (2001, 164). One need not wait on "a man," or on any of the "sons of Adam," that is, "mortals" (Ps 11:4; cf. Ps 90:3; Prov 8:4). It is not a common phrase, and there seems little reason to argue for its specific use over other epithets for the people as a whole. That it may not be specifically referring to Israelites, however, is significant. In fact, the singular form, "son of Adam" (*ben-'ādām*), refers to any human being (Ps 144:3; Jer 49:18; 95 percent of the uses of the phrase are in Ezekiel). Thus it would be hard to argue that the plural form is used exclusively of Israelites.

What does it mean to have to "wait/hope" on persons or "sons of the earth"? I have rendered the term "hope," in close analogy to many psalms that use the precise term to speak of hoping in God (e.g., Pss 33:18, 22; 42:5, 11 [6, 12]; 43:5; esp. 119:43, 49, 74, 81, 114, 147). Surely the idea of trusting in God rather than hoping for the sons of the earth serves as a criticism of human governance and raises suspicion regarding the authority (and ability!) of human leadership, which in the ancient world often claimed authority based on divine sanction—yet was based largely on the maintenance of economies, agriculture, and safety! But if the "remnant" of Jacob is involved, how is this not a "human" involvement? The answer seems clear: it is a dependence not on human *authority* but rather on those who would faithfully represent God's intention of justice and peace.

Wessels, who believes this verse is the prophet's answer to the advocates of more militant action in the previous verses, comments:

> In contrast to the emphasis on military power, this verse follows a more gentle line, and comes from the prophet. The survivors or remnant will experience peace and salvation through Yahweh's conduct and not by military aggression. Among the many nations the survivors will be a blessing like dew and showers, which come freely and are life-giving. No human is in control of these substances, they come from Yahweh. (1999, 636)

[8] Here, the image takes a definite negative turn. Virtually the same phrase opens this verse as does the previous one, again mentioning the "remnant of Jacob," but adding "among the nations" or "in the midst" of the "many peoples." Then the verse takes a different turn, drawing on an angry theme that we hear also in Isa 5:29 ("Their roaring is like a lion, like young lions they roar; they growl and seize their prey, they carry it off, and no one can rescue"). The remnant becomes a "lion." Lions, once wild in the area of Palestine, are obviously symbols of both strength and frightfulness. There are clear signs of observing lions and knowing their habits (Nah 2:11–12; Ps 17:12). Note the similar contrast of dew and lions in Prov 19:12, "A king's anger is like the growling of a lion, but his favor is like dew on the grass."

Excursus 8: A Lion among the Beasts

The "zoology" of this passage is worth further comment. Enemies are described as "lions" (Ps 22:13; Joel 1:6; Jer 4:7; cf. 1 Pet 5:8). On the other hand, peace is described in terms of either taming lions or their absence (e.g., Isa 35:9; cf. the "peaceable kingdom" passages of Isa 11:6–7; 65:25). Often the lion is used as a symbol of God's own strength and prowess (Isa 31:4; Jer 50:44; Hos 11:10). Only here in Micah, however, does there appear to be an association of Judah/Israelites as a lion against their foes. Even in Ezekiel, the kings of Judah as "lions" is a decidedly negative image: Ezek 22:25, "Its princes within it are like a roaring lion tearing the prey; they have devoured human lives." Yet ironically a lion signifies Jesus in Rev 5:5 (when Jesus is associated with the line of David), even though Jesus is otherwise overwhelmingly called "the Lamb" in Revelation (as in 5:6; etc.).

Prophetic use of "lion" imagery in the book of the Twelve is especially telling. Consider two verses in the very next book of the Twelve: "What became of the lions' den, the cave of the young lions, where the lion goes, and the lion's cubs, with no one to disturb them? The lion has torn enough for his whelps and strangled prey for his lionesses; he has filled his caves with prey and his dens with torn flesh" (Nah 2:11–12).

There seems to be a clear relationship between Nahum's use of lion imagery and its appearance here in Micah. The same terms for lion (*'aryēh*) and young lion (*kĕpîr*) are used in Nah 2:11–12 (12–13 MT) and Mic 5:8 (7). The odd phrase in Nah 2:11 (12), "no one to disturb them," is exactly matched in Mic 4:4; and the notion of lions "tearing" is common to both, as is the application of this imagery to peoples: in Micah, "lion" apparently represents Judah, and in Nah 2:11–12 (12–13), "lion" signifies enemies (cf. Amos 3, esp. v. 12). Finally, this passage in Nah 2 is immediately followed by a series of threats to destroy armaments, precisely the idea that follows the lion imagery in Mic 5. It is tempting to propose editorial activity at the time when Micah was joined to Nahum, under the influence of an attempt to "strengthen" the vengeful tone of Micah in accordance with the spirit of Nahum. Strawn has thoroughly examined lion imagery in the Bible and ancient Near Eastern contexts and comments, "Underscoring the lion's predatory dominance . . . is the observation that, in the Hebrew Bible, the most frequently mentioned victims or potential victims of the lion are human beings" (2005, 36). Strawn is furthermore certain that a major source of the Hebrew Bible's use of lion imagery is wider ancient Near Eastern usage (232, 270), specifically Assyrian iconography (378–498).

Finally, the phrase "no one to deliver" (Judg 18:28; Job 5:8 implies "deliverer" as judge). The phrase is often used with lion imagery as well (Isa 5:29; Hos 5:14, implied in Dan 8:4).

Andersen and Freedman suggest that many problems would be "fixed" if the "one of peace" in Mic 5:5a (4a) is the acting subject of these verses as well, and the one represented as a "lion" to enemies is also "dew" to the remnant (2000, 486–87). Others, however, argue that this is perhaps along the lines of a threat: the remnant will be "dew" in the best of circumstances but a "lion" in the worst situations.

There is another possibility, however remote. If we *remove* the opening phrase (first two lines shown above) of v. 8 (7), which is nearly identical to the opening phrase of v. 7 (6), then the lion imagery would refer to the "person" or "sons of the earth." In other words, one of the reasons *not* to trust in human leaders is because their idea of ruling is prowling like lions! What a contrast to be dew among the nations! If one compares this to the sentiment of Ezek 19, where the "lions" of Israel are overcome by Egypt and Babylon, one may wonder if Micah is making an unfavorable comparison here. Granted, it is major textual surgery to remove the opening phrase of v. 8 (7), which now forces us to compare and contrast the opposing sentiments in vv. 7–8 (6–7), but I am suspicious that inserting the phrase "remnant of Jacob" a second time actually forces a softening of the criticism of leadership in v. 7 (6). Finally, this tentative proposal would make far more sense of what follows. If Micah (or the later editor of Micah) intended to further Micah's criticism of human leadership for its tendency to solve everything with violence, then God's threat to disarm the nations in the verses that follow makes even more sense.

[9] After the "twin" sentiments of vv. 7 and 8, vv. 9–15 remind the reader of the wordplays on village and town names in Mic 1. Here the common terms are things that are "cut off," with a particular focus on the destruction of weaponry and foreign cult items. Verse 9 begins with the image of enemies defeated by being delivered into the "hand" of those Micah is addressing (cf. Gen 14:20; Josh 10:19; Judg 3:28; cf. Ps 21:8 [9]); it includes war against another people by "lifting a hand against" (2 Sam 20:21) and of God (Isa 26:11).

The use of the stark image "to cut off" as a way of speaking of destruction is widespread in prophetic literature, as well as in Psalms (e.g., Ps 37:9; cf. Ps 101:8; see also Isa 29:20; 56:5; Jer 44:11 KJV; Ezek 14:8; 21:3; Amos 1:5, 8; 2:3; Obad 9; Nah 1:15; Zeph 3:6, "I have cut off nations; their battlements are in ruins"; Zech 9:10, "He will cut off the chariot from Ephraim and the warhorse from Jerusalem; and the battle bow shall be cut off, and he shall command peace to the nations; his dominion shall be from sea to sea, and from the River to the ends of the earth"; cf. Zech 13:2, 8; Mal 2:12). Micah 5:9 (8) seems to begin with a summary: your enemies will be removed. But what, then, is the function of the warnings that follow? Are we to presume that Micah is now going to list the military or military-related items no longer necessary because God will deal with enemies? Or is Micah now listing the things that the foreign enemies will no longer have need of? For Wagenaar (2001, 304), the use of the verb "cut off" is an indication that this verse is a late addition, related to what he considers to be later insertions of the "extermination formulas" of 5:9–13 [8–12 MT].

[10] "On that day" in the past tense is a common storytelling technique that increases drama and is thus used in the Historical Books (e.g., Gen 33:16; 48:20; Exod 5:6; 13:8; 14:30; Num 32:10; Deut 27:11; 2 Chr 15:11). When

combined with the future tense, however, it becomes a common stock phrase for prophetic speech (e.g., Isa 2:11, 17, 20; 3:7, 18; 7:18).

Again the strong verb "cut off" appears and in this case refers to "horses and chariots." It has often been suggested that horses were not commonly used militarily by ancient Israel but were often associated with foreign armies. There are some exceptions to this, such as Solomon's stables (1 Kgs 9:19; 10:26; 2 Chr 9:25), but his acquisition of chariots stands out as unusual in the historical sources. When horses are mentioned, it is almost always in a military context. The first canonical references to chariots are found in the Joseph stories (Gen 41:43; 46:29), which are likely postexilic reedited stories in any case, and in the many references to Pharaoh's horses and chariots in the exodus accounts (Exod 14–15). Joshua 11:6, 9 portrays Joshua destroying chariots and hamstringing horses rather than taking them over for Israel's use. Indeed, chariots are typical of foreign armies (Josh 17:16; Judg 4:3, 15; 1 Sam 13:5; 1 Kgs 22:31; of Babylon, e.g., Jer 51:21; Ezek 23:23, 24; 26:7, 10, 11; Nah 2:3–4 [4–5]), as are horses (Jer 6:23). In fact, Judg 1:19 reports that the presence of the enemy's chariots impedes Judah's conquest of the plain. Also, the chariotry of Lachish is "the beginning of sin" in Mic 1:13 (NRSV).

Individual chariots are also associated with royalty in Israel and Judah. The actual use of horses and chariots is difficult to discern from the often rhetorical references to them in biblical literature. Many passages do not suggest that either warhorses or chariotry are standard issue, especially in the early monarchy; instead, they are the privileged transportation of the kings only (2 Sam 15:1; 1 Kgs 1:5; 12:18; 20:1, 33; 2 Kgs 9:21; 10:15; Jer 17:25). They are particularly associated with Egypt, from which they are often procured (so 1 Kgs 10:29; 2 Kgs 18:24; Isa 31:1; 36:9). This seems to apply also to horses (cf. Eccl 10:7; Jer 17:25; 22:4). Yet horses outnumber donkeys in the list of animals brought back to Palestine by the returning exiles (Ezra 2:66). When the Aramaeans hear chariotry, they presume the presence of foreign allies, including Egyptians (2 Kgs 7:6). David keeps only a hundred chariots from booty including many more than this (2 Sam 8:4). Later kings appear to have invested more heavily in chariotry, which is presumed in the postmonarchical judgment against conscription (1 Sam 8:12), and kings who take great pride in military procurement (2 Kgs 10:2; 13:7). Yet when many horses are needed for a rebellion against Babylon, Ezekiel's allegorical presentation accuses Zedekiah of turning to Egypt once again (17:15). The sentiments of some psalms suggests an "antichariotry" notion (Pss 20:7 [8]; 33:17).

God is said to have a mighty heavenly army of chariots (Ps 68:17 [18]; 2 Kgs 2:11; 7:6), but predictions of peace include destroying warhorse and chariotry on earth (Zech 9:10). The psalmist praises God as a good and just ruler who does not trust in weapons, including horses (Ps 147:10; cf. Hos 1:7).

It seems likely that Micah's references are to the threat of foreign armies: God will silence the means of foreign threats. However, as mentioned, Lachish is chided in Mic 1:13 for the "chariots" stationed there, and these are certainly not chariots of foreign armies. As this series progresses here in Mic 5, doubts become more and more serious about whether it is only the "enemies" of Judah that are spoken of rather than *all* nations, *including* Judah!

[11] Here the threatened destruction is more general. "Cities" and "strongholds" are two symbols of oppression, as centers of commerce and centers of military power. The first term in this verse is the verb to "cut," an action that progresses through all these verses; the second verb, "tear down," is used most often against structures. The same two terms, both the verb and the noun describing what is destroyed, appear in Lam 2:2 ("in his wrath he has *broken down the strongholds* of daughter Judah"; cf. v. 17). For the act of "tearing down," see Prov 14:1; Isa 14:17; 22:19; Ezek 13:14; 30:4. Jeremiah's assignment as a prophet is to engage in similar acts of "pulling down" the structures of oppression and replacing them with building and "planting," thus agricultural productivity over issues of control (Jer 1:10; 31:28).

"Strongholds" refers to military fortifications in a city, often combined with the term for "city" (cf. Josh 10:20; 2 Kgs 3:19; 17:9; Jer 4:5; Nah 3:14). In the context of Micah's warnings to towns in chapter 1, this series of warnings about what is to be "cut off" seems quite ominous indeed.

[12] The first phrase refers either to "sorceries" or "sorcerers," although the translations differ as to what is intended. Is this a reference to the acts of the "artistry" of sorcery (*kĕšāpîm*), or a reference to those who perform them? The Greek seems to presume the former, the art itself, rather than specifically the practitioners (thus translated as "spells" in NJB, as opposed to "sorceries" in NRSV).

The persons involved are themselves banished in Exod 22:18 (17) and Deut 18:10 (which mentions both terms used here in Micah). The art of sorcery is associated with foreigners, beginning in the biblical tradition with the stories of Moses confronting Pharaoh's "advisers" (built on the term for "wisdom") and "sorcerers" (Exod 7:11, using the same term as here in Micah), including Jezebel's Canaanite heritage (2 Kgs 9:22) and also associated with Assyria, Babylon, and Persia (Isa 47:9, 12; Dan 2:2; Nah 3:4). There are also accusations against the practice (so Mal 3:5?). It is perhaps splitting hairs to ask whether individuals, or their practices, are intended here. We are clear enough on the intention.

The Greek term is *pharmakon*, the root of the English term for medicinal practice, "pharmacy," even though it is commonly translated "sorceries" in 2 Kgs 9:22. It already appears in Sir 38:4 as "medicines" and there is seen in positive terms: "The Lord created medicines out of the earth, and the sensible will not despise them."

The second phrase is often translated "witchcraft" or "soothsayer" (cf. Lev 19:26). It is the third term in Deut 18:10's list of four: "No one shall be found among you who makes a son or daughter pass through fire, or who practices divination, *or is a soothsayer*, or an augur, or a sorcerer" (cf. Deut 18:14; 2 Kgs 21:6). In the Prophets, such practices are routinely seen as indicating foreign practices (Isa 2:6; 57:3; Jer 27:9). If these accusations are against fellow Judeans, then it presumably involves a corruption from outside religious influences. It is thus tempting to read this in the same spirit as Josiah's reforms in 2 Kgs 23, a passage that also elucidates the pagan practices of fellow Judeans in a later generation.

[13] The sequence of what God will "cut off" continues. In this case, the objects are "images" (*pěsîlîm*, already used in Mic 1:7) and "pillars" (sg. *maṣṣēbâ*). Both terms appear in the warnings of Deut 7:5, 25; 12:3, where there are further instructions to utterly destroy such religious imagery (including the highly debated term *'ăšērâ*, often understood either as an image or as the name of the female Canaanite goddess Asherah; see below). In Deuteronomy, these *pěsîlîm* are to be "burned." As to the actual appearance of the object intended by the first term, in Judg 3:19, 26 it is often translated "sculptured stones" (NRSV) and suggests some image as a territory marker for travelers.

References in Isaiah are suggestive of Mesopotamian monumental architecture (Isa 10:10, "As my hand has reached to the kingdoms of the idols whose images were greater than those of Jerusalem and Samaria"). It does not seem too far-fetched to imagine that these "greater" images may relate to the massive carved structures at the gates of Babylonian and Assyrian cities, as well as to the massive carvings typical of Persian urban architecture. Isaiah 21:9 confirms this, referring to the shattered "images" of fallen Babylon (cf. Jer 51:47, 52).

The use of the Greek term *glypta* ("idols," "images," often used to translate *pěsîlîm*) is also instructive because Wisdom of Solomon provides a fascinating political description, even if it is from a later period:

> Then the ungodly custom, grown strong with time, was kept as a law,
> and at the command of monarchs carved images were worshiped.
> When people could not honor monarchs in their presence, since they lived at a distance,
> they imagined their appearance far away,
> and made a visible image of the king whom they honored,
> so that by their zeal they might flatter the absent one as though present.
> (Wis 14:16–17)

The second noun in Mic 4:13 (12), *maṣṣēbâ* (sg.), means altars or "pillars," something set up. Jacob's stone in Gen 28:18, 22 seems to mean a stone erected for commemoration (cf. 31:13, 45). As widely recognized, Genesis does not object to Jacob's action. Such stones also appear to have importance as territorial markers (Gen 31:51–52). The "pillars" set up by Moses (Exod 24:4), with twelve symbolic stones, mark a sacred site. Yet Leviticus and Deuteronomy (again, 7:5) ban such structures, using the same terms as here in Micah (Lev 26:1, "You shall make for yourselves no idols and erect no *carved images or pillars*").

In the Deuteronomistic History, the term "pillar" is often associated with Canaanite deities (2 Kgs 3:2; 10:26; implied in 23:14). All the more interesting, then, to notice the possibility of the term being used in an acceptable manner, as something acceptable to proper worship or honoring of YHWH, as in Isa 19:19, "On that day there will be an altar to YHWH in the center of the land of Egypt, and a pillar to YHWH at its border."

The LXX employs the term *stēlē* and chooses the same term to speak of Lot's wife (Gen 19:26; Wis 10:7) and also the famous "image" in Ezekiel's vision in 8:3, where the Hebrew uses *sēmel*. The precise command "You shall not bow down" appears in the Covenant Code (Exod 20:5; 23:24; cf. Deut 5:9) and is alluded to in Ps 81:9.

[14] The verb "uproot" (*nātaš*) also appears in Amos 9:15, "I will plant them upon their land, and they shall never again be *plucked up out of the land*"; later it will have a more prominent use in the Deuteronomic tradition and thus in Jeremiah, where it is just as often used of God "uprooting" Israel from the land in the Babylonian exile (Deut 29:28 [27 MT]; 1 Kgs 14:15; Jer 1:10; and the reverse in Jer 24:6; 31:28, 40).

The object of uprooting, however, is a much more vexed and difficult term. Scholars are divided as to which occasions appear to be neutral, as simply a sacred pole or object, and which occasions may be specific references to objects associated with the Canaanite goddess Asherah. The debate warmed considerably with the discovery of the pieces of *pithoi* (Gk. for "water jugs") at Kuntillet ʿAjrûd (in the Sinai desert), where a drawing and statement suggest *ʾăšērâ* as a female consort to YHWH. But others just as strongly argue that it is simply a reference to a sacred object, a "pole," in honor of YHWH and not connected to the accompanying drawings that seem to portray a male image and a female image, presumably deities to accompany the prayer written in the clay piece.

One of the problems is the inconsistency of the use of the term *ʾăšērâ*. For example, Deut 16:21 speaks of something wooden placed next to an altar dedicated to YHWH, while Judg 3:7 speaks of two proper names for deities in Canaanite practice: Baal and Asherah (cf. 1 Kgs 18:19; 2 Kgs 23:4). Yet again Judg 6:25, reminding us of Deut 16:21, speaks of a "sacred pole" next to an altar dedicated to Baal (cf. Judg 6:28, 30). During Josiah's reform, we find a description of the removal of "the asherah" (2 Kgs 23:6 NJPS), interpreted in the NRSV as "the image of Asherah." In the very next verse, there is a reference to making "veils" apparently dedicated "to" Asherah. Most of these references

Judah over (or among?) the Nations 185

are in the Historical Books, with few references in the Prophets to this term ("sacred poles" in NRSV: Isa 17:8; 27:9; Jer 17:2; Mic 5:14 [13]).[52]

Jeremiah (44:17–19, 25) mentions "the queen of heaven," and this is widely held to be Asherah, even though she is not named in this important chapter. We are left with the general assumption that there was a Canaanite deity named Asherah whose symbol seems to have been a wooden pole or "tree" erected adjacent to an altar—either an altar for Baal or, in a practice forbidden in the Deuteronomic law, an altar for YHWH.

The verb "to destroy" (*šāmad*) has volatile overtones in the Hebrew text. As a term of exaggerated hyperbole, it naturally has strong associations with military narratives. In fact, however, it is used mainly in two contexts: ritual contexts in reference to the destruction of pagan sites (often of "high places," as in Lev 26:30; Num 33:52; Hos 10:8) and military "destruction."

When used for military destruction, it can be used both of nations "destroyed" by God (or under God's supervision: Deut 2:12, 21, 23; 7:23; 9:3; Amos 2:9) and of Israel about to be "destroyed" (Deut 4:26, 7:4; 9:8, 14, 19, 20, 25; Ps 106:23; see the "curses" in Deut 28:20, 24, 45, 48, 51, 61). Not surprisingly, it appears along with "ban/cursed to destruction" in narratives of the "conquest" (Josh 7:12; 11:20). In the Historical Books, kings talk of "destroying" rivals (1 Kgs 16:12; 2 Kgs 10:17). Taking the cue mostly from the Deuteronomic traditions, then, the prophets take up this verb of destruction mostly as threats to the Israelite people themselves (the "broom of destruction" in Isa 14:23; Ezek 25:7) or to others (Jer 48:8, 42). The concept of "total destruction" of enemies begins to enter into the later vocabulary of apocalyptic as well, beginning with the late prophets (Hag 2:22; Zech 12:9). Although the notion of specifically "destroying cities" is not as common, there are two references that seem similar enough to perhaps have been inspired by Micah's use of the phrase here: Jer 4:7 and Ezek 35:4.

[15] The phrase rendered "anger and rage" (NJB "furious rage") appears in three locations, suggesting a stream of influence: Deut 29:27, here in Micah, and finally in Ezek 5:15, "when I execute judgments on you in anger and fury, and with furious punishments." While God's "hot fury" (*ḥēmâ*) can be mentioned in connection with God rejecting pagan practices (Lev 26:28; Num 25:11; Deut 9:19), the more common use of the term is in the context of punishment. The psalmist prays that God's anger will be turned away, reduced (Pss 6:1 [2]; 38:1 [2]; 78:38; 89:46 [47]), or directed against enemies in curse formulas (59:13 [14]; 79:6). The term is typically used of God's "warrior punishment" of either the surrounding nations or Israelite kingdoms. In prophetic usage, it is similar. Prophets call for God's punishing anger against enemies

---

52. We are particularly indebted to the work of Mark S. Smith for our understanding of Canaanite (and other ANE) deities and their relationships to biblical conceptions of God. See Smith 2002; 2010.

(Isa 34:2; Jer 10:25; Ezek 36:6, 18; Nah 1:2, 6; Zech 8:2), yet God's anger is often threatened against the Israelites themselves in prophetic rhetoric (e.g., Isa 51:17, 20; 63:5–6; Jer 4:4; 7:20; 21:12; 32:31; Ezek 5:15; 8:18). Micah's use, therefore, is rather typical rhetoric for God's punishing "fury." Yet in the Wisdom tradition "anger" or "hot fury" is strongly discouraged (Prov 14:17, 29; 15:18; 22:24; 29:22; despite a reference to God's "anger" in 24:18!).

Finally, God's "vengeance" against enemies is part and parcel of this rhetoric of anger and destruction. Although Leviticus forbids taking revenge or bearing a grudge against fellow Israelites (19:18), still God is often described as taking vengeance on enemies (Deut 32:43; Ps 58:10; Isa 1:24) and celebrated as the "warrior God," wearing "clothes of revenge" (Isa 59:17; cf. Nah 1:2); in addition, individuals ask for God's help in seeking revenge (Judg 15:7; 16:28; 1 Sam 14:24; 18:25; cf. God's command through the prophet to Jehu in 2 Kgs 9:7, flatly contradicted in Hos 1:4–5). This develops, although not widely used, into the notion of the "day of revenge" (Isa 61:2; 63:4, notably left out in Jesus' reading of the passage in Luke 4! cf. also Jer 46:10).

Andersen and Freedman notice that in this (Mic 5) series of things that are "cut off," a dozen of the terms used also appear in Zech 9:9–10, suggesting an example of reusing Mican themes in the time of Zerubbabel (2000, 493). But again, one of the main controversies about this series is the question of *who* is being addressed, and thus *whose* "sorceries," "cities," and so forth are to be "cut off"? Andersen and Freedman argue that chapters 4–5 are late in Micah's life, or come from early in the Babylonian exile, but not late in the exile because there is no hint of Persian involvement (495). The idea seems to be, in their reading, that Zion will conquer other nations, and this notion is perhaps informed by memories of a "golden past" in the time of David and Solomon. They conclude that Micah looks into the past, but "glimpses the future" in a manner that transcends historical possibility (496–97).

However, if these are promises of victory over foreign peoples, some wonder whether we are hearing from the *confident opponents* of Micah once more. Wagenaar, for example, goes back to Mic 1:2; thus the punishments here are directed at the nations who "have not heard me" (2001, 201; also Wolff 1990, 160). Since he accepts Mic 1–5 as a literary unit, earlier passages in Micah can be a context for reading these threats at the end of chapter 5. Hillers, on the other hand, takes this passage as "originally a formal renunciation of inauthentic, foreign elements as a prelude to the Messianic age" (1984, 72). Thus all the threats to "cut off" sorceries, chariotry, citadels of power, and so forth *are directed against Judah*, and these are all indications of Judean emulation of foreign powers, imitations that Micah rejects in a purified Judah, claims Hillers.

Calling these verses "the divine purge," Mays states that they are unlike anything else in the book of Micah, and he does not believe they come from Micah himself. In fact, he suggests that they fit more closely with the beginning

Judah over (or among?) the Nations 187

of the exilic period (1976, 124–25). Similarly, McKane wonders if this refers to a "purging" of the messianic age after the exile (1998, 174–75). Willis believes that confidence is expressed here about YHWH's salvation: "It seems that the purpose of this passage is to encourage Israel (faced with insurmountable obstacles) to trust completely in Yahweh" (1969b, 209). Wagenaar reads the "ban formulas" in reference to passages such as Zech 9:9–10 and 13:1–2a, thus seeing these purges as a series of cleansing actions among the Judeans. They are not threats to foreigners but cleansing actions among the Judeans themselves, and thus "an announcement of judgment" (2001, 308–10).

In any case, it seems that vv. 9 and 15 (8, 14) involve threats to non-Judeans, while the material in vv. 10–14 (9–13) applies directly to the Judeans. Wagenaar believes that v. 15 (14) was inserted at a later time to redirect the previous cleansing to foreigners (2001, 311). A question is raised, however, about the final line of this entire sequence, "the nations that do not listen." First, many have suggested that the term "nations" simply does not belong here and was inserted by a "rabid nationalist" who attempts to turn away the judgment against Judah that is implied in the rest of the passage (Willis 1969c, 355). McKane (1998, 173–74) and Rudolph (1975, 103), following previous suggestions, want to read *haggē'îm* = "the proud" or "the insolent," instead of *haggôyīm*, "the nations,"[53] thus continuing the judgments that can well be directed to Judeans!

Another question remains, however. Whether directed toward Judah or foreigners, the audience is bitterly condemned for not "listening." But listening to *what*? A strong possibility is that they (whether Judeans or foreigners) do not listen to the torah of peace in 4:3! Will there be punishments for nations who continue to practice the ideology of warfare and conquest (Judah included!), as opposed to the "united nations" who gather on Zion to unlearn war? What makes this even more likely is the clear implication that Judah itself is to be stripped *of its own tools of violence* in 5:10–11 (9–10), in addition to false religious practices in vv. 12–14 (11–13). As Runions helpfully observes, the list of things "cut off" sound very much like punishments for the tools of colonization used by foreign powers (2001, 230), which therefore places the final comment in v. 15 in a helpful context.

Finally, Zapff also suggests that the book of Micah, as it now appears in the canon, features a dialogue with the books that surround it: Jonah and Nahum. For those nations willing to repent, as illustrated in Jonah, God is ready to forgive (e.g., Mic 4:1–5). But for those unwilling and intransigent, the fate discussed in Nahum awaits them, as illustrated here in 5:15 (14)! Thus Zapff suggests an interesting way to deal with the apparent "contradiction" between

---

53. In a spirited rebuttal against those who (quite properly) take offense at the language of God's vengeance, Waltke tries to defend the importance of God's anger and wrath (2007, 338–42). Waltke, however, does not consider the possibility that this could be translated differently.

the sentiments in this later section of Mic 5, such as apparent punishment of foreigners—and the sentiments that begin Mic 4, the peaceful resolution of conflict with foreigners (2003).

Micah 6:1–5 God Reconvenes the Trial

1 Listen to what YHWH says:
Stand up and state your case[a] to the mountains;
  let the hills hear your voice!
2 Listen, mountains, to YHWH's case,[a]
  and everlasting foundations of the earth!
Because YHWH disputes[a] with his people;
  he will argue[b] with Israel.[c]

3 My people, what have I done to you?
  How have I wearied you? Answer me![d]
4 For I brought you from the land of Egypt,
and ransomed you from the house of slavery,[e]
and I sent before you Moses, Aaron, and Miriam.[f]
5 My people, remember what Balak, King of Moab, had planned,
  and how Balaam, son of Beor, answered him;
[remember passing] from Shittim to Gilgal,[g]
  in order to know the righteous acts[h] of YHWH.

  a. The terms for "state case" and "dispute" are from *rîb*.
  b. In this case *yākaḥ*, rather than *rîb*.
  c. Reversing the order of the phrases for readability.
  d. Wolff (1990, 164) has "testify against me!"
  e. Reversing phrases for readability.
  f. Sweeney sweeps aside the argument that the mention of Miriam here suggests a late addition, but his citing "J" to defend this argument is now more problematic given recent work on redating J to the Neo-Babylonian Period (2001a, 397).
  g. Nothing introduces the two place-names, but most translations supply "and what happened" or something similar.
  h. Here *ṣidqôt yhwh* = "righteousness" in plural form: usually "deeds" or "acts" is supplied to complete the plural construct with the name of God.

As we noted in the introduction, there is considerable debate about chapters 6–7. Are they the work of a separate prophet? Were they added at a much later date? Do they show liturgical use at a later time? Or are they, as Strydom (1993) and others have argued, the *older* sayings of an eighth-century northern prophet contemporary to Amos and Hosea (and earlier than Micah of Moresheth)?

God Reconvenes the Trial

[1] "Listen!" This call to specific attention echoes the earlier calls in 1:2 and 3:1, 9. There is a precedent for a call from God to "listen" (Num 12:6; Ezek 18:25) and from certain individuals demanding attention (Moses in Num 16:8; 20:10; Saul in 1 Sam 22:7; Job calling on God in Job 13:6). And so it is used by prophets commanding attention for the messages they bring (Isa 7:13; Jer 5:21).

Echoing the trial of humanity by God at the opening of the book of Micah, so here God calls for the "case" or "dispute" (cf. Isa 3:13; 34:8; cf. 41:21; Hos 4:1; 12:2 [3]; Jer 2:9; 25:31). According to Andersen and Freedman, the *rîb* structure indicates that the conflict is "within the covenant relationship" (2000, 500).

However, what is critical in this passage (and the next) is precisely a matter that Wolff (1990, 164) has questioned: the passage appears to be an accusation "against" the mountains. McKane (1998, 178) does not accept Wolff's suggestion that the mountains and hills merely represent the nations, but rather McKane suggests that they are witnesses. There are many commentators who thus turn to ancient cosmology to refer to mountains as "the whole earth" (Sweeney 2001a, 396). Once again, however, it may be crucial to remember the context for Micah: he is a lowlander, directing his criticism against Jerusalem! Thus it is absolutely possible that Micah's argument is directed "against the mountains" (by which we mean Jerusalem): the hills would likely be within his sight! We can imagine his arm outstretched, his finger pointing accusingly, upward and to the northeast, as he rails against the Jerusalem elite: "Up there—the leaders in their city—in their mountain abode." That Micah could also be using cosmological language (i.e., "foundations of the earth" in the next verse) does not invalidate the political meaning of accusing the mountains in his opening remarks here.

The prophet is said to address "mountains and hills." While the two terms are often used in parallel, it is also the case that "mountains" and/or "hills" can be used of the "high places" of pagan worship as well (Deut 12:2; 2 Kgs 16:4; Isa 65:7; Hos 4:13). While this is not necessarily suggested here, it would go well with his other accusations.

Many have suggested specific steps of a *rîb* patterned dispute, such as Andersen and Freedman (2000, 509; cf. Ps 50):

1. A summons to the custodians of the covenant to supervise the dispute
2. Accusation or interrogation of the accused
3. A recital of YHWH's deeds, vindicating his side of the matter
4. A rejection of sacrifice as a means to reconciliation
5. Either a verdict or an exhortation to make the right kind of reparations

Once again, however, the genre is adapted: "Micah calls his piece a disputation, but the argument turns into an appeal for reconciliation" (511).

What seems clear, however, is that the opening of Mic 6 is intended to take up the trial that was called into session at the beginning of the book. If it is a later editor, it is certainly done with style, literally suggesting that the trial of Judah's leaders by Micah continues! Surely this is what Jeremiah also intended to communicate.

[2] Once again the mountains are addressed, but in this sentence the new phrase used in parallel is "foundations of the earth," a phrase known from Ps 82:5; Prov 8:29; Isa 24:18; and Jer 31:37. The image is intended to communicate the full range of God's creation—from the top of the mountains to the "foundations of the earth."

In addition to having a "case" with "God's people," God will "contend" (*yākaḥ*). The term is used of disputes (Gen 21:25; 31:37), even against God (Job 13:3). The noun form results in "arbitrator" (Job 9:33; Amos 5:10) or a "rebuke" (Prov 25:12; 28:23). We previously noticed "anger," which is also combined with this notion of disputation in Pss 6:1 (2) and 38:1 (2), as above. That God will "dispute" with Israel is a striking notion (Ps 50:21, "But now I rebuke you, and lay the charge before you"; cf. the nations in Ps 94:10; reproving a son in Prov 3:12; the Peace Prophecy in Mic 4:3//Isa 2:4). That a prophetic word can represent God as taking issue with Israel, opening a dispute, is echoed in Isa 1:18, but arguably not as central a theme as it appears to be in the book of Micah.

[3] God protests with a common question: "What have I done to you?" (Num 22:28; 1 Kgs 19:20), and here God asks whether God has "wearied" Israel. This is a striking use of a relatively rare term, which does turn up in other prophetic contexts, but never quite like Micah uses it here! For example, Isaiah speaks of God being weary of Israel's sins (Isa 1:14; 7:13) or the "weariness" of people who are themselves apparently tired from all their sins (of Moab in Isa 16:12, of Babylon in 47:13, and in reference to Judeans in Jer 9:5 [4]). Jeremiah speaks more than once of being "weary" of trying to hold back God's bad news (Jer 15:6; 20:9). However, on no other occasion does a prophet portray God as sarcastically asking if God has "wearied" God's people! Andersen and Freedman observe that "weariness" is an Exodus theme as well (2000, 518). The sarcasm seems complete in the demand for an answer. The LXX chooses to render this idea of "weary" with "trouble" or "annoy" (*parenochleō*), suggesting something different from the Hebrew term for "wearied," which is contrasted with "giving strength" (Ps 68:9 [10]).

[4] That God is here identified as the God who brought the Israelites from slavery draws on an ancient Hebrew theme (Ps 81:10 [11]; Lev 11:45). The Hiphil form of the verb, however, suggests "lifted up and out" (from *'ālâ*).

God Reconvenes the Trial

For the following phrase, the reference is to God having "ransomed" (*pādâ* = ransom/redeem; LXX *lytroō*). Hosea 7:13 uses the same Hebrew term as in Micah, but Isa 43:1 (the same form in Greek) uses *gā'al*.

The common phrase "house of slavery" is found in Exodus (13:3, 14; 20:2) and Deuteronomy (5:6; 6:12; 7:8; 8:14; 13:5, 10 [6, 11]) and in passages influenced by the Deuteronomistic Historian (thus Josh 24:17; Judg 6:8). This is almost always combined with the recognition of God's having brought the people "out of Egypt."

Finally, reference to Moses and Aaron is to be expected in a discussion of the exodus events, but the inclusion of Miriam is unexpected. When we are introduced to Miriam, by name, in the book of Exodus (15:20), she is called a "prophetess" (NJPS). The other major tradition we have appears in Num 12, where Aaron and Miriam criticize Moses (ostensibly for marrying a Cushite/Ethiopian woman, but the issue appears to be a question of leadership), and Miriam is punished by a seven-day case of leprosy. This is the only reference to Miriam in the entire prophetic literature. One might speculate why she is here: perhaps Micah recognizes the importance of women in local agricultural society, since he certainly acknowledges their suffering from war in the opening chapters.

[5] The plea to "remember" is reminiscent of Hezekiah's plea to God (2 Kgs 20:3//Isa 38:3) but appears in Job and Nehemiah's pleas to God as well (Job 4:7; 10:9; Neh 1:8). Here, however, the plea is from God to the people, which is unusual. It is more typical of Deuteronomic rhetoric to emphasize the importance of "remembering": Deut 5:15, "Remember that you were a slave in the land of Egypt" (cf. 15:15; 16:12; 24:18); Deut 7:18, "Remember" how God treated Pharaoh; 8:2, "Remember" being led in the desert; 8:18, "Remember YHWH your God"; 24:9, "Remember what YHWH your God did to Miriam on your journey out of Egypt."

The story of Balak trying to hire the prophet Balaam to "curse" Israel is well known from Num 22–24, but Balaam is unable to carry out the curse. The passage is particularly interesting for recognizing the prophetic gifts of a non-Israelite, which many commentators cannot bring themselves to accept ("How could Micah approve of Balaam the hireling?" [McKane 1998, 177–78]), but positive recognition is surely implied in many contexts. Even Egypt's magicians can perform wonders!

Within the Numbers traditions, "Shittim" is mentioned only in Num 25:1 as a place where the Israelites become involved in prostitution with Moabite women, although Slayton suggests that it is the same location as "Abel-Shittim" in Num 33:49 (1992, 1222). In any case, it appears that Shittim is the staging area for the entry into Canaan.

Oddly, Num 31:8, 16 blames Balaam for encouraging prostitution with Midianite women, and this is used to justify his execution by soldiers under orders from Moses, orders that place Midianites under a ban. Numbers 22–24 is a strange passage only because Balaam does not seem to be blamed *here* for anything other than his inability to see God's plan clearly in the full (and frankly quite entertaining) Balaam stories, although his negative image certainly increases in Josh 13:22, reflected in 2 Pet 2:15 and Rev 2:14. Joshua 2:1 and 3:1 refer to "Shittim" as the location from which Joshua scouted the land of Canaan before entry.

Gilgal ("circle of stones?"), on the other hand, has wider attestation in the Hebrew Bible. This is the first encampment after the entry into the land (Josh 4:19), but is also probably an important staging area during the reign of Saul (1 Sam 11:14–15; 13:4, 8, 12, 15). Kotter observes that Gilgal is seen negatively in Amos (4:4; 5:5) and Hosea (9:15), but positively in Micah (1992, 1022). The use in Micah seems to refer simply to the accomplishment of crossing from the Jordan's east side to its west side, thus establishing an Israelite presence in the promised land.

The phrase "that you may know" can be helpfully compared to Joshua (e.g., 4:24, "so that all the peoples of the earth may know that the hand of YHWH is mighty") and 1 Kgs 8:60, "so that all the peoples of the earth may know that the LORD is God; there is no other." The point from these examples is that the "nations" will know. In Micah, the Israelites are addressed.

On the "righteous" or "saving" acts of YHWH, see Judg 5:11; 1 Sam 12:7; Ps 103:6; Isa 45:24.

Finally, Hutton points out that the references to Shittim and Gilgal may include the negative as well as positive events associated with these two locations. In short, "Janus-like" they reflect the two sides of God's actions toward the people: judgment and salvation (1999).

In referring to the exodus, the central point of these verses (6:3–5) is not entirely clear. Verse 5 clearly recounts God's ability to miraculously protect the people from the harm that King Balak wants to inflict on the people through curses. Based on the opening section of Mic 6, which reconvenes the trial, God is continuing to argue God's case: "Look at what I have been able to do for you in the past! And now we are about to be given advice on what we should do in return—in gratitude for God's care in the past."

Micah 6:6–8 The Prophet Advises the Accused

6 How shall I meet YHWH,
    [and]^a bow myself to my God on high?
Should we meet him with whole offerings,
    with calves a year old?
7 Would YHWH be pleased with thousands of rams,
    with ten thousand rivers of oil?

The Prophet Advises the Accused

Should I give my firstborn [for] my transgression,
    the fruit of my womb for the corruption of my soul?
8 He has told you, mortal, what is good,
    and what YHWH seeks from you:
do[b] justice, love steadfast devotion,[c]
    and walk mindfully[d] with your God.

a. The conjunction "and" does not occur, but the opening interrogative, "how," governs both lines.

b. The Hebrew clause *kî 'im* is often rendered "but only to" or something similar, such as "rather" (*GKC* 500). It was undoubtedly intended to contrast the positive statements in v. 8 with the rhetorical questions asked in vv. 6–7. For English, however, the intervening phrase in v. 8a makes this opening clause unnecessary for a good English rendering. Inserting "instead" before "do justice" would be another option.

c. *Ḥesed*, usually translated "steadfast love" (cf. Ps 136) or "kindness," but this has a somewhat different implication in English than in the context of the Hebrew, where it usually means God's devotion to God's people, suggesting loyalty as much as "kindness" (Sakenfeld 1978). Andersen and Freedman (2000, 529) understand the "devotion" as toward God, believing that all three points relate to God. See comments below.

d. McKane (1998, 187–88) discusses the choices of translating the adverb either as "wisely" or "humbly." The term used here is also found in Prov 11:2, where it is antithetical to "arrogance" (*zādôn*). McKane suggests "walk in humility with God." I favor "mindfully" because it suggests stronger intentionality than "humbly," especially in reference to Prov 11:2.

[6] This is one of the most beloved of prophetic texts in the entire canon. The opening is almost universally compared with poems of "temple entrance" in modern analysis, often citing the Psalms.[54] Opening the passage with a question is reminiscent of the many questions characteristic of the rhetoric of the late prophetic work Malachi (e.g., 1:2, 6, 7; 2:17; 3:7, 8).

The verb to "meet" or "confront" is often used in the context of worship or in pleading for God's assistance (Deut 23:4, "because they did not meet you with food and water on your journey out of Egypt"; Pss 21:3 [4], "For you meet him with rich blessings"; 59:10 [11], "My God in his steadfast love will meet me"; 79:8, "Let your compassion come speedily to meet us").

The text uses a somewhat unusual term for "bow" (Pss 145:14, "YHWH ... raises up all who are bowed down"; 146:8, "YHWH lifts up those who are

---

54. Wolff (1990, 167) wonders whether the source of this series of ideas is Israelite worship. Sweeney (2001a, 400) compares this passage to Pss 15:2 and 24:4. Wolff also likens it to other cultic language (e.g., Lev 1:4; 7:18; 19:7; 22:23, 25, 27). Yet one can also compare traditions critical of the cult in other prophets, such as Amos 5 and Jer 7.

bowed down; YHWH loves the righteous"). Most evocative is the prophetic indictment in Isa 58:5:

> Is such the fast that I choose,
> a day to humble oneself?
> Is it to bow down the head like a bulrush,
> and to lie in sackcloth and ashes?
> Will you call this a fast,
> a day acceptable to YHWH?

The Greek uses the unusual term *antilambanō*, which can be rendered "to devote oneself to" or "come to the aid of" (e.g., Pss 3:5 [6 LXX]; 18:35 [17:36]; 20:2 [19:3]) or "uphold" (119 [118]:116). It is used as "sustain" in Isa 63:5 and "uphold" in Jer 23:14.

The more common Hebrew term (*šāḥâ*) is also used of "worship" generally, either of God or of pagan gods (as in Mic 5:13 [12 MT]; cf. Pss 5:7 [8]; 22:27, 29 [28, 30]; 45:11 [12]; 95:6; Isa 2:8; Zeph 1:5; 2:11), yet also of the political act of acknowledging superiors (Gen 23:7; 1 Sam 24:8 [9]).

The phrase "God on High" (or "most high," *'ĕlōhê mārôm*) is also somewhat unusual. The second part of the term is used to refer to "heights," as for the place where God dwells (Isa 33:5), but also as a virtual epithet for the God of Israel (Ps 56:2 [3]). The more common Hebrew phrase *'elyôn* is found frequently (e.g., Pss 7:17 [18 MT]; 9:3; 21:7; 77:10 [11]), but as a virtual replacement for references to older names for the God of Israel (note the increased use in Sirach [e.g., 9:15; 12:2] and in Daniel [7:18, 22, 25]). It is often suggested that this may reflect Persian references to the divine "most high."

The question continues, using the same term "meet" but "with offerings" (cf. Ps 66:13, "I will come into your house with burnt offerings"). Leviticus 9:2–3 refers to a calf "a year old" (NIV) as an offering, in this case for Aaron's sin. Amos 6:4 is often taken to refer to the consumption of calves by the wealthy, perhaps instead of their proper use as sacrificial animals. The references to "a year old" is far more commonly a criterion for lambs that are sacrificed (Lev 23:18–19; Num 7 throughout; 28:3, 9, 19). In the entire prophetic literature, this is the only reference to the ritual requirements for sacrificing an animal "a year old."

[7] The terms used here refer to being "pleased with" or "favorable toward" (*rāṣâ*). That a sacrifice is found to be "pleasing" or "acceptable" is a standard term in ritual descriptions both in ritual law and in prophetic references to sacrifices or offerings being "acceptable" (e.g., Lev 1:4; 7:18; 19:7; 22:23, 25, 27; esp. note Ps 51:16 [18], whose sentiment has often been compared with this famous passage in Micah; cf. Ezek 20:40, 41; Hos 8:13; Amos 5:22; Mal 1:8, 10, 13). The term can be used also of prayers being acceptable, probably related to the notion of prayer as sacrifice for the petitioner (Pss 40:13 [14]; 77:7 [8];

85:1 [2]; 119:108; 149:4). Famously, Isa 42:1 speaks of the "servant" as the one in whom God "delights."

Rams are especially treasured, and wealth is often measured in rams (2 Kgs 3:4; 2 Chr 17:11). The sacrifice of rams is often noted, but also the use of "rams" to refer to God's preference of something other than this expensive animal (so 1 Sam 15:22, "And Samuel said, 'Has YHWH as great delight in burnt offerings and sacrifices, as in obedience to the voice of YHWH? Surely, to obey is better than sacrifice, and to heed than the fat of rams'"; cf. Isa 1:11). Indeed, auspicious days are marked by the number of sacrificial animals (e.g., absurd numbers in 1 Chr 29:21, "On the next day they offered sacrifices and burnt offerings to YHWH, a thousand bulls, a thousand rams, and a thousand lambs, with their libations"; cf. the more modest numbers in Ezek 45:23; Ezra 8:35).

The number "ten thousands" is often used to increase rhetorical impact from "thousand" (e.g., 1 Sam 18:7–8; 21:11 [12]; Pss 3:6 [7]; 91:7). "Oil" is added to cereal offerings (Lev 2:15; 14:10; but not for a sin offering, 5:11) or anointing (e.g., Lev 8:10; 21:10; 1 Sam 16:1).

As for "firstborn" (*běkôr*), see Gen 10:15; 27:19, 32. Regarding Israel as God's "firstborn son," see Exod 4:22. The notion that the "firstborn" belongs to God is discussed in Num 3:13, "For all the firstborn are mine; when I killed all the firstborn in the land of Egypt, I consecrated for my own all the firstborn in Israel, both human and animal; they shall be mine. I am YHWH." In addition, it is said that the Levites "replace" this requirement (Num 3:12; cf. 8:16–18). If this is a passage critical of the sacrificial cult (cf. Amos 5; Jer 7), then this is an ironic question, coming at the end of a crescendo of sacrificial gifts (burnt offerings, then calves, rams, excessive amounts of oil—and finally a human being)? The passage seems to be suggesting the growing *absurdity* of the question by exaggerating the sacrificial gifts. The obvious case to modern readers, Abraham (Gen 22), is not mentioned here. In fact, prophetic references to the patriarchs and matriarchs of Israel are extremely rare, leading many to suspect that the Genesis traditions have quite simply not become widespread in Israelite use yet.

The term for "transgression" or, more simply, "sin" (*peša'*) is used less often than the far more prominent term for "sin," *ḥaṭṭā't* (cf. Pss 32:5; 51:2, 3 [4, 5]; 59:3 [4]), but often in combination with it, as here. The latter term is used over forty-six times in Leviticus alone. The "fruit" of a "womb" is used elsewhere (Gen 30:2; "womb" and/or "ground": Deut 7:13; 28:4, 11, 18, 53; cf. Pss 127:3; "body," 132:11). Isaiah 13:18 uses the same phrase to mean young people: "Their bows will slaughter the young men; they will have no mercy on the fruit of the womb; their eyes will not pity children."

[8] This verse begins by "answering" the ironic question proposed previously, "What should I do?" But the answer begins with what appears to be almost a scolding: We have been told! The form of "told" suggests "declare"

in the Hiphil form of the verb (Gen 3:11; Ps 111:6; Isa 41:26; 48:14). The term was used in the wordplay in Mic 1:10. The notion of God telling, of course, also suggests the ethical expectations of the Mosaic law, "spoken" by God to Moses and the entire community of the faithful.

One might argue that "humanity" in general is addressed with the term *'ādām* (cf. Isa 5:15), arguably universalizing God's expectations for all humanity. Non-Hebrews, after all, have been the subject of other pronouncements in Micah, so it seems hardly shocking that they would also be addressed for ethical expectations (cf., e.g., Jonah; Amos 1–2; 9:7). All people are to know "what is good."

The emphasis is on what God expects or seeks, or "what God cares about" (see Ps 142:4 [5]; Ezek 34:4; 1 Chr 28:9). What is first sought by God is to "do justice" (see Isa 1:17; 16:5). Wolff expounds profoundly on this phrase: "It means the orders of justice that are maintained and reinstituted by peaceful actions, by just court decisions and by conciliation within the community. Everyone in Israel is to 'know justice,' especially every official" (1990, 180). The term "justice" is here combined with the all-important verb "to do" or "perform," thus the importance of *doing* justice. Kings are to "do" justice (2 Sam 8:15; 1 Kgs 3:28; 10:9; Ps 99:4; Jer 22:3, 15; 23:5). God "does" justice (Pss 10:18; 140:12 [13]). Proverbs 21:15 calls "doing justice" the "joy of the righteous ones."

The phrase continues with the call to "love" *ḥesed*, to love kindness, as many have translated, but I have chosen a direct rendering of "steadfast devotion," partly in an effort to call attention to this very important concept that is so much more than mere "kindness." For devotion and justice together, see Ps 119:149; Isa 16:5; Jer 9:24; Hos 2:19; 12:6. God "loves justice" (Isa 61:8). *Ḥesed* communicates God's loving devotion to Israel and is most notably celebrated in Ps 136, where the phrase is repeated in every stanza: *kî lĕʿôlām ḥasdô*, "for his steadfast love endures forever!" Here again Wolff adds profoundly: "The practice of justice ... apparently has not achieved its goal if it has not accomplished the 'love of kindness'" (1990, 181).

Here the notion is not that justice is performed toward God; instead, it is how people behave toward one another. In the modern world, it is far too easy to act with terrible harshness, even violence, and justify the act by calling it "justice." Hence the next phrase is not toward God alone. How easy it would be to act cruelly toward one another and then justify it by a claim of loving devotion to God! This is precisely the hypocrisy that Jeremiah later accuses temple worshipers of engaging in (Jer 7).

The phrase about "steadfast devotion" disallows a harsh and vindictive idea about "justice." One of the characteristics we most treasure in our modern saints—Dorothy Day, Dr. Martin Luther King Jr., Cesar Chavez, Sir Apirana Ngata, Oscar Romero—is their steadfast devotion to humanity! Justice without love can become a mockery of justice itself: it becomes merely cold rules and regulations, with no thought of actually building the human enterprise. On many occasions, Jesus profoundly clarifies the necessary combination of justice with mercy and devotion. When Peter asks if we forgive our brothers and sisters even "seven times," Jesus replies with his calculation of loving mercy: not seven but *seventy*! Rulers may claim to rule by justice, but without compassionate servanthood, it is merely pagan justice (Mark 10:43). These values are clarified by what follows.

The literature on Micah always debates the rendering of this final adverb. Is it "humbly," "cautiously," "modestly"? The term normally translated "humbly" or "modestly" is used twice in the entire Hebrew Bible (*ṣānaʻ*, in the Hiphil form in Micah, otherwise in Prov 11:2). The Greek suggests "be prepared" or "ready" (or perhaps "be certain," which would suggest at Hos 6:3 something like "certain as the dawn"). So Hillers (1984, 76) suggests "wisely," highlighting what he suggests is an "intellectual quality" to this rare term.

As Wolff (1990, 181) has intimated, the sentiment suggests possible influence from Deut 10:12, "So now, O Israel, what does YHWH your God require of you? Only to fear YHWH your God, to walk in all his ways, to love him, to serve YHWH your God with all your heart and with all your soul" (cf. Jer 7:23). Andersen and Freedman end their discussion of this debate with some exasperation:

> Scholars have been so preoccupied with trying to find out the meaning of the word ... that they have missed the simple part that is as clear as day. "Walk with your God," whether humble or circumspectly or wisely or however, is not the main point. Walk with your God by doing justice and loving mercy! (2000, 560)

As in other cases in Micah, the sentiment appears clear even if all the details of the language and grammar are not.

Shaw asks, "Of whom is justice, kindness, and obedience required?" and answers, the king! (1993, 177). If so, then Micah continues to direct his withering criticism toward the central authorities.

Finally, Micah echoes the criticism of the cultic expectations with the same criticism found in Jer 7; Amos 5; and Isa 1. *In each case, cultic requirements are contrasted with justice.* If we take seriously the perennial connection between cultic and royal leadership, the twin institutions of Israelite authority, then it becomes clear that Micah's criticism is directed toward the entire Jerusalem "establishment." Like those who protest taxation without justice, Micah represents the cries of the countryside, whose precious resources (esp. livestock!) are seen as the "ideal sacrifice." Micah thunders in reply: *justice* is the ideal! Finally, I stress the association of "walking" with God in Mic 6:8 and walking with God in peace in 4:5.

Can we appreciate the sympathy with which many Judeans, generations later, would watch the spectacle of a young Galilean violently dispersing the accoutrements of the sacrificial cult in Roman-occupied Jerusalem, only to quote precisely one of these prophetic condemnations of sacrifice without justice (Jer 7:11; Matt 21:13)? We can only speculate how many were impressed that day. Perhaps some of them were impressed enough to ask who that courageous young man was who risked serious trouble with the temple authorities and their Roman overlords by attacking a source of economic oppression of the people, calling the temple a "den of robbers" rather than a "house of prayer." The spirit of Micah indeed!

Micah 6:9–16 God's Accusations of Injustice and Sentence

9 The voice of YHWH! He calls to the city,
  It is wise to fear your name.[a]
Listen, tribe![b]
  Who has assembled (has appointed) her?[c]
10 Yet still[d] a house[e] of wickedness,
  even treasures of wickedness,
  the lean[f] ephah, the hated thing?[g]
11 Can I call "pure" [the] balances that are corrupt?
  or a bag of corrupt stone weights?
12 Yet her rich are full of violence;
  she resides by speaking lies,
  with deceitful tongues in their mouths.
13 Thus, I will infect[h] and strike you,
  a ravaging[i] because of your sins.
14 You will eat, but you will not be full,
  your emptiness[j] among[k] you.
You will try to drive back, but you will not be safe;
  that which you tried to protect I will give to the sword![l]
15 You will plant seeds but not harvest;
  you will press the olive, but not anoint yourself with oil;
  you will press grapes, but not drink wine.
16[m] He [You][n] honored the statutes of Omri,[o]
  and all the works of the house of Ahab,
  and you walked according to their plans,
Therefore, I give you to destruction,
  and the residents to hissing.
You will take up my people's disgrace.

  a. This phrase is widely read as a late addition (Sweeney 2001a, 401).
  b. Wolff (1990, 185) reads "tribe" and then translates the next phrase: "And assembly of the city." McKane (1998, 194), on the other hand, renders: "Hear what is the nature of the tribe and who has appointed it."

God's Accusations of Injustice and Sentence 199

c. Andersen and Freedman want to move ʿôd from v. 10 to the end of v. 9, "Who appointed her still?" (2000, 539). Jeppesen, however, translates: "Who has made a decision about her?" with the proposed answer: God (1984b, 574).

d. I read ʿôd ha'iš as "Yet still . . . ?" It could also be rendered "Is there still . . . ?" The LXX awkwardly tries to read "fire" (pointing the Hebrew as 'ēš).

e. Many commentators prefer to read bat = a liquid measure (cf. Isa 5:10), rather than bêt = house, thus "a corrupt bat," comparable to a false liter/gallon.

f. Wolff (1990, 193) reports that the adjective is normally used in relation to the human body.

g. This is a participle built on the term for "indignation" (zĕʿûmâ), thus "one who causes indignation" or "one about whom one is indignant." This translation cuts to the heart of the matter, showing what the "indignation" is about.

h. The root verb is to "be sick" (ḥālâ), but this term is built in the Hiphil form, "to cause to be sick" (heḥĕlêtî), which I translate as "infect."

i. The term suggests a desolation from military attack.

j. The Hebrew term yešaḥ is unknown. Some have suggested "dung," and perhaps this is a reference to unsanitary conditions during a siege. Others, assuming the same context, suggest "hunger." The typical move is to retreat to the LXX and fill in "emptiness" or "darkness" (from skotazō).

k. Wolff (1990, 185) states that "within" is implied.

l. McKane (1998, 198) discusses a complex emendation to understand this as the inability to have children, and if they are born, they are given to the sword: "Though you will remove them, you will not save them."

m. This single verse (6:16) is not considered sixth century by Wolff, but everything else from 6:9 onward is (1990, 190).

n. McKane (1998, 200), in agreement with the LXX, changes this to second person to also agree with the context.

o. L. C. Allen, based partly on the LXX, amends this sentence: "and the customs of my people will be made to disappear." Note especially his replacing ʿomrî with ʿammîm, "peoples" (1973, 72). Luria, however, considers the reference to Omri to be quite significant: Omri is among those whose oppressive taxation for building is comparable to Solomon's levy of labor (1989, 71).

[9] To refer to the "voice of YHWH" suggests peril or a significant announcement of events about to transpire (cf. Voice or "sound" in Gen 3:8; Deut 5:25; Ps 29, with recurring references to "the voice of YHWH"). Note Isa 66:6, "Listen, an uproar from the city! A voice from the temple! The voice of YHWH, dealing retribution to his enemies!" Wolff comments on how unique this opening phrase actually is (1990, 190).

The voice is directed "to the city" and then again refers to the "assembly" of the city (cf. Exod 12:3, 6, 47; Lev 4:13; Num 32:4; 1 Kgs 8:5). Readers need to keep this "city" in mind because the following verses keep mentioning "her," always referring back to the city, Jerusalem. Yet many commentaries suggest that Samaria is being addressed, largely because of the references to Omri and

Ahab in v. 16.[55] Although it is true that Samaria is briefly addressed in chapter 1, Micah's particular rage is directed not only toward the northerners who practice the statutes of Omri and Ahab but his rage is also directed toward those who do not need to practice the statutes of Omri and Ahab, but choose to do so anyway: the Jerusalem elite summarized simply as "the city."

The strange interjection about the wisdom of fearing "your name" is used elsewhere of non-Hebrew nations coming to recognize God (Pss 61:5 [6]; 102:15 [16]). That "fearing God" is part of "wisdom" is also a common motif, although not expressed in precisely the form we have in Micah (Ps 111:10, "The fear of the LORD is the beginning of wisdom"; cf. Prov 1:7; 9:10; Sir 1:14; 19:20).

The final phrases of Mic 6:9 draw a parallel between "tribe" and "assembly." The term for "tribe" [*matteh*] is more common for places where the people of Israel are being described and enumerated by individual units (see, e.g., Num 10; 13; 34). Prophetic references to this subdivision of Israel into "tribes" are rare in the prophets (cf. Ezek 47:23).

The verse implies a calling of tribal representatives to Jerusalem in order to announce policies that apply to all! Micah asks, rhetorically, "Who asked you to assemble us all?" or perhaps even "How dare you presume to assemble us all as if you have the authority to get us into this political mess!" What will follow are the reasons why Micah thinks the leadership, and their city, are hardly worthy of obedience.

[10] It is common to suggest that the items of this series in vv. 10–11 all have to do with corrupt economics, thus corrupt measurements that favor the wealthy. So instead of "house," one may easily read "bath" (i.e., *bat* as a measure of liquid, as in Isa 5:10). This certainly makes sense: Micah would then be attacking unjust measurements.

However, good sense (and even richer satirical polemics) can be gained by reading this as "house," or even a double entendre. The *house* of the "wicked" can once again convey an attack on Jerusalem. For "wicked" = *rāšāʿ*, see Pss 9:5 (6); 10:2–4 (the "wicked" hunt the poor and do not believe in God); Ps 37 also lists the many evils of "the wicked." However, the term is used in Proverbs, fully a third of all occasions in the Hebrew Bible, to describe evil persons. Isaiah 11:4 contrasts the doing of justice with acting "wickedly." In mentioning the "house of wickedness," Micah perhaps is including the temple as well! Certainly the purchase of certain measures and weights for sacrifice are part of the temple economy. Indeed, "treasures" is typically used in reference

---

55. Andersen and Freedman (2000, 544) suggest that the city is Samaria. Wagenaar (2001, 53) agrees, but Wolff (1990, 190) argues that Jerusalem is being addressed, not Samaria, and cites 2 Kgs 8:27; 21:3, 13. Runions (2001, 230) goes further and asks whether the violence done to "you" in Mic 5:10–15 (9–14) and 6:13–16 can be seen as "retribution" for the colonizing violence depicted in 5:7–9 (6–8) and implied in 6:4–5.

God's Accusations of Injustice and Sentence 201

to the temple or to the king's holdings (1 Kgs 14:26; 1 Chr 26:22, 26). Clearly the attack here is on *the greed of the central institutions*.

Readers recognize that weighing is a sign of economic activity, perhaps even prosperity. However, scripture texts insist that measures must be honest (an "ephah" is a dry weight) and fair (Ezek 45:10, "an honest ephah"; cf. Deut 25:14–15). The interesting phrase here is a "wasted" or "lean ephah" (see Isa 10:16, "will send wasting sickness"; cf. Ps 106:15). The reference is to intentionally altered weights and measures—the bane of farmers throughout history! For Micah's fellow lowlanders, corrupt weights and measures are a direct attack on their livelihood and can result in further levels of economic enslavement. Hardly a wonder that Micah would refer to "that hated thing"!

Here the Greek renders "with insolent injustice," but it is widely held that the Greek should read *metron*, "measure," rather than the common *meta*, "with." The terms are similar enough to explain the confusion (see Hillers 1964, 81).

[11] The opening term suggests the question about "approving" the weights ("clean," "pure"; cf. Ps 73:13, a "clean" heart, suggesting "approved"; cf. Prov 20:9). The LXX verifies this notion, using *dikaioō*: to "pronounce righteous" that which is corrupt.

Indications of doing business by using weights and scales to pay for grains or measure precious metals appear throughout this text. Proper weights and measures are key to maintaining social justice for the village economies dependent on proper measurement of their labor, as is clear from a variety of texts (Lev 19:36, "You shall have honest [*ṣedeq*] balances, honest weights, an honest ephah, and an honest hin: I am YHWH your God, who brought you out of the land of Egypt"; Prov 11:1, "A false balance is an abomination to YHWH, but an accurate weight is his delight"; cf. 20:23).

We translate as a bag of "corrupt stone weights," but this could be rendered "bag of deceitful stones." These "weight bags" are common possessions for those who engage in business (Deut 25:13; Prov 16:11). The notion of "deceitful" bags of stones makes perfect sense, although the term for "deceit" can be used in other ways (2 Kgs 9:23; Job 15:35; 31:5; cf. Pss 17:1; 34:13 [14]; 50:19; 52:4 [6]; Isa 53:9). Throughout the prophets, "deceit" is associated with those who get rich by falsifying balances and weights (Hos 12:7 [8]; Jer 5:27, cf. 9:5; Amos 8:5). According to Sweeney, all this discussion of false business practices suggests that refugees living in Jerusalem during a crisis are being oppressed and taken advantage of (2001a, 401).[56] This is possibe, but so is

---

56. When I first drafted this section, Haitians were reeling from the 2010 devastation of the earthquake in Port-au-Prince. Particularly reprehensible were those trying to take advantage of the situation and make money from those in crisis by fake money-raising schemes in the USA and even among Haitian refugees.

traveling to sell one's produce in the markets in the capital (cf. Neh 13:15), or even engaging in local sales with representatives from the city.

[12] The "rich" are "full of violence" (cf. Ezek 7:23). The term for "violence" (*ḥāmās*) has a colorful history in the Bible, beginning in the Torah with the violence of humans that brought on the flood (Gen 6:11, 13; cf. Pss 11:5; 27:12; 35:11 CEB; Prov 3:31). In Isaiah, such violence is contrasted with peacefulness (Isa 60:18; cf. Zeph 1:9). The Greek arguably reduces the rhetorical fire and speaks of "transgressions" or "crimes" (cf. Amos 5:12, denouncing "transgressions," as in Mic 3:8; Isa 59:20; Ezek 18:31), rather than the stronger Hebrew term "violence."

The reference to "deceptive" words (using *šāqer*; cf. "speaking lies" or "lying words" in Isa 59:13; Jer 9:5 [4]; "doing" lies in Jer 8:10) echoes the commandment in the Decalogue (Exod 20:16; cf. Lev 6:2 [5:22]; "lying" lips in Ps 31:18 [19]; cf. Ps 119:69, 78). Lying is a means of oppressing the poor (Isa 32:7).

The implication is clear: in previous verses we see false economic practices, and now in v. 12 we have the lies that try to justify them. Abominable is the attempt of the oppressor to justify such behavior with the most pious of language (Prov 27:6). Wolff (1990, 195) rightly suggests that such lies are essential to the practice of violence.

[13] The Hebrew here is difficult. The root term is to be "sick" or "ill," and in the Hiphil to "make ill" or "be weakened," so perhaps "I am made ill/weak from striking you" (the term appears in Isa 14:10, "You too have become as weak as we"; cf. "weakened" or "tired themselves" in Jer 12:13, but as "grief" in Isa 17:11). Hillers renders literally: "I have made grievous smiting of you" [1964, 81 n. 1]). But see Isa 33:24 ("I am sick") and Jer 14:17 ("grievous wound"). This notion of "sickness" to describe behavior or punishment is used in Isa 1:5 ("Why do you seek further beatings? Why do you continue to rebel? The whole head is sick, and the whole heart faint").

This is related to the idea of God "striking" (Isa 5:25; 9:13 [12]; 11:4; 30:31). God's "striking" is a form of discipline, so that the people would learn, and it is usually accompanied by the theme that the people did not listen. In the later Prophets, this becomes a way to refer to the exilic events themselves, as in Isa 57:17, "Because of their wicked covetousness I was angry; I struck them"; 60:10, "In my wrath I struck you down, but in my favor I have had mercy on you"; Jer 2:30; 5:3; Ezek 7:9; Hos 6:1, "He has struck down, and he will bind us up."

The final phrase of Mic 6:13 recurs in "make desolate" or "lay waste." God's punishment will result in the sanctuary and land being "deserted" or "desolate"—surely an image that a farmer would find especially loathsome (Lev 26:31, 32, 34, 35, 43; cf. 1 Kgs 9:8; Ezek 33:28, "I will make the land a desolation and a waste"; Zech 7:14, "Thus the land they left was desolate, so that no one went to and fro, and a pleasant land was made desolate"; Ps 69:25,

"May their camp be a desolation"); a heart can be "desolated," as in Ps 143:4 (cf. Jer 2:12). Desolation is also related to the conditions of exile (Lam 1:4, 13, 16), and return from exile marks the end to desolation (Isa 49:8, 19; 54:3; cf. 61:4; Jer 33:10; Ezek 36:34; Amos 9:14). We are reminded of Mic 3:12.

[14] The idea of eating to satisfaction is a common biblical motif of peace and prosperity (Lev 26:5; Deut 6:11; 8:10; 11:15; 31:20; Pss 22:26 [27], "The poor shall eat and be satisfied"; 107:9, "He satisfies the thirsty, and the hungry he fills with good things"; 147:14, "He grants peace within your borders; he fills you with the finest of wheat"). Indeed, a sign of justice in the land is that the people are not going hungry (Isa 58:10, "If you offer your food to the hungry and satisfy the needs of the afflicted, then your light shall rise in the darkness and your gloom be like the noonday").

Therefore, threats to Israel for disobedience, including many threats with regard to the exile, mention precisely this motif (Lev 26:26, "Though you eat, you shall not be satisfied"; cf. Hos 4:10; 13:6). In the later Prophets, this lack of food becomes a common theme for the threats of exile and the promise of return (Jer 5:7; cf. Ezek 7:19). The promise of restoration includes this motif as well (Jer 50:19).

The following phrase is also difficult: the term *yešaḥ* is not attested elsewhere. The suggestion is universally "emptiness," but also "dung" is suggested, followed by the common phrase "in your midst." The Greek suggests "darkness" (cf. Ps 105:28 [104:28 LXX]; "dark" in Lam 5:17).

The last two phrases appear to speak of putting something "aside" (often used of moving or "turning back," as in Ps 80:18 [19 MT]; Zeph 1:6], but also of "turning back" or moving a boundary stone in the Torah (Deut 19:14; 27:17; cf. Prov 22:28; 23:10; Ezek 22:18 suggests "dross" or that which is "thrown aside"). The term "delivered" or "rescued" is usually rendered here "to be safe," as in safe deposits or the secure accumulation of goods.

Finally, what was thought to be safe will be given to the sword. This seems awkward as a result of trying to accumulate, but not impossible (Jer 15:9 has the precise phrase; cf. 25:27; Ps 78:62; Isa 65:12). McKane is certain that this means the attempt to protect children, who will nevertheless face the sword (1998, 198).

[15] The threat that agricultural production will not be sufficient, and that this is a punishment from God, is not only common throughout the Bible (Hag 1:6); it is also integral to the curse tradition. This is reflected, for example, in Lev 26:16 ("You shall sow your seed in vain, for your enemies shall eat it") and in the curses of Deuteronomy (e.g., Deut 28:38, "You shall carry much seed into the field but shall gather little in, for the locust shall consume it"); it is taken up in Hosea (8:7, "For they sow the wind, and they shall reap the whirlwind. The standing grain has no heads, it shall yield no meal; if it were to yield, foreigners would devour it"; cf. Hos 9:2). Thus the similarity of these thoughts may be attributed to the well-known theme of agricultural failure.

More generally, the seasonal agricultural practice of sowing and reaping serves as common imagery in many different texts, both joyful and judgmental (e.g., Ps 126:5, "May those who sow in tears reap with shouts of joy"; Prov 22:8, "Whoever sows injustice will reap calamity"; cf. Eccl 11:4), and is taken up by the prophets (Jer 12:13, "They have sown wheat and have reaped thorns, they have tired themselves out but profit nothing. They shall be ashamed of their harvests"; esp. Hos 10:12, "Sow for yourselves righteousness; reap steadfast love"; cf. 10:13; Joel 1:10?). Precisely because of the oppression of the poor, Amos echoes this tradition and, like Micah, aims it directly at the wealthy, who would normally wallow in the fat of the land. Amos speaks of the same tradition of taking taxes and levies: "Therefore because you trample on the poor and take from them levies of grain, you have built houses of hewn stone, but you shall not live in them; you have planted pleasant vineyards, but you shall not drink their wine" (5:11; echoed in Zeph 1:13).

The specific threat about oil is also taken from the curse tradition (Deut 28:40, "You shall have olive trees throughout all your territory, but you shall not anoint yourself with the oil, for your olives shall drop off"; cf. v. 51). The curses can be reversed in promises of well-being (Isa 62:8, "I will not again give your grain to be food for your enemies, and foreigners shall not drink the wine for which you have labored"; cf. Joel 2:19, 24; Jer 31:12). There is an allusion, perhaps, to the opposite of peace, where people will sit under their own vines and fig trees. Here the situation is reversed: no agricultural productivity at all.

[16] The story of Omri is briefly told in 1 Kgs 16:16–28. After a period of serious instability in the northern kingdom, Omri overcomes a challenger ("Tibni, son of Ginath") in order to reign. The perspective of the Deuteronomistic Historian, however, is relentlessly critical of the northern kingdom, relating the sins of the kings to the first insurrection of Jeroboam, who seceded from the Davidic rule in Jerusalem. The description of Omri[57] is, however, unusual: he not only "did evil in the sight of YHWH" (the typical dismissal of monarchs) but also "did more evil than all who were before him" (v. 25). Notably, this same phrase recurs a few verses later in the introduction to Ahab himself, suggesting that Ahab, finally, is judged the worst of all in the northern kingdom (v. 30).

Sweeney observes that Omri and Ahab tried to align with Aram against Assyria, but then Ahab goes to war against Aram (1 Kgs 22), and later Jehoahaz, Jehoash, and Jeroboam II restore links with Assyria. Thus Sweeney reads Micah as opposed to all such "maneuverings" (2001a, 405).

The LXX, curiously, chooses instead to mention Zimri in place of Omri. This is clearly a reference to the Zimri, "commander of half the chariot forces" of

---

57. From Neo-Assyrian sources we know that some of the rulers of the northern kingdom were identified as representing the "house of Omri," and Jehu (ca. 841?) is pictured on the famous limestone Black Obelisk as bowing low before the Assyrian monarch Shalmaneser III (858–824 B.C.E.).

God's Accusations of Injustice and Sentence

Baasha (1 Kgs 16:9–20). While this may be a simple orthographic oversight, it may also be significant to recall that Zimri led a palace revolt that wiped out the entire "house of Baasha" (1 Kgs 16:11), an act that certainly anticipates the more well-known fate of the "house of Ahab" at the hands of Jehu (2 Kgs 9). In both cases, a particular curse formula is used, namely that the "dogs will eat" anyone who belongs to the house of Baasha (1 Kgs 16:4), which is used also against the house of Ahab (1 Kgs 21:24), a curse used originally of Jeroboam, the founder of the northern secession (1 Kgs 14:11). The LXX translator, then, may simply be drawing attention to the similar fate of the two doomed "houses," Baasha and Ahab. Omri himself, notably, did not die under this kind of curse, and his son Ahab became the more famous villain of Israelite history. This reading/interpretation is further supported by noticing that the Greek uses a phrase suggesting that God will be forced to drive the people "into extinction" (*eis aphanismon*), precisely the phrase used of Jeroboam in the LXX of 1 Kgs 13:34 (even though the precise term in the MT is not the same in Mic 6:16).

Second Kings 8:18 blames King Jehoram of Judah for doing the "evil" actions of "the house of Ahab"; and 2 Kgs 8:27 also blames his son Ahaziah for following "the way of the house of Ahab." Likewise, 2 Chr 21:13 elaborates on this tradition; and 2 Kgs 21:13, in discussing the reviled Manasseh, evokes the memory of "the house of Ahab."

The stories of Ahab are told more fully in the Deuteronomistic Historian's work, focusing especially on the expropriation of Naboth's vineyard by Jezebel and Ahab (1 Kgs 21). Given Micah's angry denunciation of the abuse of the poor and the farming class of Judah, it seems hardly in doubt that this is what Micah is referring to. Hillers's hesitation on this ("the precise sense of the phrases 'precepts of Omri' and 'all the practices of the house of Ahab' escapes us" [1964, 82]) seems entirely unnecessary. Micah's angry words in relation to these two scions of oppression seem perfectly clear and logical in context (Luria 1989, 72).

Yet there is a widespread insistence that the reference to Omri and Ahab strongly suggests that the "city" in question in 6:9–16 is Samaria rather than Jerusalem. This seems odd. Of course Samaria "followed the precepts" of Omri and Ahab; they were the kings! That is bad enough. However, as we have recognized, it is more shameful and more shocking for Jerusalem to "follow" such precepts when Jerusalem (and specifically its leadership) do not need to do so!

For "plans," read "scheming" or "devices" (Prov 1:31; Jer 7:24; Hos 11:6). The LXX uses a more neutral term that can be used to speak of the "plans of God" as well as evil "plans" (Ps 33:11 [32:11 LXX], "advice" of God; but Ps 1:1, "advice" of the wicked).

You will be given to "waste"—drawing on the same traditions that undoubtedly inspired the curse formulas of Deuteronomy (Deut 28:37; cf. 2 Kgs 22:19) and certainly recurs frequently in the judgmental rhetoric of the prophets (Isa 5:9; 13:9; Jer 2:15; 4:7; 18:16; 19:8; 25:11; and later in Zeph 2:15).

As we have already noticed, the Israelites appear to be particularly susceptible to worries about their "appearance" in the eyes of other nations. Once again, this draws from standard curse formulas as used, for example, by Deut 29:24, "They and indeed all the nations will wonder, 'Why has YHWH done thus to this land?'" Specifically, to be an object of scorn or "hissing" is not an uncommon complaint in relation to judgment (1 Kgs 9:8). This is a concern that continues in the Persian-period rewriting of the history (so 2 Chr 29:8). Not surprisingly, then, being the object of "hissing," "scorn," or "taunting" is a matter of grave concern to the prophets (Jer 19:8, "I will make this city a horror, a thing to be hissed at"; cf. 25:18; so also against Edom in 49:17; against Babylon in 50:13; cf. Lam 2:15). This continues into the later Prophets as well (so Zeph 2:15, "Everyone who passes by it hisses and shakes the fist").

This same paranoia about taunting from others is seen in the use of terms for "reproach" or "scorn" (ḥerpâ): Isa 54:4, "Do not fear, . . . for you will not suffer disgrace"; Ezek 36:15, "No longer shall you bear the disgrace of the peoples" (cf. Pss 44:13 [14]; 79:4; 102:8 [9]; 119:42). The term is used, not surprisingly, by the two major prophets of the exilic period (Jer 24:9; Ezek 5:15).

Andersen and Freedman point out that the plural form "you" referring to leaders is not used in Mic 6:1–8, but YHWH addresses leaders in vv. 9–16. Thus, following the pronouns, they identify the addressees as "the people," "the leadership," "the wealthy," and "the one," with the last being a wicked king (2000, 557–60).

It is all too common for today's self-appointed media "prophets" to repeat themes of God's threats and punishments (moderns who seem especially fond of the word "wrath," presumably making their ravings sound "biblical"). Typically, however, the ancient reasons for God's threatened judgment (usually the treatment of the poor by the wealthy and powerful) are conveniently replaced with the modern policies of bigotry, sexism, nationalism, or greed. We should never allow "God's judgment" to be exploited for unjust propaganda if in any sense we are to be responsible as we read the ancient prophetic texts in the context of modern faith and practice. How can we discern an authentic modern prophet? We need look no further than Micah's prescribed measurements: do they love justice, exhibit a devotion to humanity, and walk mindfully with God?

Micah 7:1 The Farmer-Prophet's Anguish

1 Alas for me, because I am like a gatherer of summer fruit,
    a gleaner of the vintage!
But there is no cluster to eat,
    the early figs that I love.

The Farmer-Prophet's Anguish

[1] The two phrases have a similar sound at the beginning of the two parts: the first phrase begins with "Woe is me!" (*'alĕlay*), and the second phrase with "a gleaner" (*'ōlĕlōt*). The term for "summer fruit" (*qayiṣ*) is often, in slightly different forms, used for simply "summer" as a season (Gen 8:22), often contrasted with "winter" (*ḥōrep*; cf. Pss 32:4; 74:17; Prov 26:1; Zech 14:8). Yet in some contexts it refers to summer fruit itself, as found in lists of other foodstuffs (e.g., 2 Sam 16:1, 2; Jer 40:10; and famously in the wordplay of "end" and "fruit" in Amos 8:1–2). Here, combined with "gatherer" and "gleaner," the term is clear. The LXX, on the other hand, reads "straw" or "stubble" (Exod 5:12; 15:7; Job 41:29 [21 MT]), which somewhat confuses the seasons, as both gathering and winnowing straw would be a harvesttime activity.

Pentateuchal legislation allowed the poor to "glean" the last of the harvest as a form of mutual aid (Lev 19:10; Deut 24:21), and this tradition is used by the prophets (Isa 24:13, "as at the gleaning when the grape harvest is ended"; Jer 49:9, "If grape-gatherers came to you, would they not leave gleanings?"; cf. Obad 5). McKane (1998, 207) reports that Ibn Ezra already made the connection with gleaning. Are we to see by implication that Micah identifies with the poor? Is the fruit to be compared to good people? Thus no good fruit = no good people!

"Cluster" presumably refers to grapes (Num 13:23, 24; Isa 65:8), but the term can be used of other plants (Song 1:14). "Figs" or "early figs" refers to another agricultural product found in prophetic imagery (Jer 24:2, "One basket had very good figs, like *first-ripe figs*, but the other basket had very bad figs, so bad that they could not be eaten"; cf. Isa 28:4; Hos 9:10). Although it is difficult to be specific about what kind of fruit is intended here, Andersen and Freedman argue that it surely must be a fig, given the associations in the text elsewhere (2000, 566–67).

Finally, Micah speaks of something that his "soul" or "life" desires, which I have rendered as fruit "that I love." How this term (*nepeš*) is translated is often a matter of the modern reader's poetic judgment. For example, the term for "life" can often be translated poetically by using the English "soul" (in NRSV see, e.g., Ps 86:2, "life"; but Ps 119:20, "soul"). Here the sense is certainly a much stronger "desire" than merely "liking." There can hardly be a clearer moment revealing Micah's own context: he represents a people for whom agriculture is the beloved center of life. At this moment it is also worth pausing to consider whether this is a later addition to Micah, as some have argued. If so, then we have equally clear evidence that this editor/commentator on the earlier Micah material shares the same love of village farming life. It is rare for commentators to consider the humanity, hopes, and fears of the nameless Judeans who may have added to a work, to enhance its meaning for later generations.

Sweeney is particularly eloquent with his defense of the notion that we are reading about Micah and his fellow lowlander refugees in Jerusalem. Although

I do not agree that Micah is necessarily in Jerusalem for these words, I find Sweeney's descriptions worthy of serious consideration:

> A siege with its attendant starvation tends to bring out the worst in people as they struggle, even against each other, to survive. A refugee such as Micah would likely find himself on the streets of the city scrounging for food and fighting off those with whom he was forced to compete. (2001a, 407)

What is beyond question here is that the final chapter begins with a sighing acknowledgment that the world Micah knows has changed, perhaps forever, and we have a fleeting moment of drama as he wistfully speaks of a farmer's pastoral dream.

Here it is appropriate to consider the fascinating history of speculation about the entirety of chapter 7. De Moor, as mentioned above, declares his "astonishment" with the work of scholars on Micah who have proposed dividing this chapter into no less than twenty different proposed units. In reply to this, De Moor is inclined to read Mic 7 as *all* coming from a disillusioned Micah, the same prophet as producing chapters 1–3: "In my opinion the prophet Micah could have spoken these words at the end of his career. He sadly observes that there is no one who has listened to his admonitions" (2000, 164). De Moor also does not accept the view (see below) that "Lady Zion" is occasionally speaking in chapter 7 rather than Micah; instead, he argues that the textual variants replacing the feminine gender (noted below and in my translation) with the masculine gender at key points in the chapter must be taken more seriously.

Micah 7:2–6 The Prophet Describes an Unjust and Disintegrating Society

2 The faithful one has perished from the land.
  There is no upright individual[a] among humans.
All of them, they lie in wait for bloodshed,[b]
  a man against his brother—they hunt[c] with a net.[d]
3 Hands are good—at doing evil!
  The privileged[e] ask—the judgment benefits.
The great one dictates what he desires.[f]
  So they twist . . . [justice?].[g]
4 Their "good" is like a thorn from a bush;
  even the upright individual[h] is like a thornbush.
A day[i] of your sentinels, of your being mustered,[j] has come.
  Now comes confusion for them![k]
5 Do not be certain about a companion;
  do not trust a leader![l]

The Prophet Describes an Unjust and Disintegrating Society 209

Guard the doors of your mouth,
even from the one who lies in your embrace!ᵐ
6 Because aⁿ son is one who mocks a father;
a daughter rises up against a mother,
A daughter-in-law against a mother-in-law.
A man's enemies are residents of his house!

a. "Upright person" (so Wolff 1990, 200).
b. Plural form, *lĕdāmîm*.
c. The "man" and "brother" are singular, but "hunt" is plural—referring to *both* the man and the brother? Wolff reads "oppress to death" rather than "hunt with net" (1990, 201).
d. Here many want to read *ḥērem* as "total destruction" rather than as "net," thereby implying the infamous "ban" of ancient Israelite warfare theology. McKane (1998, 209) notes comparative renderings in the Peshitta, Targum, and Vulgate yet retains "net." Wolff suggests a man hunts the other "to death" (1990, 201).
e. Singular in Hebrew.
f. Mays (1976, 149) wonders if there are missing terms in this verse yet suggests that in any case it is possible to read it coherently.
g. Wolff reads "and they twist it" (1990, 200). Mays (1976, 149) runs the line into the next phrase: "they twist their good like a thornbush." Others have proposed that something is missing here—and "justice" seems a reasonable proposal.
h. Here I render *yāšār* again as "upright individual," recognizing that the same term is also found in 7:2.
i. McKane (1998, 217) proposes "day of judgment" here.
j. "Your" is a second-person singular possessive ending, but "sentinels" and "mustered" are plural. A problem here is that "day" and "has come" are separated by the two plural participles referring to guards or "sentinels," and "those who are mustered." The "individual" being addressed can be Jerusalem or perhaps the king.
k. I use "confusion," it can be "confounding for them" (*mĕbûkātām*), or "their confounding" or "their confusion."
l. Cha (1996, 117–18) cites Jer 9:3–5 and 12:6, insisting on "friend" here, as does Wolff (1990, 200).
m. I cannot improve on NRSV here.
n. Wolff (1990, 200) makes this entire series definite rather than indefinite.

[2] Mays (1976, 150) wants to read this entire section as part of the uncertainties of the exilic period. On the other hand, the descriptions of social instability could well apply to the frightful campaigns of the Assyrians, and even to the consequences of preparing against the Assyrian campaigns. Wolff (1990, 205), however, observes that "our passage is not far removed from Ecclesiastes' discovery of the corruption of all human beings."

The term "faithful" (*ḥāsîd*), built etymologically on the important concept of *ḥesed*, is also translated as "enduring" or "steadfast." It is used primarily in the religious poetry of worship (e.g., Pss 4:3 [4], "Know that YHWH has set apart the faithful for himself"; 18:25 [26], "[With] the faithful you show yourself faithful" (NIV); cf. 116:15; Jer 3:12). Notice how the complaint of the absence of "faithful" persons in Ps 12:1–2 (2–3) is accompanied, as here in Micah, with accusations of how people who are *not* faithful act: "Help, YHWH, for there is no longer anyone who is godly; the faithful [ḥāsîd] have disappeared from humankind. They utter lies to each other; with flattering lips and a double heart they speak."

Micah's response, however, is more serious, referring to those who are "lying in wait for blood." References to shedding blood as a euphemism for oppression and injustice are common in prophetic rhetoric (so Isa 1:15, "I will not listen; your hands are full of blood"; cf. Isa 33:15; 59:7; Ezek 7:23, "For the land is full of bloody crimes; the city is full of violence"; cf. Ezek 9:9; against Assyria in Nah 3:1, "Ah! City of bloodshed, utterly deceitful"). The notion of a "city of blood" is used ironically by Ezekiel against the Israelites themselves (24:6, 9). "Blood" is used to speak of injustice in Hos 4:2 ("bloodshed follows bloodshed"). The beginning of Proverbs portrays a picture of urban crime: "Come with us, let us lie in wait for blood; let us wantonly ambush the innocent" (1:11), similar to Jer 22:17, "But your eyes and heart are only on your dishonest gain, for shedding innocent blood, and for practicing oppression and violence"; cf. "innocent blood" in Deut 19 and 21). It is hard to avoid the conclusion that this is part of Micah's sense of social breakdown. In the modern era, televised pictures of towns and cities after major military attacks, riots, or earthquakes aptly illustrate Micah's descriptions of social disintegration.

In such circumstances, suggests Micah, "a man" (*'îš*) hunts his brother. Bloodshed combined with "lying in wait" means that people are plotting evil. Ambush appears in descriptions of military tactics (Josh 8; Judg 9; 16:2). In the legal tradition, it is the equivalent of premeditated murder (so Deut 19:11). Such plotting is often mentioned in relation to oppression of the poor (Ps 10:9; cf. Prov 24:15). Micah will not allow that terrible social consequences are "unintended," as modern leaders often publicly plea when they are confronted with the suffering that results from their economic or political policies.

For "net" (*ḥērem* II), see Ezek 26:5 (cf. another term for "net," *mikmār*, in Ps 141:10; Isa 51:20; *môqēš*, "snare," in Prov 18:7; 22:25; 29:6). Here the temptation to read *ḥērem* I, "ban" or "devoted to destruction" (thus referring to the famous genocidal tactic that was part of the early theology of warfare, according to, e.g., Josh 6:17–18), is resisted by most scholars.[58]

[3] The emphasis on "hands" refers to the actions of those who do evil (cf. Ps 24:4, "clean hands and pure hearts"). The term used for "skilled" or acting "skillfully" suggests premeditation and planning on the part of those whose activities exploit and oppress (cf. playing "skillfully" on a stringed instrument

---

58. Andersen and Freedman (2000) do not even consider it, while Wolff (1990, 201) lists those who insist on "net," and others (including his own translation) take the notion of utter destruction seriously.

in Ps 33:3; cf. Isa 23:16; or seeing "well/keenly" in Jer 1:12; cf. 2:33; 7:5). The LXX suggests "make ready" or "prepare" (so "prepare" weapons in Ps 7:13 [14]; or "establish" in Ps 65:6 [7]).

The term *śar* is most often used of military commanders (1 Kgs 16:16; cf. 1 Sam 8:12; Neh 2:9, "officers of the army"; cf. Isa 21:5), but it can also refer to officials in the retinue of the king (Pss 68:27 [28], "princes"; 119:161; 148:11). In prophetic rhetoric, it is often used of officials, perhaps of the king, who are corrupt and seeking payments and bribes (Isa 1:23; 3:14; Jer 1:18; in Jeremiah the term "princes" is almost always listed immediately after the king but before other officials and leaders, as in 2:26; 4:9; 8:1; 17:25; 24:1; 29:2; cf. Ezek 17:12; Hos 7:3, 5; 8:10; Amos 1:15; 2:3; but Zeph 1:8 suggests that the term does not speak literally of "princes," that is, to heirs to the throne, as they are differentiated here). Here the reading is difficult, but not impossible. Literally the *śar* "questions" or "requests." The implication suggests advisers who promote their belligerent policies. The results of their "requests," of course, are even more financial benefits for themselves.

What they seek is *šillûm*, "payment," presumed from a construction based on the root for "well-being" or "peace" (so Isa 34:8, year of "vindication"; cf. days of "recompense" in Hos 9:7). But this could be rendered differently: what the officials "inquire about," the judges "reassure," as in the common phrase "Be at peace" (Isa 39:8, reassurance from the prophet to Hezekiah; cf. "prosperity" in 54:13). Jeremiah 4:10 suggests that "peace" can be "reassurance" and "security" (also 14:13). Thus the implication is that the great and the privileged are speakers of their heart's desire.

Thus they "twist." The term can also be rendered "weave" (typically derived from the root term normally rendered "ropes" or "bindings" [e.g., Judg 15:13, 14; Pss 2:3; 129:4]; but a clue may be found in the imagery used in Isa 5:18, "Ah, you who drag iniquity along with cords of falsehood, who drag sin along as with cart *ropes*"). The LXX simply renders "rescued," a strange attempt to understand the Hebrew terminology. The previous verse, however, may have ended in "nets," and this verse ends in "ropes"; thus the notion of "weaving evil" or being "tied up" in their behavior seems to be suggested here. Hillers discusses various possibilities for a missing term here, perhaps "justice," although he finds this "unconvincing" (Hillers 1964, 84).

Although Andersen and Freedman declare that the text here is "hopeless," they acknowledge that Micah is speaking of two corrupt offices, "head administrator and chief magistrate" (2000, 569–70). Precision may be "hopeless," but clarity of thought certainly is not. "Twisting" justice to serve the ends of the powerful would be a typical image for Micah and is hardly difficult for moderns to understand! Here we are again reminded of the famous line attributed to Mark Twain: "It ain't those parts of the Bible that I can't understand that bother me, it is the parts that I do understand."

[4] The Hebrew is difficult: literally, "their good," usually translated as a superlative in reference to people, thus "the best of them are as thornbushes." The term normally rendered "thorns" is used elsewhere only at Prov 15:19 ("thorns"). The LXX goes in an entirely different direction in this first phrase and refers to that which is "eaten by moths" (cf. "moth" in LXX: Isa 33:1; 50:9; Prov 25:20; Matt 6:19–20).

For "upright individual," see "righteous deeds" in Pss 11:7 and "upright" in 37:37. The term is used in two different forms in Isa 26:7 and as "straight path" in Jer 31:9. The ending term in this phrase is then presumed to be a parallel to the ending of the first phrase, rendered "bush/hedge" (*mĕsûkâ*). The LXX refers to a "day of watching" (cf. Sir 40:6), which seems reasonable: a day clear enough to see far from a watchtower.

There is a reference to a particular event happening, the arrival of a "day" as well as to two terms that identify two groups for whom this day will be difficult, but the phrases are difficult. Some have even proposed reading "north" for one of the terms (thus *ṣāpôn* for *ṣappâ*), which would suggest a reading: "The day—those from your north." But I propose a reading based on the term "watch": thus "a day of your sentinels" (cf. 2 Kgs 9:17; cf. Isa 21:6, "a lookout"), followed by "your mustering," but some have suggested "your punishment" (cf. Isa 10:3, "day of punishment").

The sense of the final phrase seems to be the coming of "confusion" (cf. Isa 22:5, "For the Lord GOD of hosts has a day of tumult and trampling and *confusion*." The LXX speaks rather of a time of "weeping" (Isa 22:12). In either case, the confidence of the Jerusalem leadership is seriously called into question by Micah. They seem so certain of the outcome. They are wrong.

[5] The sentiment speaks of social disturbance, the opposite of a society where you have trusted friends and neighbors. Jeremiah speaks of a similar condition, probably adopting the sentiments of Micah (Jer 9:4, "Beware of your neighbors, and put no trust in any of your kin; for all your kin are supplanters, and every neighbor goes around like a slanderer"). See Prov 1:11–18 for a description of behavior that would endanger the social fabric of village and town life—typical urban corruptions.

Do not "believe/trust" in a friend (cf. Pss 78:8, 22, 32, 37, referring to those who did not "trust in" God, in God's actions, or in God's covenant; cf. Isa 28:16, "One who trusts"). For "friend" (*rēaʿ*), see Job 6:27; Ps 35:14. The second phrase is a warning known to Psalms (62:10 [11]; 146:3), so also a problem with "close friends" (Prov 16:28; Ps 55:13 [14]; "allies," Jer 13:21), but LXX reads "heads of ancestral houses" (1 Esd 5:63; 8:59).

The warning is to "observe/guard/keep" your wife (cf. 1 Kgs 8:25; Esth 2:3, "guardian" of women; Ps 34:20, God "watches over"; cf. Ps 37:37; Prov 7:1, "Keep my words"). The phrase used, however, is striking: the "one lying with you in your embrace" (cf. Deut 13:6 [7]), thus emphasizing the inability to trust

The Prophet Describes an Unjust and Disintegrating Society

even the one with whom you sleep and the one with whom you are intimate! With this person, you are to "guard the doorways of your mouth" (cf. Sir 28:25, "Make a door and a bolt for your mouth"; cf. Ps 141:3). Reicke notes a number of parallels from ancient Near Eastern texts about familial breakdown in times leading to the "end" of a city or a society, including references to brother turning against brother, daughters and mothers against one another (1967, 358–59).

[6] The son treats the father "foolishly," or "the son is a scoffer to the father" (cf. Deut 32:6; 32:21; Ps 14:1). The imagery of family breakdown continues: the daughter "rises up against" her mother (2 Sam 14:7). Next, a "bride" (Jer 2:32) against her "mother-in-law"; the latter translation of Mic 7:6b is based entirely on the use of the same Hebrew term in Ruth, (as in 1:14; 2:11, 18, 19). Finally, a man's enemies are residents of his household! The picture of disarray and internal dissent is palpable. This is cited, famously, by Jesus in speaking of the divisions that will be caused by his message (Luke 12:49–53; only Matt 10:34–36 includes this final phrase from Mic 7:6).[59]

In one reading, what Micah deeply cares about, social stability and the ability of lowlander society to continue their pastoral work, shatters before him. We need not propose that this is the result of an actual attack (thus we need not insist on a specific date of an Assyrian campaign, for example) because Micah knows that social breakdowns can result from oppressive economic conditions brought about in preparation for war, even before its actual conduct. The famous antimonarchical passage of 1 Sam 8 clearly indicates social upheaval from the very institution of the monarchy, not necessarily from any particular crisis. What is rarely acknowledged by the powerful is that their policies seep like an acid into the very bedrooms of the oppressed! Families break down. The impact, for example, of years of oppression suffered by African Americans in nineteenth- and early twentieth-century America, Maori family and tribal structures in New Zealand, and Aboriginal Australian tribal structures in Australia—such events have often resulted in catastrophic destruction of family unity and stability. In a final insult, the very same people are then blamed for the lack of stability in their families! Micah, at least, sees clearly why this has emerged in his time. Not for him are the simplistic moralizing explanations that avoid the consequences of economic policies of the elite and effectively blame the victim!

Another reading, which does not necessarily replace our previous suggestions, might stress that Micah is also mocking the royal family. Given the intrigue noted in 1–2 Kings among the royal families—assassinations, usurpations of the

---

59. It is tempting to wonder if Jesus intended to imply something different. Is he saying that former enemies will become close like family—speaking of the rearranged society as a result of his message, a society composed not of mere family loyalties but chiefly a unity built on commitment to truth—or was he simply quoting the same sentiment of disarray and division from the Micah passage, more or less as is? On this, see also Grelot 1986.

throne, and other violence—a warning not to trust your own wife would be biting satire (cf. the wonderfully entertaining apocryphal story of Zerubbabel in 1 Esd 4, which satirizes the royal bed chamber in precisely this fashion!).

Micah 7:7–13 The Vindication to Come

7 But I will watch[a] for YHWH;
   I will wait for the God of my salvation.
   My God will hear me.
8 Do not rejoice over me, my opponents!
   Because I have fallen, I will rise.
When I sit in darkness,
   YHWH will be a light to me.
9 I will carry the anger of YHWH,
   because [if?][b] I have sinned against him.
Until the time when he will judge my case,
   and bring my justice and bring me out to the light,
   I will see His righteousness!
10 My opponent will see!
   She who said to me, "Where is YHWH your[c] God?"
My eyes will see her.
   Now she will be trampled like mud in the streets.[d]
11 A day for building your garden fences,[e]
   a day for extending your boundaries.
12 That day [they] will come to you[f]
   from Assyria, from the cities of Egypt,
from Egypt to the River,
   from sea to sea,[g] from mountain to mountain.
13 And the land will become a wasteland
   to their inhabitants for the fruit of their deeds.

   a. The term echoes the "sentinels" of v. 4 above.
   b. "If" would suggest a Job-like uncertainty that a sin has actually brought this on!
   c. De Moor discusses a number of texts that have the form as masculine, "your [male] god" rather than "your [female] god." He defends the point that Micah is the one speaking throughout ch. 7 (2000, 166–67).
   d. Both McKane (1998, 221) and Wolff (1990, 198) suggest that this is an agricultural image, not an image of city streets.
   e. Wolff (1990, 212) renders this "walls," but not a common wall. See comments.
   f. Williamson argues for corruption in the term and calls for "Your flock will come" (1997, 371).
   g. McKane (1998, 227) reads "from sea to sea" as "obscure hyperbole."

The Vindication to Come

[7] The status of Mic 7:7 has received considerable attention in the commentary literature. Is it merely a "stitch" between vv. 8–13 and vv. 1–6? Part of the debate focuses on the nature of vv. 8–20, which is now widely read as a "liturgy" of sorts. Sweeney, for example, see the liturgy as follows (2000, 409):

v. 7	Introduction
vv. 8–10	Addressing the enemy
vv. 11–13	Addressing Jerusalem
vv. 14–17	Addressing YHWH
vv. 18–20	Concluding praise

The notion that there is a "liturgy" in chapter 7 is by no means settled, however. The idea seems to be focused around the possible "use" of the book of Micah in later centuries of faith and practice, and readings that end with a liturgy suggest the use of prophetic literature in worship.

One potential problem is the fact that some prophetic literature, including Micah, is highly critical of temple traditions. We need to overcome this challenge before fully embracing a liturgical use of prophetic literature. Where does a critique of temple abuses enter into the temple liturgy itself? We rarely see this kind of courage even in modern liturgy!

In Mic 7 are three phrases of contrasting attitudes:

1. The writer contrasts his attitude, "I will watch" (or perhaps "be watchful" or "remain watchful," Mic 7:7a), with the attitudes of his opponents. The opening phrase presumes a contrast with other attitudes that are either not watchful or simply watching for the wrong events!
2. The second attitude is expressed in patience: I will await "the God of my salvation" (Mic 7:7b; cf. Pss 18:46 [47]; 25:5; 27:9; 62:6–7 [7–8]; Hab 3:18). To "wait for salvation" (Lam 3:26) suggests doubt and a willingness to remain faithful in the face of things not working out in the short term (so Job 14:14).
3. God "will hear me" and "bring my justice" (Mic 7:7c, 9d; cf. typical pleas to God to "hear" prayers, as in Pss 17:6; 54:2 [4]).

If, however, Micah is intending to contrast his own "watchfulness" for YHWH against the futile military watchfulness of sentinels, then the passage becomes even more provocative and contributes to Micah's overall critique of false trust in military preparations. You "watch" in your way and toward your goals, but I "watch" for God.

[8] "Do not rejoice over me" or perhaps even "against" me (cf. Isa 14:29; Pss 13:5 [6]; 41:11 [12]). Proverbs 24:17 forbids precisely this kind of bravado: "Do not rejoice when your enemies fall, and do not let your heart be glad when they stumble."

How one translates "enemy" can make a significant difference in appreciating this passage. Foreign enemies might be the intended referent, but that is hardly certain. Ahab addresses Elijah as "my enemy" (1 Kgs 21:20), so "opponents" can just as easily be among one's own people, and for prophets they often were! McKane (1998, 218) reports that various enemies have been suggested across the history of interpretation, including Rome in the Targums, Babylon in Kimchi's interpretation, and Persia in Rudolph's reading of Micah (1975, 221). This is a fascinating exercise in the history of interpretation but does not settle the question for us. An internal enemy would be consistent with Micah's rhetoric throughout the book.

To speak of God as a "light" is an important image (Exod 13:21; Ps 27:1, "The LORD is my light and my salvation"; or light "of God," so Isa 2:5, "O house of Jacob, come, let us walk in the light of the LORD"). It is central to the beginning of John's Gospel. Similarly, darkness can be compared to death or defeat (Ps 143:3); seeing light, after being released from prison, is another motif that may refer to actual confinement or death (Isa 42:7; cf. Lam 3:6). These similarities with Lamentations and Second Isaiah have led many commentators to suggest strong ties to that time period (i.e., after 587 B.C.E.).[60]

[9] This verse seems to draw on the internal jurisprudence system in the temple, the "enemies" in this case being fellow Israelites! The classic case is Ps 35, which opens with suggestions of "national" enemies, but the discussion later alludes to fellow Israelites with whom the person lives in close communal proximity (vv. 11–14). Thus there is the tradition of being particularly disturbed with internal rivalries, taunts, and divisions (cf. Pss 55:12–13 [13–14]; 69:7 [8],"It is for your sake that I have borne reproach, that shame has covered my face"; cf. Mic 6:16 NRSV, "bear the scorn").

There is considerable discussion about Micah's confession of sin in this passage (cf. Ps 41:4 [5]), but surely this is quite compatible with the postexilic tradition of the penitential prayer, where confession is key to the entire genre:

> O my God, I am too ashamed and embarrassed to lift my face to you, my God, for our iniquities have risen higher than our heads, and our guilt has mounted up to the heavens. (Ezra 9:6)
>
> You have been just in all that has come upon us, for you have dealt faithfully and we have acted wickedly. (Neh 9:33)
>
> Then I turned to the Lord God, to seek an answer by prayer and supplication with fasting and sackcloth and ashes. . . . "We have sinned and done wrong, acted

---

60. Andersen and Freedman (2000, 576) believe that this reflects attitudes of Lamentations and Second Isaiah.

wickedly and rebelled, turning aside from your commandments and ordinances." (Dan 9:3, 5)

We have sinned before the Lord. We have disobeyed him, and have not heeded the voice of the Lord our God, to walk in the statutes of the Lord that he set before us. (Bar 1:17–18)

All of these allusions to internal disputes supports our argument against an emphasis in these verses on "national" (and thus external) enemies. Further, to ask for "my justice" and "vindication" (Mic 7:9d) relates to appeals to God for judgment (Isa 62:2; Jer 51:10; Pss 24:5; 35:23–24; 37:6). Micah's conflict is with his own leaders.

[10] The theme of others seeing vindication or affirmation is very important in ancient Israel's sociopolitical religious and worship literature (Pss 25:2, "Do not let me be put to shame; do not let my enemies exult over me"; 35:26; cf. 42:3 [4]; 127:5). This can be accompanied by questions from adversaries, but the calls to God seem to suggest that God ought to be concerned about God's reputation (Pss 42:10 [11], "They say to me continually, 'Where is your God?'"; 79:10; 115:2).

In fact, the reference to a feminine subject suggests an urban location, most likely the central city. The writer is speaking of gaining the upper hand over the power of "the city."[61] The question "Where is YHWH your God?" refers to vindication: if you are right, then where is the proof? Here the interesting reference to "YHWH your God" reminds us that this phrase is used in the Hebrew Bible some 300 times, but nearly half of those are in Deuteronomy alone (many more in DH). The suggestion of Deuteronomic influence in these words seems difficult to avoid.

As we have observed, there is a rich vocabulary of terms for shame and dishonor (Pss 35:4, 26; 40:14–15 [15–16]; 71:13; cf. Isa 41:11). In Isaiah are many uses of the concept of "shame," but almost always on enemies or on taking away the shame of Israel. Jeremiah, on the other hand, often shares Micah's sentiment (Jer 3:25, "Let us lie down in our shame, and let our dishonor cover us; for we have sinned against the LORD our God"; 6:15; 8:12; 9:19; 11:13, "altars to shame you"; 22:22; 23:40; against others in 46:24, "Egypt"; 48:1, "Moab").

In military terms, David brags of "stamping down" his enemies "like the mire of the streets" (2 Sam 22:43//Ps 18:42; cf. Isa 41:25, "[Cyrus] shall trample on rulers as on mortar, as the potter treads clay"; and in reference to Jeremiah's prison, in Jer 38:6). Note also the association with military preparations (Nah 3:14, "Draw water for the siege, strengthen your forts; trample the clay, tread the mortar, take hold of the brick mold!"; cf. Zech 10:5, trampled enemies like "mire in the streets," *běṭîṭ ḥûṣôt*).

---

61. Andersen and Freedman suggest that the feminine singular implies confrontation between two cities (2000, 584).

[11] The most common term for "wall" (*ḥômâ*) is often used in Isaiah in reference to Jerusalem (presumably because he is resident there; see Isa 22:10, 11; 36:11; 49:16; 60:10, 18; 62:6; cf. Prov 18:11) and is used of the city walls of Jerusalem and other major cities (1 Sam 31:10, etc.) and thus of defensive constructions (Nehemiah 1:3; 2:8 and many times, so Ezek 26:9). On the other hand, the term here in Micah (*gādēr*) is used in a manner that may suggest a parallel to the major type of city wall (Ezek 13:5; 22:30) but is more often used for agricultural fencing (Ps 80:12 [13]; Prov 24:30–31; Isa 5:5; Hos 2:6). Even in Amos 9:11, the "hut" of David, whose "walls" will be fixed, is the "hut" of an agricultural worker (so Isa 1:8; cf. Andersen and Freedman 2000, 586). The suggestion, once again, is that Micah is familiar with village life, Isaiah with the city.

Note the term "statutes" (sg. *ḥōq*) throughout Ps 119 and Deuteronomy (e.g., 4:1), paralleled with "commandments" (but cf. Jer 5:22). The translation of "expanding borders" is thus a guess unsupported by the LXX, which also tries to render the Hebrew with a reference to "customs" or "laws," but uses the verb "to rub away." Hillers presumes the use of "distant" in Isa 33:17 to defend the NRSV translation, even though "land" or "borders" do not appear in the MT here in Micah (1984, 88).

[12] The procession-of-the-nations theme reminds us of Mic 4:8. References to both Assyria and Egypt in the same thought are relatively rare in the Bible, but do occur in some prophetic texts, presumably at a time when both major powers present threats to the Israelite peoples, or as a collective reference to major threats of the past. In this case, note especially the famous passage in Isa 19, which takes up events in the future that involve both Egyptians and Assyrians, but may also refer to Israelites *from* those locations (cf. Isa 7:18; 52:4). Hosea also refers to both powers as false saviors of Hebrew people who may appeal to either of them for assistance (Hos 7:11; 9:3; 11:5, 11; 12:1 [2]; later taken up in Jer 2:36). More often the two powers are used as symbols of the "far reaches" of the earth, where Israelites have been exiled and from which they will be gathered (e.g., Isa 11:11, 16; 27:13; echoed in the later work of Zech 10:10, "I will bring them home from the land of Egypt, and gather them from Assyria"). Related to this, then, are the generic references "sea to sea" and "mountain to mountain," reminiscent of the prayers for the expanded rule of the king in Ps 72:8, "May he have dominion from sea to sea, and from the River to the ends of the earth."

[13] This verse presents some problems. Is it to be considered the final word of the section starting at v. 7, or the first thought in the next section, concluding at v. 20, the end of the book? The idea here is a land that becomes a "wasteland" or "desolation." The threat is part of the curse tradition in the Torah (Lev 26:33) and is picked up as a warning in the Prophetic Books (e.g., Isa 1:7, "Your country lies desolate"). The term "desolation" is used almost

A Final Prayer for Deliverance 219

entirely by prophets, however, and especially in the sixth century in reference to the events of the Babylonian conquest. Of 58 occasions, the majority occur in Jeremiah and Ezekiel—in Jeremiah most often of the Judean people and lands, in Ezekiel often of God's punishment of foreign lands. The appearance of the term in Mic 7:13 suggests a bookend with its use in 1:7, but the contexts are rather different. Furthermore, warnings about destruction often parallel the land "and the inhabitants" to affirm the total destruction (Isa 24:1; Jer 25:9).

Echoing the first section of the book (3:4), here in 7:13 are references to fruits of labor or work. Finally, the literal phrase "fruit of their deeds" is used in a positive manner in Isa 3:10, but the same phrase used for negative deeds, undoubtedly influenced by Micah, appears in Jer 21:14 and 32:19.

It is hard to avoid a sense of impending vindication in this passage. But as we have observed elsewhere, everything turns on the identified parties! Is Micah defending himself against those in his society who resist his criticism? Is he addressing fellow Judeans? Or is Micah, like other prophets (including Jeremiah and Second Isaiah), directing his anger at the external threats and enemies who always think they have the upper hand against Judah? The latter is possible, but the tone of the book (including this chapter) pushes toward an internal debate with opponents among his fellow Judeans.

Micah 7:14–20 A Final Prayer for Deliverance

14 Shepherd your people with your scepter,
    a flock that is your inheritance,
dwellers alone,[a]
    a forest in a garden.
Lead to Bashan and Gilead,
    as in the days of old.
15 As in the days when you brought [us] out from[b] Egypt,
    Show us wondrous things![c]
16 The nations will see you and be ashamed,
    from all their military power.
They will put a hand to a mouth;
    their ears will be silent.
17 They shall lick dust like a snake,
    or like crawling things of the earth.
They shall come trembling from their fortresses[d] to YHWH our God;[e]
    they will be in dread and fear of you.

18 Who is a god like you,
    pardoning sin and passing over transgression
    for a remnant that is your inheritance?

He does not hold on to anger forever,
   because He delights in kindness.
19 He will again show compassion to us;
   he will overcome^f our sins.
   He will throw all our sins to the bottom of the sea.
20 Give faithfulness to Jacob,
   kindness to Abraham,
   as you promised to our fathers in former days.

a. For *šōknî lĕbādād*, cf. Num 23:9, "Here is a people living alone [*lĕbādād yiškōn*] and not reckoning itself among the nations!"

b. With Wolff (1990, 214) I omit "land of" Egypt. LXX lacks "land," but Andersen and Freedman (2000, 592) point out that "land of" Egypt is a common phrase.

c. MT: "I will show him." But "show us," a common amendment here, preserves possible liturgical use (McKane 1998, 230). "I will show him" reads *'ar'ennû*, but "show us" reads *har'ēnû*, the difference of merely the opening letter. Shaw, on the other hand, preserves the first person and suggests that God is acting here (1993, 195).

d. Hebrew *mimmisgĕrōtêhem*; cf. Ps 18:45 (46).

e. Many propose to omit reference to God here, as does Wolff 1990, 212.

f. Gordon (1978) argues for "pardon" here.

[14] The people are to be led with "staff" or "scepter." The term is used in a variety of circumstances, referring to different items (royal symbol/scepter in Gen 49:10; Ps 45:6 [7]; Isa 14:5; Amos 1:8; shepherd's staff in Lev 27:32 and likely Ezek 20:37; "rod of discipline" in Prov 22:8, 15; "rod" of oppression in Isa 9:4; cf. 10:5, 15, 24; "rod" of God's anger in Lam 3:1). The wordplay on a shepherd's staff and a ruler's scepter seems intentional.

"Inheritance" is the portion that belongs to the Israelite tribes, normally as a portion of land. Here the image is of "God's inheritance," a concept that does have a history in other uses. Exodus 15:17 refers to "the mountain of your inheritance" (NIV). Psalms praises the people of God as God's "inheritance." Notice the connection with God as shepherd in Ps 28:9, "O save your people, and bless your heritage; be their shepherd, and carry them forever" (cf. Pss 68:9 [10]; 74:2; 106:5), as well as Isa 63:17, "for the sake of the tribes that are your heritage," and especially in Joel 2:17, "Spare your people, YHWH, and do not make your heritage a mockery, a byword among the nations."

The notion of "living alone" seems to be an indication of peace, not harassed by imperial regimes or neighbors (cf. Num 23:9; cf. Jer 49:31). Bashan is almost always associated with herding and well-watered growth (Deut 32:14; Ps 22:12 [13]; Ezek 39:18; Zech 11:2), and "garden" (*karmel*, Carmel?) is either a garden or a specific location, often associated in the same poetic phrases with greenery or natural beauty (Nah 1:4; Isa 33:9; Jer 50:19).

A Final Prayer for Deliverance

For Wolff (1990, 226), the idea of "dwellers alone" suggests that the sentiment comes from a people "hemmed in" in Jerusalem and thus not able to take flocks to the fertile areas such as Bashan and Gilead. He also thinks that *karmel* is not a place-name here.

Finally, the reference to "days of old" or "former times" is a clear indication of the importance of a tradition that can be appealed to. What form this tradition takes, of course, is quite controversial, but what is clear is that a tradition can be appealed to (Amos 9:11; Mal 3:4; Ps 44:1 [2], "We have heard with our ears, O God, our ancestors have told us, what deeds you performed in their days, in the days of old"; cf. Ps 143:5; Lam 1:7; Isa 63:11). We are reminded that the use of history can serve many purposes. Early Israelite tradition can justify arguments raised against kingship just as much as support kingship (certainly stories like David and Bathsheba, or the revolt of Absalom, preserve traditions of criticism).

[15] The reference to the exodus motif here also draws on historical tradition, both in Exodus and in the Deuteronomic tradition, where God is identified by the act of bringing out slaves from Egypt (Deut 5:6); this deliverance is even used as part of the motivation clause for certain actions and celebrations (16:3, "because you came out of the land of Egypt in great haste"). Associated with this is praise of a God who will "do wonders," lauding God's abilities, especially in confronting national enemies (Josh 3:5, "Sanctify yourselves; for tomorrow YHWH will do wonders among you"; Job 5:9; 37:5, 14; Ps 72:18, "Blessed be YHWH, . . . who alone does wondrous things"; cf. Pss 86:10; 98:1; 136:4). A key point here must be that God's "wonders" are considered miraculous acts rather than crediting humans, including human abilities to engage in impressive military campaigns. Moses calls on the people to "stand and watch" when God engages battle (Exod 14:13–14 S-C). Consequently, 1 Sam 8 suggests that choosing a king is rejecting God (vv. 7–9).

[16] In this case, however, the reaction of the nations is particularly important. What the nations will do is "be ashamed," and this is related directly to descriptions of their power. That nations will see something significant about God is known from prophetic tradition (e.g., Isa 62:2, "The nations shall see your vindication, and all the kings your glory"; Ezek 39:21, "All the nations shall see my judgment that I have executed"). Even the proud will be silenced in shame (esp. Job 29:9). The term for "powerful" or "warrior" suggests the power of violence (*gibbôr*, "warrior," as in Pss 33:16; 89:19 [20]; 127:4; Joel 3 [4]:10; and even Ps 24:8, God is "mighty in battle"). According to Andersen and Freedman, the phrase means that they are to be "deprived" of their military might (2000, 593). Some have argued that Mic 7:13 appears to take away a glimmer of hope for the nations that is held out here in vv. 16–17; at least here they come to realize their mistakes. McKane, on the other hand, does not accept the notion that these verses speak of a conversion (cf. Jonah) but only their defeat by YHWH (1998,

232–33). Are defeat or conversion the only alternatives? What about the recognition of past mistakes as a breakthrough to the idea that new relationships between diverse peoples can be formed? Surely this is precisely the basis of forging new national relationships in a United Nations or a European Union. Such was the dream, for example, behind Prime Minister Kevin Rudd's 2008 official apology to Aboriginal Australians. Is it pointless to hope for such recognition of past sufferings by peoples in the recent, and even distant, past? Not to them it isn't!

The nations will also be embarrassed or humiliated (Ps 86:17; Isa 26:11; 45:24). The act of covering one's mouth is seen as a sign of accepting that one has either been wrong, accepting orders without question, or a sign of shock at the fate of others (Judg 18:19; Job 21:5, "Look at me, and be appalled, and lay your hand upon your mouth"; cf. Job 40:4; Prov 30:32; even as late as Sirach, in 5:12). Similarly, the act of covering the ears is a sign of people not wanting to hear something that might contradict what they think or hope for (Isa 33:15; cf. Jer 6:10; Zech 7:11).

Isaiah 52:15 famously combines both speechless surprise and humiliation in the context of the vindication of one who was so badly treated: "so he shall startle many nations; kings shall shut their mouths because of him; for that which had not been told them they shall see, and that which they had not heard they shall contemplate." It seems hardly surprising that the first Christians read the experience of Jesus into these words.

Despite doubts about the notion of *hope for the foreign nations* expressed by some recent commentators, it seems hard to avoid the possibility that this is precisely what is intended, especially in a book characterized by other such possibilities of hope (e.g., Mic 4:1–5). There is also the close association with the book of Jonah (compare the theme of the sailors' "fear" in Jonah 1:16 and the "fear" of the nations in Mic 7:17, the very next verse here). The foolishness of harsh military policy (and even personal relationships!) is often based on the inability to believe that "others" can come to think differently, that mutual recognition of past mistakes may begin to build bridges of trust. The critical point to be made in these final verses is that enemies can come to recognize past mistakes. Here we are very close to the spirit of the later book of Jonah, but even more can be said. Jesus' famous conversation with the Roman centurion (Matt 8:5–13) is made possible by the Roman's own humbled recognition that he, as an occupying soldier, is unworthy! His confession of colonialist guilt builds a bridge to Jesus. What might modern confessions of colonial guilt accomplish in our relations with otherwise hostile developing world nations?

[17] To "lick dust" is a phrase that comes from the tradition of the procession-of-the-nations theme that became prominent among the eighth-century prophets and shows signs of development in other literary contexts. In some cases, the theme of licking the dust appears negatively (Ps 72:9; Isa 49:23), but

there is debate as to the source of this imagery. In his commentary on Isa 40–55, Baltzer, for example, presents this as not necessarily a negative image. He suggests a "carnival image" where perhaps even children play the "role" of foreign kings and queens falling down and bowing, certainly a unique reading of the "lick the dust" reference in Isa 49:23 (2001, 330, but see also Ps. 2:12 and Gen 42:6 suggest other possible allusions). Others seem just as positive that this example of bowing comes from Persian practice, although it seems beyond doubt that the famous Black Obelisk presents an illustration of precisely the act of subservience described here: King Jehu is depicted bowing before the Assyrian monarch Shalmaneser III, the greater political authority.

If this is the case, then one might ask whether "rising from the dust" is an example of political independence rather than simply improving one's general condition of being downtrodden (Isa 52:2, "Shake yourself from the dust, rise up, O captive Jerusalem; loose the bonds from your neck, O captive daughter Zion!"). It is possible that there are some conceptual connections between the book of Jonah (3:8–10, where the Assyrians are portrayed as recognizing their past sins of violence) and the acts of contrition depicted here in Mic 7:16. A snake crawling in the dust seems to the modern reader to be a clear reference to the entire narrative of the serpent "eating dust" in the Adam and Eve narrative (Gen 3:14, 19), but it is quite impossible to know how "old" the Genesis materials really are. Suffice it to say that judgments about evil persons compared to snakes make their point, and repentance compared to those "snakes" crawling in the dust (an image of bowing in contrition) equally make their point!

To come out of strongholds "trembling" (Deut 2:25; 2 Sam 22:46; Ps 18:45 [46]) and similarly to "tremble" before God are both common themes of reversal of fortune (Ps 99:1; cf. Isa 64:2, "so that the nations might tremble at your presence"; Jer 33:9). Furthermore, there is a profound sense of hope in the idea that enemy peoples will indeed come to realize the true nature of God and their own culpability in opposing God's intended plan for humanity. In fact, this is a critically important point. Throughout the ages those who hope for peace are typically accused of naïveté on this point. However, even pacifists are not blind to the guilt of those who have so blatantly promoted oppression and warfare; hence in these cases, the repentance of the guilty is such a powerful theme. The tradition of the Truth and Reconciliation discussions made famous in South Africa is partly premised on the idea and action of perpetrators publicly admitting to their horrendous behavior. Contrast this to the frequent legal decisions in the United States where public figures, companies, and politicians agree to court-imposed terms "without admitting guilt."

Recognition of the horrific mistakes of the past is not only crucial but often a major stumbling block in modern conflict resolution. Such recognition calls for acknowledging the suffering of the Others and recognizing their humanity. The resistance to such acknowledgment, as in governmental refusals to acknowledge the suffering of indigenous peoples or violent earlier mistakes toward minorities, stands in the way of progress in many conflicts around the world. History must be attended to because it is part of contemporary relationships and identities. Micah already understands this.

To "fear God," however, may well refer to foreigners not only frightened by God's ability to defend the Israelites but also actually coming to have faith in the God of the Israelites, as a kind of recognition, perhaps even conversion! Solomon's dedication prayer in the temple clearly shows signs of postexilic editing, so that the following passage appears precisely at the point when the writer refers to foreigners praying to the God of Israel:

> Then hear in heaven . . . and do according to all that the foreigner calls to you, so that all the peoples of the earth may know your name and fear you, as do your people Israel, and so that they may know that your name has been invoked on this house that I have built. (1 Kgs 8:43)

In relation to the Micah passage, Hagstrom clarifies: "While the response begins with a boast over their enemies, the master of their foes is clearly Yahweh rather than any human leaders. After that, the community acknowledges the basis of their salvation: YHWH's forgiveness and faithfulness" (1988, 122).

[18] Those who argue that within its verses Mic 7 contains some form of public liturgy can cite the final verses of the book as their strongest evidence. The rhetorical question "Who is like our God?" is not common in biblical literature yet is often paired with a sentiment similar to that expressed here in Mic 7:18 (1 Kgs 8:23; cf. 2 Chr 6:14; Pss 77:13 [14], "What god is so great as our God?"; 35:10, "YHWH, who is like you?"; cf. Pss 71:19; 86:8; 89:8 [9]; Jer 10:6–7). In addition to the question, however, the verse affirms God as typified by forgiveness, often expressed, as here, in conjunction with *ḥesed*, "loving-kindness" or "faithful love" (see comments above at Mic 6:8; cf. Exod 34:6–8; Pss 78:38; 85:2 [3]).

The passage furthermore expresses God's "delight" in forgiveness and mercy, also a prominent theme in the Psalms and in celebratory praises of God in the Prophets (Ps 35:27; Hos 6:6, "For I desire steadfast love and not sacrifice, the knowledge of God rather than burnt offerings"; Jer 9:24; famously Ezek 18:23, 32; 33:11).

The reference, again, to a "remnant" has often suggested to modern readers an exilic or even postexilic context for this section. Although this is quite plausible, a concern for survivors of the violent crises of the late eighth-century devastations could be in mind here just as much as the later violence of the sixth century B.C.E.

A Final Prayer for Deliverance

[19] Micah says that God will "again" have compassion. This seems a reasonable rendering of the verb to "turn/repent" (*šûb*). The notion of God "changing God's mind" is sometimes used when God decides against destruction. Typically, the anger of God will not be "turned away" (Ezek 18:21; Jer 30:24), but not so in Joel 2:14, and notably in Jonah 3:9, where the "Ninevites" hope that God may change God's intentions of destruction.

Once again, however, this theme is associated with redemption from imperial conquest in the earlier Prophets and in the penitential prayer tradition after the exile and into the Persian period, so the prayer asks: "Forgive your people who have sinned against you, and all their transgressions that they have committed against you; and grant them compassion in the sight of their captors, so that they may have compassion on them" (1 Kgs 8:50; cf. 2 Kgs 13:23, where it is directly associated with Abraham, Isaac, and Jacob; Pss 102:13 [14]; 103:13). God's compassion *after* punishment is a frequent theme in later portions of Isaiah (e.g., 14:1), and *even the idea of including Gentiles* in a new era of God's grace is occasionally found (Isa 60:10).

God will tread mistakes under foot, casting sins to the farthest imagined places, such as under the sea. Ironically, the term for "tread under foot" can also be used for military conquest (2 Sam 8:11, "all the nations he subdued"), but in later use it appears more often of "reducing" people to slavery, such as in 2 Chr 28:10; Neh 5:5; Jer 34:11, 16. Furthermore, God is said to "cast" or "throw" the "iniquities" of the people. The same term, significantly, is used of the people being "cast out" of the land in Deuteronomic curses (Deut 29:28; cf. Jer 52:3), but Isaiah also speaks of God having "cast all my sins behind your back" (38:17). The reference, then, to casting the sins into the "depths" seems surely an allusion to the destruction of Pharaoh's forces at the exodus, given that this same imagery is repeated in the penitential prayer tradition (Exod 15:5; cf. Neh 9:11, "You threw their pursuers into the depths, like a stone into mighty waters"). The two terms for "sin" and "iniquity" (NRSV) appear together frequently (Hos 8:13; cf. 9:9, "He will remember their iniquity, he will punish their sins").

Micah contrasts military defeat with the "defeat" of sin and corruption. One thinks of military language put to new uses, preeminently in Wisdom of Solomon's "spiritual armaments" (5:16–23), taken up so powerfully in Paul's imagery in Eph 6:12–17. These ideas are also evident in modern uses, as in General Booth's Salvation Army; William James's notion of *The Moral Equivalent of War* as a unifying "battle" against poverty, suffering, or moral decline; President Lyndon B. Johnson's War on Poverty; and so forth.

[20] The use of the name "Jacob" to refer to the entire people becomes common among the eighth-century prophets and continues in later prophetic tradition. It is often used in parallel with "Israel" (e.g., Ps 147:19; Mic 3:8; Isa 14:1; 44:21; 65:9). Referring to both Abraham and Jacob in the same thought is much rarer, as indeed are any references to the patriarchal tradition in the Prophets.

However, Jacob and Abraham do appear in texts that suggest at least some familiarity with basic themes of the patriarchal stories, including a lineage for Abraham through Jacob (Isa 29:22; 41:8). The mention of patriarchs, however, is a strong indication of a postexilic context, given tendencies now to date Genesis material to a post-587 context.

Referring to the land as that which God "swore" to ancestors (sometimes explicitly naming Abraham) is a common phrase (Gen 24:7; 50:24, Exod 13:5, 11, 19; 32:13; 33:1), but especially typical of Deuteronomy (Deut 6:10, 18, 23, and at least 24 additional verses in Deut alone). Notably, occasions for making such "vows" increase in the narratives about royalty as they make pronouncements (vow by Saul—1 Sam 19:6; David—2 Sam 3:35; Solomon—1 Kings 2:23) The theme is repeated in the poetry of worship, especially in reference to asking God to act on God's promises to the line of David (Ps 89:3, 35, 49 [50]). References to the "land" that God "swore" is not as common in the Prophetic writings, however (e.g., Jer 11:5; 32:22, although "gave" to ancestors is clearly related to the theme, thus Jer 3:18; 7:7). However, the references to "the ancestors" takes a more judgmental turn in the prophets (Hos 9:10) and especially the sixth-century prophets and later (Jer 2:5; 7:25; 16:11; 34:14; 44:9, 10; Ezek 20:18, 27, 30, 36; Zech 1:2, 5). This surely provides a background to the rise of the penitential prayer form, especially evident in the Persian period (1 Kgs 8:40; Neh 9:36; Ezra 9:7; Bar 1:15–20; cf. Ps 106:6). Micah's use is either an addition from a later period (as many have argued for this entire chapter and more) or it is early enough not to be influenced by the more negative turn in later references to the sins and mistakes of the ancestors. What is clear, however, is that it is decidedly not a reference to any promises to the royal house!

The Hebrew reads, literally, "give truth to Jacob." This, too, relates to the penitential prayer tradition, so "You acted truthfully" (Neh 9:33 S-C), although "speaking truth" may relate to acting justly (Zech 8:16, "These are the things that you shall do: Speak the truth to one another, render in your gates judgments that are true and make for peace").

Andersen and Freedman observe that these final verses present the writer as a kind of "intercessor" for the community, and Mic 7 summarizes many of the themes of the entire book of Micah (2000, 600–601). I am not entirely in agreement, however. Although the ending is certainly hopeful and trusting in God's preservation of the people for the future, it certainly does not "summarize" the fiery attitude of the prophet toward leaders and their politics and policies of destruction. Proposed "happy endings" ought not to be allowed to blunt the critique of authority that actually typifies this book as a whole.

As we have indicated, there is considerable discussion about the possible "liturgical form" of the verses of chapter 7, although how much of the chapter is

A Final Prayer for Deliverance

to be included in this analysis remains controversial. It must be asked, however, whether the assignment of these sentiments to a "public liturgy" has the impact of protecting later readers from the subversive nature of this book as a whole. Can a public liturgy be so severely critical of the tradition?

The tradition of the penitential prayer, to which we have alluded many times, certainly suggests that at least those famous prayers (e.g., Ezra 9; Neh 9; Dan 9), which surely had a public or even liturgical form, could be critical of previous generations (e.g., the "sins of our ancestors"). In contrast to Micah, contemporary Christian spirituality can often be shallow and artificially positive. A liturgical form that warns the powerful, empowers the weak, and disdains militaristic bravado would characterize a worship service more in keeping with the spirit of the book of Micah—that is, chapters 1–6 as well as chapter 7!

Finally, however, one wonders whether the closing verses of Micah echo a tendency in some of the other prophetic voices of the Twelve to close with an edited Hollywood-style ending, with a happy and promising note at the end. Amos, for example, famously features the final five verses of hope, quite contrary to the spirit of the rest of the book (and featuring a positive word about the house of David, contrary to Amos 6:4–7). Here in Micah we find a similar controversy about whether someone has provided a hopeful end for a book that is otherwise deeply critical.

Perhaps modern preachers should take the book's *ending* as Micah's parting advice. Like the book of Revelation, even at the end of a severely critical book (or sermon), one should end with God's enduring promise of forgiveness and hope. Unlike the postexilic tradition we know as the penitential prayers (Dan 9; Neh 9; Ezra 9), which most certainly name the sins of the ancestors, the promise of forgiveness at the end of Micah should not tempt us to suppress a clear memory and spoken acknowledgment of those actions that require our penitence in the first place. Such an honest prayer of confession, before an assurance of God's forgiveness, would then truly be in the spirit of the angry man of Moresheth.

INDEX OF SCRIPTURE AND OTHER ANCIENT SOURCES

OLD TESTAMENT

Genesis
2:3	115
2:9	83, 85
2:10	131
2:13	131
2:17	85
3:6	83
3:8	199
3:11	196
3:14	223
3:19	223
3:24	100
4:4	156
6:11	123, 202
6:13	123, 202
7:11	53
8:22	207
9:23	95
10:8	172
10:15	195
11:8	129
14:20	180
15:1	124, 133
15:4	133
16:5	133
19:26	184
21:17	81
21:25	190
22	195
22:17	74
23:2	62
23:7	194
24:7	226
24:60	74
25:23	167
26:35	74
27:3	127
27:19	195
27:28	177
27:32	195
27:40	85
28:11	117
28:18	183
28:22	183
29:15	124
29:22	61
30:2	195
30:23	158
30:32	124
31:13	183
31:19	77
31:29	82
31:36	55, 75
31:37	134, 190
31:45	183
31:51–52	184
31:52	133
32:31	146–47
33:16	180
34:14	158
34:21	
34:29	161
35:19	73, 166
35:21	151
37:26	161
38:12	77
38:23	118
41:3	73
41:43	181
41:48–49	61
42:6	223
45:7	149
46:29	181
48:7	73
48:20	180
49:10	220
49:17	114
49:19	162
50:10	62
50:17	55, 120
50:20	82
50:24	226

Exodus
	190
2:23	25, 111
2:23–24	81
2:25	156
3:5	115
3:8	52, 153
4	57
4–5	54
4:22	195
5:6	180
5:12	207
5:22–23	148
6:6	153
7:11	182
9:25	147
10:28	49
11:1	62
12:3	199
12:6	199
12:34	95
12:36	153
12:47	199
13:3	191
13:5	226
13:8	180
13:11	226
13:14	191
13:19	226

Exodus (continued)		34:11	49	23:10	75, 92
13:21	216	34:24	76	23:18–19	194
14	53	34:26	75	23:22	92
14–15	181			25	83, 154
14:13–14	221	**Leviticus**		25:3–4	56
14:30	180	1:4	193n54, 194	25:36	114
15:3	147	1:16	74	26:1	60n10
15:5	225	2:12	75	26:21	66
15:7	147, 207	2:15	195	26:33	60, 105
15:9	76	4:7	51	26:1	184
15:14	69	4:13	199	26:5	203
15:17	220	4:18	51	26:6	137
15:18	139	4:25	51	26:16	203
15:20	191	4:30	51	26:26	203
17:7	124	4:34	51	26:28	185
18:4	153	5:2	102	26:29	110–11
18:8	153	5:11	195	26:30	185
18:19	152	6:2	85, 110, 202	26:31–32	202
18:21	161	6:4	85	26:33	218
19:4	77	6:10	73	26:34–35	202
19:8	138	6:28	111	26:43	202
19:10	115	7:18	193n54, 194	27	154
19:16	137	7:21	102	27:11	102
20:2	191	8:10	195	27:32	220
20:5	184	9:2–3	194		
20:16	52, 103, 202	10:11	138	**Numbers**	
20:17	83	10:12	74	3:12–13	195
22	95	11:6	102	6:3	103
22:2	88	11:45	190	7	194
22:5	56, 127	13	62	8:16–18	195
22:9	95	13:45	118	10	200
22:18	182	14:10	195	10:7	146, 152
22:25	114	16:16	55, 120	10:9	152
22:26	97	16:21	120	11:11	148
22:26–27	97, 97n25	17	111	11:17	52
22:27	81	18	57	11:23	92
23:8	123	19:7	193n54, 194	11:33	66
23:19	75	19:10	207	12	191
23:21	49	19:13	85, 110	12:6	189
23:24	184	19:17	134	13	200
24:4	184	19:18	186	13:23–24	207
26:1	82	19:26	183	15:22	138
26:31	82	19:36	201	16:8	189
28:6	82	20	57	16:14	127
32:12	87	20:7	115	16:15	145
32:13	226	20:24	76	18	83
32:30	55	21:10	195	20:10	189
33:1	226	22:23	193n54, 194	20:15	148
34:6–8	224	22:25	193n54, 194	20:17	56
34:7	55, 120	22:27	193n54, 194	21:5	118

Index of Scripture and Other Ancient Sources

21:6	114	6:11	203	16:3	221		
21:8	114	6:12	49, 191	16:12	191		
21:22	56	6:18	92, 122, 226	16:19	124		
22–24	191–92	6:23	226	16:21	74, 184		
22:28	190	7:1	156, 172	17:4	130		
23:9	220	7:4	185	17:8	62		
24:14	152	7:5	60, 147, 183–84	18	84		
25:1	191	7:8	191	18:4	75		
25:11	185	7:13	195	18:7	138		
27:18	95	7:18	191	18:10	116, 182–83		
28:3	194	7:23	185	18:14	116, 183		
28:9	194	7:25	60, 183	18:20	138		
28:19	194	7:26	122	18:22	138		
31:8	191	8:2	191	19	52. 210		
31:9	161	8:7	53	19:8	70		
31:16	191	8:8	137	19:11	210		
32:4	199	8:10	203	19:14	90, 203		
32:10	180	8:11	49	20	27		
33:49	191	8:14	191	21	210		
33:52	185	8:17	161	21:5	62		
34	200	8:18	191	21:9	92		
35:24	133, 156	9:3	185	21:16	167		
35:30	52	9:8	185	21:19	74		
35:33	156	9:14	149, 185	22:1	148		
		9:19	185	22:30	57		
Deuteronomy	76, 226	9:19–20	185	23:3	166		
1:16	134	9:21	134	23:4	193		
1:37	121, 124	9:25	185	23:18	60		
2:1	185	10:12	197	23:19	124		
2:21	185	10:17	123	23:20–21	114		
2:23	185	11:15	203	24	95		
2:25	223	11:16	49	24:6	88		
3:4	88	12:2	189	24:9	191		
3:13	88	12:3	60, 183	24:12–13	97		
4:1	135, 218	12:9	101	24:14	85		
4:5	135	12:13	49	24:18	191		
4:9	49	12:19	49	24:21	207		
4:10	135	12:23	49	25:4	160		
4:14	135	12:25	92	25:13	201		
4:20–21	84	12:28	92, 122	25:14–15	201		
4:23	49	12:30	49	26:5	149		
4:26	51, 185	13:5	191	26:6	148		
5:1	135	13:6	212	26:10	75		
5:6	191, 221	13:10	191	27:11	180		
5:9	184	13:14	130	27:17	90, 203		
5:15	191	13:18	92	27:20	57		
5:20	52	14:1	162	27:25	124		
5:21	83	15:6	156	28:4	195		
5:25	199	15:9–10	148	28:11	195		
6:10	226	15:15	191	28:12	156		

Deuteronomy (continued)

28:18	195	6:10	152	24:12	100
28:20	112, 185	6:15	86	24:17	191
28:24	185	6:16	152	24:18	100
28:29	110	6:17	161	24:19	120
28:33	85	6:17–18	210		
28:37	86, 205	6:20	152	**Judges**	
28:38	203	6:21	161	1:19	181
28:40	204	7:6	73	1:31	75
28:45	185	7:13	115	2:6	84
28:48	85, 185	7:12	185	3	76
28:49	77	7:21	83	3:1–2	135
28:51	185, 204	8	210	3:7	184
28:53	195	8:26	161	3:19	183
28:59	66	8:28	55n4	3:26	183
28:61	66, 185	10	76	3:28	180
28:64	105	10:3	76	4:3	181
29:24	206	10:5	76	4:15	181
29:27	184–85	10:10	66	5:11	192
29:28	225	10:19	180	5:19	161
29:29	57	10:20	66, 182	6:8	191
30:1	148	10:23	76	6:9	100
30:4	148	10:24	85, 107, 109, 121	6:11	73
30:9	69	10:28	86	6:15	167
30:19	51	10:34	76	6:24	73
31:18	86	10:35	161	6:25	184
31:19	68	10:37	76	6:28	184
31:20	203	11:6	181	6:30	184
32:2	177	11:9	181	8:12	137
32:6	213	11:20	185	8:27	73
32:14	220	11:23	84	8:32	73
32:21	213, 75	12:15	76	9	137, 210
32:43	186	12:17	62	9:5	73
33:10	124	12:19	62	11:6	109, 121
33:29	50	13:21	172–73	11:11	109
33:29c	52	13:22	192	11:33	66
		14	88	13:4	103
		15:33–47	71	13:7	103
Joshua	76	15:35	71, 76	13:8	133
2:1	192	15:38	71	14:18	135
2:10	161	15:44	75–76	15:7	186
2:11	53	15:59	71	15:8	66
2:15	88	17:16	181	15:13–14	211
3:1	192	18–20	88	16:2	210
3:5	221	19:13	16	16:28	186
3:11	161	19:29	75	18:7	98
3:13	161	19:45	16	18:19	222
4:14	86	20:4	74	18:28	179
4:19	192	21:24–25	16	**Ruth**	166
4:24	192	22:8	88	1:2	73
5:9	158	23:10	175	1:14	213
6:5	152	24:1	61	2:11	213

Index of Scripture and Other Ancient Sources

2:18–19	213	18:7–8	195	1:45	105		
3–4	154	18:25	186	2:23	226		
3:4	57	19:6	226	2:29	74		
3:7	57	20:19	74	3:3	55		
4:11	73, 165	21:1	137	3:28	196		
		21:11	195	4:21	166		
1 Samuel		22	76–77	4:25	98, 137		
1:10	74	22:1	76	4:28	74		
1:15	103	22:3–4	76	8:5	199		
1:19	82	22:7	189	8:23	224		
2:10	169	24:8	194	8:25	212		
3	47	24:11	82	8:40	226		
3:7	57	24:12	134	8:43	224		
3:12	86	24:13	86	8:46	134		
3:21	57	24:15	134	8:50	55, 120, 225		
3:31	202	25:1	62	8:56	101		
4:3	154	25:2	77	8:60	192		
4:5	105, 152	25:9	138	9:8	56, 202, 206		
4:10	66	28:3	62	9:15	100		
4:13	137	31:10	218	9:16	69, 75		
5:2	74	**2 Samuel**		9:19	151, 181		
6:2	116	1:17	87	10:9	196		
6:13	130	1:20	68, 72	10:19	74		
6:19	66	3:35	226	10:26	181		
8	24–25, 213	5:2	168	10:29	181		
8:7–9	221	5:20	105	11:7	55		
8:12	135, 181, 211	6:20	57	12:7	93		
9–10	55	8:4	181	12:18	181		
11:2	158	8:11	225	12:21–24	101		
11:14–15	192	8:15	196	12:22–24	23		
12:7	192	12:15	66	12:31–32	55		
13:4	192	14:7	213	13:2	55		
13:5	181	14:13	148	13:32	55		
13:8	192	14:13–14	82	13:34	205		
13:12	192	15:1	181	14:11	205		
13:15	192	15:2	168	14:26	201		
13:20	69	15:12	152	15:19	124		
13:20–21	135	16:1–2	207	15:23	119		
14:15	137	17:2	137	16:4	205		
14:24	86, 186	17:10	53	16:5	119		
14:30	66	19:9	154	16:9	61		
15:21	75	20:21	180	16:9–20	205		
15:22	195	21:17	77n15	16:11	205		
15:29	77n15	22:35	129, 135, 160	16:12	185		
16–17	166	22:43	161, 217	16:16	61, 211		
16:1	195	22:46	223	16:16–28	204		
16:4	137	23:13	76	16:25	204		
17	72	**1 Kings**	213	16:27	119		
17:8	68	1:5	181	16:30	204		
17:12	167, 172	1:12	152	18:19	184		
17:46	82			18:28	156, 162		

1 Kings (continued)		10:15	181	19:27–28	28
18:32	138	10:17	185	19:31	149
19:20	190	10:26	184	19:32–34	29
20:1	181	12:9	74	19:35	13
20:21	66	13:7	160, 181	20:3	191, 200n55
20:33	181	13:12	119	20:12–18	146
21	84, 205	13:23	225	21:6	183
21:20	216	14:7–10	10	21:13	200n55, 205
21:24	205	14:15	184	21:14	82
22	46, 90, 204	14:19	10	22:19	205
22:5	133	14:24	10	23	183
22:11	37, 46, 162, 164	14:25	16	23:4	184
22:15	103	14:26–27	10	23:5	55
22:17	103	15:10	11	23:6	161, 184
22:17–18	23	15:19–20	6	23:7	60
22:19	133	15:20	11	23:8–9	55
22:22–23	103	15:29	11, 58	23:13	55
22:24	163	16	11	23:14	184
22:25	86	16:3	76	23:15	55, 161
22:28	46, 51, 133	16:4	189	23:19–20	55
22:28b	46	16:7–8	7	23:35	10
22:31	181	16:8	124	24:14–15	58
22:45	119	16:9	58	25:4	53
		16:15	82	25:11	58
2 Kings	213	16:20	45	25:15	10
1:1	54, 120	17	12	25:21	58
2:11	181	17:1–5	12		
2:24	138	17:3–6	12n1	1 Chronicles	2
3:2	184	17:6	58	4:4	166
3:4	195	17:9	182	4:14	71
3:5	54, 120	17:11	58	4:41	45
3:19	182	17:17	81	5:18	129, 136
4:34	174	17:23	58	13:9	148
6:20–23	23	17:24	146	16:40	82
6:28–29	110n33	18	18	19:19	135
7:1	133	18–19	12, 28, 175	21:13	205
7:6	181	18:1–21	45	21:19	138
8:18	205	18:4	134	21:23	135
8:20	120	18:13–16	13, 29, 137	22:8	10
8:27	200n55, 205	18:13–19:37	13	26:22	201
9	23, 205	18:14	10, 13	26:26	201
9:7	186	18:14–16	12	28:9	196
9:14	61	18:17–19:37	13		
9:17	212	18:24	181	2 Chronicles	2
9:21	181	18:26–27	13	6:14	224
9:22	182	18:27	111	7:18	166
9:23	201	18:31	13, 24, 69, 98, 137	9:18	74
9:36	133	19:4	129	9:25	181
10:2	181	19:21	152	11:5–10	17
10:9	61	19:25	166	15:6	135
				15:11	180

Index of Scripture and Other Ancient Sources 235

15:16	161	9:3	226	18:2	160		
16:9	10	9:11	225	19:3	117		
17:11	195	9:24	80	21:4	92		
20:27	106	9:33	216	21:5	222		
20:37	76	9:36	226	22:6	88		
22:9	101	11:20	84	23:5	160		
26:6–7	10	11:30	76	24:3	88		
26:9–16	10	12:46	165	24:9	110		
27:3–6	10	13:15	202	26:14	160		
27:7	10	13:17	85	28:23	160		
28	11, 48	13:25	138	29:7	74		
28:9–15	23	**Esther**		29:9	221		
28:10	225	1:6	88	30:1	118		
28:12–15	101	1:14	172	30:28	117		
28:15	64	2:3	212	30:29	65		
28:17–18	11–12	2:6	58	31:5	201		
28:27	45	8:8	138	31:33	75		
29:8	206	8:10	74	36:8	88		
29:21	195	8:14	74	37:5	221		
32:3	162	9:5	66	37:14	221		
32:27–29	122	**Job**		38	52		
33:15	129	2:8	214	38:28	177		
34:7	134	2:12	194	39:15	160		
Ezra		4:7	73	40:4	222		
2:1	159	5:5	191	41:29	207		
2:66	58	5:8	161				
5:10	181	5:9	179	**Psalms**			
6:22	106	5:11	221	1:1	205		
7:14	171	5:12	117	2:3	75, 211		
8:31	172	5:17	159	2:9	163, 174		
8:35	154	6:20	134	2:12	223		
9	195	6:27	117	3:5	194		
9:1	148, 227	7:21	212	3:6	195		
9:4	166	9:33	75	3:7	96, 163		
9:6	137	10:9	134, 190	4:3	209		
9:7	216	11:19	191	5:2	49		
9:9	226	12:17	138	5:3	156		
10:3	55n4	12:19	65	5:5	80		
Nehemiah	137	13:1	65	5:7	194		
1:3	159	13:3	160	6:1	134, 185, 190		
1:8	218	13:6	190	6:8	80		
1:9	191	13:15	49, 189	6:10	117		
2:8	148, 168	13:23	134	7:1	175		
2:9	218	14:14	75, 120	7:6	96		
2:17	211	14:17	215	7:13	211		
5:3	55n4	15:3	75	7:17	169, 194		
5:5	83	15:20	134	8:5	101		
5:11	225	15:35	153	9:5	139		
9	83	16:10	201	9:6	55n4, 200		
	148, 227		163	9:7	150		

Index of Scripture and Other Ancient Sources

Psalms (continued)							
9:19	96	21:13	85, 119, 169	33:16	221		
10:2	82	22:5	117	33:17	181		
10:2–4	200	22:8	153	33:18	178		
10:9	210	22:12	220	33:22	178		
10:12	96	22:13	179	34:11	132		
10:15	147	22:14	50	34:13	201		
10:16	139, 150	22:24	112	34:20	212		
10:17	51	22:26	112, 203	35:4	82, 118, 217		
10:18	196	22:27	165, 169, 194	35:10	110, 224		
11:4	52, 178	22:29	194	35:11	202		
11:5	123, 202	23:1	169	35:11–14	216		
11:7	212	23:4	163	35:14	212		
12:1–2	210	24:2	131	35:15	147		
12:6	194	24:4	193n54, 210	35:19	109, 156		
13:1	112	24:5	217	35:23–24	217		
13:5	215	24:7	174	35:26	118, 156, 217		
14:1	213	24:8	221	35:27	224		
14:4	80	24:9	174	36:4	82		
15:2	193n54	25:2	118, 217	37	200		
15:5	114, 124	25:4	133	37:6	217		
16:6	89	25:5	215	37:9	180		
16:11	133	25:7	54	37:37	212		
17:1	51, 201	25:8	122	38:1	134, 185, 190		
17:6	215	25:10	133	38:6	117		
17:12	178	25:19	109	38:15	178		
18	135	25:20	175	38:19	109		
18: title	154, 175	27:1	216	39:8	75		
18:1	153	27:2	111	40:13	194		
18:4–5	89	27:9	112, 215	40:14	118		
18:6	52	27:11	133	40:14–15	217		
18:17	153, 175	27:12	103, 202	41:4	216		
18:25	210	27:14	177	41:7	109		
18:34	160	28:3	80	41:11	152, 215		
18:35	194	28:5	160	42:3	217		
18:42	217	28:7	169	42:5	178		
18:45	220, 223	28:9	220	42:9	117		
18:46	215	29	199	42:10	217		
18:48	175	29:8	153	42:11	178		
19:8	122	30:5	82	43:5	178		
19:14	154	30:7	112	44:1	221		
20:2	194	31:15	153, 175	44:5	52		
20:5	138	31:18	202	44:7	117		
20:6	119	31:21	162	44:13	206		
20:7	181	31:24	178	44:14	86		
21:1	169	32:1	54, 120	44:15	91		
21:3	193	32:4	207	44:19	65		
21:7	194	32:5	75, 195	44:24	112		
21:8	180	33:3	211	45:6	139, 163, 220		
21:11	82	33:10–11	159	45:11	194		
		33:11	205	45:17	139		

Index of Scripture and Other Ancient Sources

46:1	169	66:1	152	78:35	154
46:4	129	66:5	132	78:37	212
46:5	82	66:13	194	78:38	185, 224
46:5–7	144	66:16	132	78:51	75
46:8	55, 132	67	169	78:52	151
46:9	135, 147	68:2	50	78:55	89
46:10	144	68:9	190, 220	78:62	203
48	129, 136	68:16	129	78:68	129
48:2	129	68:17	181	78:70–72	168
48:4–6	144	68:27	211	79:1	56, 124
48:14	139	69:4	109	79:1b	55
49:6	161	69:7	216	79:4	206
49:10	161	69:18	154	79:6	185
50	189	69:25	202	79:8	193
50:10	125	70:2	118	79:10	217
50:19	201	71:4	154	80:1	152, 169
50:21	134, 190	71:13	217	80:2	119
51:2–3	195	71:19	224	80:8	137
51:10	130	71:24	118	80:9	100
51:16	194	72	169	80:12	106, 218
51:17	147	72:4	85	80:18	203
52:2	82	72:6	177	81:9	184
52:3	109	72:8	169, 218	81:10	190
52:4	201	72:9	222	82:5	190
54:2	215	72:14	154	83:4	132
55:2	49	72:16	177	83:17	118
55:12–13	216	72:17	169	85:1	195
55:13	212	72:18	221	85:2	224
55:21	174	73:13	201	85:8	170
56:2	194	73:17	160	86:2	207
56:9	108	74:2	154, 220	86:6	51
57:5	85	74:12	166	86:8	224
57:11	85	74:17	207	86:10	221
58:2	123	75:4	147	86:17	222
58:10	186	75:10	160	88:13	82
59:3	195	76	136	88:14	112
59:9	169	76:3	147	89:3	226
59:10	193	76:3–7	144	89:8	224
59:13	185	77:5	166	89:9	166
59:16	82	77:7	194	89:19	221
60:6	152	77:10	194	89:23	135
60:12	50, 52	77:12	112	89:32	163
61:1	51	77:13	224	89:35	226
61:5	200	77:15	154	89:37	51
62:6–7	215	78:7	112	89:39–45	163
62:10	85, 110, 212	78:8	212	89:40	105
63:11	162, 166	78:13	53	89:41	158
65:6	119, 123, 130, 211	78:16	131	89:46	112, 185
65:8	82	78:22	212	89:49	226
65:13	152	78:32	212	89:50	158

Psalms (continued)		107:35	55	130:7	69
90:3	178	107:42	162	131:3	150
90:5	82	108:5	85	132:8	101
90:14	82	108:13	50, 52	132:11	195
91:7	195	109:10	55n4	132:14	101
92:2	82	111:6	196	132:17	77n15, 160
92:6	160	111:8	122	135:10	156
92:11	156	111:10	200	135:15	60n10
94:10	134, 190	112:8	156	136	193
94:21	162	113:1–2	169	136:4	221
95:1	152	113:2	150	137:7	57
95:3	150	114:2	151	139:9	82
95:6	194	114:7	153	140:2	82
97:5	50, 53, 161	115:2	217	140:4	82
97:7	60n10	115:4	60n10	140:12	196
98	169	115:18	150	141:3	213
98:1	221	116:15	210	141:10	210
98:2	57	118:10	138	142:4	196
98:3	165	119	218	143:3	216
99:1	223	119:20	207	143:4	203
99:4	196	119:42	206	143:5	221
101:8	180	119:43	178	143:7	112
102:2	112	119:49	178	143:8	82
102:8	206	119:61	89	143:9	153
102:13	225	119:69	202	144:3	82, 178
102:15	200	119:74	178	144:5	52
103:4	154	119:78	202	145:1–2	139
103:6	192	119:81	178	145:13	151
103:13	225	119:108	195	145:14	193
103:22	151	119:110	114	146:3	212
104:29	112	119:114	178	146:8	193
105:11	89	119:116	194	147:2	148
105:28	203	119:128	133	147:10	181
105:33	137, 147	119:141	167	147:14	175, 203
105:36	75	119:147	178	147:19	225
106:5	220	119:149	196	148:11	211
106:6	226	119:161	211	149:4	195
106:10	154	119:176	114		
106:15	201	120:7	116n35	**Proverbs**	
106:23	185	121:8	150	1:6	86
106:36	60n10	124:8	138	1:7	200
106:38	60n10, 156	125:2	150	1:11	210
106:40	122	125:3	163	1:11–18	212
106:43	153	126:5	204	1:19	161
107:2	154	127:3	195	1:31	205
107:9	203	127:4	221	2:7	122
107:13	111	127:5	217	2:13	122
107:16	147	129:4	211	2:15	122
107:19	111	130:2	51	2:21	122
107:33	55	130:6	82	3:12	190

Index of Scripture and Other Ancient Sources

5:3	91	19:9	52	**Ecclesiastes**	
5:16	129	19:10	78, 100	4:8	85
6:7	109	19:12	178	8:11–12	81
6:19	52, 103	19:25	160	9:16	119
7:1	212	19:26	118	9:17	166
8:4	178	19:28	52	10:7	181
8:14	119	20:9	201	11:4	204
8:29	190	20:16	88		
8:34	174	20:23	201	**Song of Solomon**	
9:10	200	21:13	119	1:14	207
10:9	122	21:15	196	2:13	137
10:17	114	21:16	114	3:8	136
11:1	201	22:8	123, 163, 204, 220	18:20	138
11:2	193, 197	22:15	163, 220	18:22	138
11:3	92, 122	22:22	74, 110	34:6	66
11:5–6	92, 122	22:24	186	**Isaiah**	8, 18, 29n8, 48,
11:11	92, 122	22:25	210		125n39, 133
11:14	152	22:28	52, 90, 203	1	197
11:15	85, 110	23:10	90, 203	1–39	136
12:16	114	23:13–14	163	1:1	116
12:17	52, 103	23:32	114	1:2	138
13:10	153	24:6	153, 176	1:2–3	51
13:24	163	24:8	81	1:4	81
14:1	182	24:15	210	1:5	202
14:2	92	24:17	156, 215	1:7	218–19
14:5	52	24:18	186	1:8	56, 124, 151, 218
14:9	122	24:28	52	1:10	109, 121, 133
14:10	74	24:30	56, 127	1:10–17	133
14:11–12	122	24:30–31	218	1:11	195
14:17	186	25:12	190	1:11–17	53
14:22	114	25:20	212	1:14	190
14:25	52	26:1	207	1:15	122, 210
14:28	77	26:3	163	1:16	112
14:29	186	27:6	202	1:16–17	81
14:35	118	28:6	122	1:17	20, 196
15:1	119	28:16	109, 161	1:18	134, 190
15:18	186	28:23	190	1:21	119
15:19	212	28:24	110	1:23	124, 211
15:22	152	29:6	210	1:24	186
15:27	109, 161	29:15	163	1:26	153, 153
16:11	201	29:18	116	1:28	54
16:12	81	29:22	186	1:29	118
16:28	212	29:26	166	2	21–22, 130
17:5	118, 156	30:4	61	2:1	45
17:8	124	30:14	110	2:2–4	24, 136, 139, 141
17:23	124	30:17	77	2:2–5	142–44
18:7	210	30:18	172n46	2:4	135, 190
18:11	218	30:32	222	2:5	139, 216
18:15	160	31:16	56	2:6	183
19:5	52	31:10–31	56	2:6–22	141

Isaiah (*continued*)

Reference	Page
2:7–8	119
2:8	60n10
2:10	101
2:11	181
2:17	86, 181
2:18	60n10, 172
2:19	101
2:20	60n10, 86, 181
3:2	116
3:6	121
3:7	181
3:10	219
3:12	114
3:13	168, 189
3:14	211
3:15	20
3:18	181
3:26	87
4:1	158
4:2	86
4:3	168
4:4	122
5	20, 84n17, 137
5:1–7	56
5:2	57
5:3	134
5:5	105–6, 218
5:7	57n6, 109
5:8	83, 125
5:9	206
5:10	199–200
5:11	82, 103
5:15	196
5:17	126
5:18	54, 89, 211
5:20	109
5:21	160
5:22	82, 218
5:25	202
5:26	134
5:28	160
5:29	178–79
6:11	60
7	57n6
7:13	108, 189–90
7:18	86, 181, 218
7:20–21	86
7:23	86
8:6	129
8:17	112
9:3	88
9:4	163, 220
9:6	153, 170, 172
9:7	130
9:12	87, 202
9:15	114
9:17	87
10:2	110
10:3	212
10:5	163, 220
10:5–13	52
10:10	60n10, 183
10:15	163, 220
10:16	201
10:20	86
10:21–22	81
10:24	163, 220
10:27	85–86
10:27–33	71
10:27b–32	71
10:32	151
10:33	147
11:2	119, 153
11:4	129, 134, 163, 200, 202
11:6	170
11:6–7	179
11:11	218
11:12	147–48, 147n44
11:16	218
12:2	169
13:1	47
13:3	115
13:6	64
13:7	53
13:8	153
13:9	206
13:16	101
13:18	195
13:19–21	125
13:22	65
14	147
14:1	225
14:2	109
14:5	163, 220
14:10	202
14:17	182
14:22	96
14:23	55n3, 185
14:27	113
14:29	215
14:30	20
14:31	111
15:3	64
15:4–5	111
16:3	148
16:5	130, 196
16:10	152
16:12	190
16:14	76
17:1	56
17:8	185
17:9	60
17:11	66, 202
17:14	88
17:16	66
18:5	135
19	147, 218
19:1	60n10
19:3	60n10
19:8	87
19:11–12	153
19:16	58, 137
19:19	184
19:20	154, 175
19:22	134
19:25	83
20	63
20:3	64
20:3–4	59
21:3	153
21:5	107, 143, 211
21:6	212
21:7	51
21:9	60, 147, 183
21:16	76
21:17	138
22:1–4	109
22:2	153
22:3	109
22:5	212
22:10–11	218
22:12	212
22:19	182
22:25	138
23:1	63
23:16	211
23:17–18	60
23:18	124

Index of Scripture and Other Ancient Sources

24:3	138	33:1	212	41:15		161
24:5	156–57	33:5	150, 194	41:17		112
24:12	55n4, 74, 135	33:9	220	41:18		53
24:13	207	33:15	122, 124, 210, 222	41:21		189
24:14	169	33:17	218	41:25		217
24:15	169	33:23	88	41:26		196
24:18	190	33:24	202	41:28		153
24:20	56, 124	34:1	51	42:1		119, 195
24:23	118	34:2	161, 185	42:7		216
25:2	55n3, 153	34:4	137	42:13		152
25:8	138, 158	34:5	161	42:14		153
25:10	166	34:8	189, 211	43:1		154, 191
26:7	122, 133, 212	34:11	76, 126	43:5		104, 168
26:8	133	34:11–17	125	43:6		169
26:11	180, 222	34:13	65	43:13		82, 154
26:18	106	34:13–15	126	43:14		154
27:2–3	56	35:2	76	43:20		65
27:9	185	35:7	65	43:25		120
27:13	218	35:9	179	43:27		120
28	136	36–38	28	43:28		161
28:6	119	36–39	13	44:6		154
28:7	103, 114	36:1	29	44:21		225
28:11–12	101	36:5	119	44:22–24		154
28:16	212	36:9	181	44:25		116
28:17	55	36:11	218	44:26		55n4
28:21	96	36:12	111	44:28		168
28:23	49, 51	36:14–15	154	45		7
29:3	172	36:16	24, 137	45:2		122, 160
29:6–7	53	36:18–20	154	45:7		69
29:14	153	37:11	161	45:13		93, 122
29:20	180	37:11–12	154	45:22		165, 169
29:21	134	37:22	151–52	45:24		192, 222
29:22	226	37:27	92	46:3		109
30:3	91	37:29	175	47		64n12
30:13	106	37:32	149	47:1		78
30:15	119	37:33–35	175	47:3		58, 64
30:19	111	38:3	191	47:4		154
30:22	60	38:6	154	47:8		78
30:27	169	39:8	211	47:9		182
30:28	53	40–55	216n60, 223	47:12		182
30:31	53, 163, 202	40–66	38	47:13		190
31:1	181	40:3	93, 122	48:5		60n10
31:4	52, 179	40:11	151	48:14		196
31:4–5	53	40:31	77	49		132, 136
31:5	175	41:5	137	49:1		51
31:7	60n10	41:7	135	49:5		147
32:6	20, 156	41:8	226	49:8		112, 203
32:7	202	41:9	169	49:11		133
32:14	151	41:11	217	49:16		218
32:18	101, 170	41:14	154	49:19		203

Isaiah (*continued*)

49:23	222–23	60:5	131	2:7	55, 83		
49:26	111	60:10	202, 218, 225	2:9	189		
50:6	163	60:13	76	2:12	203		
50:9	212	60:17	170, 172	2:15	206		
51:4	133	60:18	175, 202, 218	2:21	137		
51:17	186	60:21	56	2:26	118, 211		
51:20	186, 210	60:21–22	165	2:30	202		
52:2	85, 151, 223	60:22	150, 167	2:32	213		
52:4	218	61:2	186	2:33	211		
52:7	170, 172	61:3	56, 137	2:36	218		
52:9	55n4, 154	61:4	55n4, 203	3	157		
52:10	165	61:8	109, 196	3:12	210		
52:12	105	62:2	217, 221	3:14	87		
52:15	156, 222	62:4	60	3:18	226		
53:1	57	62:6	218	3:22	87		
53:2	101	62:8	204	3:25	91, 217		
53:7	77	63:4	186	4:4	112, 186		
53:9	201	63:5	194	4:5	182		
53:12	88, 120	63:5–6	186	4:7	55nn3–4; 179, 185, 206		
54:3	203	63:11	166, 221				
54:4	206	63:17	220	4:8	62, 64, 87		
54:5	161	64:1	52	4:9	86, 211		
54:7	104, 168	64:2	223	4:10	211		
54:13	211	64:10	60	4:27	60		
55:1	124	65:7	189	4:31	151, 153		
56:5	180	65:8	207	5:3	202		
56:7	133	65:9	225	5:4	108		
56:8	148, 168	65:12	203	5:7	203		
56:12	103	65:25	170, 179	5:13	95		
57:3	183	66:1	101–2	5:17	137		
57:15	148	66:2	137, 148	5:21	189		
57:17	202	66:5	137	5:21–22	108–9		
58:1	120	66:6	199	5:27	201		
58:5	194	66:12	131	5:31	103n27		
58:7	64	66:20	168	6:2	151		
58:9	112	66:24	54	6:4	115		
58:10	203			6:8	55, 60		
59:1	92	**Jeremiah**	29n8, 38, 104–5, 109, 112, 133, 149, 219	6:10	222		
59:3	122			6:11	119		
59:7	122, 210	1:2	133	6:12	83		
59:8	122	1:6	108	6:13	161		
59:11	134	1:10	182, 184	6:14–15	113, 118		
59:12	120	1:11	108	6:15	114, 217		
59:13	202	1:12	211	6:19	51		
59:17	186	1:13	108	6:23	151, 181		
59:19	169	1:18	211	6:24	153		
59:20	202	1:19	154	6:25	69		
60	132	2:4	109	6:26	68		
60–62	41	2:5	226	7	133, 193n54, 195–97		

Index of Scripture and Other Ancient Sources 243

7:5	211	16:5	87	25:31	169, 189
7:6	20, 85	16:6	87, 162	26	30
7:7	139, 226	16:11	226	26:3	112
7:11	133, 198	16:15	148	26:9	138
7:20	186	16:19	169	26:16–19	26
7:23	197	17:2	185	26:18	34, 46, 155
7:24	205	17:18	147	26:20	138
7:25	226	17:25	181, 211	27–28	37
7:28	153	17:26	15	27:2	85
7:29	70, 77, 87	18:11	85	27:8	85
7:33	130	18:16	206	27:9	183
8:1	211	18:18	82	27:11–12	85
8:3	148	18:21	57	27:13	138
8:7	108	18:22	162	27:20	58
8:10	161, 202	19:8	66, 206	28	27, 80, 90–91, 125n39
8:12	114, 217	19:9	111, 190		
8:19	146	20:10	147	28:2	147
9:3–5	209	20:13	154	28:4	207
9:4	190, 202, 212	21:12	82, 110, 186	29:1	58, 168
9:5	201	21:14	219	29:2	211
9:11	55n4, 65, 126	22:3	196	29:4	58
9:19	87, 217	22:4	181	29:4–10	27
9:22	160	22:8	156	29:7	58
9:24	196	22:15	196	29:11	85, 159, 170, 172
10:6–7	224	22:17	161, 210	29:14	58, 104, 168
10:10	150	22:22	217	30:8	85–86
10:19	66	22:23	153	30:10	138
10:22	55n3, 60, 65	23:1–4	105	30:12	66
10:25	186	23:2	148, 168	30:17	148
11:5	226	23:3	149, 168	30:24	225
11:13	217	23:5	196	31:7	149
11:19	82	23:14	194	31:8	60–61, 148
12:6	209	23:16	116	31:9	212
12:10–11	60	23:22	112	31:10	151
12:13	202, 204	23:32	114	31:12	131, 204
12:15	84	23:35	138	31:15	87
13:17	151	23:40	217	31:22	87
13:21	153, 212	24	137	31:28	182, 184
13:24	105	24:1	58, 211	31:37	190
14:2	117	24:2	207	31:38	148
14:13	108, 211	24:6	184	31:40	184
14:14	116	24:9	158, 206	32:15	83
14:17	66	25:5	112	32:19	219
15:6	190	25:6	148	32:22	226
15:9	118, 203	25:9	161	32:31	186
15:13	124	25:11	206	32:37	147, 168
15:18	62, 66, 75	25:18	158, 206	33:6	170, 172
15:20	154	25:27	203	33:8	120
15:21	154	25:29	148	33:9	223
16:4–6	62	25:30	52	33:10	203

244 Index of Scripture and Other Ancient Sources

Jeremiah (continued)							
34:11	225	49:17	66, 206	3:30	163		
34:14	226	49:18	178	4:3	65		
34:15	93	49:25	153	4:4	101		
34:16	225	49:28	96	4:13	122		
34:18	95	49:31	220	4:16	88		
38:6	217	49:33	60, 65	5:2	83		
38:11–13	89	50:12	118	5:5	85		
38:17	225	50:13	66, 206	5:6	171		
39:2	53	50:15	152	5:17	203		
39:9	168	50:16	135				
39:17	86, 154	50:19	203, 220	**Ezekiel**	38, 58n7, 63, 105, 109, 112, 133, 149, 178, 219		
40–41	153	50:37	58				
40:7	153	50:38	60				
40:10	207	50:43	153	1:15	74		
40:11	149	50:44	179	1:18	159		
40:13	153	51:3	161	4:2	162		
40:15	149	51:8	63	4:14	108		
41:5	162	51:10	217	5:10	105		
41:8	153	51:11	143	5:14–15	158		
41:17	166	51:21	181	5:15	185–86, 206		
42:2	149	51:29	159	6:4	147		
42:15	149	51:30	58, 119	6:4–6	60n10		
42:19	149	51:37	65, 126	6:6	147		
43:5	149	51:44	129, 131	6:14	60		
44:7	149	51:47	60, 183	7:9	202		
44:9–10	226	51:51	158	7:15	153		
44:11	180	51:52	60, 183	7:19	203		
44:12	149	52:3	225	7:23	202, 210		
44:14	149			7:26	153		
44:17–19	185	**Lamentations**	216n60	8:3	184		
44:22	112	1:4	203	8:18	186		
44:25	185	1:5	101	9:2	74		
46:3–4	143	1:6	101	9:9	210		
46:10	186	1:7	221	10:6	74		
46:24	217	1:8	65	10:9	74		
46:27	138	1:13	203	10:16–17	130		
47:3	160	1:16	203	10:19	130		
47:5	162	2	151	11	111		
48:1	217	2:2	182	11:2	82		
48:8	138, 185	2:8	85	11:5	119		
48:20	63	2:9	116, 133	11:13	149		
48:25	160	2:11	101	11:17	104–5, 147, 168		
48:38	87	2:15	206	11:24	119		
48:40	77	2:17	182	12:20	60		
48:42	185	2:19	101	12:22	86		
49:4	87	3:1	220	12:24	116		
49:5	105	3:6	216	13:4	55n4, 65		
49:9	207	3:9	162	13:5	218		
49:14	96	3:25–36	163	13:6	45		
		3:26	215	13:14	57, 182		

Index of Scripture and Other Ancient Sources 245

13:16	115–16	21:7	53, 91	34:12			151
14:8	180	21:12	64	34:13			168
14:15–16	60	21:15	53, 105	34:15–16			169
14:22	168	22:2	122	34:17			134
15:8	60	22:4	158	34:23–24			169
16	60	22:12	124	34:25		170, 172
16:7	73	22:12–13	161	34:28			138
16:22	73	22:18	203	34:29		56, 91
16:31	60	22:25	179	35–36			51
16:33	124	22:28	138	35:4		55n4, 185
16:34	60	22:29	110	35:5			57
16:39	73	22:30	218	36:6			186
16:40	59n9	23:7	60n10	36:6–7			91
16:41	60	23:23–24	181	36:15		91, 158, 206
16:44	86	23:29	73	36:18			186
16:52	91	23:30	60n10	36:23			159
16:54	91	23:37	60n10	36:24		104, 168
16:63	91	23:39	60n10	36:30			158
17	137	24	111	36:34			203
17:2	86	24:3	86	37:1			119
17:12	211	24:6	210	37:21			168
17:15	181	24:9	210	37:26		170, 172
18:2–3	86	24:17	119	38:10		82, 86
18:8	114	24:22	119	38:14			86
18:12	88	24:26–27	86	38:16			159
18:13	114	25:7	185	39:18			220
18:16	64	26:2	147	38:18–19			86
18:17	114	26:5	210	38:23			156
18:21	225	26:7	181	39:21			221
18:25	189	26:8	172	39:26		91, 138
18:30	163	26:9	218	39:28			168
18:31	202	26:10–11	181	44:23			124
19	180	26:11	160	45			84
19:11	163	26:17	87	45:10			201
19:14	163	26:20	55n4	45:23			195
20:8	60n10	27:24	88	46:13–14			82
20:16	60n10	28:12	87	47:23			200
20:18	60n10, 226	29:10	60	48:14			75
20:27	226	29:12	60				
20:30	226	30:4	57, 182	**Daniel**		86, 151, 159
20:34	104, 168	30:9	86, 137	2:2			182
20:36	226	30:13	60n10	3:15		80, 82, 154
20:37	220	31:4	57n6	4:37			133
20:40	75	32:24–25	91	6:22			162
20:40–41	194	32:30	91	7:18		139, 194
20:41	104	33:28	202	7:22			194
20:46	103	34	139	7:25			194
20:49	86	34:4	196	8			160
21:2	91, 103	34:10	169	8:4			179
21:3	180	34:11–19	105	9		148, 227

Daniel (continued)

9:3	217
9:5	217
9:16	158
11:3	168

Hosea

39–42, 47–48, 58n7, 188

1:1	47, 133
1:4	23
1:4–5	186
1:5	86
1:7	181
2:3	58
2:6	218
2:10	154
2:12	125, 137
2:16	86
2:18	86, 147
2:19	196
4:1	189
4:2	210
4:10	203
4:13	189
5:14	154, 179
6:1	202
6:3	197
6:6	53, 224
7:1	162
7:3	211
7:5	211
7:11	218
7:13	118, 191
7:15	82
8:3	87
8:7	203
8:10	211
8:13	194, 225
9:1	60
9:2	203
9:3	218
9:7	211
9:9	225
9:10	137, 207, 226
9:15	112, 192
10:1	137
10:8	185
10:11	74, 160
10:12	204
10:13	123, 204
11:4	88
11:5	218
11:6	205
11:8–9	63
11:10	179
11:11	218
12:1	218
12:2	189
12:3	112
12:6	196
12:7	85, 201
12:10	116
13:6	203
14:9	122

Joel

41

1:1	47–48, 133
1:6	150, 179
1:7	137
1:10	204
1:18	151
2:5	150
2:10	117
2:14	41, 225
2:17	158, 220
2:19	158, 204
2:22	137
2:24	204
2:26	169
3:8	134, 138
3:9	115
3:10	135, 141, 143–44, 221
3:13	52
3:15	117
3:19	60
4:1–3	144
4:2	88
4:8	134
4:9–12	144
4:13	135

Amos

41–42, 48, 188

1–2	172, 196
1:1	47–48
1:3	75, 160
1:5	147, 163, 180
1:6	75, 95, 105
1:8	163, 180, 220
1:9	75, 95, 105
1:11	75, 95, 105
1:13	75
1:15	211
2:1	75
2:3	180, 211
2:4	75
2:6	75
2:8	82, 97–100, 98n27
2:9	185
2:12	82
2:13	160
3:1	138
3:6	137
3:12	179
4:1	20, 85
4:3	106
4:4	82, 192
4:13	50
5	193n54, 195, 197
5:5	192
5:10	122, 134, 190
5:11	82, 204
5:12	202
5:13	85
5:15	109, 149
5:16	87
5:21–24	112
5:21–25	133
5:22	194
5:24	53
6:1	75
6:1–6	20
6:4	20, 194
6:4–7	227
6:6	82
7:1	87
7:16	91, 103
7:17	102
8:1–2	207
8:5	201
8:9	86, 117
9:7	196
9:11	86, 165, 218, 221
9:14	203
9:15	184

Obadiah

63, 156

1:1	47, 116
1:4	130
1:8	86
1:9	180

Index of Scripture and Other Ancient Sources

1:12	156	1:10–16	67–79, 71–72	3:6	117
1:18	138	1:12	74, 74n14	3:7	118, 119n38
Jonah	41–42, 187,	1:12b	69	3:8	103, 116, 119–20,
	196, 221	1:13	22, 136, 181–82		202, 225
1:1	47–48	1:14	16	3:9	93, 108, 122,
1:16	222	1:14–15	69		129, 189
3:8–10	223	1:15–16	22	3:9–10	127
3:9	41–42, 113, 225	1:16	66, 77, 100	3:9–11	27
4:11	40	2	33, 93, 108, 152	3:9–12	38, 121–28
Micah	29n8, 30, 38, 41,	2:1	2, 17, 20, 74n14,	3:10–11	22
	48, 58n7, 78,		80–81, 104n29	3:11	20, 74n14,
	190, 192	2:1–2	125		104n29, 152
1	15, 30, 46, 58, 78,	2:1–5	35, 38, 76, 89,	3:11–12	127
	138, 180, 182, 200		79–91	3:12	25–26, 34, 43,
1–2	33	2:2	20, 84, 100		48, 50, 53, 55–56,
1–3	27, 33–34, 74n14,	2:3	74n14, 82, 139n42		78, 124–26, 131–33,
	155, 208	2:3a	38		135, 142, 203
1–5	33–34, 38, 186	2:4	22, 87–89, 157	4	21–22, 116, 130,
1–6	227	2:5	88		136, 160
1:1	3, 45–49	2:6	95, 101, 103	4–5	33–34, 36,
1:1–4:10	150	2:6–7	37, 90–94		154, 186
1:2	38, 49, 52, 54,	2:6–8	93	4–7	33
	108, 186, 189	2:6–11	38	4–8	1
1:2a	46	2:7–10	32	4:1	135, 146
1:2–4	50	2:8	22, 43, 94, 116	4:1–3	141
1:2–7	35, 48–61	2:8–9	4, 20, 88, 96, 101	4:1–4	34, 136
1:2–16	33	2:8–13	94–107	4:1–5	25, 34, 38, 43,
1:2–3:12	33	2:9	15, 20, 59, 78,		24–26, 52, 56,
1:2–5:15	37		85, 99–100		98, 125, 127–45,
1:2b–3a	53	2:10	102		138n40, 164, 174,
1:3	22	2:11	91, 103, 103n27		177, 187–88, 222
1:3–5a	38	2:12	34, 38, 147,	4:1–10	142
1:4	18, 57		151, 168	4:1–5:1	164
1:5	62, 107	2:12–13	3, 33, 95,	4:2	132
1:5–6	56		104–6, 104n28	4:3	69, 134–36, 138,
1:6	25, 43, 48, 53,	2:13	106		187, 190
	56–57, 78, 125–26,	3	109n32, 111	4:3–4	22
	132, 135	3–5	143	4:4	13, 137–38,
1:6–7	64	3:1	114, 121, 189		146, 179
1:7	58, 60–61,	3:1–3	127	4:5	138–39, 141, 197
	134, 183	3:1–4	22, 38, 107–13	4:6	104, 148
1:7b	61	3:1–5	4	4:6–7	151
1:8	22, 59, 64–65	3:1–4:8	33	4:6–7a	38
1:8–9	61–69, 77	3:1–5:14	143	4:6–8	34
1:8–16	35, 38	3:2	74n14, 109	4:6–10	145–55
1:9	66	3:3	111	4:8	23, 34, 146,
1:10	196	3:4	108–9, 112,		156, 218
1:10–13	69		112n34, 219	4:8–9	152
1:10–15	32, 66	3:5	22, 37, 46, 88	4:9	146, 152, 163
		3:5–8	38, 113–20	4:9–10	38, 153

Micah (*continued*)		6:1–2	192	7:18–19	123
4:9–5:15	33	6:1–5	188–92	7:20	166, 218
4:10	3, 146, 156	6:1–8	206		
4:10–11	23	6:1–7:7	33–34	**Nahum**	41–42, 187
4:11	52, 58, 87, 91,	6:2	108	1:1	47, 116
	146, 157, 159	6:3	88	1:2	186
4:11–13	142–44, 164	6:3–5	192	1:4	220
4:11–5:1	155–65	6:4–5	23, 200n55	1:5	53
4:14–5:5	174n51	6:5	88	1:6	186
4:13	23, 37, 46, 156,	6:6–8	133, 192–98	1:9	82
	161–62, 164,	6:7	75, 111	1:13	147
	177, 183	6:7–8	139	1:15	180
5	29n8, 30,	6:8	90, 133, 139n42,	2:3–4	181
	182, 186		197, 224	2:5	131
5:1	23, 38, 146,	6:9	51, 108, 200	2:11–12	178
	163–64, 166	6:9–12	32	2:11–13	179
5:1–2	31n9	6:9–16	198–206	3:1	122, 210
5:1–6	175	6:10–11	200	3:3	135
5:1–8	141	6:12	202	3:4	182
5:2–3	167	6:13	202	3:5	65
5:2–4	170	6:13–16	200n55	3:7	63
5:2–5a	165–71	6:14	23	3:10	100
5:4	34	6:16	51, 88, 199–200,	3:14	162, 182, 217
5:4–6	23		205, 216	3:18–19	40
5:4b–5	174	7	33, 208, 215,	3:19	66
5:5	146, 173		224, 226–27		
5:5–6	170–76	7:1	206–8	**Habakkuk**	
5:5a	179	7:2	23, 93, 209,	1:1	45
5:5b–6	47		210n58	2:6	86
5:7	146	7:2–6	208–14	2:7	114–15
5:7–8	38	7:4	93	2:9	161
5:7–9	200n55	7:6	213	2:12	122
5:7–15	176–88	7:6b	213	3:8–13	53–54
5:8	23, 125, 179	7:7	215, 218	3:9	73
5:8–9	52	7:7–13	214–19	3:12	160
5:9–14	141	7:7–20	33	3:18	215
5:9–15	187	7:8–10	52		
5:10	23, 74, 146	7:8–20	33–34	**Zephaniah**	
5:10–11	179	7:9d	217	1:1	47, 133
5:10–14	38	7:10	23, 217n61	1:5	194
5:10–15	200n55	7:11–12	32	1:6	203
5:12	174–75	7:12	23	1:8	211
5:13	194	7:13	219, 221	1:9	202
5:14	108, 185	7:14	34	1:9–10	86
5:15	23, 38, 49	7:14–20	219–27	1:11	63
6	138, 190	7:16	119, 223	1:12	148
6–7	33–34, 38–38,	7:16–17	23, 221	1:13	161, 204
	188	7:17	222	1:18	154
6:1	18, 143	7:18	45, 83, 224	2:9	149, 168
				2:11	194

Index of Scripture and Other Ancient Sources

2:13–15	125	8:17	82	2:12	180
2:15	206	8:20–23	25, 132, 141	2:17	193
3:4	133	9:9	152	3:4	221
3:5	82	9:9–10	186–87	3:5	182
3:6	180	9:10	169, 180–81	3:7–8	193
3:11	86	9:16	86		
3:13	138, 149	10:2	116	**APOCRYPHA**	
3:14	152	10:5	217		8
3:16	86	10:8	168	**Tobit**	
3:19	145, 147–48, 168	10:10	171, 218	13:11	169
		10:11	163	**Judith**	
3:20	104	11	169	2:5	161
Haggai		11:2	220	11:1	161
1:1	133	11:6	135, 154	11:7	161
1:6	203	11:9	111	13:17	139
1:12	149	12:2–9	144	16:3	162
1:14	149	12:3–4	86	16:15	50
2:11	133	12:6	86, 160		
2:22	185	12:8–9	86	**Wisdom of Solomon**	
2:23	86	12:9	185	5:16–23	225
		12:11	86	9:15	194
Zechariah	38	13:1–2a	187	10:7	184
1:1	47, 133	13:1–2	86	12:2	194
1:2	226	13:2	180	14:16–17	183
1:4	112	13:3	138	16:9	173
1:5	226	13:4	86	17:2	82
1:18	130	13:6	66		
1:18–19	160	13:8	180	**Sirach**	
1:21	137, 160	14:1	88	1:14	200
2:1	130	14:1–3	144	5:12	222
2:11	86, 156	14:2	100, 147	8:7	156
3:1	156	14:4	86	14:5	85
3:9	156	14:5	73, 162	14:8	85
3:10	86, 137	14:6	86	14:10	85
4:14	161	14:8	207	19:20	200
6:5	161	14:8–9	86	28:25	213
6:13	172	14:11	161	38:4	182
7:10	82	14:12–15	144	38:25	135
7:11	222			40:6	212
7:14	202	**Malachi**		49:10	40
8	136, 138n40	1:1	47		
8:2	186	1:2	193	**Baruch**	148
8:6	149	1:3	60, 65	1:15–20	226
8:10	124	1:4	55n4	1:17–18	217
8:11–12	149	1:6–7	193		
8:12	137, 177	1:8	194	**Prayer of Azariah**	
8:13	109	1:10	194	1:16–17a	148
8:14	148	1:13	110, 194	**Susanna**	
8:16	170, 172, 226	2:6	123	1:31	78

1 Maccabees		
2:36	162	
3:22–23	147	
14:12	137	
2 Maccabees		
12:38	77	
1 Esdras		
4	214	
5:63	212	
8:11	172	
8:59	212	
8:85	139	
4 Maccabees		
18:24	139	

NEW TESTAMENT

Matthew	
1:5	166
5:23–24	112
5:39	163
6:10	152
6:19–20	212
7:22	86
8:5–13	222
9:24	118
10	151
10:34–36	213, 213n59
11:5	149
20:25–28	120
21:5	152
21:12–13	133
21:13	198
23:39	138
25:31–46	134, 160
26:52	67, 107
Mark	
4:1–9	160
10:30	83
10:43	197
12:17	152
14–15	163
Luke	
4	186
4:1	119
6:29	163
7:22	149
8:53	118
10:12	86
12:49–53	213, 213n59
17:31	86
19:45–48	133
20	151
21:8	138
21:14	149
John	
10	169
12:15	152
15	137
18:36–37	152
Acts	
1:8	169
6:3	119
6:5	119
9:1–9	47
11:24	119
13:47	169
Romans	
11	137
12:17–19	163
1 Corinthians	
16:21	108
2 Corinthians	
10:1	108
Galatians	
1:5	139
5:2	108
Ephesians	
3:21	139
6	53
6:12–17	225
Philippians	
4:20	139
Colossians	
4:18	108
1 Thessalonians	
5:3	153
2 Thessalonians	
3:17	108
1 Timothy	
1:17	139
Hebrews	
1:8	139
James	93
2	133
5	89–90
1 Peter	
4:11	139
5:8	179
5:11	139
2 Peter	
2:15	192
Revelation	151, 227
1:6	139
1:18	139
2:14	192
4:9–10	139
5:5	179
5:6	179
5:13	139
7:12	139
7:17	169
13:3	62
13:12	62
19	53

PSEUDEPIGRAPHA

Enoch	51

DEAD SEA SCROLLS

	167
Texts of or on Micah	
from Wadi Murabba'at	31
1QpMic (1Q14)	31–32, 50
4QpMic (4Q168)	31–32
4QMic frg. 5	31, 31n9
4QXIIf	167
4QXIIg	31, 41
8ḤevXIIgr	31–32, 41
Rule of the Community	
1QS 8.5	137

RABBINIC SOURCES AND SCRIPTURE TEXTS

Ibn Ezra	88n21
Kimchi	88n21

Masoretic Text 31 (*see also* Dead Sea Scrolls)
Pirqe Rabbi Eliezer 40–41
Rabbi Yoḥanan ben Zakkai 140
Septuagint 31–32, 31n10 (*see also* Dead Sea Scrolls)

ANCIENT NEAR EASTERN EVIDENCE

fertility dolls 14–17, 15n4, 20
Kuntillet ʿAjrûd water jugs 184
LMLK jar stamps 14–17, 14n2, 15n3, 20, 76
Mandaean amulet 173
Sefire Treaty, Stela I A 32–33 126
Tel Sandakḫannah 76
Tell ed–Duweir (Lachish) 16–17, 16n6, 20
Tell Judeideh (Moresheth) 15–16
tomb of Micah 15n5
trading weights 16

Akkadian
literature 45

ANEP
124–25 59n8
130–31 16

ANET
284–85 12n1
307 139n43
564 7

Babylonian
incantations 173n50
Murašu archive 8
Nippur, Aramaic incantation 173
royal inscriptions 161

Egyptian
Palette of King Narmer 59n8

Neo-Assyrian
annals 24
Black Obelisk, Shalmaneser III 204n57, 223
Esarhaddon treaty, *ANET* 529 125
iconography 179
inscriptions 159
Orders of the king 6
panopticon 159
reliefs
 fall of Lachish 17–18, 59, 78
 of kings 3–4, 159
 from Sargon's Palace, Khorsabad 59n8

Sennacherib's battle descriptions 17, 17n7
sources 204n57
warfare iconography 59

Ugaritic
CTU
I.119.26–36 174
V.3.1.3–4 173
female warrior deities 162
Holy Mountain motifs 50
incantations 173
Keret Epic 174
literature 173n49

EARLY CHRISTIAN SOURCES

EUSEBIUS

Onomasticon
134.10 15n5

GREGORY THE GREAT
77–78

GRECO-ROMAN LITERATURE

HERODOTUS

Histories
3.68–71 173n48

INDEX OF SUBJECTS AND AUTHORS

Aaron, 191, 194
Abel-Shittim, 191
Abraham, 195, 225–26
Abrams, Ray, 117n37
Achaemenid Empire. *See* Persian Empire
Achzib, 75–76
'ādām (humanity), 171–72, 178, 196
address, changes in, 109n32
Adullam, 76, 77
agriculture. *See* farming
Ahab, 84, 200, 204, 205, 216
 house of, 205
Ahaz, 7, 11–12, 76
Ahaziah, 205
Ai, destruction of, 55n4
Alfaro, Juan, 30, 97
Allen, Leslie, 34, 105, 171, 199
Amaziah, 10
ambush, 210
Amos, 42, 47
 antimilitarism in, 102
 Oracles against the Nations in, 75
Anath, 162
ancient Near East
 end of society in, 213
 incantations of, 173
 lions in, 179
 mourning practices in, 63–64
 primordial battle myths in, 53
 shepherd imagery in, 168
 war in, 100, 115
Andersen, Francis, 32, 33, 35, 47, 48, 49, 50, 51n2, 57, 57n6, 62, 63, 65, 68, 69, 70, 71, 73, 73n13, 75–76, 81, 83, 87–88, 91, 95, 96, 97n24, 98, 100, 104n28, 109, 109n32, 111, 115, 117, 117n36, 119n38, 122, 126, 129, 130, 131, 136, 138n40, 148, 153, 161–62, 162n45, 163, 167, 172, 175, 179,
186, 189–90, 193, 197, 199, 200n55, 206, 207, 210n58, 211, 216n60, 217n61, 220, 221, 226
anger, 185–86
animals
 similes featuring, 62, 65–66, 77
 as symbols of de-creation, 55n3, 65, 76, 125–26
antimilitarism, 1–2, 20–26
 in folk songs, 21–22
 laborers and, 21–22, 99, 101, 128, 144–45
antimonarchical speech of Samuel, 24, 213
apocalyptic
 astrology in, 51
 darkness in, 117
 "on that day" in, 86
 visions in, 47
apostrephō (turn away, apostatize), 87, 112–13
archaic perfect, 68
'āšaq (oppression, exploitation), 80, 84–85
'ăšērâ (Asherah, asherah pole), 183, 184–85
Ashur. *See* Neo-Assyrian Empire
astrology, 51
'āṣûm (strong, mighty), 149–50
authority, 178
'āwen (evil), 80
'āwōn (corruption, wickedness), 54, 81
Azal, 73
Azariah. *See* Uzziah
Azariah, Prayer of, 148

Bach, Alice, 35
bākô (weeping), 68
Balaam, 191–92
Balawat door braces, 59
baldness, 77–78
Baltzer, Klaus, 223

bāmôt (high places), 50, 55, 121, 125, 185, 189
ban. *See ḥērem* (total destruction, net)
barefoot, going, 62, 64
Bashan, 220
Becking, Bob, 130
bĕhēmôt (animals), 125
Bentham, Jeremy, 158
Ben Zvi, Ehud, 35, 49–50, 52, 89n22, 126, 131
Berlin Wall, 140
Berrigan, Daniel, 140
Berrigan, Philip, 140
Beth Etzel, 73–74
Bethlehem, 165, 166
  symbolism of, 30
bêt marzēaḥ (house of mourning), 87
Biddle, Mark, 107
birth imagery, 167–68
Bissett, Jim, 128
"bite," 114–15, 171, 173
  of insect, 173
Black Obelisk, 204n57, 223
Blenkinsopp, Joseph, 137
bloodshed, symbolizing injustice, 122, 123, 124, 128, 210
"borders," 175
Borowski, Oded, 14
bôš/bōšet (shame), 91, 114, 117–18
boundary lines, 89
"bow down," 193–94
Bozrah, 105, 106
breaching of walls, 53, 95, 105–6
bribery, 123–24
Brin, Gershon, 95, 105
Brueggemann, Walter, 142
Bryant, David, 156, 166, 167, 174, 174n51
building projects, 7, 128
  and imperial gaze, 159
  taxation and, 123, 199
Burbank, Garin, 128
Byrne, Ryan, 15

Callaway, Phillip, 32, 167
call to war, 96–97, 99, 143, 160
calves, consumption of, 194
Campbell, Edward, 11
cannibalism, 110–11
  economic, 107–13
Carroll, Robert, 1, 58, 120
"carry away," 80, 81, 83

Cathcart, Kevin, 173–74, 175
Cha, Jun-Hee, 27, 62, 68, 70, 103n27, 113, 114, 118, 130, 209
chariots, 74, 181–82
  expense of, 75
chiasm, 35
children
  glory of God and, 101
  loss of, in wartime, 15, 78, 203
  of privilege, 70, 78
  suffering of, in wartime, 100–101
Christianity
  contemporary, 67, 227
  in developing world, 89
  lament and, 67
  pacifism in, 140–41
  and prophetic preaching, 79
cities
  destruction of, 55n4, 56
  as feminine, 57, 65, 157, 162, 217
  gates of, 72, 74
  symbolizing oppression, 182
  terms for, 153
  turned into farmland, 57
Clifford, Richard, 50
coherence of Micah, 32, 36–39, 43
"collateral damage," 67, 79
colonialism, violence of, 2, 84, 89, 171, 200n55, 213, 222
commanders, 107, 109, 122, 211
conflict resolution, 136, 223–24
confusion, 212
conquest, 6, 59, 161
  of Canaan, 84, 173, 192
  depictions of, 3–4, 16, 59, 100–101
  as disruption of economic systems, 89
  "peace" through, 164
conscription, 79, 97, 99, 116, 181
Contention and Conciliation, Book of, 33
Cook, J. M., 8
corruption, 114
  economic, 200–201, 202
  leading to destruction, 102
  political alliances leading to, 61
  privilege leading to, 120
  of temple, 200–201
cosmological language, 189
"counselor," 152–53, 176
coveting, 83
crushing, 147–48, 160–61
"cry out," 111–12, 112n34, 152

Index of Subjects and Authors

cultic language, 54, 133, 193n54, 197
curse traditions, 65, 110–11, 125–26, 204, 205–6, 218–19
"cut off," 180, 181, 182, 183, 186–87
Cyrus II, 7

dārak (tread), 50, 52–53
darkness, 117, 199, 203
dating texts, 148
   in Micah, 32, 34, 36, 38, 48, 105, 126, 129, 154, 172–73, 174n51, 186, 188
   transgenerational trauma and, 44
David, 172
   Bethlehem and, 166
   as man of war, 10, 136
   retreat of, 76, 77
Davidic dynasty, 143, 152, 167
   Micah opposed to, 46, 165
   punishing nations, 141
   replacement of, 30, 167, 169, 174
day, 212. *See also* "on that day"
Day, Peggy, 59n9
Dead Sea Scrolls, 31, 167
   the Twelve among, 41
death, mourning, 63–64
debate with false prophets, 36–37
   lack of markers for, 37
Decalogue, 83, 202
deception, 75–76, 103, 201, 202
   as oppression of poor, 202
de-creation, 55, 60, 76
deliverance, 175, 179, 190–91, 221
   concluding prayer for, 219–27
Dempsey, Carol, 89n22
deportation, 4, 12
desolation, land as, 60, 202–3, 218–19
Deuteronomistic History
   antimilitarism in, 24
   critical of Northern Kingdom, 204, 205
   God's plans in, 166
   Josiah's reform in, 55, 60
   tribal allotments in, 84
Dever, William, 20–21
"dew," 177, 178, 179
Dickens, Hazel, 21
disability, 148
distributive justice, 83–84, 86, 88, 89
divination, 116, 121
dominion, 151–52
Doom, Book of, 33, 161
"double effect," 79

Doukhobors, 131
"Down by the Riverside," 21–22
drama, Micah as, 37
"drivel," 91, 95, 102, 103
"drive out," 100
Dubovský, Peter, 159
dust, 73
   licking, 222–23
   rising from, 223
"dwelling alone," 220, 221

eagle, 65, 77–78
earth
   as addressee, 51
   far reaches of, 218
   foundations of, 190
   God's presence throughout, 101–2
East German peace movement, 140–41
eating, 114–15, 203. *See also* cannibalism
economics
   cannibalism imagery and, 110
   conquest and, 6–7, 89
   distributive justice and, 83–84, 86, 88, 89
   and exploitation, 80, 85, 89, 110, 200–201, 213
   of rural Judah, 18–21
Edelman, Diana, 17
Eden narrative, 223
editing of Micah, 32, 34, 35, 43, 44, 104–5, 208
   Deuteronomistic, 46
Edom, slave trade and, 105, 106
egeirō (raise up), 115
Egypt, 218, 220
   slavery in, 25
"eight," 172, 174
Ekron, 17
'ēl (God, power), 82
'ĕlîlîm (idols), 60n10
Elisha, 23
elites
   apostasy of, 88
   authority of, 178
   judgment on, 121–28, 160, 168–69
   like lions, 180
   luxuries of, 101, 103
   Micah's direct address to, 108–9
   as militant patriots, 89, 94–107
   oppression by, 79–90, 103, 110, 113, 122, 170, 202
   responsible for justice, 109
   war benefiting, 99

'elyôn (height/high), 56n5, 194
"ends of the earth," 169–70, 175
enemies
    "cut off," 180
    fellow Israelites as, 127, 216, 217, 219
    feminizing, 58
    as lions, 179
    in one's own household, 213
    treading/stamping upon, 52–53, 217
English Digger Movement, 128
Ephrata, 165, 166
epitēdeuma (deeds), 112
'ēṣel (next to), 73–74
"establish," 130, 133, 211
'ēt (plowshare), 69, 74, 135
eternity, 139, 150–51
ethics, 39, 140, 196
    and the ideal future, 130, 131
    religion and, 133
Eusebius, 15n5
evil
    economic, 85
    and evildoers, 80
    God bringing, 69, 74
    hands skilled at doing, 210–11
    love of, 109
    and those who conceive evil, 81–82
    time, 85
exile, 51, 58–59, 78, 86, 154
    Abrahamic promise and, 226
    as being stricken by God, 202
    desolation and, 203
    God initiating, 95, 105
    and postexilic restoration, 155–65
    "remnant" and, 149
    and sense of being watched, 86–87
exodus motif, 53, 148, 190–91, 221, 225
exposing enemies, 51, 57–59
Ezekiel
    call narrative of, 159
    empathy of God in, 63
    school of, 38
    sexualized punishment in, 58n7

Fales, Mario, 5, 13
false prophets, 102–3
    fate of, 117–18
    judgment on, 121–28
    lacking empathy, 67
    leading people astray, 114
    as liars, 103
    Micah's debate with, 36–37, 90–94, 104, 108, 143, 152, 153, 160, 162, 164, 175, 186
    Micah's denunciation of, 94–107, 113–20
    modern, 206
    predicting peace, 28, 46, 115, 116, 152
    "rest" prophesied by, 101
    soothsaying of, 174
    visions and, 45
    visions of, 116–17
    war of, on their people, 115–16
family breakdown, 210, 212–13
farming
    abundance and, 136–37
    and agricultural metaphors, 56–57, 124, 125, 160
    love of, 207
    and protest movements, 128, 144–45, 170–71
    unproductive, as punishment, 203
    as usefulness, 25, 56–57, 124–25, 126, 127
    war contrasted with, 24
    and worker's hut, 50, 55–56, 124, 218
"Farms Not Arms," 145
fearing God's name, 200
feminist biblical criticism, 57–59, 157
fencing, 218
fertility. *See also* pillar figurines
    importance of, in wartime, 15
fields, 56, 153, 155
figs, 207
fire of judgment, 51
firstborn, 195
first fruits, 75
first-person speech, 63
flaying, 95, 108, 111, 127
flood narratives, 53, 202
forced labor, 8, 128
    military service as, 99
foreigners
    fearing God, 224
    resolution of conflict with, 188
    sorcery and, 182, 183
    threats to, 187–88
forgiveness, 197, 224, 227
form criticism, 35
"former days," 166, 167
"former times," 221
Foucault, Michel, 158

Index of Subjects and Authors 257

foundations, 51, 57
Fox, George, 123
Freedman, David Noel, 32, 33, 35, 47, 48, 49, 50, 51n2, 57, 57n6, 62, 63, 65, 68, 69, 70, 71, 73, 73n13, 75–76, 81, 83, 87–88, 91, 95, 96, 97n24, 98, 100, 104n28, 109, 109n32, 111, 115, 117, 117n36, 119n38, 122, 126, 129, 130, 131, 136, 138n40, 148, 153, 161–62, 162n45, 163, 167, 172, 175, 179, 186, 189–90, 193, 197, 199, 200n55, 206, 207, 210n58, 211, 216n60, 217n61, 220, 221, 226
"friend," 212
Friends, Society of, 2, 123, 128
fruit, 207
"fruit of a womb," 195
"fruit of their deeds," 219
Frye, Richard, 8
fury. *See* anger
future
　ideal, 131
　near *vs.* far, 130
　"on that day," 181
　oracle of, 86

gā'al (redeem), 146, 154, 191
gālâ (uncover), 51, 57–59, 70
garden, 220, 221
"garment," 95, 97, 98–99
gates, 72, 74
　open, symbolism of, 174–75
Gath, 10, 14, 16, 17, 72
gathering, 61, 147, 147n44
gāzal (tear), 110
gāzaz (shave, shear), 77
"gaze," 156–59
gdd (gash, muster), 156, 162
geber (young, strong man), 80, 85
Gedaliah, 27, 149
gender, 57–59, 65, 157
genre stereotyping, 35
"genuine sayings" of Micah, 33
Gilgal, 192
gleaning, 207
"glory of Israel," 76–77, 77n15
God
　abandoning people, 112–13
　answering cries, 112
　as breacher of walls, 95, 105–6
　bringing evil, 69, 74

　changing God's mind, 225
　as creator and judge, 55
　as deliverer, 175
　descent of, 52
　empathy of, 63
　fear of, 200, 221–22, 223, 224
　fury of, 185–86, 187n53
　inheritance of, 220
　Israelites punished by, 104, 105–6, 148
　as king, 150, 151–52, 165, 169
　kingdom of, 120, 151–52
　legal language and, 52, 138, 188–92
　as light, 216
　military might of, 181–82
　nations as agents of, 52, 55
　plans of, 85, 86, 130, 131, 159, 166
　as planter, 56–57, 137
　pleasing, 192–98
　policy and, 92
　power of, 139
　scattering people, 105
　speech of, 138
　spirit of, 119
　walking with, 138–39, 143, 193, 197
　as warrior, 147, 186
　wonders of, 221
"God most High," 194
Goffman, Erving, 158–59
gōlâ (exile), 51, 58, 70
good, hating, 109
"good words," 93
Gordon, Robert, 220
gôyīm rabbîm (many nations), 132, 134
Grabbe, Lester, 12n1
grapes, 207
greed, 61, 88, 201
Green Corn Rebellion, 21, 101
Gregory the Great, 77–78
Gysi, Klaus, 140

Haak, Robert, 92
Hagstrom, David, 74n14, 172, 224
hair, 64, 70, 77
Haiti, earthquake in (2010), 201n56
hālak (walk), 90, 139, 139n42
ḥālaq (parcel out), 87, 88
ḥāmad (covet), 83
Hananiah, 27, 29n8, 90, 91, 125n39
hands, 210
　representing power, 80, 82–83

ḥānēp (pollute, profane, godless), 156, 157
Hannah, prayer of, 169
ḥāpēr (disgrace), 117–18
Haran, Menahem, 50
ḥāšab (think, conceive), 81–82
ḥāsîd (faithful). *See* ḥesed (steadfast love, loyalty)
ḥaṭṭā'â/ḥaṭṭā't (sin), 54, 119–20, 195
haughtiness, 85
Haupt, Paul, 32
ḥăzôn (vision), 45
head of household, 85
ḥebel (cord, line, rope), 88
ḥērem (total destruction, net), 156, 161, 209, 210
Herodotus, 13
ḥerpâ (shame, humiliation), 157, 206
ḥesed (steadfast love, loyalty), 193, 196, 209–10, 224
Hezekiah, 146
 opposition to, 13–14
 religious reforms of, 14
 revolt of, 1, 12–15, 24, 28–29
high places, 50, 52, 55, 121, 125, 185, 189
 Jerusalem as, 55
ḥîl (writhe), 69
Hillers, Delbert, 1, 49, 50, 68–69, 70, 90, 91, 94, 95, 96, 125, 126, 129, 130, 142, 145, 146, 152, 155, 156, 163, 168, 171–72, 174, 186, 197, 202, 205, 211, 218
historical context, 2, 3–31
historical-critical method, 2
history, use of, 221
Hobbs, T. Raymond, 142
Hoffman, Yair, 43
Holladay, John, 27
holy, making, 60, 114, 115
Holy Mountain. *See* mountains
"holy places," 53
"holy temple," 52
holy war, 115, 156, 160, 164
homes, 100
honor-shame, 87
hooves, 160–61
hope, 178
ḥōq (statutes), 218
ḥorbâ (ruins), 55n4
horns of iron, 37, 46, 160, 162, 164
horses, 74, 160–61, 181

Hosea
 prostitution imagery in, 42
 time references in, 48
 violence condemned by, 23
Hosea-Amos-Micah, 41
Hoshea, 12
House, Paul, 42
"House of Israel," 109
"house of slavery," 191
"house of the wicked," 200
Houston, Walter, 18–19
hôy, 80
human sacrifice, 110, 111, 122, 195
humiliation, 90, 91, 118, 163, 206. *See also* shame
 māšāl and, 87
 over loss of land, 88
humility, 193, 197
hunger, 199, 203
 as punishment, 203
hut for farmworkers, 50, 55–56, 124, 218
Hutton, Rodney, 112n34, 192

'î (worker's hut), 50, 55–56, 124, 218
Ibn Ezra, Abraham, 114, 207
idolatry, 55, 60, 61, 112, 177, 183–84
 "cut off," 180, 183
 terms for, 60n10
images, 183. *See also* idolatry
"imperial gaze," 157, 158, 159
impurity, 156, 157
incantations, 47, 173–74, 175
inclusio, 49
inequality, militarism leading to, 20–22, 23, 24, 46, 75, 144, 170
infection, 199
"inheritance," 69, 220
injustice
 bloodshed symbolizing, 122, 123, 124, 128, 210
 God accusing people of, 198–206
 in Jerusalem, 123, 201–2
inspiration, 47
insults. *See* humiliation
interest, collection of, 114–15, 124
international context of Micah, 3–8
"The Internationale," 22, 102
International Workers of the World (IWW), 21
interpretation
 bias in, 3, 142

Index of Subjects and Authors

models of, 1
readers' context and, 2–3, 139–41
socioeconomic context for, 1, 3, 20–26, 127
translation as, 32, 56, 152
interrogative particles, 50
intertextuality, 71, 141–43
Isaiah and, 132, 141–42, 144
Jeremiah and, 26–28, 34
Joel and, 141, 143–44
New Testament and, 213, 213n59
Isaiah
agricultural metaphors in, 56
encouraging Hezekiah, 13, 28–29
like Hananiah, 29n8, 125n39
nakedness of, 64
Peace Prophecy in, 132, 141–42, 144
"remnant" in, 149
school of, 38
Servant Songs of, 119, 222
vineyard metaphor of, 105–6, 137
visions in, 45
Israel
appearance of, before nations, 206
and conflict with Judah, 10, 11–12, 88
deportation of, by Assyrians, 12n1
dominating world, 138n40, 143
God punishing, 104, 105–6, 148
as inheritance of God, 83
insurrection in, 11
Jacob and, 107, 225
as "mighty nation," 149–50
plotting with Egypt, 12
rulers of, 9
usurpations in, 6, 9, 11
as vassal, 6, 11

Jacob, 107, 119–20, 146, 147, 183, 225–26
Jacobs, Mignon, 33, 123, 162
James, Epistle of, 89–90
Jehoash, 10
Jehoiachin, 7
Jehoram, 205
Jehu, 204n57, 205, 223
Jeppesen, Knud, 33, 34, 132, 177, 199
Jeremiah, 1–2
God's punishment in, 104, 106
Hananiah and, 27, 29n8, 90, 91, 125n39
letter of, to exiles, 27, 168
Micah's influence on, 26–28, 34, 106, 114, 144, 155

Oracles against the Nations in, 118
school of, 38
Jeroboam I, 204, 205
Jeroboam II, 10
Jerusalem. *See also* elites
Babylonian destruction of, 127
ceding territory, 76
as center for peacemaking, 132
daughter of, 152
fall of, to Israel, 10
injustice in, 123, 201–2
inviolability of, 29, 36, 46
judgment on, 34, 43, 48–61, 65, 67, 125–28, 199, 205
military preparations in, 14–15, 122, 144
mountain imagery for, 18
"plowing" of, 25, 26, 124, 127, 131
refugees in, 201, 207–8
siege of, 12, 28–29
vengeance of, 161–62
Jesse, 167, 172
Jesus
centurion and, 222
citing Micah, 213, 213n59
as corrective to Davidic dynasty, 169
and interpersonal justice, 112
linking justice and mercy, 197
mocking of, 118
resisting empire, 152, 171
revolutionary subordination of, 120
striking of, 163
and the temple, 197–98
on violence, 107
warring against evil, 53
Jezebel, 205
Joel, 41, 42, 48, 141, 143–44
Jonah, 175, 222, 223
empathy of God in, 63, 225
placement of, in the Twelve, 41, 42, 187–88
universalism of, 40
Jones, Barry, 41, 146
Jonker, Gerdien, 4
Joseph cycle, 82, 149, 181
Josiah's reform, 55, 60, 111, 183, 184
centralization of worship in, 61
Jotham (king), 10, 48
Jotham's Fable, 137
Jubilee, 83

Judah
  and conflict with Israel, 10, 11–12, 88
  crimes of, 75
  frontier of, 17–18
  lowland violence in, 19, 72
  over the nations, 176–88
  and Philistines, 17, 72
  rulers of, 9
  rural economics of, 18–20
  as vassal, 6, 12
"judge between," 133–34
"judge of Israel," 163, 164
judgment
  against Jerusalem, 34, 43, 48–61, 65, 67, 125–28, 199, 205
  and salvation, in Micah, 34–37, 38, 41, 104, 192
  against Samaria, 48–61, 67, 125–27, 128
  theophany and, 53
justice
  abhorring, 122
  cult contrasted with, 197
  elites responsible for, 109
  love and, 196–97
  mišpāṭ as, 119
  peace as component of, 196
  pleasing God by doing, 196
  "twisting," 211
"just war," 79, 137

Kang, Sa-Moon, 115
karmel (Carmel, garden), 220, 221
kata- (prefix), 118
kātat (beat), 134–35
Keret Epic, 174
Kimchi, David, 69, 104
kingdom of God, 120, 151–52
kingship
  antiroyalism and, 24, 213, 221
  in Assyrian thought, 159
  chariots and, 181
  and ideal king, 165–71, 177, 197
Kletter, Raz, 17
Kotter, Wade, 192
Kuhrt, Amélie, 159
Kuntillet ʿAjrûd, 184

Laato, Antti, 13
labor movements and antimilitarism, 21–22, 99, 101, 128, 170–71

labor pains, 153
Lachish, 72, 74, 75, 78–79
  economic importance of, 16–17, 20
  LMLK jar stamps in, 14
  size of, 16n6
  strategic importance of, 16
"Lady Zion," 208
"lame," 146, 147–49, 154
lament, 61–68, 73, 79
  abandonment themes in, 112–13
  denunciation and, 81
  terms for, 62, 63, 64, 68, 87
land
  as God's possession, 84
  grants, 69, 75–76
  loss of, 72, 84, 84n17, 86, 87, 88, 89, 128
  productive, 126, 127
  promise of, 226
"latter days," 25–26
"laughingstock," 118
leaders. *See* elites
legal language, 52, 138, 188–92
  and Micah's advice to the accused, 192–98
"lick dust," 222–23
"lift up," 190
light, God as, 216
Limburg, James, 142, 143
lion imagery, 178–80
Lipschitz, Oded, 15n3, 28
listen, command to, 49, 51, 189
literary formats, 35, 39
liturgical texts, 34, 139, 141, 146, 150, 215, 220, 224, 226–27
Liverani, Mario, 4–5, 6
LMLK jar stamps, 14–15, 20, 76
  dating, 15n3
"Lord of the whole earth," 161
Luria, B. Z., 199
luxuries, 78

Maccabeans, 77
magic, 15n4, 173–74, 175, 182
makkâ (wound), 66
Malachi, rhetoric of, 193
mamlākâ (kingdom), 151
Manasseh, 205
Maori, 84n18
Mareshah, 76
mārôt (bitterness), 69, 70, 74

Index of Subjects and Authors

Marrs, Rick, 136
māšāl (saying, byword, taunt, proverb), 81, 86–87, 157
Masoretic Text (MT), 31
maśśā' (oracle), 47
maṣṣēbâ (pillar), 183–84
maṭṭāʿ (place of planting), 56
maṭṭeh (tribe), 200
Mays, James Luther, 34, 49, 61, 70, 76, 86n19, 91, 93, 94, 95, 96, 104, 127, 155, 160, 164, 166, 172, 186–87, 209
Mazar, Amihai, 16, 16n6
McKane, William, 34, 49, 51n2, 56, 68, 69, 80, 83, 84, 84n18, 88n21, 98, 104, 107–8, 113, 121, 122, 126, 129, 132, 138–39, 141, 142, 143, 146, 150, 155, 156, 171, 177, 187, 189, 193, 198–99, 203, 207, 209, 214, 216, 221
Melcher, Sarah, 148
Menahem, 11
Mennonites, 2, 131
Merchant of Venice (Shakespeare), 115
messenger formula, 80
messianism, 30, 186, 187
metaphor, agricultural, 56–57, 124, 125, 160
methodology, 1, 2–3, 139–45
  genre stereotyping and, 35, 39
  theological focus of, 39
Micah (book)
  cited in Jeremiah, 26–28, 34
  coherence of, 32, 36–39, 43
  dating, 32, 34, 36, 38, 48, 105, 126, 129, 154, 172–73, 174n51, 186, 188
  development of, 37–38
  divisions of, 32–39, 43, 104–5, 208, 224
  "happy ending" of, 226, 227
  historical context of, 2, 3–31
  judgment and salvation in, 34–37, 38, 41, 104, 192
  liturgical texts in, 34, 139, 141, 146, 150, 215, 220, 224, 226–27
  "message" of, 35–36, 39, 42, 43
  as revolutionary text, 30–31, 43, 227
  textual versions of, 31–32
  in the Twelve, 39–42, 46, 47, 48, 143–44, 187–88
  use of, in worship, 215
Micah (name), 45–46
Micah (prophet)
  confession of sin by, 216–17
  as critical populist, 1
  identity of, as prophet, 119, 120, 207
  lamenting destruction, 63, 67, 206–8
  opponents of (*see* false prophets)
  period of activity of, 48
  as poor, 207
  as rural person, 45, 48, 89
  tomb of, 15n5
  as village elder, 21, 25, 36, 75
Micaiah ben Imlah, 23, 37, 46, 51, 90–91, 162, 164
Migdal-Eder, 146, 151
militarism, 3, 113. *See also* war
  as beginning of sin, 75, 78, 136
  chariots and, 74, 75, 181–82
  corruption and, 115
  of elites, 89
  foolishness of, 222
  horses and, 74, 160–61, 181
  inequality and, 20–22, 23, 24, 46, 75, 144, 170
  as lack of trust in God, 175
  Micah's suspicion of, 21, 93–94, 97
military-industrial complex, 117n37
military preparations, 14–15, 16, 18, 20–25, 122, 144
millenarian movements, 1
Miller, Charles, 99
"mindfully," 193, 197
minorities, subordinate status of, 28
Minor Prophets. *See* the Twelve
Miriam, 188, 191
Miscall, Peter, 130, 143
misogyny, 58, 73
mišpāḥâ (tribe), 86
mišpāṭ (justice), 119
Mizpah, 27
Moabite women, 191–92
Moberly, R. W. L., 46
monarchy, 169, 213
  Samuel's speech against, 24, 213
Moor, Johannes de, 33, 208, 214
Moresheth, 1, 46
  excavated at Tell Judeideh, 15, 16
  as frontier town, 15–18
  proximity of Lachish to, 10, 15–16
morning, 82
môšēl (ruler), 165, 166
Moses, 172, 173, 182, 184, 191, 192

mountains
  cosmological symbolism of, 189, 190
  and Holy Mountain motif, 50
  Jerusalem elites represented by, 18, 54, 189
  melting, 53, 54
  and "mountain of God," 129, 130, 131–32, 133
mourning rites, 63–64, 70, 73, 77. *See also* lament
"moustache," 118–19, 119n38
Murašû archive, 8
murmuring, 124
mustering for war, 96–97
  as violation of poor, 99
"my people," 88

Na'aman, Nadav, 14, 16–17, 68, 69
Naboth's vineyard, 84, 205
nāgaʿ (disease, assault), 62
nāhâ (lament), 87
naḥălâ (tribal allotment, inheritance), 80, 83–84, 89
Naḥal Ḥever, 31–32
nāhār (river), 129, 131
Nahum, 179
  judgment of Nineveh in, 40, 41, 47, 63
  nationalism in, 42
  placement of, in the Twelve, 40–42, 187–88
  theophany in, 53
nakedness, 51, 57–59, 59nn8, 9; 64–65, 72, 99
names, 45–46
  and acting in name of deity, 138
nāśā' (carry, lift up), 80, 81, 130, 135
nāṭap (preaching, driveling), 91, 95, 102, 103
nātaš (uproot), 177, 184
nationalism, 23, 28, 36, 79, 137, 162, 187. *See also* false prophets
  and holy war, 160
  in Isaiah, 29
  and reading the Bible, 170
  in the Twelve, 41, 42
  wealth and, 134
  and Zion theology, 36
nations
  assembled against Zion, 155, 156, 157–59
  fearing God, 221–22, 223, 224
  Israel humiliated before, 206
  Judah over, 176–88
  procession of, 218, 222
  punishment of, 34, 141–42, 177, 187

recognizing Zion, 136
  shame of, 221, 222
  as sheaves, 160
Nebuchadnezzar, 7, 8, 16
Neo-Assyrian Empire, 3–8, 218
  administration of, 6
  as code for other empires, 171, 173
  curse against, 171–76
  end of, 7
  as God's agent, 52
  international relations of, 4–5
  propaganda of, 3–4, 16, 59, 111, 159, 161
  standing army of, 6
  western interests of, 5–8, 9
Neo-Babylonian Empire, 7, 8
  Jeremiah and, 27–28
  judgment of, 55n3
  in Micah, 154, 155
  punishment of, 64n12
nepeš (soul, life, breath), 207
net, 209, 210
new society, 145–55
nĕ'um-yhwh (YHWH says), 146
Niditch, Susan, 115
Nimrod, 172, 174
Nineveh
  condemned in Nahum, 40, 41
  repentance of, 40, 41, 223
Nineveh reliefs, 3–4, 16, 18, 59, 69, 78
nonviolent resistance, 3, 21, 28, 107, 155, 170–71
number parallelism, 172

Obadiah, 42, 63
  visions in, 47
Oberforcher, Robert, 167
Oded, 11, 23
oil, lack of, 204
Olyan, Saul, 147
Omri, 199–200, 204
  house of, 204n57
"on that day," 86, 146, 180–81
Ophrah, 73
oppression, 79–90, 103, 110, 113, 122, 170, 202
  and cry of the oppressed, 112
  foreign, 80
oracles, 47
oral rhetorical style, 35
  first-person speech and, 63
  as performance, 52, 68, 70

Index of Subjects and Authors

ostrich, 65
the Other, suffering of, 224
owl, 62, 65

pacifism, 140, 223
Palestine, provinces of, 172
Palette of King Narmer, 59n8
Pannell, Randall, 29n8, 30, 156, 165, 167, 174
panopticon, 158
parabolē (saying, byword, taunt, proverb), 86
pāsîl (image, idol), 60
"path, way," 133, 139
patriarchy, 58
patriotism
    idolatrous, 79
    survival as, 28
Patton, Corrine, 58
Paul, 108
Pax Assyriaca, 5
peace, 165–66, 179, 223
    Assyrian language of, 5
    economy of, 128–39
    God's presence leading to, 138
    ideal ruler bringing, 170, 172
    "living alone" as indication of, 220
    open gates symbolizing, 174–75
Peace Prophecy, 24, 128–45, 177
    agricultural implements in, 56
    ancient context of, 141–43
    in Isaiah, 132, 141–42, 144
    and judgment on Jerusalem, 34, 43, 131–32
    modern context of, 139–41
    seen as pipe dream, 25–26, 130–31
Pekah, 11–12
Pekahiah, 11
penitential prayer traditions, 55, 148, 158, 216–17, 225, 226, 227
Persian Empire, 7
    economic policies of, 8
    "humanity" of, 8
    influences of, 194
pešaʿ (rebellion, sin), 54, 119–20, 195
pĕsîlîm (images), 183
Peter, 107
Pham, Xuan Huong Thi, 63–64
Philistines, battles with, 10, 72
pillar figurines, 14, 15
pillars, 183–84
Pirke de Rabbi Eliezer, 40–41
Piro, Joseph, 159

Pixley, Jorge, 30, 88
"plan, scheme," 82, 85, 89, 153, 205
planting imagery, 56–57, 137
"pleasing," 194–95
pleasing God, 192–98
plēgē (plague, mortal wound), 62
"plotting," 81, 82, 210
plowing, 57
    of Jerusalem, 25, 26, 124, 127, 131
plowshares, 56, 69, 74, 135
Plowshares 8, 140
plunder, 161, 164
political policy, 92
ponēros (evil, bad), 85
poor
    cloaks of, 97, 97nn24, 25; 98–99
    comfort for, 170
    gleaning, 207
    suffering of, 89, 97, 100, 113, 148–49, 210
populism, 20–26. *See also* antimilitarism
"pouring stones," 57
power, 119
praise, 150
"preach," 91, 95, 102, 103
Premnath, D. N., 127
priests, corruption of, 123, 124
prisoners of war (POWs), 51, 58–59, 64–65, 72, 86, 99
    as slaves, 105, 106
procession of the nations, 218, 222
profiteering, 116
propaganda, 3–4, 16, 59, 111, 139, 159, 161
prophets
    economic concerns of, 20
    identifications of, 47
    opposed to war, 23
    true *vs.* false, 46
"prostitute's wages," 60–61, 67, 124
pruninghooks, 135. *See also* spears
Pul. *See* Tiglath-Pileser III
punishment
    of Babylon, 64n12
    corresponding to sin, 74n14
    desolation of land and, 55, 60, 65, 202–3, 218–19
    of nations, 34, 141–42, 177, 187
    sexualized, 57–59, 59n9, 73
    unproductive farming as, 203
    war as, 66–67, 148
Purver, Anthony, 69, 98, 98n26

qāšab (heed, pay attention), 49
qāṣar (reap), 92
qāṣîn (commander), 107, 109, 122
qayiṣ (summer, summer fruit), 207
qînâ (dirge, lament), 87
Quakers, 2, 123
  biblical translation by, 98n26
  meetinghouses of, 128
  peace and, 131
quartering of soldiers, 84, 97
"Queen of Heaven," 185

rāʿaʾ/rāʿâ (do evil, evil), 81–82, 108, 145
rabbinic tradition, 84n18, 88n21, 104
  antiwar sentiments in, 140
Rabshakeh, 13, 98, 111, 137, 154
Rad, Gerhard von, 115
"raise up," 115, 172
rams, consumption of, 195
"ransom," 191
rāšāʿ (wicked), 200
Rashi, 104
rāʿ (evil), 69, 74, 74n14, 80
readers
  context of, 2–3, 139–41
  invited to dialogue, 42
  oppressed communities of, 2
reading. See interpretation
Reagan, Ronald, 140
rēaʿ (friend), 212
reconciliation, 222, 223
redemption, 146, 154, 225
refugees, 201, 207–8
regional context of Micah, 8–20
Rehoboam, 93
Reicke, Bo, 213
"rejoice against," 215–16
religious language, use of, 93
"remember," 191
"remnant," 34, 147, 149, 160, 168, 177, 178, 224
Renaud, Bernard, 62
rešaʿ (wickedness), 81
"rescue," 153–54, 203, 211
rēʾšît (first, best), 75
"rest," 101
restoration, postexilic, 155–65
revolutionary subordination, 120
rhetoric
  drama of, 37, 80, 195

oral, 35
questions and, 193
rîb (state case, dispute), 188, 189–90
righteousness, 188, 201
"rise up," 96–97, 101
ritual worship. See cultic language
robbery, "tearing" as, 110
Robinson, Theodore, 71, 84n17
"rod," 163–64, 220
Rogerson, John, 3, 99
rope, 88–89
Roux, Georges, 6
royal family, mocking, 213–14
Rudd, Kevin, 222
Rudolph, Wilhelm, 142, 146, 187
"rulers," 108–9, 129, 165, 166
Runions, Erin, 58, 66, 69, 146, 151, 152, 156, 157, 162, 187, 200n55
Ruth, 166

sacrificial meal, 111
šādad (ruin), 87, 87n20
śādēh (field), 125
safety, 203
saints, 196
salvation, judgment and, 34–37, 38, 41, 104, 192
šāmad (destroy), 185
Samaria, judgment on, 48–61, 67, 125–27, 128
Samaria ivories, 20
šāmaʿ (listen), 49
šammâ/šěmamâ (ruins), 55n4
Samuel, antimonarchical speech of, 24, 213
sāpad (lament, mourn), 62, 63, 87
śāpām (cover to upper lip, moustache), 118–19
śar (commander, prince), 211
Sargon II, 7, 12, 14n2, 59n8
satire, 164–65, 176
scepter. See "rod"
"scheme," 82, 85, 89, 153, 205
Schniedewind, William, 14n2, 17n7
Schultz, Richard, 131, 139, 141
Schwartz, Michael, 128
"scorched-earth" policy, 8
ṣěbāʾôt (armies, hosts), 138
Sedlmeier, Franz, 129, 131
Sefire Treaty, 126
Sellin, Ernst, 97n24

Index of Subjects and Authors

Sennacherib, 7
  Judah campaign of, 13, 17, 71–72, 78, 174n51
  tribute paid to, 24
Septuagint (LXX) of Micah, 31, 147–48
  as interpretation of Hebrew, 32, 56, 112
šeqer (falsehood, false witness), 103, 103n27
Servant Songs (Isaiah), 119, 222
"seven," 172–73, 174
sexualized punishment, 57–59, 59n9, 73
Shallum, 11
Shalmaneser, 12
shalom
  false, 28, 46, 116
  removal of, 95, 95n23
  wordplay on, 95, 97, 97n24, 98
shame, 87, 91, 114, 157–58, 217
  of false prophets, 117–19
  of Israel, before nations, 91, 157–58, 206
  nakedness and, 64, 69, 73
  of nations, 221, 222
Shaphir, 69, 73
sharecropping, 83, 88n21
Shaw, Charles, 49, 62, 70, 97, 125, 197, 220
sheep imagery, 105
Shemaiah, 23
Shephelah
  as context for Micah, 8–20
  threatened by war, 70–71
shepherd imagery, 148, 167, 168–69, 174, 176, 220
Shittim, 191–92
sickness, 199, 202
sieges, 74, 162, 208
  cannibalism and, 111
šillûḥîm (land grant, inheritance), 69, 75–76
šillûm (payment), 211. *See also* shalom
śîm (make, set), 55
śimlâ/śalmâ (garment), 95, 97
sin, 119–20
  "beginning" of, 75
  communal, 54
  God casting away, 225
  punishment corresponding to, 74n14
Sinclair, Lawrence, 31, 32
Sirach, folk-blessing in, 40
skilled hands, 210–11
slave trade, 105, 106
Slayton, J. C., 191
Smith, Ralph, 127

snake, 223
social chaos, 208–14
"social facilitation," 158
social identity and trauma, 44
social psychology, 157, 158–59
Soelle, Dorothy, 99
šôlāl (go barefoot), 62, 64
Solomon
  as man of peace, 101, 170
  as môšēl (ruler), 166
  Prayer of, 55, 101, 134, 224
  reign of, as Golden Age, 98
  stables of, 181
Song of the Vineyard (Isaiah), 56
"son of Adam," 178
soothsayers. *See* magic
šôpār (horn), 73, 73n13
sorcery, 182–83. *See also* magic
sorting people, 160
sowing and reaping, 204
spears, 135
Stade, Bernhard, 33
Stager, Lawrence, 7–8
Stansell, G., 29n8, 46, 50, 53, 91, 102, 125, 125n39
Starr, Edwin, 22
statutes, 218
Stolper, Matthew, 8
stones, deceitful, 201
Stover, Fred, 21
straight, 92–93
  made crooked, 122
Strawn, Brent, 179
"stray, astray," 114, 148
"strike," 163–64, 202
stripping (nakedness), 51, 57–59, 59nn8, 9; 64–65, 72, 99
Strydom, J. G., 188
šûb (turn, return), 60–61, 81, 225
  apostasy as, 87–88
subjectivity, 2
sûg (overtake), 90, 91
superscription of Micah, 45–48
survival as patriotic, 28
survivors. *See* "remnant"
Susanna, 78
Sweeney, Marvin, 21, 34, 54, 70, 104–5, 106, 108, 110n33, 122, 130, 141, 143, 144, 146, 188, 193n54, 201, 204, 207–8, 215

swords, 107, 129, 134, 135, 174, 175. *See also* Peace Prophecy
and "given to the sword," 203
synagō (gather), 61
syntribō (broken, crushed, lame), 147–48
Syro-Ephraimite War, 10, 11–12
systrephō (align against), 61

Talmon, Shemaryahu, 131
tan (jackal?), 62
taunting, 89–90, 206. *See also māšāl* (saying, byword, taunt, proverb)
taxes and taxation
in Israel, 24–25, 199, 204
in Persia, 8
prophets critiquing, 46, 204
of vassal states, 11, 20
Tell Judeideh. *See* Moresheth
temple, 101, 133
cleansing of, 133
corruption associated with, 200–201
critique of, 215
temple entrance poems, 193
"ten thousands," 195
terror of war, 137–38
Te Whiti o Rongomai, 128
theophany, 50, 53
thornbushes, 212
Tiglath-Pileser III, 4, 5, 6, 8
time references, 48, 146–47. *See also* future; "on that day"
torah, 133
Israelites as teachers of, 129
total institutions, 158–59
trade
compared to prostitution, 60
limited by Neo-Assyrian Empire, 6
trampling enemies, 217
trauma, 44
"treading," 50, 52–53, 160, 225
Treaty of Waitangi, 84n18
"tremble," 137, 223
tribe, 86, 198, 200
and restorative justice, 154
and tribal property, 80, 83–84, 89
trust, lack of, 212–13
truth, 120, 213n59, 226
Truth and Reconciliation talks, 223
tryphera (pleasures), 78

Twain, Mark, 211
the Twelve, 39–42, 143–44, 187–88
coherence of, 41
identifications of prophets in, 47
Micah redacted for, 45–46
theological divergence among, 40–41
time references in, 48
U-shaped trajectory of, 42
"twist," 211
Tyre, 60

Uffenheimer, Benjamin, 29n8, 141–42
Ugaritic texts, 50
uncovering, 51
as euphemism for sexual intercourse, 57
universalism, 134, 141. *See also* Jonah
"upright," 92–93, 209, 212
"uproot," 177, 184
Ussishkin, David, 14, 15n3, 16n6
Utzschneider, Helmut, 37, 49, 63, 69, 70, 138
Uzziah, 10, 45, 48

Van de Mieroop, Marc, 7
Vanderhooft, David, 7, 64n12
van der Woude, A. S., 36, 37, 104, 104n29, 106, 143, 152, 160
vassalage, 6
vengeance, 161–62, 186, 187n53
Via Maris, 52
vindication, 214–19
"vine and fig tree," 136–37
offered by Rabshakeh, 13, 24, 69, 98, 137, 170
vine clippers, 56
vines, 56–57
vineyards, 56, 105–6, 137
violence
Bible used to justify, 140
colonialism and, 2, 84, 89, 171, 200n55, 213, 222
against poor, 97, 110, 202
visions, 45, 47, 116–17
Micah having, 47
Visions, Book of, 33
"voice of YHWH," 199
Volkan, Vamik, 44

Wadi Murabbaʿat, 31

Index of Subjects and Authors

Wagenaar, Jan, 32, 37–38, 39, 50, 86, 90, 95, 105, 119, 129, 138n41, 139, 144, 151, 164, 166, 170, 173, 174, 178, 180, 186, 187, 200n55
"waiting," 177–78
walking, 90, 139, 139n42
  with God, 138–39, 143, 193, 197
walls, 218
Waltke, Bruce, 45, 97n24, 100, 187n53
war
  benefiting elites, 99
  bloodshed in, 122
  call to, 96–97, 99, 143, 160
  "collateral damage" of, 67, 79, 208–14
  combatant suffering in, 79
  defeat in, 225
  failure in, 77
  financial strains of, 116
  of God, 52–53, 115, 156
  horrors of, 100
  imperial goals of, 4
  learning, 129, 135–36
  pastoral support for, 117n37
  personal exemptions from, 27
  preparations for, 14–15, 16, 18, 20–25
  primordial battle and, 53
  prisoners of, 51, 58–59, 64–65, 72, 86, 99, 105, 106
  as punishment, 66–67, 148
  sieges and, 74, 111, 162, 208
  veterans of, 149
warfare, spiritual, 53, 225
Warren, Nathanael James, 111
"War—What Is It Good For?," 22
wasteland, 55, 55n3, 60, 126, 205–6, 218–19
watchfulness, 215
watching and being watched, 156–59
waters, "splitting" of, 53–54
wax, 50, 54
wealthy. *See* elites
weapons
  destruction of, 130, 134–35, 136, 147, 169, 179, 180, 187
  transformation of, 24
"weariness," 190
"weave," 211
Weems, Renita, 58
weights and measures, 199, 200–201
Wellhausen, Julius, 132, 136

Wessels, Wilhelm, 30, 36, 164–65, 174, 178
Westermann, Claus, 35
"Who is like God?," 45, 224
Wildberger, Hans, 141
Williamson, H. G. M., 35, 214
Willis, John, 33, 34, 129, 139, 156, 177, 187
"Will Jesus Wash the Bloodstains from Your Hands?," 21
"wine and strong drink," 103, 114
Winstanley, Gerard, 128
Wisdom literature
  associated with elites, 110
  counselors in, 152–53, 176
  "hating evil" in, 109–10
  power in, 119
  "straightness" in, 122
witchcraft. *See* magic
witness (legal terminology), 52
Wolff, Hans Walter, 1, 20–21, 34, 45, 46, 50, 51n2, 68, 69, 84, 88, 90, 93, 97, 97n25, 104, 108, 110, 114, 116n35, 122, 125, 127, 131–32, 136, 142, 143, 145–46, 147, 155, 156, 165, 171, 177, 188, 189, 193n54, 196, 197, 198, 199, 202, 209, 210n58, 214, 220, 221
women
  abuse of, 51, 57–58
  sexuality and, 58
  symbolizing strength, 151, 152, 162
  vulnerability of, 100
Wood, Joyce Rilett, 37
wordplay, 69, 70, 73
word use, 38
worship, 194
  hypocritical, 133
  local aspect of, 61
wounds, 62, 66
Würthwein, Ernst, 32

yād (hand), 80, 210
yaḥēl (wait, hope), 69
yākaḥ (argue, contend), 188, 190
yālal (wail), 62, 64, 87
yāšār (straight, correct, upright), 92–93, 209
yaʿănâ (owl?), 62
yešaḥ (unknown meaning), 199, 203
yĕsôd (foundation), 51
yeter (those who are left, survivors), 168
"YHWH of Armies," 130, 138

"YHWH your God," 217
ykḥ (decree, reprove), 134
Yoder, John, 120
yoke, 80, 85
yrš (take possession, conquer), 45, 76

Zaanan, 69, 73, 74
Zajonc, R. B., 158
Zapff, Burkard, 34, 40–42, 187–88
Zechariah (book), 47
Zedekiah (false prophet), 37, 46, 162, 164
Zedekiah (king), 91, 137, 170, 181
Zimri, 204–5
Zion
    birthing new king, 167–68
    daughter of, 151
    Psalms, 139
    retribution of, 161–62
    theology, 29, 36, 46, 104, 136, 164
    as "Tower of the Flock," 151